Christian Faith Seeking Historical Understanding: Essays in Honor of H. Jack Forstman

H. Jack Forstman

Christian Faith Seeking Historical Understanding: Essays in Honor of H. Jack Forstman

Edited by

James O. Duke and Anthony L. Dunnavant

Mercer University Press
Macon, Georgia
1997

©1997 All rights reserved
Mercer University Press
6316 Peake Road
Macon, Georgia 31210

First edition.
Published in association with
the Disciples of Christ Historical Society.

Jacket design by Mary Frances Burt
Jacket Illustration: Caravaggio's Supper in Emmaus

∞The paper used in this publication meets the minimum
requirements of the American National Standard for
Information Sciences—Permanence of Paper for Printed
Library Materials, ANSI Z39.48-1984.

Library of Congress Cataloging-in-Publication Data

Christian faith seeking historical understanding: essays in honor of H. Jack
Forstman / edited by James O. Duke and Anthony L. Dunnavant. —First
edition.
p. cm.
Includes bibliographical references.
ISBN 0-86554-560-X
1. Theology. 2. History (Theology) 3. Christian Church (Disciples of Christ) 4.
Resotration movement (Christianity) I. Forstman, Jack, 1929– . II. Duke, James
O. III. Dunnavant, Anthony L., 1954– .
BR50.C518 1997
230'.66—dc21   97-31310
CIP

Christian Faith Seeking Historical Understanding
Essays in Honor of H. Jack Forstman

PART II "THE NEW REFORMATION" OF THE DISCIPLES OF
CHRIST, ALWAYS REFORMING

Reflections on Theology and the Church

Reflections on Worship

Reflections on Unity, Division, and the Ecumenical Quest

*The publication of this book was possible in part
due to the generosity of a subvention from
The Disciples of Christ Historical Society
of Nashville, Tennessee.*

Editors' Introduction

The essays in this volume deal with challenges facing Christians who acknowledge that their efforts to understand the meaning of the faith they affirm take place under the laboratory conditions of human history. This acknowledgement does not come especially easy to Christians. They are tempted like everybody else to make their way through history as though little if anything mattered except that times are good or that times are troubled. They are also tempted, however, to presume that their faith in God and the gospel exempts their accounts of that faith's meaning from the influences and limits—and mistakes!—characteristic of every human attempt to understand how things were, now are, and will be hereafter. Overcoming these temptations is not a once-and-for-all accomplishment but an on-going effort prompted by faith itself. Since the rise of historical consciousness in the eighteenth century, the Christian church's willingness to deal honestly, and well, with its own historical conditionality has been under constant testing.

These studies have been written in honor of Jack Forstman, for whom "faith seeking historical understanding" has been the signature theme of his career as a theologian and church leader. In his books on John Calvin, Friedrich Schleiermacher, German Protestant theologians "in the shadow of Hitler," and ecclesiology, as well as scores of articles and reviews, Forstman has gained distinction for scholarship of exceptional breadth, insight, and literary elegance. As a teacher, he has encouraged students at Randolph-Macon Women's College, Stanford University, and Vanderbilt University's Divinity School (where he served for a decade as Dean as well as professor of theology), to learn from the history of Christian thought without recourse to traditionalism by means of critical, self-critical, and constructive thinking. In his home church, the Christian Church (Disciples of Christ), and in ecumenical settings, he has pointed out paths beyond denominational gridlock while advising against easy answers to complex issues. The varied strands of his lifework, which is still very much in progress, reflect his devotedness to the task of Christian theology in the sense of seeking a genuinely historical understanding of the nature and implications of Christian faith. Each of the chapters that follow is in its own way devoted to the pursuit of this task as well.

The inquiries Jack Forstman has undertaken in his teaching, writing, and church service are first and foremost explorations of the meaning of Christian faith for today in light of probing reassessments of ever-changing understandings of faithfulness to the gospel at crucial junctures in Christianity's theological tradition.[1] Thus the title of this volume, *Christian Faith Seeking Historical Understanding*, by beginning with the reference to "Christian faith," is meant to locate these essays within a theological conversation that takes into account Forstman's view that "the task which always confronts the theologian ... is to find that basis for theology most conducive to the full understanding of faith and least likely to obscure faith's meaning."[2] Further, that "historical understanding" is sought here is consistent with Forstman's affirmations that because Christian faith originated in the past, the task of understanding it today is "first of all a historical problem" and that "what the church speaks and does, indeed what the church is, will be genuine and dependable only when it stems from an understanding on the part of Christians that prompts that special speaking and doing."[3]

This collection of essays is organized under two distinct yet interrelated headings, "Faith Seeking Understanding in Modern History" and "Disciples of Christ on 'The New Reformation,' Always Reforming." In a time often characterized as "postmodern" and "post-denominational," it may seem quaint, ironic, or even comic to speak of exploring the meaning of Christian faith today by way of fresh inquiries along such lines. If so, it is apt nonetheless, and for truly theological, and thus anti-antiquarian and trans-denominational, i.e., ecumenical, reasons. One of the gifts Jack Forstman has offered his students and readers has been his unusual clarity and candor about the ways that quaintness, irony, and comedy accompany Christian theologies at their best—those self-aware that they are human efforts to speak of God and in this respect examples of transcendental jest. (Christian theology at its worst is never quaint, ironic, or comic at all,

---

[1] James O. Duke, with Joseph D. Driskill, "Disciples Theologizing Amid Currents of Mainstream Protestant Thought, 1940 to 1980: Sketchbook Observations," in *A Case Study of Mainstream Protestantism: The Disciples' Relation to American Culture, 1880-1989*, ed. D. Newell Williams (Grand Rapids: William B. Eerdman's Co.; St. Louis: Chalice Press, 1991) 156.

[2] H. Jackson Forstman, *Word and Spirit: Calvin's Doctrine of Biblical Authority* (Stanford, CA: Stanford University Press, 1962) 156.

[3] H. Jackson Forstman, *Christian Faith and the Church* (St. Louis: Bethany Press, 1965) 35, 21.

but unremorsefully and too often deadly in its seriousness.) Likewise, "the church is inherently funny in its incongruity"[4] in that divided and often self-serving churches proclaim faith in God's good news for all the world and the oneness of the church of Jesus Christ on earth. To his credit, Forstman makes good on this theological observation by his own readiness to laugh.

A distinction is to be made, however, between the dismissive "bellow" of the "outsider" and the "smile" of the "insider" in relation to the comedic character of the church.[5] Perhaps then a parallel distinction is worth drawing with regard to where one stands in relation to questions about the significance of both "modern" Christian thought and denominational heritage. The recognition that such questions are so frequently considered passé should give those of us still concerned with them self-critical pause, provoke the self-deprecating smile, and remind us to frame our explorations in humility. Yet as Forstman's analysis of early theological responses to the lure of Hitlerian National Socialism reveals with exceptional poignancy, self-critical pause applies to ventures of appeal because of their contemporaneity or future hopes no less than any others.[6] The point of investigating how previous generations of Christians have understood the life and thought of the church is not to turn back the clock, perpetuate the status quo, or retreat from contemporary challenges. It is an aid to understanding the meaning of faith in the gospel as adequately as possible so that Christians here and now might distinguish between what to accept and what to resist, whether past, present, or future.

The essays in Part 1, then, address major thinkers, topics, and issues that have played significant roles in "modern" theology's fitful struggles first to acknowledge that theology and the church are not timeless but historical and then to search out the meaning of Christian faith in light of its still-unfolding history and by means of responsible historical inquiry. This struggle has been multifaceted. Critical reappraisals and transformative reconstructions of the biblical-theological heritage of Reformation Protestantism by European

---

[4]Ibid, 183, See also ibid.,177-90; and Jack Forstman, *A Romantic Triangle: Schleiermacher and Early German Romanticism*, American Academy of Religion Studies in Religion, ed. Stephen Crites, no. 13 (Missoula: Scholars Press for the American Academy of Religion, 1977) 1-33, 95-111.

[5]Forstman, *Christian Faith and the Church*, 186.

[6]Jack Forstman, *Christian Faith in Dark Times: Theological Conflicts in the Shadow of Hitler* (Louisville: Westminster/John Knox Press, 1992).

scholars and African American leaders alike are among the episodes in the quest for historical understanding of Christian faith treated in these pages.

Jack Forstman's participation in denominational studies of the Disciples of Christ has been marked by a measure of reluctance[7] and an even larger measure of significant contributions and influence. The reluctance, including his studied avoidance of billing as a "denominational historian," as well as his influence on Disciples historians are related to his awareness of the particular vulnerabilities associated with denominational scholarship. One such vulnerability is that which Claude Welch has pointed to by the phrase "domestic chronicles," that is, the tendency for studies of denominational history to be parochial and insufficiently critical.[8] This legitimate concern about isolating denominational studies from the "larger conversation" underway in religious and theological studies is one that Jack Forstman has handled by his approach to the Disciples heritage. This approach has been neither provincial nor uncritical, but attentive always to the larger context in which Christian faith seeks historical understanding.

It is noteworthy that Jack Forstman has remained an active member and leader in the Christian Church (Disciples of Christ). An equal and opposite reaction to the danger of denominational parochialism is a "scholarly" aloofness and on occasion arrogance that withholds commitment to the church. Forstman holds, however, that "faith in ... God means the union of commitment and criticism."[9] Furthermore, this union is to be worked out not in intellectual abstraction but in the course of actual involvement with one's denominationally particular community of faith. This is, Forstman has noted, "an unusual union." Whereas loyalty to many causes and communities is tested by the standard love it or leave it, one deals in the case of Christian faith with "a commitment which, if one is to be

---

[7]Note Jack Forstman's language relative to being "drawn into a project about my own denomination" in Martha Lyle Reid, "Unfinished Business," *Spire: Vanderbilt University Divinity School and Oberlin Graduate School of Theology* 18/2 (Winter 1996): 4.

[8]Claude Welch, *Graduate Education in Religion: A Critical Appraisal*. A Report of a Study Sponsored by the American Council of Learned Societies with a Grant from the Henry Luce Foundation, Inc. (Missoula, MT: University of Montana Press, 1971) 249-50.

[9]Dean H. Jackson Forstman, "Commitment and Criticism: A Program for Christian Ministry, Installation Address," *Spire: Newsletter of Vanderbilt University Divinity School and Oberlin School of Theology* 5/1 (Fall 1979): [4].

true to it, calls for the most rigorous criticism."[10] Thus a critical memory of the longer and wider relationships in which Disciples stand is necessary if the history of the Disciples is to be set in its proper context. Relationships to European Christianity, the Reformed tradition, the ecumenical movement, and "modernity" along with its cultured despisers become important in this connection. These relationships are among those receiving significant attention in this volume's studies of the faith, order, life, and work of the Christian Church (Disciples of Christ).

This book's bifocal attention on "Faith Seeking Understanding in Modern History" and "Disciples of Christ on the 'The New Reformation,' Always Reforming" cuts across some of the standard, well-worn grooves of disciplinary specialization. This of course is precisely the point—at least in part. One dimension of the richness of Jack Forstman's teaching ministry with Disciples students was that he led them to encounters with the longer and broader Christian tradition that enabled them see their own story in fresh and illuminating ways. The essays in Part 1, then, serve to replicate that experience for readers in the Disciples of Christ as well as in other particular denominational traditions. Disciples readers will turn to Part 2 with an expanded field of vision for understanding their own church. For readers outside the traditions of the "Nineteenth-Century Reformation," critical explorations of this movement form a case study of a Christian community whose own particularized history illustrates in many and varied ways, some inspirational and others cautionary, a truly ecumenical lesson: as Forstman puts it, "understanding is so difficult and misunderstanding so easy." For this community, the goal of faithfulness to the gospel of Jesus Christ has proved to demand not one reformation but a commitment to be always reforming. Christian faith and human history alike prompt Disciples and other Christians as well to recognize that inasmuch as theology is at root faith seeking understanding, the understanding to be sought and gained is historical in character.

It is especially fitting that this volume appear under the auspices of the Disciples of Christ Historical Society, which marks the conclusion of the academic year (1996-97) of Jack Forstman's retirement from the Vanderbilt University Divinity School by this sign of solidarity in common cause with that school, the American Society of Church History, and Mercer University Press. For his

---

[10]Ibid.

manifold contributions to this project, heartfelt and unbridled thanks go to Peter M. Morgan, President of the Disciples of Christ Historical Society. Special thanks are due also for the generous support of the Council on Christian Unity of the Christian Church (Disciples of Christ), and for that of Paul Crow, its President, and his wife Mary, who honor Jack Forstman as mentor, partner in Disciples and ecumenical theology, and devoted friend. Much of the "conspiratorial" and celebrative fun that goes into the making of a *Festschrift* depended in this case on the aid of Dan Moseley, Forstman's pastor at Vine Street Christian Church, Nashville, Tennessee.

—James O. Duke and Anthony L. Dunnavant

PART ONE

FAITH SEEKING UNDERSTANDING

IN MODERN HISTORY

Is Friedrich Schleiermacher Passé?

by

Edward Farley

Brian Gerrish, responding to Emil Brunner's extensive critique of Friedrich Schleiermacher, asks, "Has Schleiermacher been disposed of?"[1] This essay repeats that question. Not one, but several things might be responsible for rendering Schleiermacher passé. The first is the long tradition of caricature and misreading that invents a "Schleiermacher" whose thought is so obviously wrong-headed that it collapses before the most facile of criticisms. The second is the shifting scene of culture, church, philosophy, and theology. Here Schleiermacher's voice is silenced by renewed biblicism, hermeneutics severed from critical historical orientations, anti-apologetic and neo-confessional theologies, and philosophies that would eliminate all traces of fundamental ontology of human beings. Let us first address the tradition of Schleiermacher caricature.

I usually try to avoid the grammar of superlatives when making historical statements, words such as most, least, greatest, worst, first, best, most profound, and so forth. If I did proffer a superlative, it would be that Schleiermacher is of all major European theologians the most caricatured. Has Schleiermacher survived his caricaturists? I distinguish here between caricatures that invite easy dismissal of Schleiermacher and serious critics. Caricaturists pass along traditions of criticism with only a minimum (if any at all) technical engagement with Schleiermacher's texts. Serious critics (such as Karl Barth and Regin Prenter) work from that engagement. Caricatures and serious misreadings of Schleiermacher began in his own lifetime and evoked from him at least one major response.[2] Caricatures have continued in mainstream and conservative Protestant theology from that time to the present.[3] These caricatures unite in a single theme, virtually

---

[1] Brian Gerrish, *Tradition and the Modern World: Reformed Theology in the Nineteenth Century* (Chicago: University of Chicago Press, 1978) 29.

[2] Friedrich Schleiermacher, *On the Glaubenslehre: Two Letters to Dr. Lücke,* trans. James Duke and Francis Fiorenza (Chico: Scholars Press, 1981).

[3] For a summary account of a few major misreadings of Schleiermacher, see Richard

constituting a kind of "heresy" of Schleiermacher interpretation. This misreading is so basic that it constitutes a serious obstacle to any serious study of Schleiermacher. I speak of the almost standard interpretation of Schleiermacher as a psychological reductionist, a theologian who would derive Christian beliefs and their contents from the religious feelings of believers, or who regards those feelings as the norm for authentic belief. On the basis of this misreading, it is easy to pronounce Schleiermacher an individualist, a romantic, a mystic, a Cartesian (and we all know how bad that is!), and a Feuerbachian.[4]

R. Niebuhr, *Schleiermacher on Christ and Religion: A New Introduction* (New York: Charles Scribners, 1964) 6-13.

[4]In 1872 Charles Hodge described Schleiermacher as mysticism's most distinguished and influential advocate, a theme to be later picked up by Emil Brunner. Hodge went on to say that to theologize for Schleiermacher means "to interpret his own Christian consciousness; to ascertain and exhibit what truths concerning God are implied in his *feelings* (emphasis mine) toward God; what truths concerning Christ are involved in his feelings toward Christ." See Hodge's *Systematic Theology* (New York: Scribner's 1872), 1:9.

Passing over Schleiermacher's distinction between the "feeling (Gefühl) of dependence" and the "feeling of unqualified dependence" or piety, A. H. Strong criticizes Schleiermacher for identifying religion with the "feeling of dependence," thus omitting God. *Systematic Theology* (Philadelphia: Judson Press, 1907), 20. For Strong, Schleiermacher sees "theology as a mere account of devout Christian feelings, the grounding of which in objective historical facts is a matter of comparative indifference." 14 His citation here refers not to Schleiermacher, but to K. R. Hagenbach, who says that Schleiermacher sees doctrines as "the perpetual expression of the feelings common to believers." *A History of Christian Doctrine*, trans. E. H. Plumptre (Edinburgh: T. and T. Clark, 1881) 3: 268. He also represents Schleiermacher as interpreting religion as "*a* feeling, in distinction from knowledge or action." (emphasis mine) 269.

In an important book in the 1930s, H. R. Mackintosh passes this interpretation on to subsequent generations. Instead of apprehending feeling as Schleiermacher defines it, as immediate self-consciousness, a structural aspect of human world engagement, he defines it as "laying hold by the soul of a trans-subjective Reality," "*an* experience on the part of Self." (emphasis mine). *Types of Christian Theology: Schleiermacher to Barth* (London: Nisbet, 1937), 65. And ignoring the tripartite referentiality of theological statements (God, world, pious self-consciousness), he says that a doctrine is a "statement about our feeling, not about God." 64 Also writing in the 1930s, the more philosophically oriented E. A. Burtt sets forth the feeling of utter dependence as a "*sense* of being unqualified dependent." (emphasis mine) It would seem from this interpretation that "unqualified dependence" is the object of some sort of perception or awareness, an experience of something about our consciousness. *Types of Religious Philosophy* (New York: Harpers, 1939), 297. He then says that this makes God "an aspect of man's religious consciousness," 298.

The tradition of interpreting Schleiermacher's *Gefühl* (feeling) as an actual, empirical, and specific feeling, something like an emotion, continues in twentieth century historical and theological texts. For Otto Weber, Schleiermacher's view is that the subject as absolutely dependent experiences itself as "being touched and conditioned by a trans-subjective essence" with which it is thus united. *Foundations of Dogmatics*, trans. D. L. Guder (Grand Rapids: Eerdmans, 1981), 137. Thus in feeling God and the human being are simply merged. Helmut Thielecke's interpretation also renders *Gefühl* into something psychological. In his view, Schleiermacher thinks that "the existential feeling of absolute dependence is first there in my consciousness." *The Evangelical Faith*, trans. G. W. Bromiley (Grand Rapids: Eerdmans, 1974) 1:44. For Wolfhart Pannenberg, Schleiermacher makes "subjective belief the basis of dogmatics." and the "subjective faith-consciousness" the sole criterion of dogmatic articulations. *Systematic Theology*, trans. G. W. Bromiley (Grand Rapids: Eerdmans, 1991) 1:42.

The psychological interpretation continues in twentieth-century evangelical theologians. Carl F. H. Henry, following Burtt, sees Schleiermacher as correlating God with "inner spiritual experience." *God, Revelation, and Authority, vol. I, God Who Speaks and Shows* (Waco, TX: Word Books, 1976) 80. Thus, the essence of religion is an "inner feeling," (452) and the meaning of God is "derived from our inner experience" (81). Donald Bloesch, possibly picking up the theme of mysticism from Hodge and Brunner, sees Schleiermacher as a "mystical" theologian. For Bloesch, "Schleiermacher described the mystical experience as 'immediate self-consciousness.'" *Toward an Evangelical Theology of Revelation* (Grand Rapids: Eerdmans, 1971), 143. In similar vein Millard Erickson says that for Schleiermacher, religion is not a matter of doctrine but rather of feelings. *Christian Theology* (Grand Rapids: Baker Book House, 1984), 2: 803.

Some members of the so-called Yale School have made their own contribution to the religious-psychological interpretation of Schleiermacher. George Lindbeck does this subtly by way of a typology of theologies which enables him to assign Schleiermacher to one of the types. The "experiential-expressive" type of theology (of which Schleiermacher is the proto-type) sees religion as located "in the pre-reflective experiential depths of the self." *The Nature of Doctrine: Religion and Theology in a Postliberal Age* (Philadelphia: Westminster Press, 1984), 21. Thus, doctrines "are constituted by harmony or conflict in underlying feelings, attitudes, existential orientations or practices." 17 If this is an interpretation of Schleiermacher, it is one that has little to do with Schleiermacher's account of doctrines in his *Brief Outline of Theological Study*_or his *Glaubenslehre*. The irony of this criticism is that Lindbeck's preferred type of theology, the cultural-linguistic type, is very close to Schleiermacher's own program of describing and doing justice to the particularity of religious communities. William C. Placher says that for Schleiermacher "*a* feeling of absolute dependence" is "at the basis of all my experiences." (emphasis mine). *A History of Christian Thought: An Introduction* (Philadelphia: Westminster, 1983), 274. So goes what appears to be an on-going tradition of psychological interpretation of Schleiermacher. These interpretations all construe §3 and §4 of Schleiermacher's *Glaubenslehre* to be about feelings, a feeling, an experience, a consciousness of, experiences. Thus, they pass over Schleiermacher's careful distinction between *Gefühl* (feeling) or immediate self-consciousness, *Frömmigkeit* (piety), and expressions of piety at the level of actual human states, in short, Schleiermacher's archaeology of dogmatics. To describe this level, Schleiermacher does not use the term *Gefühl*, or immediate self-consciousness but has another vocabulary: "expressions of piety" (*Äusserungen der Frömmigkeit*), "essence of piety" (*fromme Erregungen*), "pious feeling states" (*Gefühlzustände*) such as a

The reason it is a misreading is that it confuses what is a transcendental-ontological structure of the human being with occasional psychological experiences, emotions, and feelings, and, ignoring the predominance of the actual historical religious community in Schleiermacher's thought, it makes the "feelings" bear the whole weight of his theory of religion, Christianity, and dogmatics. In just a few sentences, this interpretation renders Schleiermacher passé. And it persists in the face of a generation of Schleiermacher scholarship in which both the ontological character of his "propositions borrowed from ethics" and the centrality of the determinate, historical community again have a place.[5]

Have shifts in culture, religion, and modern religious thought rendered Schleiermacher passé? The question breaks into two parts. Is it important to interpret (Christian) faith *critically*, that is, without

---

penitence or joy in God, and "certainty (*Gewissenheit*) about the feeling of utter dependence. Schleiermacher, like Jonathan Edwards, (whom one would think would be similarly targeted by these critics and who does see religion as carried in the affections), does thus speak of specific religious emotions and states, but this speaking is not his "feeling of utter dependence." By identifying *Gefühl* with psychological states, these interpreters can then say that Schleiermacher roots religion, faith, theology, or doctrine in "feelings."

[5]Some of the "corrections" of the psychological caricatures are found in texts that advance serious theological criticisms of Schleiermacher. One thinks especially of Karl Barth, not so much for this early caricatures of Schleiermacher, but in his later serious engagement as expressed in his Göttingen lectures. *Karl Barth: the Theology of Schleiermacher*, ed. D. Ritschl and trans. G. W. Bromiley (Grand Rapids: Eerdmans, 1982). In these lectures Barth moves beyond the polemics of his own early writings and opposes Brunner's appellation of Schleiermacher as mystic. He also corrects psychologizing charges that Schleiermacher based his dogmatics on a general theory of religion or on human feelings. Rather, the only basis of Glaubenslehre is its presentation. For a collection of essays that analyze Barth's relation to Schleiermacher, see the *Festschrift* written for Hans W. Frei. James O. Duke and Robert F. Streetman, eds., *Barth and Schleiermacher: Beyond the Impasse* (Philadelphia: Fortress Press, 1988). Another critically oriented but close analysis of Schleiermacher can be found in Regin Prenter's *Creation and Redemption*, trans. T. I. Jensen (Philadelphia: Fortress Press, 1967). Prenter uncovers the ambiguity of Schleiermacher's concept of *Gefühl* and argues that he combines transcendental and psychological levels.

Other texts that correct the psychologistic interpretation are Claude Welch, *Protestant Thought in the Nineteenth Century*, vol. I, 1799-1870 (New Haven: Yale University Press, 1972) 57-86; Robert Williams, *Schleiermacher the Theologian: The Construction of the Doctrine of God* (Philadelphia: Fortress Press, 1978); Terrence N. Tice, "Schleiermacher's Theological Method," 2 vols. (Th.D. diss., Princeton Theological Seminary, 1961; Richard R. Niebuhr, *Schleiermacher on Christ and Religion*, and Brian Gerrish, *Tradition in the Modern World*.

presupposing premodern interpretations that carry with them the baggage of "Christian cosmology," absolute textual authority, and literalistic ways of understanding doctrines? And, is it important to interpret faith *apologetically*, that is, in such a way that the "reality" and power of faith is made alive in and for contemporary settings? A critical and apologetic re-articulation of the Protestant form of (Christian) faith in the face of a powerful Enlightenment discreditation of "positive" religious faiths is what we have in Schleiermacher's *The Christian Faith* (or *Glaubenslehre*).[6] As critical thinker, Schleiermacher drew from the Enlightenment. As apologist, he critically confronted the Enlightenment. As theologian, he advanced a powerful criticism of the "natural religion" of the Enlightenment. Is there a sense in which Schleiermacher's combination of criticism, apologetics, and confessionalism is a positive legacy?

We must acknowledge from the outset that the European cultural and religious environment is highly fragmented and has expanded its horizons to include global and multicultural issues. There may not be a single "situation" in which theologians re-articulate (Christian) faith. Thus, there may be no identifiable "cultured despisers" to be likened to the circle of romantic intellectuals whom the young Schleiermacher addressed. North American societies seem to have no one identifiable group that could be called "intellectuals." In place of such a group has arisen a class of cognitive specialists (in both universities and corporations) and another class of specialized professionals (psychologists, lawyers, clergy, managers, physicians, etc.). Neither group participates in an "intellectual" way in the legacies of learning, aesthetics, or politics. Except for their now-growing fundamentalist populations, postmodern societies blur older distinctions between believers and nonbelievers or between an intellectual elite and rank and file members of society.

At the same time there has arisen in contemporary Euro-Western societies a large population for whom the very phenomenon of religion and religious faith makes little sense. This population should not be identified with the non-churched. In that population are active Catholics, Protestants, and Jews whose attitude toward religion is not so much positive and confident belief or unbelief as a puzzlement (or even indifference) about the phenomenon. Displacing belief and unbelief is a professionalist, therapeutic, or self-oriented pragmatic

---

[6]Friedrich Schleiermacher, *The Christian Faith*, trans. H. R. Mackintosh and J. S. Stewart (Edinburgh: T. and T. Clark 1928).

construal of what religion is about. For a great many postmodern scientists, professionals, corporate leaders, rank and file workers, and academic specialists, religion is neither relevant nor real. They suspect that religion requires of them a suspension of their critical faculties and belief in various "fantastic" notions. For many the only authentic ways of being religious are the largely anti-Christian and secularized new age experiments in "spirituality" or the fervent, exclusive, and sometimes even entertaining, congregations of fundamentalism. Thus, some find their religious home in new age religious groups or in "non-denominational" fundamentalist congregations. The one appeals to the essentially therapeutic orientation of secularized faith, the other to needs for certainty and for an intimate community felt so desperately in a time of cultural malaise and demise. Of course, countless other voices would be heard: neo-confessionalists, feminist, African American, womanist, and liberation theologians, the muted (even if radical) "liberalisms." But these primarily literary voices may only rarely engage the postmodern "cultural despiser" for whom religion means either fundamentalism or new age therapeutic.

In the face of this situation, it may be useful to review Schleiermacher's apologetic response to his own situation. In making this review, we need not assume that Schleiermacher's apologetic is simply something to be appropriated. In its original form, it is probably a meal postmoderns are unable to digest. But, to change the metaphor, there may be some point in a serious engagement with that apologetic, especially as it is fashioned in Schleiermacher's *Glaubenslehre*. This apologetic turns on three motifs, the first of which is only minimally articulated and the other two of which are textually explicit: a critical hermeneutic, the onto-transcendental anthropology, and the principle of religious positivity or particularity.

I

The first theme of Schleiermacher's apologetic sets the task of the other two themes. Standard interpretations of Schleiermacher's program tend to begin (and frequently end) with the second theme, the onto-anthropological turn. This is not surprising in view of the fact that Schleiermacher (in the *Glaubenslehre*) says little about his actual theological method, and hence does little to thematize the very thing that sets for him his apologetic and theological task? This unthematized theme, presupposed in virtually every passage of this work, is his "critical hermeneutic"; that is, his critical orientation toward what Catholic and Protestant theology regarded as the straightforward deliverance of truth in the texts of Scripture (the Protestant view) or in the accumulating and official texts of tradition (the Catholic view). Here theology works from and makes use of the authoritative texts in exegesis, citation, and application. It does not apply criticism *to* these texts.

Several things combine to hide this aspect of Schleiermacher's apologetic. First, his explicit theological style tended to be non-polemical. He is thus less concerned to display the incoherencies, ambiguities, and arbitrariness of a doctrine than to uncover the way that doctrine connects with and expresses the faith of the community. Second, the interpreter of Schleiermacher may miss the fact that the *Glaubenslehre* proceeds by way of a new hermeneutic or regards dogmatics itself as a hermeneutic because Schleiermacher wrote a piece on textual hermeneutics important in its own right.[7] Thus, the sense in which the *Glaubenslehre* was itself a new hermeneutic is obscured by the importance of Schleiermacher's important work on textual interpretation. In the *Glaubenslehre*, dogmatics becomes a work of interpretation (of Christian faith) and it also contains a particular version of that interpretation. Further, Schleiermacher finds a way to incorporate virtually all of the (Protestant) doctrines, a retention that may hide the subtle ways in which each doctrine is reinterpreted.

How then do we know of the existence of this critical hermeneutic? First, it is present, though with minimal methodological comment, in Schleiermacher's work on texts.[8] Second, we become aware of Schleiermacher's critical hermeneutic when we realize what is *not* present in the *Glaubenslehre*. We do not find what might be called a cosmological way of representing what the doctrines of faith are about. Absent is a description of creation, eschatology,

---

[7]Friedrich Schleiermacher, *Hermeneutics: The Handwritten Manuscripts*, ed. H. Kimmerle; trans. J. Duke and J. Forstman (Missoula, MT: Scholars Press, 1977).

[8]Schleiermacher directed his critical-historical skills toward both texts of Scripture and texts of the history of doctrine. Examples of his biblical interpretation are his essay on Luke and his life of Jesus. *Critical Essay on the Gospel of St. Luke*, trans. C. Thirwall (London: John Taylor, 1825), [original date, 1817]; and, *The Life of Jesus*, trans. S. M. Gilmour (Philadelphia: Fortress Press, 1975), [original lectures, 1982]. On the history of doctrine, see his "On the Discrepancy between the Sabellian and the Athanasian method of Representing the Doctrine of the Trinity, *Biblical Repository and Quarterly Observer*, 5 (April and July, 1935) [original date, 1822].

providence, or incarnation as supernaturally originated events that constitute a universal cosmic narrative. Schleiermacher does not talk about "demythologizing" (or decosmologizing), but he does demythologize. For instance, Schleiermacher's interpretation of the work of Christ makes no use of objective and penal substitution theory to describe a transhistorical transaction going on between the Son and the Father. What Schleiermacher has done is to demythologize, decosmologize, even deconstruct, with a kind of Ockham's razor, the whole package of Christian doctrines, but without an explicit formulation of this activity as a principle or method.

If Schleiermacher's critical hermeneutic remains more or less hidden in the *Glaubenslehre*, it does obtain some thematization in his lectures on theological encyclopedia, the first version of which was published ten years prior to the appearance of *The Christian Faith*. Even in this text, Schleiermacher hesitates to articulate any grounds for a critical handling of traditional texts except to say that historical organisms (e.g., the Christian community) are liable to disease.[9] In the *Brief Outline* we find the most explicit formulation of dogmatics **as a** hermeneutic and of the hermeneutic principles at work in the *Glaubenslehre*. The psychologistic caricatures of Schleiermacher tend to make his *Addresses on Religion* the interpretive key to the *Glaubenslehre*.[10] Thus, the Introduction to the *Glaubenslehre* (the onto-anthropological propositions "borrowed from ethics") is regarded as a repetition of the "sense and taste for the infinite" found in the Addresses. Such a move thus misses Schleiermacher's restatement of hermeneutic principles (in the *Brief Outline*) and thus also the historical aspect of his apologetic program.

What is the hidden hermeneutic of the *Glaubenslehre* that finds some expression in the Brief Outline? Simply put, it is the principle that beneath the empirical-historical phenomenon of Christianity is a *Wesen* or essential structure obtainable and describable by "philosophical theology." With this distinction between a total historical movement and its enduring *Wesen*, modern or post-authority theology is born. This is not to say that premodern Christian theology had no ways of distinguishing what is central and

---

[9]Friedrich Schleiermacher, *Brief Outline of the Study of Theology*, trans. T. Tice (Atlanta: John Knox, 1966), §54. [Tice translates the 1830 edition of this work.]

[10]Friedrich Schleiermacher, *On Religion: Adddresses in Response to its Cultured Despisers*, trans. Terrence N. Tice, Research in Theology, ed. Dietrich Ritschl (Richmond, VA: John Knox Press, 1969).

necessary from what is peripheral and dispensable. Conciliar documents and church confessions attest to that.[11] But for pre-modern approaches, this is not so much an ongoing historical task as the proper formulation of the divinely given truths present in texts of Scripture or a divinely guided dogmatic tradition. The vehicle on which theology works is that which preserves authoritative texts, not "Christianity." And what the theologian would discern is not the *Wesen* or nature of Christianity, but the eternally true revelation. Discerning what is central in this sense is a matter of exegesis, not the historical sifting of a complex and multiple-traditioned community. Additionally, it seems that Schleiermacher did not create this critical hermeneutic out of a mere curiosity. Once he subjected the authoritative texts to historical scrutiny (as others of his time had begun to do), he had to acknowledge the historical and, therefore, nonauthoritative character of any and all specific texts. At this point, he confronted what for many Enlightenment thinkers seemed to be the only two alternatives: drop religion altogether (since its ancient texts were now desacralized) or rediscover religion as a general human phenomenon over and above specific religious communities. Schleiermacher rejected both options, and in their place constructed a third, a critical hermeneutics oriented to the *Wesen* of actual religious communities.

This hermeneutic had far-reaching implications, many of which have yet to be examined and developed. Also it posed a new and frightening problem for theology itself. For now the theologian must walk a thin rope stretching over an abyss. The abyss is what gapes before us when the vehicles of authority (scriptural texts, magisterium, church confessions) disappear. Karl Barth looked into this abyss, saw the grinning face of Feuerbach staring back from its depths, and drew back. Many options offer the theologian ways to traverse the thin rope of uncertainty. Select some past period (e.g., the Patristic age) as definitive and normative and let it guide the journey. Show that Christian traditions express the truths of a universal metaphysics. Extract from the texts and history of the Christian movement whatever pertains to individual morality or

---

[11]Thus, William Adams Brown's history of the search for the essence of Christianity begins with the ancient church. He argues that the very name, Christianity, attests to a consciousness of something to be differentiated from other religious communities. For Brown the Reformation is the second period of re-formulating true Christianity. *The Essence of Christianity: A Study in the History of Definition* (New York: Scribner's Sons, 1902).

radical social transformation. Replace the normative texts with appeals to human existential religious experience. In spite of the caricaturists who insist that Schleiermacher opted for "religious experience," I must say that Schleiermacher rejected all of these responses. His response—which I refer to as the Schleiermacher apologetic—combined three themes: the more or less unexplicated critical hermeneutic, the rooting of theological contents with actual human religiousness, and the placing of both in the setting of a determinate, actual, corporate religious community. I turn now to the second theme, the onto-anthropological dimension of his apologetic.

II

In authority theologies, determining what is divinely true rests on a confidence (certainty) in the validity or authenticity of the authoritative text or canon of texts. Insofar as this confidence is grounded, it has some reason for thinking that the authoritative texts embody something true and normative. Accordingly, at the very core of authority, theology is not simply scripture, tradition, etc., but a paradigm (inherited from the past along with the texts themselves) that specifies how and why these texts are necessarily truth-bearing. For this reason some believers experience a loss of the whole thing, faith itself, when a historical attitude disrupts the paradigm. For everything the believer possesses as belief, including salvation itself, appears to be given in and through this paradigm and the certainty that comes with it. Without the text-plus-paradigm, faith itself seems to fall into the abyss that opens up with paradigm-destroying historical thinking. The alternatives seem to be either the authority (with the paradigm) or faithlessness.

In the face of this alternative, Schleiermacher denies that faith comes and goes with or has its existence from its own inherited *ways* of construing (its paradigms) authoritative texts. It is not, in other words, utterly dependent on the work of human and historical *paradigms* of authority. In place of the relation of certainty to a theory or paradigm of authority, Schleiermacher substitutes the facticity of piety or religiousness itself. And with this substitution everything changes—the nature of religio-theological judgments, the character of dogmatics, the place of religious emotions, the status of natural theology, and the role of the religious community in theology.

Here we confront in a direct way the issue posed by the reductive and psychologistic interpretations of Schleiermacher. Did not

Schleiermacher say that "Christian doctrines are accounts of the Christian religious affections"?[12] Is it not evident that Schleiermacher has thus exchanged the objective contents of "revelation" for emotions? What this hasty and oversimplified conclusion misses is simply Schleiermacher's complex archaeology of Christian dogmatics. This archaeology emerges quite clearly when we read the *Glaubenslehre* backwards from §31 to earlier sections. In §31, Schleiermacher speaks of "the system of Christian doctrine" which is the form dogmatic thinking takes when it grasps the doctrines in relation to each other. At this level systems of doctrine fall into comprehensive historical types, e.g., Roman Catholic and Protestant. Of what is a system of doctrine comprised? His answer is, dogmatic statements (*Sätze*). But what is a "dogmatic statement?" It is what results when faith-statements (*Glaubenssätze*) are subjected to rigorous (*wissenschaftliche*) thinking for didactic purposes.[13] In dogmatic statements, the convictions, claims, and attestations of faith take on a form suitable to instructive communication. What are these faith-statements (*Glaubenssätze*) and where do they come from? They are the linguistic expressions of the religious or pious affections (*Gemütszustände*). What these faith-statements express is the certainty and salvific happiness (*Seligkeit*) that comes with redemption through Christ.[14] These piety-based, faith-statements also make up the units of Christian preaching.

In saying that faith-statements are expressions of religious affections, has Schleiermacher made the subjective world of feelings the norm and content of dogmatics? Here we must continue to track Schleiermacher's archaeological analysis. What are these "Christian affections" and how do they originate? In a psychological perspective they are simply whatever emotions religious people have when they worship, pray, preach, grieve, etc. For Schleiermacher they themselves are expressions of a determinate structure, a structure that is externally referential. First, they are "religious" only if they are

---

[12]Schleiermacher, *Christian Faith*, §15.

[13]Ibid. §16.

[14]Ibid. In this rooting of dogmatics in faith-statements and finally in religious piety itself, Schleiermacher has mediated what Congar calls Franciscan and the Thomist ways of thinking of theology; that is, theology as a hiatus of knowledge and relation to God, and, theology as a more distanced, argued enterprise of demonstration. When Schleiermacher would place "theological study" in the university system, he again performs a mediatorial task, putting together theology's practical aspect, its service of clergy education with its scholarly aspect, thus, the determination of the essence of Christianity.

located in and share the character of the *Gefühl* (feeling, immediate self-consciousness) of utter dependence. But Schleiermacher is quite clear that there is no such thing as a general "feeling of utter dependence?" The following statement from the *Glaubenslehre* should have warned interpreters not to confuse the abstracted feeling of utter dependence with anything that is actual. "Since the feeling of absolute dependence, even in the realm of redemption, only puts in an appearance, i.e., becomes a real self-consciousness in time, insofar as it is aroused by another determination of the self-consciousness and unites itself therewith."[15] (In other words, piety, the utter dependence that structures the immediate self-consciousness, is actual only in connection with the particularity of the human being's actual world and historical relations. It exists in other words only as Christian piety, Jewish piety, etc.

This means that the religious affections are expressions of a determinate Christian religiousness, which for Schleiermacher means a state of the sensible self-consciousness as it undergoes the transition from sin to redemption through Christ. Religious emotions unaffected by that determinacy are not the affections Schleiermacher is talking about. For Schleiermacher, religious affections are not simply whimsical, idiosyncratic, autonomous orgies of emotion. They arise with, and are expressions of, the facticity of redemption. This is why they are referential. Once Schleiermacher has reconnected the abstracted feeling of utter dependence with the actual (sensible) self-consciousness, thus, with the determinate religiousness of the Christian community, he can argue that (Christian) piety is directed both to God and to worldly conditions. Thus arises the triune referentiality of the faith-statements (*Glaubenssätze*). He explicitly says that while their primary form is given by their connection to the affections, they refer at the same time to both God and world. The reason that contents of God and world adapt to the basic form is that they originate in the first place in the transition from sin to redemption through Christ. If the "anthropological" reference were not their basic form, then faith-statements would not be statements of *faith* but would be objective-speculative statements based on arguments, evidences, and speculations. And because the religious affections are expressive of a piety already shaped by the event and community of redemption, they possess in an intrinsic way a content that eschews what he calls the natural heresies of Manicheanism and

----

[15]Ibid., §14,1.

Pelagianism.

But this archaeology does not stop with determinate piety, the redemptive modification of the immediate self-consciousness. For this historically determinate piety is not simply externally imposed on the human being, but arises in connection with a structural aspect of human immediate self-consciousness. To explicate Schleiermacher borrows propositions from "Ethics" or a generic account of human reality. In order to show that redemptive modifications are neither violations of human reality nor mere superficial and arbitrary supplementations, Schleiermacher connects them to certain features of individual human reality. In the *Dialektik*, he argues that (human) "life" is comprised of thinking, willing, and immediate self-consciousness. In both the *Dialektik* and the *Glaubenslehre*, he undertakes an exceedingly dense account of the way *Gefühl* (feeling), or immediate self-consciousness, attends both self-initiating activity and passive receptivity. In this account, Schleiermacher discovers that about the human being which orients it to that with which religious communities are concerned—the unqualified (even if unembodied) dependence of the immediate self-consciousness. The referent of this dependence remains (in the propositions borrowed from Ethics) formal until some actual historical faith renders it determinate. There is a certain ambiguity about what Schleiermacher is doing in this analysis. Is he making a transcendental deduction? If so, the *Gefühl* of utter dependence is the transcendental condition of the possibility of actual piety. Or, is he generalizing in a speculative way from observations of various types of religious faiths? Whichever is the case, Schleiermacher need not be asserting some sort of pre-grace autonomy that takes control of piety or redemption in advance. He is certainly not asserting some actual religious experience and set of emotions to which "God," the gospel, redemption, and Christ can all be reduced? To uncover a generalized consciousness structure of utter dependence can function both as a way to deny the chauvinistic claim that Christianity is the one and only true religiousness and as a way to show that the redemption that Christian piety undergoes savingly modifies, rather than violates, the human being.

Such is Schleiermacher's archaeology of dogmatics. It presses from the dogmatic *system* to dogmatic *statements* (*Sätze*), to faith-statements (*Glaubenssätze*), to religious affections, structured already by a determinate Christian *piety* (*Frommigkeit*), which as determinate is dependence on God in the situation of the transition from sin to redemption through Christ, to a general feature of human self-consciousness. For Schleiermacher, the alternative to making faith-statements rooted in affections structured by the undergoing of redemption is to make them into logical or perceptual statements.[16] This archaeology of dogmatics discloses the reason for Schleiermacher's onto-anthropological turn. If keeping the individual and its experiencings in the picture is "Cartesian," then it is a Cartesian turn. But we should remember that the individual Schleiermacher has in mind, with its *Gefühl* of utter dependence, its affections, and its statements, is one whose piety arises from and with a faith-community by whose determinate witness the piety is already shaped. This being the case, Schleiermacher's criteria for dogmatics are not the religious affections in some psychological sense, but the corporate piety expressed in those affections. This turn is clearly correlational in the sense that the contents and claims of a historical faith, thus its meaning of God, redemption, evil, and the like, correlate with a more universal structure of human reality. In sum, what we have in the *Glaubenslehre* is a post-authority apologetic in which relation to external authority (verified by the Holy Spirit?) is replaced by the very facticity of redemption in the concrete life of the religious community and its individuals—a redemption which, while not demonstrable in universal terms, is related in a positive way to human reality. This kind of apologetic has continued in such theologians as Karl Rahner, Paul Tillich, and David Tracy.

III

Psychological reduction caricatures Schleiermacher on two counts. First, confusing an onto-transcendental structure with an empirical emotion while suppressing Schleiermacher's archaeology of dogmatics, they reduce the contents of faith to religious emotions. Second, they suppress the other main motif of Schleiermacher's apologetic—the salvific efficacy of a specific, historical religious faith. The young Schleiermacher included this motif in his addresses to the "cultured despisers" of religion.[17] Many interpreters of Schleiermacher have been so fascinated with his address on the nature of religion and his phrase "the sense and taste for the infinite" that they have virtually ignored the final two addresses.[18] But even as the

---

[16]Ibid., §28,3.

[17]See the last two, i.e., the fourth and fifth addresses, of Schleiermacher's *On Religion*.

[18]An exception is Albrecht Ritschl who would correct the prevailing focus on Schleiermacher's so-called subjectivism. *A Critical History of the Christian*

"feeling of utter dependence" has no existence except in connection with the sensible self-consciousness, so no general religion exists apart from actual, social, and historical communities. The Enlightenment "romantics" whom Schleiermacher addressed would have readily acknowledged the existence of "positive" religions. In their view, religion itself is a "spiritual disease," hopefully besetting only isolated individuals and virulent in any corporate form.[19] Schleiermacher thus confronted the Enlightenment proposal to replace actual religions with a general and natural religiousness. Without the fourth and fifth addresses, Schleiermacher's *Addresses* would have capitulated to this proposal. Parallel to the Enlightenment view is the modern (or postmodern) suspicion of all actual religion. Surely there is something warranted in this suspicion since it is just at the point of actual social life and practice that religions are corrupt and corrupting. When they control a society, they become one more excuse and motivation to constitute outsiders as enemies. To assure their own survival, their policing of the beliefs and practices of their members prompts them to defend literalized myths and to close themselves to internal and external criticism. Heirs of the Enlightenment continue to ask, is not hierarchy, cognitive idolatry, arbitrary casuistries, various chauvinisms, and false certainties too high a price to pay to have religious particularity? At the present time, with the re-emergence of religious fundamentalism over much of the globe, the question takes on a new intensity. Many postmoderns share the Enlightenment longing to replace actual religious communities with something more psychologically ideal and philosophically general. Disillusionment and contempt with religious particularity did not disappear with the Enlightenment.

In the face of what seems to be a warranted contempt for actual religions, Schleiermacher advances a defense of religious positivity. But Enlightenment modes of thinking, especially historical thinking, clearly dispose the way he makes this defense. Both Roman Catholic and Protestant faiths are historically particular. Each also has a characteristic way of subjecting its social actuality to theological interpretation. In Roman Catholicism, a divinely originated structure (the magisterium) presides over and guarantees faithfulness to Catholicism's doctrinal, liturgical, and institutional legacy. This legacy as protected by the magisterium is what is factically posited or

---

Doctrine of Justification and Reconciliation, trans. J. Black (Edinburgh: Edmonston and Douglas, 1872) 443-44.

[19]Schleiermacher, *On Religion*, 207.

given to theological interpretation. In Protestantism, the religious community ever reforms itself by subjecting its preaching, polities, and institutions to scriptural texts. Authoritative scriptures and (for some traditions) an official confessional interpretation of such is the factical given presupposed by theological interpretation. In both versions religious positivity is a mixture of what is historically actual (scripture, tradition, magisterium) and divinely authoritative.

I offer these facile summaries in order to say that Schleiermacher's way of defending religious positivity abandoned these givens, these syntheses of the historical and the divine. In Schleiermacher's view, scripture and tradition do play an indispensable role in the religious communities of Christendom and their theologies. But the given with which theology works is not infallible and authoritative texts, but Christianity itself as the medium and matrix of redemption. More basic than scripture or tradition is the sheer facticity of redemption that brings about and shapes the religious community. This is what engenders basal affections that find expression in faith-statements (*Glaubenssätze*) and from that dogmatic claims and systems. Christianity's *Wesen* (essential and distinctive reality) is not an external authority to be appealed to but the constitutive reality presupposed by any and all theological attempts to interpret, clarify, or systematize. Thus, for Schleiermacher the "positivity" or determinacy of (Christian) religion is not simply the bare fact that a religious group is historically identifiable, but the theological fact that it is a corporate, redemptive existence. Given that, theology has both something to interpret and a norm for its assessments. And it is just this facticity that prevents theology (or Christianity itself) from being abolished by the discreditation of textual authorities or the corrupt character of actual religious institutions.

IV

Is Friedrich Schleiermacher passé? First, have Schleiermacher's caricaturists successfully eliminated him from the canon of important Western theological texts? In place of pyschologizing caricatures, I have set Schleiermacher's total apologetic: his attempt to identify the power and validity of what history bequeaths (the *Wesen* of Christianity), his re-connection of what seem to be simply objectivized and external truths to the way human beings experience matters of religion and his connecting of that to the structure of human reality, and his way of retaining the specific religious community and its traditions. In this apologetic, Schleiermacher found a way to acknowledge the relativity and fallibility of what is historical, and at the same time articulate something historical as the matrix and deliverer of redemption. It may not be an exaggeration to say that the key to Schleiermacher's apologetic in the *Glaubenslehre* is the way Schleiermacher understands how these three themes come together. How does he relate the actual historical religious community, its *Wesen*, to human reality (especially as *Gefühl* of utter dependence) and to religiousness both as a generic feature of human reality and as a particular way a historical form of faith reappears in individuals? In my view, what unifies these various motifs in Schleiermacher is the facticity of redemption. The determinate religious community Schleiermacher has in mind is a community of redemption. The transition from sin to redemption, built on the supposition of God, and taking place through Jesus, is the *Wesen* (the being, reality, power) of Christianity. The particular modification of generic piety or *Gefühl* of utter dependence is dependence on God in the mode of redemption through Christ. The archaeology of dogmatics finds its deepest stratum in redemptive piety that is already incorporated into the community and experienced (by its individuals) through affections, or, as Karl Jaspers would say, in the mode of *Existenz*. When we press the archaeology beneath redemptive piety, we find ourselves in the sphere of the abstract and generic, that which has no actual existence in itself. In the light of this archaeology and the three-fold apologetic, we must conclude that the Schleiermacher of psychologizing reduction is a terrible caricature. If this is so, the caricaturing literature has only apparently rendered Schleiermacher passé.

Is Schleiermacher passé in the face of the momentous shifts in culture, religion, philosophy, and theology that have taken place since Schleiermacher's *Addresses On Religion*? Our answer cannot but be dialectical. On the one hand, we must acknowledge that Schleiermacher's thought (like all theologies) has the character of an attempt, not a definitive accomplishment. Thus it is not without its unclarities, ambiguities, aporias, and parochialisms. Two queries may illustrate this point. First, *is* it the case that the most general structure we find at work in all actual religions, that which makes them religious, is a certain way of being *dependent*? One can at least imagine an inductive and generalizing argument that all religious faiths share in common a relation of dependence on whatever they designate as sacred, ultimate, or important. But does an onto-transcendental analysis of the human way of being a "self-consciousness" yield an "immediate self-consciousness" (*Gefühl*), one element of which is an unqualified dependence? A trace of this theme may be at work in Heidegger's notion that a structural feature of *Dasein* is its "thrown-ness," its being in the world as not from its own activity and initiation.

Could it be that Schleiermacher's proposed "unqualified dependence" as (abstractly) *the* meaning of religiousness is a transcendental inversion of the natural theology arguments he would avoid? The arguments of natural theology would show in an objective way the world system as dependent on God. Has Schleiermacher permitted this motif of dependence in the natural theology literature to invade and shape his onto-transcendental analysis of human being? It may be that the way the human being is oriented to what is beyond itself is not so much a structure of dependence as a passion (*conatus, eros*, desire). This is the Tillichian, and even Blondelian, modification of Schleiermacher. Schleiermacher took one step toward this motif when he replaced spheres of cognition and moral experience with the immediate self-consciousness as the anthropological locale of religiousness. But another step was needed. It does seem to be the case that immediate self-consciousness has a primacy to (is presupposed by) and mediates knowing and willing (doing). But to focus on this function and on the way it attaches to spontaneity and freedom tends to empty it of passion and turns it into an abstract dependence. At best this "feeling" is an existentially diluted passion.

The second query concerns the role and function of the retrieved *Wesen* of Christianity as normative for theological discourse. Let us grant to Schleiermacher the relativization of Christianity itself, and with that, its variety of periods, types, claims, and pieties. If the *Wesen* of all this is also a historically originated and perduring shape or accomplishment, why is it too not subject to relativization? What precisely gives the *Wesen* the status of a theological norm? Schleiermacher's texts contain a response to this question. The *Wesen* is normative not just as a neutral content of an essence-oriented historical inquiry, but as a redemptive facticity. Historical Christianity, Christendom and its branches, is a matrix and carrier of a specific type of redemption that actually takes place. This redemption carries with it certain internal norms, the departure from which are the "natural heresies." In addition, two other norms are at work in any interpretation of this redemptive facticity. The one, resulting from Schleiermacher's privileging of anthropology, is a general criterion. Religion (and redemption) must have a supplemental or fulfilling relation to the reality of the human being.

Generic religiousness as an element in human self-consciousness is Schleiermacher's basis for this norm. The second norm, flowing indirectly from this anthropology, is the negative theology that arises from the fact that the referent of religiousness is fundamentally irreducible to the world. This being the case, Schleiermacher has a norm to apply to all actual pieties, to various world religions, and to Christian faith itself. Negatively expressed, the interpreter would inquire into the degree to which a piety makes mundane the referent (the Whence, God) of utter dependence.

Do these moves suffice to render the *Wesen* of Christianity, namely, the facticity of redemption, normative? They do articulate certain principles needed by any theology: negative theology, nonviolation of the human being, nondeparture from the *kind* of redemption that is taking place. But what assures us that the kind of redemption attested to in the *Wesen* (justification, sanctification, etc.) is in fact redemptive? Is the referral of redemption to the general structure of piety as dependence a sufficient answer to this question? Can the thin and general norm of an onto-transcendental piety serve to specify concretely just what redemption accomplishes and why it is redemptive? At this point Schleiermacher had a resource for the exploration of redemption that he made little use of—the reference of all faith-statements to what he called the world. Uncovering just the way sanctification, the redemptive re-making of the human being, has to do with human reality, with social, biological, intersubjective dimensions, is the task Schleiermacher did not take up? Restricting his "borrowed propositions" from Ethics to his Introduction and to his account of generic piety, he had no way to relate his account of specific redemption to the concrete realities of human individuality or sociality. Thus, correlation in Schleiermacher remained a general structure, and was not employed in specific explorations. The result was a kind of historicism, a falling back to historical-descriptive accounts of determinate piety. The historical *Wesen,* thus, is normative not because it expresses what redemption actually does but, because it is simply historically determinate.

To repeat the question at hand, have historical and interpretive developments of (post)modernity rendered Schleiermacher passé? My review of the Schleiermacher apologetic may help make the question more precise. Does Schleiermacher's critical hermeneutic, the anthropological turn, and the retention of religious positivity have anything at all to say to us? Even if we find no way of retrieving Schleiermacher's actual proposals, there may be one sense in which the Schleiermacher texts retain their pertinence. The three elements of his apologetic response to the relativizations of modernity are together a kind of model for confronting the issues these relativizations pose. Far from disappearing, relativism has become in the (post)modern period ever more radical. In Schleiermacher's day the de-absolutization of religions placed them all on the same plane. Further, all historical mediations, including their definitive texts and official interpretations, were relativized.

In our day, under the impact of untrackable diversity, the hermeneutic that has arisen with such relativizations more and more has reduced issues to local and constituency expression. Theologies, philosophies, cultures, and religions tend to disappear into these diversities and into the atomism of difference: into gender, age-groupings, first, second, and third worlds, Euro- and non-Euro-traditions, elites and the poor, and untold varieties of religious fundamentalism. More than any time in human history, the peoples and groups of our era may need some way to adjudicate difference, to exist in open, critical dialogue with each other. But the grounds for the exploration of mutuality seem to be rapidly disappearing, held captive by difference, tribalism, and individualism. The unities we have are not sensed commonalities, but desensitized cultures of consumerism and nationalism. Seemingly gone are "religion," religiousness, humanity, religious types ("Christianity," "Hinduism"), human nature, symbols, "reality," moral experience, any and all phenomena expressible in unitary or mutual terms. The unities fall to historical and particularizing thinking, scientific experiment, and linguistic deconstruction.

These new and intense forms of relativism leave us with questions not unlike those with which Schleiermacher struggled. *Is* there a way that religious faiths can address and become embodied in the social and individual dynamics of the "human being," and if so, in what sort of discourse? *Do* these dynamics in any way connect with, presuppose, or modify anything about the human being? Is it possible to think of particular social groups and their traditions as in any way embodying and preserving something useful to future generations? Is it possible to engage in a critical hermeneutic ever open to the requirements of difference and detail that can at the same time identify and retrieve something that persists through difference as a positive legacy and a contemporary resource? Can actual religious communities survive their own idolatries, corruption, and foolishness, or are (post)moderns forced into one of three options: fundamentalism, new age natural religion, or aggressive antireligion? Can the particularity of religious faith be in any sense important and positive, or is it fated for such irrelevance and corruption that it has no place at all in the "brave new world" of advanced capitalism and post-industrial societies? These questions, with their issues, flow directly out of Schleiermacher's apologetic. In this apologetic, we have something of a model for a critical apologetic in the situation of radical relativism. That apologetic still summons us to think religious particularity, human reality, relativity and difference, and religiousness in relation to each other. If these questions are in any way pertinent, perhaps Friedrich Schleiermacher is not passé.

The Fellowship of the Mystery: The Category of Faith in Friedrich Schleiermacher

John P. Plummer

> To me, who am less than the least of all the saints, this grace was given, that I should preach among the Gentiles the unsearchable riches of Christ, and to make all see what is the fellowship of the mystery which from the beginning of the ages has been hidden in God who created all things through Jesus Christ.
>
> Ephesians 3:8-9

> For I do not seek to understand that I may believe, but I believe in order to understand. For this also I believe, –that unless I believed, I should not understand.
>
> St. Anselm, *Proslogium*
> (used as the epigraph for the German
> edition of the *Glaubenslehre*)

I. Introduction

Anyone who reads Reformed theology has surely been struck by the predominance of the category of faith. In Calvin, Edwards, Bushnell, Barth, the Niebuhrs—it echoes like one long peal through the ages. However, when one turns to one of the finest sons of this tradition, Friedrich Schleiermacher, one is shocked at the infrequency of any mention of "faith." Such a conspicuous absence should arouse our attention. In order to understand this situation, we will first consider how he defines faith. Then, we will see how this faith comes about. Third, in examining the relation of "faith" to other theological categories in Schleiermacher, we will discover why it occupies the place it does in his work. Finally, we will see what lessons lie hidden for contemporary theology in the way Schleiermacher deals with faith. We will draw primarily on *The Christian Faith* (or the *Glaubenslehre*), with some occasional help from the sermons collected in *Servant of the Word* and the open letters to Dr. Friedrich Lücke in *On the "Glaubenslehre"*.

II. The Definition of Faith

Before we can attempt to determine how "faith" fits into Schleiermacher's system and why it is so infrequently mentioned in his works, we must examine how he defines faith when it is discussed. Schleiermacher makes a number of approaches to a definition of faith. One is reminded of H. Richard Niebuhr's comparison of faith to a cube, of which one side is always visible, other sides variously appear according to one's perspective, and the bottom and inner sides remain always hidden.[1] With Schleiermacher, we will consider the cube from several different, but not contradictory, angles. First of all, faith involves a kind of certainty.[2] "But since each can only enter [into the Christian fellowship] through a free resolve of his own, this must be preceded by the certainty that the influence of Christ puts an end to the state of being in need of redemption, and produces that other state; and this certainty is just faith in Christ."[3]

This certainty is different from ordinary certainty in that it corresponds to a higher level of consciousness, but it is not any less certain for that. "The faith of which we are now speaking . . . is a purely factual certainty, but a certainty of a fact that is entirely inward."[4] It should be clear that Schleiermacher is not speaking of a certainty corresponding to propositional knowledge, but of that corresponding to the experience of a mode of self-consciousness. Perhaps the best analogy is the prereflective certainty we have of ourselves.

In the same section of the *Glaubenslehre* where he discusses faith as certainty, Schleiermacher distinguishes faith in God, much more broadly found, from faith in Christ. Faith in God is "nothing but the

---

[1] H. Richard Niebuhr, *Faith on Earth: An inquiry into the Structure of Human Faith*, ed. Richard R. Niebuhr (New Haven: Yale University. Press, 1989) 12.

[2] Compare what follows to John Calvin, *Institutes* III.ii.7: "Now we shall possess a right definition of faith if we call it a firm and certain knowledge of God's benevolence toward us, founded upon the truth of the freely given promise in Christ, both revealed in our minds and sealed upon our hearts through the Holy Spirit." *John Calvin, Institutes of the Christian Religion*, ed. J. T. McNeill, trans. F. L. Battles (Philadelphia: Westminster, 1960) 2: 551.

[3] Friedrich Schleiermacher, *The Christian Faith*, eds. H. R. Mackintosh and J.S. Stewart (Edinburgh: T. and T. Clark, 1989) §14,1.

[4] Ibid.

certainty concerning the feeling of absolute dependence, as such, i.e. as conditioned by a Being placed outside of us, and as expressing our relation to that Being." Note that faith in God is more than the feeling itself; it is "certainty concerning" it. Faith in Christ is more specific; here we deal only with those who have realized their need for redemption and its accomplishment in Jesus of Nazareth.

But the term 'faith in Christ' here (as the term 'faith in God' formerly) relates the state of redemption, as effect, to Christ as cause . . . And so from the beginning only those people have attached themselves to Christ in his new community whose religious self-consciousness had taken the form of a need for redemption, and who now become assured in themselves of Christ's redeeming power.[6]

Faith is a certainty joining our religious affections (whether of the more general or particularly Christian sort) to their divine cause. While some characteristics of faith, like certainty, apply both to faith in God and faith in Christ, it seems best to regard Schleiermacher's mentions of faith as applying primarily (and in some cases exclusively) to specifically Christian faith.

Within the body of the *Glaubenslehre*, faith is given its most full treatment under the topic of conversion. Proposition 108 reads: "Conversion, the beginning of the new life in fellowship with Christ, makes itself known in each individual by Repentance, which consists in the combination of regret and change of heart; and by Faith, which consists in the appropriation of the perfection and blessedness of Christ."[7] In repentance, we turn away from our old, sinful life, and in faith we begin the new life in Christ. Schleiermacher says that the two are bound together in unity by the "desire to receive the impulses of Christ."[8]

As Schleiermacher recognizes, there is some danger in treating faith under conversion. One might think that faith is something that must be worked before the new life can begin, or that it constitutes only a moment of origin and not a continuing state. The

---

[5] Ibid. Schleiermacher, in a footnote, refers the reader to his description of the feeling of absolute dependence, and of God as the "Whence" in §4.4.
[6] Ibid., §14,1.
[7] Ibid., §108.
[8] Ibid., §108,2.

appropriation of the blessedness of Christ, which is only the beginning act of faith, is what really falls under conversion.

> For appropriation, taking possession, is a single act; whereas faith in its duration is the resulting, abiding consciousness of being in possession. Thus the beginning of divinely created faith essentially belongs to conversion; its duration is the constant basis of the new life.[9]

Thus, faith might be rightly placed under (or above?) both conversion and sanctification.

It should be more than ever clear that, as we noted above, Schleiermacher's vision of faith is not propositional in any sense, especially not the assent to propositions taught by the Church, or even by Jesus.[10] Faith is "something completely different from a mere acceptance of teaching and law from the Redeemer."[11] It is a movement of the heart, which in turn moves the mind and the will. The learned theologian and the churchly busybody are never found to be better Christians than the one with a burning heart who is perhaps deficient in mind and will.

> It is a serious misunderstanding when one does not rightly distinguish doctrine and faith. The faith we are concerned with is quite simply nothing but the ever renewed movement of the heart that accepts the living fellowship offered to us by Christ.[12]

Using more stationary language, Schleiermacher elsewhere defines faith as "the inward condition of one who feels content and strong in fellowship with Christ."[13] The juxtaposition of his different expressions helps us to remember that this "inward condition" is 'ever renewed movement,' and that this movement as ever renewed constitutes an abiding condition as the foundation of the new life in Christ.

---

[9] Ibid., §108,1.

[10] Schleiermacher suspects, somewhat correctly, the Roman Church of such a conception of faith, see *Christian Faith*, §108:1. He could never have taught a notion of "lifeless faith" which is still real faith, as in St. Thomas.

[11] Friedrich Schleiermacher, *Servant of the Word: Selected Sermons of Friedrich Schleiermacher*, trans. Dawn De Vries (Philadelphia: Fortress, 1987) 54.

[12] Ibid., 148.

[13] Schleiermacher, *Christian Faith*, §108,1.

Because of its experiential nature, faith can take many forms, much like the feeling of absolute dependence which is never found in itself, but always in combination with various human states. Both conversion and the course of the spiritual life can take different forms according to temperament and external conditions, not to mention the working of God. "Faith is nothing other than the incipient experience of the satisfaction of that spiritual need by Christ: there can still be very diverse ways of experiencing the need and the succor, and yet they will all be faith."[14]

We should note that "they will *all* be faith." Whatever the diversities of its manifestation, faith remains ever the same.[15] This identity of faith not only applies to all Christians today, but to all who have ever experienced Christian faith.

But here again we must recall our fundamental proposition, that the whole procedure in redemption, the same for all races, Jew and Gentile, is also the same for all ages, and that the essential identity of redemption and of the Christian fellowship would be imperiled if our faith had either another content or another origin—the one implies the other—than it had in the case of the first disciples.[16]

In the experience of faith, we have a contemporaneity with those who have gone before us. As H. Richard Niebuhr puts it, "There is a kind of foretaste of the resurrection of the dead in the community of faith."[17] Here we come to the question: Since the origins of our faith must be the same as for the first disciples, how does faith arise? Is it our work? The work of God? Some combination of the two? What is its relation to the church? Having hopefully traced enough of the

---

[14] Ibid., §14,2.

[15] Cf. Schleiermacher, *Servant of the Word,* 68: "Faith must be exactly the same in all of us." See also *Christian Faith,* §109,4: "For just as the union of the divine with the human nature in Christ remained the same through all experience and development, so our union with Christ in faith remains always the same."

[16] Schleiermacher, *Christian Faith,* §108,5.

[17] Niebuhr, *Faith on Earth,* 113. Niebuhr goes on to speak of "that contemporaneity of the life we live in faith, when we find those who are dead yet speaking to us, because they are in the same situation personally in which we are. The church of the past is a present church, not to perception but in our life of trust and loyalty." Niebuhr's *Faith on Earth,* while not without criticisms of Schleiermacher, has tremendous affinities with him.

contours of faith to make its countenance recognizable, we now turn
to its provenance.

III. The Production of Faith

In considering the origins of faith, a student of Schleiermacher
must first say that faith never sprang from proof but from
preaching.[18] Such proclamation is how faith was delivered to the
earliest Christians, and it is how faith must be delivered to us. Without
the power of the Word, there is no faith, no conversion, no
Christianity. The only difference between us and the apostles is
"simply that the self-revelation of Christ is now mediated by those
who preach Him; but they being appropriated by Him as His
instruments, the activity really proceeds from Him and is essentially
His own."[19]
The person of faith is able to give testimony to others of the need
for redemption and the succor in Christ, which he or she has come to
experience. "Such preaching must always take the form of testimony;
testimony as to one's own experience, which shall arouse in others
the desire to have the same experience."[20] The focus on personal
experience should not deceive one into thinking the preaching is pure
subjectivity. Rather, it always "includes descriptions of Christ and His
work."[21] One's interior self-consciousness of redemption is never,
whether in one's own inner counsel or in public testimony, separate
from the historical Jesus of Nazareth.[22]
The encounter that arouses faith in Christ is not simply the
encounter of preacher and hearer. It is much broader. John C. Weborg
says that Schleiermacher's notion of faith is "an ecclesi-

---

[18] Schleiermacher, *Christian Faith*, §14,3.
[19] Ibid., §108,5; note there also: "The influence of Christ, therefore, consists solely
in the human communication of the Word, in so far as that communication embodies
Christ's word and continues the indwelling divine power of Christ himself."
[20] Ibid., §14,1; one should recall §108,2: "...the desire to receive the impulses that
come from Christ . . . binds regret and faith together and represents the true unity of
conversion."
[21] Ibid., §14,1.
[22] Cf. ibid., 108, 5: "For if it be allowed that there are divine workings of
converting grace in no actual historical relation to the personal efficacy of Christ
(even though it is as workings of Christ that they come to consciousness), there
would be no security that this inward mystic Christ was identical with the historical
Christ." I think that it is from such a passage that one could begin a refutation of Emil
Brunner's accusing Schleiermacher of "mysticism."

ological-sociological category.[23] The whole community of faith bears witness

> ... that faith of itself carries with it that participation [in the Christian communion]; and not only as depending on the spontaneous activity of the man who has become a believer, but also as depending on the spontaneous activity of the communion (Church), as the source from which the testimony proceeded for the awakening of faith.[24]

The whole church gives the testimony, which brings us to faith, which in turn incorporates us into the church, joining its witness.

Many Christians, including many late twentieth-century Christians, cart out various "evidences" for Christian faith. If anything, the fondness of our "scientific" age for proofs and facts has only exacerbated this tendency, which springs ever anew from our desperate need to be in control. Though Schleiermacher never had to deal with Josh McDowell and the like, he did have words concerning the attempt to produce faith in Christ on the basis of miracles, the fulfillment of prophecies, or the divine inspiration of the Scriptures. Schleiermacher's axe to cut through this thicket is the following: "that the efficacy of these things somehow always presupposes faith, and therefore cannot produce it."[25] We only give credence to miracles and prophecies where faith is already present.

> ... if faith in the revelation of God in Christ and in redemption through Him has not already arisen in the direct way through experience as the demonstration of the Spirit and of power, neither miracles nor prophecies can produce it, and indeed ... this faith would be just as immovable even if Christianity had neither prophecies nor miracles to show.[26]

---

[23] John C. Weborg, "A Study of Schleiermacher's Concept of Faith," *Covenant Quarterly* 36 (Fall 1978): 46. Weborg is opposing this "ecclesiological-sociological" idea of faith to faith as "pneumatological category" in the Reformers. He needs to consider that, for Schleiermacher, the ecclesiological *is* the pneumatological. Of course, there is the difficult question of whether, in Schleiermacher's theology, there is a Holy Spirit beyond the common spirit of the church. Here again, comparison with H. Richard Niebuhr would be fruitful.
[24] Schleiermacher, *Christian Faith*, §14, postscript.
[25] Weborg, "Schleiermacher's Concept of Faith," 71.
[26] Schleiermacher, *Christian Faith*, §14, postscript.

Schleiermacher also lays aside "proofs" from scripture considered as inspired, because the faith was spread for a couple of centuries without a canonical New Testament, and because of the divorce of such an exercise from the Christian religious affections.

Having seen that faith comes through preaching, through the testimony of the whole church, and not by means of miracles and such, we turn to the question of whose agency is active in the production of faith. Here Schleiermacher is a good son of Luther and Calvin. At the most fundamental level, faith is no human work, but the grace of God.

But since faith arises only through the agency of Christ, it is clearly implied in our theorem that no natural constitution of man, nothing that takes shape in him independently of the whole series of gracious workings mediated by Christ, alters his relation to God, or effects his justification, and that no merit of any kind avails for this.[27]

Human instruments may be used, but it is God who acts. It is only possible for faith to arise when "the glory of the only begotten Son of the Father fills the soul."[28] This is God's gift.

Nonetheless, Schleiermacher speaks of our "free resolve," "some activity of the self," and so on.[29] What are we to make of this? He seems to hold two points in tension. On the one hand,

It seems obvious, then, that here no causal agency can be attributed to the person who is being taken up into fellowship, for the higher form cannot be in any way derived from lower stages of life as present either in the individual or in a group of people yet to be converted.... Even the consent accompanying the reception of the Divine Word, as far as it is directed to what is essential and characteristic in it, can be ascribed only to the antecedent work of grace.[30]

Barth himself could hardly have made this point more strongly (although he might have used more capital letters and exclamation points!). Schleiermacher, however, adds something:

---

[27] Ibid., §110,4.

[28] Schleiermacher, *Servant of the Word*, 68.

[29] Schleiermacher, *Christian Faith*, §14,1 and §108,1.

[30] Ibid., §108,6.

To assume an entire lack of relation between man's personal activity and the higher operation of Christ therefore yields no satisfactory result, and the problem remains to find room for an activity in real relation to the work of Christ, and yet neither cooperation nor resistance.[31]

Schleiermacher never gives a really satisfactory explanation of our role in faith and redemption. (Who ever has?) Preparatory grace is not a complete invasion, but heightens something which is already present, "though pushed back to the very frontiers of consciousness": our desire for fellowship with God, which is part of our original perfection, and is "never entirely extinguished" in fallen humanity.[32] While this desire is not exactly activity but rather potentiality or "susceptibility," it is kindled to activity by grace.

Like virtually all treatments of faith of which I am aware, Schleiermacher's is at base an antinomy, whatever his attempts at logical consistency. Faith comes only as a gracious gift from God, yet human beings have some role in it, even "free resolve." These two assertions cannot be logically wed, and yet both seem necessary for Christians to hold. Perhaps it is best for the theologian simply to state this situation, rather than straining at unsatisfying formulations in an attempt to encompass both insights.[33]

While it is not as directly related to the production of faith, having considered the role of human activity in faith, it seems only appropriate to consider the related issue of faith and works. Here again Schleiermacher is heir to the Reformation. He may be the "founder of modern liberal protestantism," but whether he is more identified with those who went before or those who came after, seems

---

[31] Ibid.

[32] Ibid.

[33] The best definition of antinomy I have encountered is from Sergei Bulgakov: " ... an antinomy differs both from a logical and a dialectical contradiction. An antinomy simultaneously admits the truth of two contradictory, logically incompatible, but ontologically equally necessary assertions. An antinomy testifies to the existence of a mystery beyond which the human reason cannot penetrate. This mystery, nevertheless, is actualized and lived in religious experience. All fundamental dogmatic definitions are of this nature." Bulgakov, Sergei, *Sophia: The Wisdom of God*, (Hudson NY: Lindisfarne, 1993) 77, n.18. The removal of antinomy is the perpetual temptation of systematic theology. Schleiermacher perhaps succumbs to this temptation by making things a bit too pat, but his restriction of dogmatics to the setting forth in speech of Christian religious affections is itself an act of humility and an acknowledgment of mystery.

an open question to me (much like the question whether the magisterial Reformers are medieval or modern).

Anyone who holds that good works are necessary to blessedness because for him faith is mere knowledge is using a different vocabulary from ours, or holding an entirely different doctrine of redemption. . . . Anyone who does truly good works has blessedness already in his faith, and therefore cannot find himself wanting first to rely upon his works.[34]

Faith comes as a gift, but issues immediately in spontaneous activity. Christ is purely active, and so activity must characterize our fellowship with him.[35]

... our union with Christ in faith is, though not as completely, yet quite as essentially, an active obedience as His life was an active obedience of the human nature to the indwelling being of God within Him; and our reception into living fellowship with Him is the fruitful germ of all good works in the same way as the act of uniting was in His case the germ of all redeeming activity.[36]

Of course, all our good works in this life carry sin along with them. God is pleased by our good works only for the sake of our persons regarded in Christ.[37] What is important is our incorporation into living fellowship with Christ, not so much the works that will inevitably, and inevitably imperfectly, follow.

Thus, faith is produced in us by God, but not without some activity on our part, by means of the Word in preaching and the testimony of the Church, into which we are incorporated by that same faith.

---

[34] Schleiermacher, *Christian Faith*, §112,1.

[35] Ibid., §108,6.

[36] Ibid., §112,1. It is worth noting that this is yet another instance of Schleiermacher speaking of the faithful person *in persona Christi*. At the risk of filling this page with long quotations, the reader is asked to indulge another from §112,1, perhaps the strongest on this topic: "Allowing ourselves to be taken up into living fellowship with Christ, we are laid hold of by the union of the divine with the human nature in His Person, and consent to this becomes a constant and active will to maintain and extend this union." The Church is here, as classically, the continuation of the Incarnation. Peter Vogt has suggested to me that such passages imply an invisible church of the truly faithful within the state church of all citizens.

[37] Ibid., §112,3.

Human good works in no way supplement faith, but issue spontaneously from it, and are regarded graciously by God for the sake of the person now living in Christ. Schleiermacher reaffirms many characteristic Reformation emphases, and clearly regards faith as of the highest importance. ("There is no other way of obtaining participation in the Christian communion than through faith in Jesus as the Redeemer.")[38] Nonetheless, any glance at the index of the *Glaubenslehre*, or at the notes to this paper, will reveal that the discussion of faith is quite small. What sense can be made of this situation?

IV. The Relation of Faith to Other Terms

One possibility, which has been proposed from various quarters, is that Schleiermacher has made an equation of faith with other terms and discusses it under them. One even reads that Schleiermacher offers "nothing but a doctrine of faith."[39] Thus, we will now consider a number of candidates for faith's *alter ego*: piety, revelation, and living fellowship with Christ.

In their introduction to Schleiermacher's open letters to Dr. Lücke, James Duke and Francis Fiorenza observe, "Although Schleiermacher refers to his dogmatics as the *Glaubenslehre* or doctrine of faith, it is piety (*Frömmigkeit*) rather than faith which assumes the central place in the work."[40] Both his Moravian pietist background and his Reformed heritage (Calvin's emphasis on *pietas* which joins reverence and love, and without which God is not known) no doubt contribute to his affinity for the term. Very early in *The Christian Faith*, we learn that piety is a modification of immediate self-consciousness (or feeling) and the basis of all religious

---

[38] Ibid., §14.

[39] George Hasson Thomas, "Revelation, Faith, and Doctrine: A Study Based on the Theology of John Calvin, Friedrich Schleiermacher, and Karl Barth," (Ph.D. thesis, Vanderbilt University, 1961), 156. This assertion, which I take as a bit too strong, may be influenced by Karl Barth's suggestion that Schleiermacher's work might be taken as a theology of the Holy Spirit, especially when one adds that faith and the work of the Spirit tend to be tightly connected in Reformed theology. Cf. Barth's "Concluding Unscientific Postscript on Schleiermacher," in *Karl Barth: Theologian of Freedom*, ed. C. Green (Minneapolis: Fortress, 1989), 66-90 (esp. 88-90).

[40] Friedrich Schleiermacher, *On the "Glaubenslehre"*, trans. James Duke and Francis Fiorenza (Atlanta: Scholars Press, 1981), 11.

communion.[41] In the letters to Lücke, it seems to be identical with God-consciousness, and he calls it "the original expression of an immediate existential relationship."[42] Piety appears to be, on a strictly definitional level, identical to faith. In practice, however, Schleiermacher uses "piety" more broadly, tending to speak of "faith" primarily in relation to the need for redemption and its accomplishment in Jesus.[43]

Now we come to revelation. After more than fifty pages of exposition on Schleiermacher's theology of revelation, George Thomas asserts, "I could just as well have discussed all of the preceding material of this one chapter under the heading of faith as to have discussed it under the heading of revelation as did."[44] Revelation is discussed even less than faith in the *Glaubenslehre*, and it would be another project to draw out his usage of the term. However, the definition in §10 should suffice for our purposes:

> Accordingly we might say that the idea of revelation signifies the *originality* of the fact which lies at the foundation of a religious communion, in the sense that this fact, as conditioning the individual content of the religious emotions which are found in the communion, cannot itself be explained by the historical chain which precedes it.[45]

Revelation, like faith, is not doctrine or propositional knowledge. It refers to the divine causality behind the modification of immediate self-consciousness. Again, we have a term very close to faith. I suggest, however, that revelation points more to the causality in God not explained by history, and faith more to what happens to a person as the consciousness of sin begins to be replaced by that of grace, as a result of that causality. Moreover, the sections on revelation are so meager that, even if one made a strict identification of revelation and faith, these sections would not much further our understanding of faith.

My own candidate for the *alter ego* of faith in Schleiermacher's *Glaubenslehre* is "living fellowship with Christ." As an exercise, one

---

[41] Schleiermacher, *Christian Faith*, §3.

[42] Schleiermacher, *On the "Glaubenslehre,"* 40, 45-46.

[43] Perhaps in practice, "piety" often equals the more general "faith in God," as opposed to "faith in Christ." See above, for this distinction.

[44] Thomas, "Revelation, Faith, and Doctrine," 156.

[45] Schleiermacher, *Christian Faith*, §10, postscript.

could go through the quotes from Schleiermacher on faith in this paper alone, marking every time that he refers to fellowship with Christ in that context. One would use quite a lot of ink in doing so. Further, this category includes all his references to the church, as the union of Christians with each other "rests so entirely on their union with Christ that the union of an individual with Christ is unthinkable apart from his union with believers."[46] Finally, we quote from his discussion of the Lord's Supper:

> The general expressions for the effects of participation [in the Supper] which stand out most clearly are confirmation in faith, and the nourishment of the new man or the passing over of Christ's life into ours. Essentially both are the same, for living faith in Christ is simply the consciousness of our union with him.[47]

Schleiermacher himself all but equates the two in this passage.

Having considered these synonyms and/or near-synonyms for "faith," we must ask why Schleiermacher did not use the category of faith more extensively. The rather simple answer lies in §108: "it is unfortunate ... that in ordinary life this same word 'faith' is so often used for a conviction that is without either influence on the will or adequate foundation."[48] He is willing to retain the word *Glaube* because it is the ordinary translation for the Scriptural word *pistis*, and because it has acquired great significance in the Protestant-Catholic conflicts over good works. He is, after all, writing a church dogmatics. However, there is no escaping the fact that faith has been associated with intellectual assent and doctrinal orthodoxy ("The Faith").

Schleiermacher spent much of his theological career trying to move away from such conceptions, creating a dogmatics grounded in Christian religious affections. As his early book *On Religion: Addresses in Response to its Cultured Despisers* shows, he was much concerned with apologetics to the unbelievers of his day.[49] Why open the door to possible confusions, when other, less suspect categories

---

[46] Ibid., §141,1.

[47] Ibid. Perhaps Schleiermacher's Moravian background comes into play in the importance of "living fellowship with Christ." My Moravian friend Peter Vogt has reminded me of the importance of "daily interaction with the Savior" in Zinzendorf.

[48] Ibid., §108,1.

[49] Friedrich Schleiermacher, *On Religion: Addresses in Response to its Cultured Despisers,* trans. Terrence N. Tice, Research in Theology, ed. Dietrich Ritschl (Richmond, VA: John Knox Press, 1969).

will do the job as well? (This also explains why revelation does not figure largely.)[50] This is a notable example of how context can shape a theological system.

V. Concluding Remarks
(A Postliberal Appreciation of Schleiermacher!!)

We now see that, for Friedrich Schleiermacher, faith (laying aside its more general use) is primarily living fellowship with Jesus Christ, caused by God, but not without something of our own activity. It is related to (or even identical to) a number of other theological categories (revelation, piety, living fellowship) which carry some of its weight, due to contextual reasons.

Schleiermacher's manner of treating faith is not only a dusty curiosity to be put back in the drawer after examination: "How quaint!" Hidden within it lies a valuable lesson for the contemporary theologian. Schleiermacher is responsive to his context and its usage of Christian language. However, in his responsiveness, he does not allow himself to be ruled by that context. (At least not in regard to faith.) One of the premier strategies that the Tempter suggests to the theological mind is founded in the desire to be understood. All too often, this results in the "translation" of Christian language into a secular tongue. Tillich is a stunningly brilliant example of how to do this. Despite all the best intentions, this strategy always ends in betrayal of the particularity of the Gospel.

When faced with a situation like that of Schleiermacher— widespread misunderstanding of a piece of Christian language like "faith"—the theologian who chooses not to translate from Church to World seems to have two options. First, she or he may strenuously work to make the proper definitions clear to Christians. Barth can be read as such a striving for grammatical and linguistic clarity. However, one can also translate the misunderstood term, not into the World's language, but into variants within the Church's language. If it seems (pastorally) inadvisable to talk too much of faith, then one can talk of revelation, piety, living fellowship with Christ and with all believers in him. I think any theologian who attempts to speak from

---

[50] In our so-called postmodern age, "faith" has perhaps lost some of the connotations that Lutheran, Reformed, and Roman orthodoxies had given it in the early nineteenth century. Today's shadow-side of faith is more likely to be the anti-intellectual emoting of *some* fundamentalist and charismatic groups. At the risk of speculating, if Schleiermacher had felt free to write a theology of faith, I think it would look much like H. Richard Niebuhr's *Faith on Earth*, only more systematic.

within Christian faith, and not from some neutral standpoint, should (and probably already does) employ both these options. Perhaps, in the odd providence of God, we find Barth and Schleiermacher here together in embrace under the sign of faith.[51]

---

[51] I owe a final debt of gratitude to Jack Forstman, Peter Vogt, and Susan Windley who read and commented on an earlier draft.

Who's Afraid of Ludwig Feuerbach?
Suspicion and the Religious Imagination

Garrett Green

> . . . an object first takes on its true intrinsic dignity when
> the sacred nimbus is stripped off; for as long as a thing or
> being is an object of religious worship, it is clad in borrowed
> plumes, namely, the peacock feathers of the human
> imagination.
> —Ludwig Feuerbach, *Lectures on the Essence of
> Religion*

> We . . . need be afraid of no Feuerbach.
> —Karl Barth, *Church Dogmatics*

Ludwig Feuerbach appears condemned to play the historical role of
"influence." We read other thinkers of the nineteenth century
today—Hegel, for example, or Kierkegaard, or Marx—for their ideas,
for the insights they continue to bring to contemporary issues at
the end of the twentieth century. But Feuerbach is nearly always
studied primarily because of the influence he has exercised on other
thinkers—the ones who still attract readers today. James Livingston,
for example, concludes his treatment of Feuerbach in *Modern
Christian Thought* by noting how his "influence on modern thought
far exceeds that of thinkers of much greater reputation and
popularity." He mentions Feuerbach's contributions to now familiar
themes in existentialism, to the psychological theories of Sigmund
Freud and Erich Fromm, and to the I-Thou philosophy of Martin
Buber, before coming at last to the "most significant of all" the
influences: the role that Feuerbach's ideas played in the development
of Karl Marx's thought, both early and late.[1] Even the critical
edition of Feuerbach's works—produced, significantly, in the Berlin of
the German Democratic Republic—pays tribute to him primarily as
"one of the most outstanding philosophical materialists of the pre-
Marxist period . . . and above all as one of the immediate

---

[1]James C. Livingston, *Modern Christian Thought*, 2d ed. (Upper Saddle River,
NJ: Prentice Hall, 1997) 1:228-29.

philosophical predecessors of Marx and Engels."[2]
Although hardly wishing to deny the importance of such influences, Van Harvey, in his recent study *Feuerbach and the Interpretation of Religion*, wants more. Convinced that Feuerbach has been the victim of persistent misunderstandings, he wants to rehabilitate him so that his voice can be heard in the dialogue about the meaning of religion today. To this end, Harvey proposes to undertake a "rational reconstruction" of Feuerbach's philosophy of religion, not simply an historical account of his thought in the context of his own time and place (116 ff.).[3]   Two themes in particular emerge from his attempt to reconstruct Feuerbach's treatment of religion that invite further reflection and response from late twentieth-century readers, not only from those who study religion academically, but also from those for whom the interpretation of religion is a matter of *theological* importance. Since I belong to both groups, I propose to take seriously the implications of Feuerbach's theory of religion for both religious studies and historical theology. The first theme highlighted in Harvey's reading of Feuerbach is *suspicion*. Harvey claims in effect that Feuerbach is the forgotten founder of the hermeneutics of suspicion, whose omission from the canonical list of "masters of suspicion" stems from a failure to understand and appreciate his mature theory of religion. The second theme to emerge from Harvey's retrieval of Feuerbach is the central role of *imagination* in his account of the origin and continuing power of religion in human life and history.

Feuerbach: Neglected Master of Suspicion

One of the more perceptive questions raised by Harvey concerns that now-classic category of Paul Ricoeur, the hermeneutics of suspicion. Why, asks Harvey, is not Feuerbach included along with Marx, Nietzsche, and Freud as one of "the masters of suspicion," those revolutionaries of nineteenth-century thought who changed forever the way we read the authoritative texts of our traditions, including especially our religious traditions? He notes that Ricoeur is

---

[2] Werner Schuffenhauer, preface to *Gesammelte Werke*, by Ludwig Feuerbach (Berlin: Akademie-Verlag, 1981) 1:vii. In the same opening sentence, the editor also pigeonholes Feuerbach as "one of the prominent representatives of classical German *bourgeois* philosophy."

[3] Van A. Harvey, *Feuerbach and the Interpretation of Religion* (New York: Cambridge University Press, 1995); page references to this work are provided parenthetically in the text.

not alone in denying to Feuerbach a place among the suspicious elite and offers some reasons why this should be so. First of all, Feuerbach's influence on subsequent thinkers has not been as great as that of Marx, Nietzsche, and Freud; and second, his critique "was not part of a larger theoretical framework that was widely appropriated by secular intellectuals and integrated into what we now call the behavioral sciences" (7). More important than either of these factors, however, are a number of widely held misinterpretations of Feuerbach's critique of religion, and it is largely to show that they *are* misinterpretations that Harvey has written his book. He is persuaded that "all of these conventional judgments are partial and misleading truths," and he proposes "to challenge and, if possible, to correct them" (11).

Chief among the misreadings of Feuerbach, according to Harvey, is the exclusive identification of his theory of religion with *The Essence of Christianity* (1841), an interpretation that leads either to the neglect of his later works or else to the assumption that they merely refine or clarify the theory already articulated in the 1841 book. In fact, according to Harvey's interpretation, in the mature Feuerbach, religion "is no longer explained in terms of self-consciousness alone but in terms of a contingent self confronted with an all-encompassing nature upon which it is absolutely dependent" (162). Harvey is quite definite in his judgment that the later theory is better (163); it is new and "truly original" (169), he claims, and best of all it breaks finally with the lingering Hegelianism of *The Essence of Christianity*. The later theory "assumes, as the earlier did not, that believers have intellectual grounds, albeit mistaken, for their beliefs" (199). Harvey thinks that Feuerbach makes a useful contribution to the modern academic study of religion because he really "listen[s] to what believers themselves say" (309). (Harvey's hermeneutical "charity" toward Feuerbach may occasionally overreach itself; believers might be excused for not appreciating a careful listener who concludes that their hymns, prayers, hopes, and beliefs all amount in the end to no more than "the religious illusion.") But Harvey's point is that Feuerbach deserves a hearing for his mature attempt to "let religion itself speak" and then to offer his own interpretation. *Feuerbach and the Interpretation of Religion* is an invitation to do just that, to engage in serious dialogue with one of the most important critics of religion in the modern age; and by offering us a fresh and insightful account of Feuerbach's later theory of religion, Harvey's book helps to advance that dialogue.

Feuerbach and the Theologians

One of the criteria for rational reconstructions that Harvey borrows from Richard Rorty (whom he credits with originating the distinction between rational and historical reconstructions) is that "they are dominated by questions that have come to prominence in some recent work." Professor Harvey assures us that his reconstruction of Feuerbach's thought springs from just such contemporary concerns; he is also explicit about the fact that in his own case the questions arise "in the field of religious studies in contrast to theology." Despite his own disinterest in theological questions, he nevertheless makes an intriguing observation about Feuerbach's reception by the theologians. "Strangely enough," he remarks, "Feuerbach's work for the most part has been taken seriously only by Marxist philosophers and Protestant theologians and has been virtually neglected by scholars in religious studies" (20). For just this reason he undertakes to explore the implications of Feuerbach's thought for religious studies, by which he evidently means non-theological religious studies. Since I have a rather different take on what properly constitutes the field of religious studies (and how it is related to theology), I want to remove the brackets that Professor Harvey has placed around theological questions. Religious studies is the legitimate domain of all scholars who—out of whatever religious, anti-religious, or extra-religious motivations and interests—wish to engage in the serious, public, and academic investigation into the nature, function, and value of religion. For this reason, I do not find it strange that theologians (not to mention Marxist philosophers) should be among the first to take Feuerbach's critique of religion seriously. They, after all, are the ones with the biggest stake in the outcome. The attempt to separate the study of religion from theological questions (something, incidentally, that Feuerbach never dreamed of doing) inevitably leads to the neglect of the inescapable question of the *truth* of religious teachings, and hence the integrity of religious believers. Nowhere are these issues more sharply focused than in the themes of suspicion and imagination, especially at their point of convergence. Professor Harvey's rational reconstruction of Feuerbach's interpretation of religion, perhaps in spite of his own intentions, sheds a revealing light on just these issues, including their theological implications.

Harvey's observation about theological interest in Feuerbach requires some qualification as soon as we look more closely at the theological landscape since the last century. Of the leading twentieth-century theologians, only Karl Barth has devoted serious attention to Feuerbach.[4] More remarkable than the general theological neglect of Feuerbach, however, is the character of this one exception: for Barth's treatment of Feuerbach's theory of religion is overwhelmingly positive. The primary reason for Barth's affirmation of Feuerbach is that he sees him as an ally (though admittedly an unwitting one) in his struggle to free theology from its dangerous infatuation with religion. Barth takes him to be, in the words of John Glasse, "the man whose query does nothing less than locate the Achilles heel of modern theology," a flaw that is most obvious in the case of Schleiermacher, but which also afflicts other theologians, including Schleiermacher's critics.[5] Barth mentions specifically G. Menken, J. A. L. Wegscheider, W. L. DeWette, A. Tholuck, and P. Marheineke as other theologians of the day who left themselves open to Feuerbach's reduction of theology to anthropology. He doesn't stop with the generation of Schleiermacher, but includes as well later theologians who had the benefit of hearing Feuerbach's critique yet nevertheless persisted in doing theology in a way that perpetuated the "apotheosis of man," thus remaining vulnerable to the Feuerbachian reduction. This history of shame in nineteenth-century theology reaches its culmination in 1900 in the crowning irony of Adolf von Harnack's public lectures on *The Essence of Christianity*, the same title under which Feuerbach had already demonstrated the disastrous consequences of the very path proposed by Harnack to his listeners.

Barth's endorsement of Feuerbach is decidedly qualified in one respect. Although crediting him with drawing the inevitable consequence of the theological enterprise of his day, he nevertheless refers to it as "Feuerbach's trivial conclusion," wondering how these theologians could have left themselves vulnerable "to that mean insinuation, that "slander.""[6] Feuerbach may be right in important respects, says Barth, but his theory of religion remains shallow, "a

---

[4]For bibliographical references to theological responses to Feuerbach in the first part of the century, see the superb article by John Glasse, "Barth on Feuerbach," *Harvard Theological Review* 57 (1964): 69-96, esp. n. 1.

[5]Ibid., 72.

[6]Karl Barth, "An Introductory Essay," in *The Essence of Christianity*, by Ludwig Feuerbach (New York: Harper and Row, 1957), xx-xxi. This essay, used as an introduction to the English translation of Feuerbach's most famous work, was translated by James Luther Adams from a lecture Barth gave in Münster in 1926, later published as a chapter in *Die Theologie und die Kirche* (Zollikon-Zürich: Evangelischer Verlag, 1928).

platitude," "at bottom trite beyond compare."[7]
It is surely overstating the case, however, to say, as Harvey does in his introduction, that Barth treats Feuerbach simply "as a *reductio ad absurdum* of liberal theology since Schleiermacher" (20). In the first place, Barth hardly thinks that the identification of religion with human projection is an absurdity, for he endorses this position himself as the negative moment of the dialectic of religion and revelation in his own theory of religion in the *Church Dogmatics*.[8] In the second place, Barth by no means restricts his appreciation of Feuerbach to his role in unmasking the error of modern[9] theology. For even his negative comments about Feuerbach are set in the context of a generous appreciation of Feuerbach's intentions. He says, in effect, that if one is going to turn man into God, Feuerbach's way of doing it is at least more honest than the theologians. Moreover, it does greater justice to the concrete reality of human life in the world than do the spiritualizing abstractions of the theologians. Feuerbach has a "head start over modern theology" because of what Barth calls (negatively) "his resolute anti-spiritualism" or (positively) "his anthropological realism." Barth calls special attention to the communal nature of Feuerbach's humanism. Perhaps for this reason he treats Feuerbach with greater deference than that other notorious nineteenth-century despiser of Christianity, Friedrich Nietzsche. Whereas Nietzsche represents for Barth the great champion of the isolated individual, of "humanity without the fellow-man,"[10] Feuerbach affirms the unity of human bodily and spiritual reality "in the relation of the I and the Thou" ("It is just because religion is concerned with the assertion of this unity," Barth comments, "that it makes sense and not nonsense" for Feuerbach.)[11]   The supreme example of this communal anthropology is surely Feuerbach's interpretation of the Christian doctrine of the Trinity, which Harvey cites. The Trinity, Feuerbach argues,

---

[7]Ibid., xxvii.
[8]For an account of Barth's theological theory of religion, see Garrett Green, "Challenging the Religious Studies Canon: Karl Barth's Theory of Religion," *Journal of Religion* 75 (1995): 473-86.
[9]Harvey also errs in assuming that Barth thinks Feuerbach unmasks the secret only of *liberal* theology. Barth makes quite clear that the judgment falls on virtually all theologians, including many of the most conservative of the day.
[10]Barth, *Church Dogmatics*, vol. 3, pt. 2, ed. G. W. Bromiley and T. F. Torrance, trans. Harold Knight et al. (Edinburgh: T. & T. Clark, 1960) 231-42.
[11]Barth, "Introductory Essay," xxiv.

is the secret of the *necessity of the "thou" for an "I"*; it is the truth that *no being*—be it man, God, mind or ego—*is for itself alone a true, perfect*, and *absolute* being, that *truth* and *perfection* are only the *connection and unity* of beings equal in their essence. The highest and last principle of philosophy is, therefore, the *unity of men with men*.[12]

This social understanding of the Trinity shows striking similarities to Barth's own theology, so his admiration is perhaps not surprising. Not only does Feuerbach work "with human honesty and real seriousness"; Barth is willing to say even that "he works, as it were, with a Christian realism." So "Feuerbach—however badly he may have done his work—was and is really stronger than the great majority of modern and most recent theologians."[13] Barth's concern is finally not to pass judgment on Feuerbach—who, after all, does not claim to be doing Christian theology—but rather on those thinkers who do make such a claim. "Why has Christian theology," he asks, "not seen these things earlier and better than Feuerbach, things that it certainly must have seen if it really knew the Old and New Testament?" Barth is unwilling to join in the self-serving tut-tutting of the theologians about Feuerbach's atheism until they have put their own house in order. Barth in effect agrees with Harvey's judgment that Feuerbach "believed that religion was too important a subject to leave to the theologians"(6). Barth believes it too—rather, he believes that *theology* is too important a subject to leave to the theologians, for "the attitude of the anti-theologian Feuerbach was more theological than that of many theologians."[14]

Suspicion and Imagination in Feuerbach's Theory of Religion

Feuerbach and the Interpretation of Religion ought at the very least to alter the way scholars henceforth understand the nineteenth-century roots of religious studies. For Harvey demonstrates convincingly that the hermeneutics of suspicion begins with Feuerbach—and not merely because of his influence on Marx. Indeed, Feuerbach's ideas on religion lead more directly to the Freudian than

---

[12]Feuerbach, *Principles of the Philosophy of the Future*, cited by Harvey, 179.
[13]Barth, "Introductory Essay," xxiv-xxv.
[14]Ibid., x.

to the Marxian or Nietzschean version of suspicion.[15] The all-important concept of projection originates with Feuerbach, a debt acknowledged by Freud, who first turned it into a powerful and influential (if also problematic and controversial) tool in the interpretation of religion. (A portion of the credit also belongs to George Eliot, who rendered Feuerbach's cumbersome philosophical term *Vergegenständlichung* in the arresting metaphor of *projection.*)[16] Likewise pointing towards Freud's later theory is Feuerbach's emphasis on the role of desire in religion, eventuating in the *Glückseligkeitstrieb*, a term rife with proleptic Freudian overtones.

More important than these adumbrations of later nineteenth-century theory, however, is Feuerbach's account of the engine of religious projection. By identifying imagination as the "organ of religion," Feuerbach opened a perspective on religion whose significance is only beginning to be grasped at the end of the twentieth century. If he had possessed even an inkling of the possibilities inherent in this thesis—and nothing is more obvious from Harvey's book than that he did not—his treatment of religion might well have taken on a proto-Nietzschean cast. For the importance of Feuerbach's thesis, that the imagination is the key to understanding how and why human beings are religious, lies beyond the horizon of his own narrowly positivist epistemology and stolidly modernist temperament. All one has to do in order to bring out the possibilities of his thesis is to bracket just one unreflected assumption that Feuerbach always takes for granted and (therefore) never attempts to justify: the axiom that *imagination* and *reality* comprise an unproblematic duality, that they are opposed and mutually exclusive terms. In more fashionably contemporary terms, one could call this move a deconstruction of Feuerbach's concept of *Einbildungskraft/ Phantasie.*

The crucial connection is the one that links suspicion to imagination. Feuerbach's descriptive thesis is that religion is the product of imagination. But his evaluative thesis is more revealing; *because* religion is produced by the imagination, he claims, we are justified in treating it with suspicion. Why is Feuerbach suspicious of

[15]Merold Westphal detects three layers in Feuerbach's critique of religion: an explicit Hegelian one, a proto-Freudian one, and a more obscure Marxian strain, later radicalized by Marx himself. See *Suspicion and Faith: The Religious Uses of Modern Atheism* (Grand Rapids, Mich.: Eerdmans, 1993) 123-33, esp. 125.

[16]It is ironic testimony to the success of Eliot's translation that her term has found its way back into German discourse about religion in the twentieth century in the form of *projizieren* and *Projektion.*

religious ideas and sentiments? Because they are the fruits of imagination and *therefore* cannot be true. Nothing could have been more obvious to Feuerbach; and nothing makes more obvious to us how much the intellectual world has changed in a century and a half. In reviewing his intellectual development at the start of the *Lectures on the Essence of Religion*, Feuerbach contrasts his own position with Hegel's in a way that brings out forcefully the dualism of reason and imagination in his thought. Philosophy, he writes, deals with thought (*Denken*) or reason (*Vernunft*), while religion has to do with emotion (*Gemüt*) and imagination (*Phantasie*). Whereas in Hegel religion "merely translate[s] speculative ideas into emotionally charged images," Feuerbach insists on a sharp dichotomy between them. For he believes that Hegel missed something important in religion, "an element that is distinct from thought" and which constitutes the "very essence" of religion, which he calls sensuousness (*Sinnlichkeit*).[17] In Hegel, religion occupies precisely the mediating role between the pure sensuousness of art and the pure conceptuality of philosophy; its defining feature is this ability to mediate between the realms of intellect and sense, a form that he calls *Vorstellung*—traditionally translated "representation" but actually closer to "imagination" in English, as I have argued elsewhere.[18]

From the vantage point of the late twentieth century (whether one thinks of post-Kuhnian philosophy of science or of postmodern critiques of the metaphysical tradition), Feuerbach's move hardly seems an advance over Hegel. For although Hegel can be faulted for ultimately subordinating religious *Vorstellung* to the philosophical *Begriff*, thus perpetuating the long-standing Western prejudice for intellect over sense, Feuerbach does it undialectically and from the outset. For him the essence of religion is sensuousness, *not* intellect; and since "emotion and imagination are . . . rooted in sensibility," imagination can yield *only* illusion, leaving the field of truth to pure reason, now stripped of sensuousness—that is, of all relation to the body. So Feuerbach's sensuous anthropology, much praised even by Karl Barth, is not quite what it seems. After wisely noting that

---

[17]Ludwig Feuerbach, *Lectures on the Essence of Religion*, trans. Ralph Manheim (New York: Harper and Row, 1967), 12; *Vorlesungen über das Wesen der Religion: Nebst Zusätzen und Anmerkungen*, ed. Wolfgang Harich, *Gesammelte Werke*, vol. 6 (Berlin: Akademie-Verlag, 1967) 18. I have followed Harvey's practice of using shortened titles in references to this work (see p. x for a list), first to the English translation and then to the German original.

[18]See Garrett Green, *Imagining God: Theology and the Religious Imagination* (San Francisco: Harper and Row, 1989) 14-16.

Sinnlichkeit includes "not only the belly, but the head as well," Feuerbach proceeds to exempt the head from the limitations of *Sinnlichkeit* by presupposing a disembodied faculty of purely intelligible *Denken* and *Vernunft* that evidently gazes directly upon the truth. So in the end, for Feuerbach—*Sinnlichkeit* notwithstanding—the head thinks truth, while the belly imagines illusion.

The Beam of Projection and the
Grid of Imagination

Professor Harvey titles his book *Feuerbach and the Interpretation of Religion*—rather than, say, *Feuerbach's Interpretation of Religion*—for good reason. His interest is not simply a historical one, for he thinks that studying Feuerbach not only illumines the origins of religious studies in the nineteenth century but can also help us understand religion today. This constructive and contemporary motivation comes most clearly to the fore in chapter seven, the book's longest, entitled "Feuerbach and Contemporary Projection Theories." Here Harvey attempts to cash out the new and improved critique of religion in the later Feuerbach by showing its usefulness for the theory of religious projection, a task he carries out by bringing his "ideal Feuerbach" into "the modern conversation" about the meaning and truth of religion. For reasons that I find puzzling, Harvey has chosen to modernize Feuerbach by focusing on projection—the very concept on which Feuerbach relied so heavily in *The Essence of Christianity* but then abandoned in his later theory (the one Professor Harvey himself finds to be superior). Harvey's strategy—as I hope to demonstrate—leads him to make a problematic distinction between two types of projection, which he dubs the "Beam" theory and the "Grid" theory. I believe that the issues become clearer, both in the later Feuerbach and in the contemporary discussion, if we limit the term projection to the Beam model and see Grid theory as one way (a rather unclear one, in my judgment) of thematizing the role of imagination in religion. This approach recommends itself because it focuses on a term that was crucial both for Feuerbach (late as well as early) and for religious studies today. The term "imagination" not only describes religion more accurately, but also does so in a less tendentious way than the problematic term "projection."

One of the most useful, and as far as I know original, aspects of Harvey's book is the careful distinction he draws between Feuerbach's early and late critiques of religion.[19] The well-known theory in *The Essence of Christianity*—the version that so impressed the young Karl Marx—was an "inversion of Hegel's philosophy of Spirit" in which religion is "regarded as an involuntary projection inherent in and necessary for complete self-consciousness." In the *Essence of Religion and the Lectures on the Essence of Religion*, Feuerbach (in Harvey's paraphrase) sees religion instead as "an erroneous, belief-like interpretation of the all-encompassing and mysterious nature upon which the self knows itself to be dependent, an interpretation that springs out of the confrontation of the I with the not-I and the desire for recognition by this other" (229). The twofold occurrence of the word "interpretation" is not accidental; rather, it captures the main thrust of the new theory as Harvey presents it. Two other, briefer, summary statements make the point even more directly. Whereas in *The Essence of Christianity*, Harvey summarizes, "Feuerbach proposed that religion is a stage in the development of self-consciousness and must, therefore, evolve into philosophy," the later Feuerbach sees religion as "not an involuntary reflex of the self but an interpretation. ...." Even more pithily, Harvey can say that the early theory was "largely a function of ... the notion of projection," while in the later theory "religion is an interpretative response" to external forces (231). Note that in Harvey's own most careful formulations "projection" is a feature of the early Feuerbach, while his later theory is described by "interpretation." The contrast, in other words (this time mine, not Harvey's), is between two ways of imagining God: in the projected ideal image of the human species, or in the image of a personified nature. Harvey is surely right that these two theories are incompatible with one another, though he is less convincing in his claim that the later one is more persuasive. What remains problematic is Harvey's persistence (unlike Feuerbach) in trying to conceive the issues in terms of projection. In projecting, one begins subjectively and then moves to conceive external reality—precisely the direction of religious "alienation" in the early Feuerbach. What is new about the later theory is the reversal of direction: Feuerbach now sees the religious person as beginning with an experience of the outside world ("nature") and then "processing" or organizing that experience in a particular way. Such a move is

---

[19]It should be noted, however, that Glasse anticipated Harvey's thesis over thirty years ago: "In the latter work [*Lectures on the Essence of Religion*] Feuerbach viewed God not so such as the essence of man as the essence of Nature" ("Barth on Feuerbach," 93 n.47).

rightly called (by Harvey, in discussing Feuerbach) interpretation, not projection. As Harvey says, this kind of religion is an "interpretive response" rather than an "involuntary reflex of the self." Feuerbach's own term *imagination*, despite some serious problems in the assumptions he makes about it, therefore offers a more promising way of talking about religion and its relation to human life and thought.

The "Beam metaphor" requires little comment, since it encapsulates just what Feuerbach, Freud, and most other people have long meant by "projection." Something inward, unconscious, or subjective is displaced as something outward and taken (i.e., *mis*-taken) by the intending subject to be objective. That, after all, is just what the early Feuerbach said: his word was *vergegenständlichen*, to objectify. The assumption that such a move produces illusion rather than truth appears to be so directly implied by the "Beam metaphor" itself that attempts to use "projection" to describe religion without at the same time precluding its truth have had a difficult time of it.

More interesting and far more problematic is what Harvey calls the "Grid theory." The problem appears in his very first sentence about it, where he describes this option as "another type of projection theory," an assumption that begs the question at stake. He defines "Grid theory" accordingly in terms of "the symbolic or conceptual forms that human beings *superimpose* on their experience in order to make it intelligible" (246; my emphasis). Implied by this metaphoric language is the assumption that people first have experience that is *un*formed (outside "symbolic or conceptual forms") and then proceed to "superimpose" forms upon it—forms that are evidently alien to the "experience itself," that is, qualitatively other than the "pure" experience prior to the act of imposition. Simply putting the issues this way should make plain why I find Harvey's presentation of "Grid theory" unsatisfactory. Here is not the place to rehearse the arguments, but such appeals to unformed pre-linguistic experience have (for good reason) not had an easy time of it in recent philosophical and social scientific thought.[20] Whether one appeals to

<hr>

[20]For an insightful treatment of the relationship between experience and the concepts used to interpret it, see Wayne Proudfoot, *Religious Experience* (Berkeley and Los Angeles: University of California Press, 1985). Though Proudfoot, like Harvey, is concerned to expose the errors of "religious apologists," the argument cuts both ways: just as it is illegitimate to appeal to religious experience to justify the concepts that believers use to interpret it, so it is equally untenable to presuppose an essentially non-religious experience lying behind the language of piety. If "religious beliefs and practices are interpretations of experience, and ...

Wittgenstein's refutation of private language and demonstration of the *Gestalt*-like holism implicit in our perception and language; or to philosophers of science like Kuhn, Lakatos, and Feyerabend, who have shown the essential role of models and paradigms in the natural sciences; or to post-Heideggerian philosophers like Gadamer, Rorty, and Derrida, who have exposed the inherent contradictions in appeals to "pure presence" and other claims to have "unformed" access to reality apart from linguistic commitments to already existing traditions and forms of life—whichever of these voices one attends to will make it extremely difficult ever again to think of our relation to the world in terms of merely "subjective" images imposed upon an "objective" reality, however it may be conceived.

Feuerbach's Two Theories of Religious Imagination

One of the most frequent concepts found in Feuerbach's writings, especially in English translation, is *imagination.* When one returns to the primary texts after reading Professor Harvey's book, one is struck by the persistence of the term through all the twists and turns of Feuerbach's developing philosophy of religion. Worthy of particular note is the fact that imagination plays the key role in *both* the early projection theory *and* the late "existential" theory. So pronounced is this consistency in Feuerbach that it ought to relativize our understanding of the change of position highlighted by Harvey. It is no doubt both interesting and important that Feuerbach changed his mind about *how* religious people imagine the world; but even more significant is the fact the Feuerbach never wavered in his conviction *that* religion is fundamentally imagination—*and* that for this very reason it is suspect. To see how basic this strain of Feuerbach's thought really is, we need to look at what he says about religion and imagination both in *The Essence of Christianity* and in his later theory, presented most fully in the *Lectures on the Essence of Religion.*

First, a comment on terminology. In discussing German philosophical texts in English, one often faces the difficulty that various German terms—*Einbildungskraft* and *Phantasie* are the most

---

themselves fit objects of interpretation" (Proudfoot, 41), the same holds for non- or anti-religious interpretations of experience, such as those proposed by Feuerbach—and by Harvey himself. *All* data are theory-laden, not just the data cited by religious apologists. For Harvey's treatment of Proudfoot, see 93 ff.

important—correspond to "imagination" in English. In Kant, for example, the technical term for imagination is *Einbildungskraft*. In Hegel (and also in the thought of the Young Hegelians, such as David Friedrich Strauss), religious imagination is characterized as *Vorstellung* (in contrast to the conceptual purity of the *Begriff*).[21] Feuerbach employs all of these terms (though *Phantasie* is his favorite), and Eliot has rendered all of them "imagination" in most cases. The question therefore arises, whether the translation might be obscuring distinctions made in the original, and whether he might have used the terms differently in his earlier and later writings. Fortunately, Feuerbach himself provides compelling evidence for identifying all of these terms, especially *Einbildungskraft* and *Phantasie*, under the single concept *imagination*. Not only does he alternate in his use of the terms, but more than once he places them in an apposition that clearly shows they are meant as synonyms. This passage from *The Essence of Christianity* is typical: "God exists in heaven, but is for that reason omnipresent; for this heaven is the imagination."[22] In the first two editions, Feuerbach uses *Phantasie*; but in the third and final edition of 1849 he appends the word *Einbildungskraft*, so that heaven is identified as *"die Phantasie, die Einbildungskraft"*— obviously two words for the same thing. One could cite numerous other passages where both terms are employed, but none is plainer than this one. Furthermore, the same usage appears repeatedly in the later Feuerbach. In the twentieth *Lecture on the Essence of Religion*, for example, where he is ridiculing the "fetishism" of what he calls "savages [*die Wilden*]," he asks, . . ."what impels men to make gods of snail shells, crab claws, flags, and pennants?" His answer: "Their imagination, whose power is proportional to their ignorance." The one word "imagination" in the translation stands for *"Die Phantasie, die Einbildungskraft"* in the original; and he repeats the appositive when he generalizes the example to all religion: "The theoretical cause or source of religion and of its object, God, is therefore the imagination [*die Phantasie, die Einbildungskraft*]."[23]

A passage from *The Essence of Christianity* cited by Harvey (42) is characteristic of the younger Feuerbach's theory of religious

---

[21]See Green, *Imagining God*, chap. 1.
[22]*The Essence of Christianity*, trans. George Eliot (New York: Harper and Row, 1957), 203 n; *Das Wesen des Christentums*, ed. Werner Schuffenhauer and Wolfgang Harich, *Gesammelte Werke* (Berlin: Akademie-Verlag, 1973), 5:345 n. I have followed Harvey's practice of using shortened titles in references to this work (see p. x for a list), first to the English translation and then to the German original.
[23]*Lectures*, 178; *Vorlesungen*, 201.

imagination. After referring to "the impression which the imagination [*Phantasie*] makes upon the feelings [*das Gemüt*]," he specifically declares that the "imagination is the original organ of religion."[24] Feuerbach's actual words are "organ and essence [*Organ und Wesen*] of religion." Eliot's omission from the translation of the key word *Wesen*, the title concept of the book, is a rare but significant lapse, for Feuerbach announces here that the essence of religion—all religion, and not just Christianity—is the imagination. Specifically, he locates religion at the point where the emotions impact the imagination. The job of the imagination is to *represent* the contents of emotion, a task that it carries out by means of images taken from the world of the senses. Another passage, not cited by Harvey, makes clear just how central this imaginative task is to Feuerbach's view of human nature. "Man, as an emotional and sensuous being," he writes, "is governed and made happy only by images, by sensible representations."[25] Feuerbach in fact uses the singular and emphasizes it: human beings are satisfied, he insists, "only [by] the *image* [*Bild*]." Then follows the definition that Harvey cites (43): "Mind [*Vernunft*] presenting itself as at once type-creating [*bildlich*], emotional [*gemütlich*], and sensuous [*sinnlich*], is the *imagination*."[26] Here is the hinge where Feuerbach's description of religion turns to suspicion, for this triple characterization of the imagination—*bildlich*, *gemütlich*, and *sinnlich*—provides three reasons for Feuerbach's prejudice against it. Harvey's language is not too strong: "imagination *cheats* reason. Feuerbach, he writes, believes that the imagination . . . is deceptive in the nature of the case, especially when it becomes allied with feeling and wishing. It can and often does cheat the reason" (43). Even this paraphrase is not strong enough: for Feuerbach, imagination can and *always* does cheat reason. Feuerbach's hermeneutic of suspicion, in other words, is rooted in his prejudice against images, feelings, and—most striking of all in this philosopher of sensuousness—the senses as sources of truth. This prejudice, as we will shall see, in no way disappears or even weakens in Feuerbach's later theory of religion.

One more feature of the early Feuerbach's interpretation of the religious imagination is worth noting; and this point is one that he will abandon in his later thought. The context for the definition of imagination cited above from *The Essence of Christianity* is

---

[24]*Christianity*, 214; *Christentums*, 360.
[25]*Christianity*, 75; *Christentums*, 153.
[26]Ibid.; Harvey cites the passage on 43.

christological. It appears as part of Feuerbach's treatment of "The Mystery of the Logos and Divine Image." Immediately following the tripartite definition of imagination, he makes this comment: The second Person in God, who is in truth the first person in religion, is the nature of the imagination made objective.[27] More literally translated, Feuerbach says that the Second Person of the Christian Trinity "is the *objective essence of the imagination* [*das gegenständliche Wesen der Phantasie*]" (Feuerbach's emphasis). So Christ is the projection of the human imagination; in Christ the imagination imagines itself as divine. (It is intriguing passages like this one in *The Essence of Christianity* that make me hesitant to agree with Harvey that Feuerbach's later theory is necessarily an improvement.) Here is an interpretation that might indeed provide the basis for a productive dialogue between Feuerbach and Christian theologians today, especially after Feuerbach's overhasty dismissal of the imagination is called into question.

When we turn to the later Feuerbach with the question of imagination in mind, we discover the same basic premise at work. As Harvey notes, "Although the concept of the imagination plays an important role in the *Lectures*, as it did in *Christianity*, it is not treated any more systematically in the latter, unfortunately, than in the former" (181). It is nevertheless quite clear that the theory of religion presented in the *Lectures on the Essence of Religion* presupposes the very duality of emotion and thought, imagination and truth, that runs throughout *The Essence of Christianity*. Summarizing his own views in the second lecture, for example, Feuerbach maintains that "the difference between religion and philosophy is ineradicable, for philosophy is a matter of thought, of reason, while religion is a matter of emotion and imagination."[28] Later on, in a discussion of animal cults, he argues for his new theory that underlying all religion is "the feeling of dependency," which causes religious believers to propose "a chaos of the most baffling contradictions." "For what reason?" he asks rhetorically. The answer: "Out of superstition." Then follows the familiar dualism: In religion "the alternative between fortune and misfortune, well-being and suffering, sickness and health, life and death depends in *truth* and *reality* [*in Wahrheit und Wirklichkeit*] on certain objects of worship, and on others only in *imagination,* in *faith,* in the *mind* [*in der Einbildung, im Glauben, in*

---

[27]Ibid.
[28]*Lectures*, 12; *Vorlesungen*, 19.

der Vorstellung]."[29] Feuerbach is able to distinguish with such alacrity between superstition (*Aberglaube*) and truth because he presupposes that the former employs imagination (*Einbildung*, which he immediately equates with *Glaube* and *Vorstellung*) while the latter conforms to "truth and reality."

Feuerbach Reconstructed: Implications for Religious Studies and Theology

What would it take to make of Feuerbach a genuine dialogue partner in our own late twentieth-century attempts to interpret religion? Harvey has done us a service—including those of us whose interest in religious studies is motivated by a theological passion—by his painstaking efforts to reconstruct Feuerbach's interpretation of religion in terms that make contact with our contemporary questions. In conclusion, I want to suggest some points at which this "ideal Feuerbach" might contribute to our own theorizing as scholars of religion. Like most theorists, his chief virtues are closely linked with his vices; but even the vices of great thinkers can be instructive.

Feuerbach's greatest contribution (his chief "virtue"), I take to be his insight into the fundamentally imaginative nature of religious belief and practice. In his passion to reverse the effects of Hegelian spiritualizing, he saw with refreshing clarity the concrete, sensuous substance of religious life—its intrinsic connection to the earth, the body, and the natural world generally. Both secular religion scholars and theologians can surely applaud this emphasis in Feuerbach, for it is a trait as rare in the philosophers of his day as in the theologians. He knew and taught what it has taken religious studies another century to discover, that religion is not, first of all, a matter of ideas and ideals, but of images and practices. The corresponding "vice" has already been noted: his unquestioned assumption (so typical of his age in this regard) that such a product of the sensuous imagination could not possibly be the bearer of truth. So the scholar of religion must say to Feuerbach, *Yes*, the imagination is indeed the source of religion, but *No*, religion is not thereby disqualified from the search for truth.

In a time when we have learned that even the physicist, not to mention the anthropologist, must engage the imagination in order to gain rational insight into the world, the scholar of religion today will be more reluctant than Feuerbach to preface "imagination" with

---

[29]*Lectures*, 43-44; *Vorlesungen*, 53 (Feuerbach's emphasis).

"mere." The dialogue between Feuerbach and the theologians will be more complex and even more interesting, for he will remind them that religious teachings, whatever their truth value, can never be exempt from critical examination because they are rooted in imagination and, therefore, implicated in the complex tangle of human desires and mixed motives. Theologians, in turn, will want to ask Feuerbach how he can be so sure that believers do not imagine the world rightly. Here Barth has shown the way—praising Feuerbach for his "Christian realism" while chastising him for his trivialization of the Christian imagination. But Feuerbach will also be a warning to theologians not to suspend their suspicion too hastily in the endeavor to "retrieve" the religious truths of the past. Along with Marx, Nietzsche, and Freud, Feuerbach offers a salutary reminder to theologians that imagination and desire are inevitably intertwined in a complex web of conflicting motives, not all of which lead to truth. Imagination is surely more than a garb of "peacock feathers" adorning mundane reality; but the temptation to strut about in "borrowed" religious finery must always be resisted. The issue that emerges from this dialogue, therefore, is the hermeneutics of imagination. If the imagination is not only the source of error, as Feuerbach believed, but can serve the cause of truth as well—indeed, is necessary to our apprehension of truth—how can we tell the difference? Suspicion of imaginative excess is deeply rooted in religious tradition: "The heart is deceitful above all things," says the prophet (Jer. 17:9). Not whether to imagine, but how to imagine rightly, is the central theological question to emerge from the conversation with Feuerbach.

Another potential contribution that a reconstructed Feuerbach could make to religious studies and theology involves a less obvious, but nevertheless intriguing, theme in his writings. Like others before and after him who were influenced by Hegel, Feuerbach understands religion in the framework of an historical process. This theme, too, reveals both strengths and weaknesses in his interpretation of religion. Potentially useful to scholars of religion is an historical-cultural thesis, evident in a number of passages from both the early and the later Feuerbach, which represents a kind of parallel to Nietzsche's meditations on the death of God. One of the strongest indications that religious objects are unreal, Feuerbach argues, is that each religion demythologizes the gods of earlier ages. "What the present regards as reality [*für Wirklichkeit hält*], the future recognizes to be imagination [*erkennt . . . für Phantasie, für Einbildung*]," he writes the *Lectures*. "Some day it will be universally recognized that the objects of

Christian religion, like the pagan gods, were mere imagination [*nur Einbildung waren*]."[30] Setting aside for a moment the epistemological questions raised by this statement, we can extract a historical thesis that there has been a progressive weakening of the religious imagination over time, something akin to Max Weber's demystification of the world. The thesis that the imaginative force of religion (presumably only in Europe and North America?) has been progressively replaced by rational explanations could be investigated empirically by scholars of religion without necessarily accepting Feuerbach's deprecation of imagination. Less acceptable today, surely, is the evolutionary scheme and cultural prejudice that form one aspect of Feuerbach's historical thesis. He assumes that "naïve primitive peoples ... were close to the origin and hence to nature."[31] Such assumptions, of course, were nearly universal among scholars of the nineteenth and early twentieth centuries, including many of those theorists most influential in the development of religious studies as a discipline, and they can no more be used to discredit his entire theory of religion than theirs.

As in the case of Nietzsche, the implications of Feuerbach's "death-of-God" (or "cooling of religion") theme are especially interesting and potentially fruitful for the dialogue with theology. Like Nietzsche, Feuerbach frequently shows more sympathy for orthodox believers than for rationalizing modernist theologians. He compares them as follows:

> The more man is dominated by his imagination, the more sensuous is his god. ... The difference between the Christian God of the rationalists, of those whose faith is tempered by thought, and the Christian God of the older total believers, is merely that the rationalists God is more sophisticated, more abstract, and less sensuous than the God of the mystics or orthodox believers, that the rationalists faculty of abstraction restricts their imagination, whereas the old believer s imagination is stronger than his powers of conceptual thinking. In other words: the rationalists's [*sic*] faith is determined, or rather limited, by reason ... whereas the orthodox believer's reason is dominated

---

[30]*Lectures*, 195; *Vorlesungen*, 219-20.
[31]*Lectures*, 89; *Vorlesungen*, 102-3. The English translation makes the problem worse: Feuerbach speaks not of "primitive people" but of *Naturvölker*; in other passages (see above) he does, however, refer to *die Wilden* and regularly assumes their ignorance.

by his faith.[32]

In the *Essence of Christianity,* he even goes so far as to insist that the "Church was perfectly justified in adjudging damnation to heretics and unbelievers." In a wonderfully apt phrase, he accuses "the believing unbelief of modern times" with hiding "behind the Bible" while opposing "the biblical dicta of dogmatic definitions, in order that it may set itself free from the limits of dogma by arbitrary exegesis." In this situation, he notes, "faith has already disappeared, is become indifferent, when the determinate tenets of faith are felt as limitations."[33]   Here, too, we might ask (with Barth) why the theologians did not discover this truth for themselves, rather than learning it from the mouths of their secular opponents.

More than three decades after his initial engagement with Feuerbach's critique of religion in the 1926 lecture, Karl Barth returned to the topic in volume four of the *Church Dogmatics.*[34]   At the culmination of his discussion he remarks (according to the published translation) that we can venture the "good confession of the prophecy of Jesus Christ . . . without embarrassment, and need be afraid of no Feuerbach."[35]   In fact, Barth's reference is not to fear but to shame: "*. . . und werden wir uns . . . vor keinem Feuerbach zu schämen haben.*" The brief excursus that follows this remark offers a clue to its meaning, for Barth mentions the so-called ontological argument of Anselm of Canterbury, and frankly acknowledges the circularity of theological argument against skeptical critics like Gaunilo and Feuerbach. But this circle, he maintains, is not vicious but virtuous, "a *circulus virtuosus.*" Our reconstruction of Feuerbach's theory of religious imagination, with Professor Harvey's expert help, suggests why the believer can affirm the truth of revelation, without shame or embarrassment, in spite of its imaginative character. Feuerbach saw clearly that imagination was the engine of religion, but

---

[32]*Lectures,* 192; *Vorlesungen,* 216-17.

[33]*Christianity,* 251-52; *Christentums,* 416-17. Eliot omits one important term from her English translation: Feuerbach speaks of "*die Charakterlosigkeit, der gläubige Unglaube der neuern Zeit,*" thus, explicitly identifying the bad faith of theologians as a character flaw.

[34]For a detailed analysis of the continuities and differences in Barth's early and late treatments of Feuerbach, see Glasse, "Barth on Feuerbach," esp. 82-91. Also to be commended are Glasse's thoughtful concluding remarks (92-96).

[35]Barth, *Church Dogmatics,* vol. 4, pt. 3, ed. G. W. Bromiley and T. F. Torrance, trans. G. W. Bromiley (Edinburgh: T. & T. Clark, 1961) 85. For the German original, see *Die kirchliche Dogmatik,* vol. 4, pt. 3 (Zürich: TVZ, 1959) 94.

he also—like so many others, including theologians of his own time and ours—found the imagination to be a source of embarrassment. Now it is time to subject this suspicious thesis itself to a dose of suspicion. This "deconstructive" move will make it harder for secular scholars to dismiss theological claims out of hand, just as Harvey's book makes it harder for theologians to dismiss Feuerbach out of hand.

The Bitterness of Theism? Brecht, Tillich, and the Protestant Principle

Cynthia Stewart

In the turbulent decades following the First World War, many young German intellectuals were struggling to understand their place in the world. Their country was in ruins, as was their cherished way of life; the intellectual framework received from preceding generations no longer seemed adequate to deal with their universe. By necessity more than by choice, these young Germans began creating new patterns of thought in many different areas of intellectual interest. Among those who chose to present their new reality through fiction, Bertolt Brecht holds a place of honor. His work as a playwright gained him international fame: he brought a freshness and a vigor to the stage that reflected his own idealism and disillusionment. German theology of this era witnessed the rise of a number of luminaries, prominent among them Paul Tillich. Tillich's emphasis upon the ultimate concern as the ground of being and upon the No of judgment coupled with the Yes of possibility helped revitalize religious thought—and gave to many who had witnessed the destruction of every belief and value a way of staying within Christianity. Nevertheless, many of the German intelligentsia believed Christianity, and indeed theism of any kind, to be irrelevant to the new world they were creating. They did away with the concept of God in the political realm, but not all were able to eradicate the concept of a deity from their lives and works. In the poetry and prose of Bertolt Brecht, the bitterness of the author's struggle with theism is evident—so much so that bringing Tillich's views regarding the ground of being to a reading of Brecht's work provides deep insights into Brecht's constant and torturous crisis of faith. The reader can see that these two men would have understood each other well: although Brecht and Tillich may have walked away with different visions of how to create the future, their ideas were formed by staring into the same chasm.

Bertolt Brecht is best known as the author of such modern classics of the theatre as *The Threepenny Opera* and *Mother Courage and Her Children*, but his talents stretched beyond the stage to the page. He was an accomplished short story writer and a prolific poet whose work mirrored his own life struggle. In fact, he was first known outside his native Southern Germany as the author of the short story "Bargan Gives Up," a startling tale of good and evil in which the two concepts are twisted together in such a way as to lose all meaning. By intermingling the concepts so inextricably, Brecht shows the completely subjective nature of good and evil and the lack of an objective referent for either.

I. Bargan and Theology

Bargan, the title character of the story, is the leader of a company of thugs who, when the reader is first introduced to them, are in the process of pillaging a town, raping the women and killing the men. Nevertheless, Bargan is immediately identified with the good: he is "as good as God Almighty"[1] when it comes to getting his bearings from the stars. Even when Bargan's astronomical omniscience is called into question, his identification with the Deity is not. Later in the story, there is a problem with navigation: "Somehow or other we must have lost our way. God was wrong about the stars" (7). Bargan leads his company "like a swarm of kids" (3) and loves one of his men "like a child" (5). All of this, coupled with his omniscience, identify him as a Divine Father-figure.

Bargan's identification with "God Almighty" as Father does not define the limits of Brecht's portrait of him; he is also a Christ figure who endures suffering for the sake of a loved one. In fact, this is the basic theme of the tale: Bargan loves a man named Croze, and during the course of the story, Bargan gives up everything else that is dear to him in order to keep Croze. The beloved Croze is not a model of sweetness and light; in fact, to say that Croze represents evil is an understatement—Croze *is* pure unmitigated evil. He is only once clearly labeled as the Devil (8), but his actions provide strong evidence for such an identification: he argues with Bargan over possession of a woman, and when Bargan turns the woman over to Croze, the latter kills her; Croze knowingly and wrongly accuses a mate of stealing, and demands that Bargan have the man lashed; Croze desires—and receives—the massacre of seventy people of the village that the company pillaged; time and again, Croze plans and tries to implement the destruction of the entire company, including its leader Bargan. Brecht clearly delineates the dichotomy between

---

[1]Bertolt Brecht, "Bargan Gives Up," in *Bertolt Brecht, Short Stories, 1921-1946*, ed. John Willett and Ralph Manheim (London: Metheun, 1983) 3. Page references hereafter are inserted in the text.

Bargan and Croze, but at least on Bargan's side this dichotomy does not result in hatred, nor even in an essential feeling of otherness: God tries, by his acts of love, to win over the Devil.

Despite the clear animosity and unprecedented evil of Croze, Bargan continues to champion him against the rest of the company, who want to remove such a dangerous presence from their midst. In his role as God-figure, Bargan obviously has the greater power, but he refuses to use this power against Croze because such an action would not be consistent with his love. Thus we see Bargan's dual role as both Almighty Father and Loving Son: although he has the ability to destroy the sinful humanity represented by Croze, Bargan chooses rather to give his love unconditionally to the one who can never deserve his love, so much so that Bargan-as-Christ is willing to suffer and die rather than abandon the evil Croze.

The identification of Bargan as a Christ-figure is never stronger than near the end of the tale, when the men of the company realize that Bargan is not blind to the heinous faults of his cherished Croze, but rather loves him in spite of (or perhaps even because of) his despicable nature: "Then it suddenly dawned on our men how matters stood with Bargan, that he knew it all better than they did and still didn't want to abandon that fat dog, God knows why" (11). Bargan-as-Christ has chosen the most morally and physically repugnant of the bunch as he to whom all faithfulness shall be extended. Croze's election is *not* dependent upon his works, for those are one and all loathsome; neither is it connected to his own loyalty to and love for the Christ-figure, for Croze displays absolutely none; rather, Croze is loved because he is Croze. The Christ of faith shows his love for the world not only by living a life of service, but also by dying for sinful humanity; thus Bargan, in his role as Christ-figure, must do the same for Croze. At one point late in the story, Croze sets out Bargan as a shield, the sight of whom hopefully will inspire the narrator and his company to cease their attack upon the ship containing Croze. The narrator reports that they did indeed halt their fire, for "We didn't yet realize that we were doing him wrong when we stopped shooting because it was him" (12)—they do not yet understand that Bargan's identification with Christ must extend to a death for, and even caused by, the beloved.

Although the narrator never distinctly states that Bargan is to be identified as the Christ, the metaphorical language and situational constructs into which Brecht places the character suggest that Brecht wishes the reader to make such an identification. What the narrator notes clearly is that Bargan is a sacrifice made by and to God:

For all of a sudden I understood God, who, for a scabby fat dog not worth wasting your knife on, that you wouldn't have butchered but should have left to die of hunger, sacrificed a man like Bargan who was incomparable, who was just made for conquering Heaven. And who now, merely because he needed something he could be useful to, had attached himself to this lump of mange and given up everything for him, and was probably even glad that it wasn't a good man he loved but an evil, gluttonous child that sucked him dry like a raw egg in a single draught. For I'll be hanged, drawn and quartered if he didn't actually enjoy destroying himself and everything that was his for the sake of that little dog he'd set his eyes on, and that's why he gave up everything else (15).

Just as God sent Jesus to die for humanity, so did the Deity send Bargan as a sacrifice for Croze. The narrator has grasped that neither of those being saved has *merited* the effort, and in his satirical way, Brecht implies that neither is *worth* it, either. God does not come off too well in this schema, for he seems in both cases to have made a bad trade. The narrator may finally understand God, but he does not seem to value the Deity, nor to like him too much.

Brecht's continuing preoccupation with Christianity is apparent not only in the theological concepts suggested by the author's creation of a God/Christ figure and in his use of biblical allusions throughout the tale, but also in the manner of speaking that Brecht creates for the narrator of the tale. For instance, at one point the narrator is describing why the women in the town that is being pillaged are all in their shifts: "it all happened so damned quickly, with God turning his face away from them to have a look at the harvest in Brazil instead" (4). Thus, Brecht reveals his narrator as a theist who does not believe in the goodness of the Deity precisely because his own actions are allowed by that Deity. One of those actions is rape, and even this vicious deed does not escape the narrator's theological similes: "A shark would have thought we were dying for it like God for a repentant sinner" (4). Given this pattern of speech, the reader is not surprised to learn later in the tale that when the company find themselves in a potentially fatal situation, "we waited till morning like a sinner on Judgment Day waiting for God's voice to give him permission to go through the right-hand door into that famous state of bliss" (9).

Brecht has the narrator use such theological concepts not only in his metaphorical speech, but also in his own thought processes. The narrator judges the men in his company by the way they respond to Bargan, but his judgment extends farther than just to a statement of his own like or dislike—he sees those who do not share his own devotion to Bargan as fundamentally flawed: a few of the company "weren't too keen on Bargan because they were born with rotten souls" (5). The narrator knows that for this company, Bargan is and must be God; those who cannot perceive this must be fundamentally flawed beings.

The identifications that the narrator employs in describing the characters of the tale are constantly changing, and can be confusing to the reader who attempts a coherent theological reading of "Bargan Gives Up." Bargan is clearly identified as "God Almighty" at the beginning of the tale, but this rendering of the captain as the Divine Father does not preclude the reader from seeing Bargan as a Christ-figure. Croze is once named as the Devil (8), an identification that the reader will heartily endorse, but the narrator notes that to the bunch of rotten-souled thugs whom Croze gathers around him, Croze is "their God Almighty." Even "that famous state of bliss" does not escape the narrator's shifts in definition. At one point as the company passes through a narrow passageway, they find themselves being bombarded with stones from on high. There is little doubt that the perpetrators of this deed are friends of Croze and that their objective is to kill the company. The men of the company have to hide beneath their vehicles and wait "till Heaven showed us some sympathy or ran out of stones" (7). Heaven, when composed of Croze's thugs, is obviously neither just nor merciful. The rain of stones ceases only when someone has the brilliant idea to push Croze out from under his vehicle in order to display him to those throwing the stones. "That was a clear signal from Heaven" (7), the narrator tells us. Within the space of a few lines, Heaven has changed from being a decidedly hostile group of humans to a designation for Divine Providence.

These constantly changing identifications become far more startling, however, when the reader realizes that there is no objective standard, including the being of God, upon which these identifications are based. Bargan is God, but this is a God whose "wisdom and knowledge of human nature" is recognized in the context of his brilliant idea to string together some women and have his company rape them, so that the men of the town to which the women belong will rush out in their rage over the treatment of the women and be "slaughtered like young lambs" (4). For his part, Croze is the Devil, but a Devil whose temptation to evil is answered by Bargan, not out of any sort of greed, but rather out of love. Although Croze demands many atrocities, it is generally Bargan who carries them out —evil committed by a Christ-figure for the sake of a beloved and sinister man. The narrator, as we have seen, is a theist, but a theist who is none too fond of God. There is little to no stability in any of the theological concepts or identifications presented by Brecht in "Bargan Gives Up"; rather, Brecht seems to assent to, and to actually create, the sort of confusion of ideas delineated by Archibald MacLiesh in his play *J.B.*? "If God is God he is not good; If God is good he is not God ...." For Brecht, "God" and "good" are not part of a natural connection, and neither are "Devil" and "evil".

Thus, it is clear that the concepts "good" and "evil" are hopelessly intermingled in "Bargan Gives Up." The ability to distinguish between the two has been lost, although why that loss occurs is not revealed to the reader. The time frame of the story is never given, and it is unclear who exactly is this company of rapists and murderers whom Bargan leads. One might speculate a figurative setting of World War I, the horror which devastated the world of the German intelligentsia to which Brecht belonged, and that the band of men led by Bargan are a company of soldiers. In this reading, we may surmise that any true understanding of "good" and "evil" has been lost in the midst of the inhumanity of bullets, bombs, and mustard gas. For Brecht and his generation, all ground of hope has been tainted, if not lost altogether, by this war to end all wars; one can find security in nothing, certainly not in goodness. As the narrator notes, "you get assaulted in broad daylight, that's how secure we all are on this planet" (15).

II. Brecht, Tillich, and the Protestant Principle

Paul Tillich understood this complete lack of security. He also was part of the generation that lost its bearings in the aftermath of World War I, and as a nay-sayer to Hitler's regime, Tillich was one of the first professors to lose his position when the halls of academia were purged of dissidents. Tillich's theological position rendered him unable to give his own unqualified Yes to any State because to him it seemed clear that while God's Yes is given to the strivings of the human spirit, human actions—such as those encapsulated in a government— always fall under a resounding No. The endeavors that call forth the

Yes are those that attempt to express the Unconditioned—the ground of all being, what we may call God—in new ways. However, every human construct is susceptible to demonic distortions, and Tillich surely saw tell-tale signs of such distortion in Hitler's rise to power.[2]

In his struggle toward the Yes, Tillich turned to religious socialism—indeed, he helped found the party in Germany. He was able to find a grounding for life in a revitalized Christian faith that leads to political action. Bertolt Brecht faced the same political and intellectual chaos that led Tillich to search for the Yes; he too tried to find something that would hold his world together. Brecht's quest led him to an atheistic communism; he heard the Yes, but saw no religious value in it, no Divine Presence standing behind it. Rather, he saw the progression of the human spirit and the possibility of the rising of the oppressed, and to these things he gave his talents. Both Brecht and Tillich turned to politics as a way of ordering their world; we may even say that both gave their allegiance to a religious form of politics. This is evident, of course, in Tillich's religious socialism, but it is almost as apparent in Brecht's choice. His form of communism was atheistic, that is, it denied the existence of a God. In choosing to speak about the existence or nonexistence of God, however, this communism showed itself to be concerned with the particular question of theism.

Brecht formally renounced theism, but it is evident from "Bargan Gives Up," and from much else in his writing, that his soul was scored with bitterness toward a God: he denied God reality, but at the same time he continued to actively fight against his own conception of God. His was no simple divorce of a human from his Feuerbachian religious projection, but rather a searing and ongoing struggle to envision a life without God. Tillich annexes such serious challenges to God's existence into his own system of theism under the rubric of "the Protestant principle."[3] This principle, which is expressed in the doctrine of justification by faith, stands as both an understanding of the reality of Protestantism and as a means of critiquing it. Protestantism has its roots in the Reformation, a period of struggle in which the reformers used the founding myths of Christianity to analyze the Church of their time; based upon the model given in the

---

[2]Jack Forstman, *Christian Faith in Dark Times: Theological Conflicts in the Shadow of Hitler* (Louisville: Westminster-Knox, 1992) 105. Forstman's presentation of Tillich's thought thoroughly informs my discussion of Tillich, and thus will not be specifically noted again.

[3] Paul Tillich, The Protestant Era (Chicago: University of Chicago Press, 1948) xii.

founding myths, the reformers were able to formulate a critique of (current) Christianity in the name of (true) Christianity. In Tillich's view, the Protestant principle is valid not only for the Reformation, nor just for the continuing lives of the Protestant churches; rather, it "is the ultimate criterion of all religious and all spiritual experiences; it lies at their base, whether they are aware of it or not." As Tillich defines it, spiritual experience includes doubt about, and even renunciation of, belief in the existence of God; thus, doubt and renunciation are also subject to the Protestant principle:

> the principle of justification through faith refers not only to the religious-ethical but also to the religious-intellectual life. Not only he who is in sin but also he who is in doubt is justified through faith. The situation of doubt, even of doubt about God, need not separate us from God. There is faith in every serious doubt, namely, the faith in the truth as such, even if the only truth we can express is our lack of truth. But if this is experienced in its depth and as an ultimate concern, the divine is present; and he who doubts in such an attitude is 'justified' in his thinking. So ... he who seriously denies God, affirms him. ... If all this comes together and you are desperate about the meaning of life, the seriousness of your despair is the expression of the meaning in which you still are living. This unconditional seriousness is the expression of the presence of the divine in the experience of utter separation from it (xiv-xv).

According to Tillich, then, Bertolt Brecht's deep and continuing existential angst over the lack of a God demonstrates the absolute reality of God. His choice of atheistic communism proves that the thought of God was a part of his political life; the many references to God and the biblical themes that emerge in his tales and poetry show the hold this thought had over his creativity. It is obvious that Brecht's whole existence was permeated with the idea of God; Brecht perfectly embodies Tillich's understanding of justification through doubt in the religious-intellectual life.

III. Bargan and Justification

Having seen the theological implication in "Bargan Gives Up," and an inherent religiosity in the mind of the author that expressed itself even in atheism, we can now turn back to the tale and view it through the lens of Tillich's Protestant principle; in doing so, we may come to understand the serious questioning of God that Brecht undertakes in "Bargan. The Protestant principle, Tillich tells us, is the measure that judges all of history—it judges facts in the name of truth. But does it judge God himself? This seems to be what Brecht ventures in "Bargan Gives Up. "

In Tillich's terms, Bargan's actions would certainly have rated God's No, but one may wonder if the strivings of this particular spirit would ever have merited a Yes. The main motivation behind most of Bargan's actions is his great love for another human, and surely unconditional love is a movement of the spirit that calls forth God's Yes. After all, the Fourth Gospel has Jesus telling his disciples that "Greater love hath no man than this, that a man lay down his life for his friends" (John 15:13, KJV)—something that Bargan is certainly willing to do for the treasured Croze. Nevertheless, most of those actions that Bargan undertakes for the sake of Croze are heinous and destructive to others. Can we therefore say that while the actions stand most emphatically under the No, the striving calls forth the Yes? Brecht, I think, would not accept this evaluation, but would rather reverse the process and ask himself and his readers to which of God's actions humanity can give its assent.

Brecht has created a God who has lost the right to judge because his "justice" is so obviously nonexistent. Tillich's principle has its basis in the idea of a God who is the ultimate ground of being; it breaks down in the face of a Deity who would turn "his face away from [the women of the town] to have a look at the harvest in Brazil instead" (4). When the morality of God himself is called into question, then his Yes and No no longer have value. God is not absent from the world of the tale; indeed, he is far too present, present enough for the reader to see that this God seems to look with indifference, if not with favor, upon rape and murder. One may argue that Brecht's depiction is distorted, that this is not the Christian God; nevertheless, the narrator, through whose eyes we view this God, obviously employs a Christian vocabulary in his descriptions of the Deity—and of the God-figure Bargan. Were Paul Tillich to read this tale, he would perhaps see that God himself has become a demonic distortion.

Despite this highly negative view of the divine, the Protestant principle remains a useful tool for understanding Brecht's tale. It gives the reader a way to comprehend the role that the narrator's God does not play, and the way in which the characters—especially Bargan—cannot be judged by a normal good—evil frame of reference. In trying to apply Tillich's Yes and No to "Bargan" that the reader discovers that this God is distorted—perhaps as distorted as the rest of the world. The narrator obviously believes in God; he has faith in God's existence, although perhaps not in his abilities. Yet it is God who sacrificed the narrator's beloved Bargan for the sake of the scoundrel Croze. Is the narrator justified? Would he care to be justified in the sight of a God whose moral ambiguity is even greater than his own? God, whose *ability* to order the universe is unquestioned but whose right to do so is doubtful, would most certainly stand under the narrator's No.

Tillich draws Brecht into theism, but Brecht no more wants to be justified by this sort of a God than does his narrator. Brecht's narrator does not doubt the existence of God, but perhaps Tillich would prefer doubt to the sort of ironic and disdainful belief that the narrator displays. In the end, Brecht's bitterness toward the God he so desperately wishes to exorcise may show, as Tillich says, that Brecht still grounds his life in an ultimate concern that truly is God. Brecht himself knows that God is not banished by an act of the will; rather, this God of good and evil continues to show himself in the anguish and misery that ceaselessly follow humanity:

Many of us say you are not—and a good thing too.
But how could that thing not be which can play such a trick?
If so much lives by you and could not die without you—
Tell me how far does it matter that you don't exist?[4]

In "Bargan Gives Up," Bargan gives up everything for the sake of Croze, and the narrator gives up trying to save Bargan; but Bertolt Brecht could not give up trying to save himself and his world anymore than Paul Tillich could give up the hard-won faith that gave meaning to his life. We, the readers, must determine for ourselves whether to give up faith in a God who seems generally indifferent and sometimes evil, as does the narrator's God in "Bargan Gives Up"; or whether it is in faith in Tillich's God, a God whose No indicts the demonic in every age, that the world can be saved from self-destruction. Whatever we choose in the end, both Tillich and Brecht would understand the struggle into which the writings of both men place the reader, for it is the struggle to which both gave their lives: the struggle to give a world that is rampant with strife a basis for moving toward the truth.

---

[4]Bertolt Brecht, "Hymn to God" in *Bertolt Brecht, Poems 1913-1956*, ed. John Willett and Ralph Manheim (London: Metheun, 1987) 9.

Universalist and Particularist Perspectives On Zion (Jerusalem) in Biblical Texts

Walter Harrelson

Introduction

Jack Forstman and I have long engaged in conversation and debate over the question whether Rudolf Bultmann underestimated the dimensions of universalism in the Hebrew Scriptures.[1] I maintained, and still maintain, that he did, but Forstman has caused me to look again at the question and at the texts that I have used to support my position. I wish to continue this look in the following pages.

By the terms "universalism" and "particularism," we mean quite simply whether the religious community responsible for what we Christians call the Old Testament offered the world a religious understanding that could become a world faith, or whether the concentration upon the covenant people and its Law and upon the land of Israel and its holy sites, especially Jerusalem, ruled out such a development. We will be examining only one facet of the question of Israel's universalism: the question whether the place of the city of Jerusalem, often called Zion, does or does not offer such a universal perspective. If, however, it turns out that the Zion materials in the Hebrew Bible lend support for the development of a world faith, one might argue as well that Israelite understandings connected with the other specific Israelite terms such as covenant, Torah, and the promise of land may not need to rule out the development of a universal faith.

We are, of course, talking about possibilities, not about exactly how the Israelite community at particular times understood and affirmed the themes presented by the community's poets and prophets. The possibilities inherent in a religion are not restricted, of course, to what the community discerned and affirmed within its religious tradition. The question of possibility, however, is of

---

[1]See Bultmann's essay in Bernhard W. Anderson, ed., *The Old Testament and Christian Faith* (New York: Harper, 1963).

immense importance for those who, for many additional reasons, find their life and faith continuingly illuminated by the faith of the Israelite community and by the outgrowth of that faith in the Jewish and Christian communities. The universal perspectives of Christian faith, I maintain, have their counterparts in the Hebrew Scriptures. For this reason and for many others, Christianity and Judaism, both drawing upon the same multifaceted Israelite religious outlook, are inseparably linked in their understandings of the ultimate purposes of human life, even though those understandings differ significantly and materially. Universalistic themes in both Judaism and Christianity have their origin and the guidelines for their development in the Hebrew Bible. The following pages seek to support this assertion.

I. Zion's History in Biblical Perspective

We begin with a brief sketch of what is known of Jerusalem historically.[2] The site has been occupied, probably continuously, since at least the middle of the fourth millennium. The oldest written references to the city come from Egypt. Texts from the Middle Kingdom (2000-1700 BCE approximately) refer to the site as a part of the territory over which Egypt exercised control. The town (perhaps spelled Rushalimum) almost surely was located near the spring that provided the chief water supply for the city during the whole of biblical times (called today the Virgin's Fountain) at the southeast end of the site of the old city of David. The Tell el-Amarna Letters, also found in Egypt but written in Assyro/Babylonian cuneiform (with the use of many Canaanite terms), place Jerusalem among the several strongly fortified city-states of Late Bronze Age Canaan (1550—1200 BCE approximately). Jerusalem is far from the most important of these city-states (Shechem, Megiddo, Gezer are all larger and stronger by far than is Jerusalem). But the city is known as Uru-salim (either "the foundation of the deity Salim" or "the city of the deity Salim") and, in the letters, is making its appeal to Egypt for assistance to ward off its enemies. The Canaanite city-state continued on into the beginnings of the Iron Age (1200 BCE), although it probably was a considerably weakened town when David conquered it in the tenth century.

David first gave the city the political and religious prominence

---

[2]See Philip J. King's essay on Jerusalem in the *Anchor Bible Dictionary*, vol. 3 (Garden City, NY: Doubleday, 1992) 747-66.

that it continued to maintain until the present time. He did so by moving to the site the Ark of the covenant, perhaps the most sacred surviving object associated by tradition with Moses. David also managed to get the tribes of Israel to join in a united monarchy with its headquarters, political and religious, in Jerusalem. The prophet Nathan solidified David's religious connection with the city by affirming God's promise that descendants of David would always occupy the throne of David there (2 Samuel 7).

Solomon's enlargement of the city and his construction of the temple assured that Jerusalem would continue to be the religious capital of the community of Israel, even though Jeroboam I would lead a revolt against the kingdom of Solomon's son Rehoboam and establish shrines at Dan in the far north and at Bethel, located near the southern border of the northern kingdom. The prophets continued to see the community of Israel as one, and the Jerusalem temple had central meaning for the northern kingdom and its citizens, despite all that the leaders of the north could do. One telling event confirms this assertion: after the city's fall to the Babylonians in 587, pilgrims from many of the northern towns gathered at Shechem to make their way to the site of the ruined city and temple (see Jeremiah 41:41-8) to mourn their loss.

During the eighth to sixth centuries, the city's standing among the prophets of Israel took shape. It consisted in two complementary positions: As the site of God's abiding presence, Jerusalem and its religious shrine were gravely wounded by the community's acts of faithlessness to God. The result was that the deity stood ready to bring devastating punishment upon city and populace, should they not heed the warnings of the prophets. Isaiah could declare that the faithful city had become a harlot (Isaiah 1:21). Micah (3:12) and Jeremiah (chapters 7 and 26) could threaten the city and temple with utter destruction by God.

On the other hand, the prophets could not finally believe that God would leave the city unprotected and let it fall into ruin. Isaiah offers assurance that the city, or portions of it, will be spared, and many of the prophets of the period shortly before and during the Babylonian Exile spoke confidently of Zion's restoration once God's judgment had run its course. There was very considerable variation in the expressed hopes for Jerusalem by these prophets. Some spoke more forcefully about the restoration of the *people* than they did about the city (Jeremiah, for example). Some placed equal emphasis upon the land as a whole and upon the city of Jerusalem and its temple (Ezekiel, including Ezekiel 40-48, which may be later than Ezekiel).

At the same time, the significance of the Zion traditions continued to grow in the religious thought of the community of Israel. That phenomenon is what we want especially to focus upon in the present study.

II. The Ideology of Zion

First, we should say a word about the term *Zion*. No certain etymology proposed thus far has claimed wide acceptance. We must go by the usage. The term refers, concretely, to the southeast hill of Jerusalem, the early "city of David" (see 2 Samuel 5:7). It clearly does not refer primarily to the temple or its precincts, for the usage is closely connected with the community's hopes for the continuation, or the reinstatement, of the kingship of David, as promised in 2 Samuel 7. In 2 Samuel 7, in fact, a distinction is made between the "house" that David wished to build for the deity and the "house" that God would build for David. The later temple of Solomon was built outside the walls of David's Jerusalem, over or near to the site for a temple that David had earlier selected. That site was the threshing floor of Araunah (2 Samuel 24), purchased by David from Araunah, where David offered sacrifices to God. Zion, therefore, is not first and foremost the locale within the city of Jerusalem at which sacrifices and offerings are made, and therefore characterized more as a place of cult and worship than as a seat of government. Rather, Zion is the place from which God exercised rule over the people of the covenant, a locale always associated with David, the very David whose hands were deemed too bloody to be suitable for the building of a place of worship for the LORD.

The distinction, however, must not be overdrawn. Temples in the ancient world, and in Israel, were critical for all aspects of the life of a people. The cult had in view the renewal of life on earth, a renewal in which the community was permitted by the deity to share. Temples were repositories of important treasures and documents, were centers of learning, and were the sites from which advice and guidance were sought from the deity on regular and special occasions. When the term Zion was used to refer to the temple, the expression usually was "mountain of Zion" (see Isaiah 8:18). The point, however, is that the term Zion in Israelite ideology is firmly connected with the political and historical realities of the life of the community of Israel. Zion is the term for David's city, Jerusalem, and David receives a divine promise that his "house" will endure, even when Jerusalem itself may fall. Zion thus becomes a metaphor of God's abiding presence with the people of the covenant. Zion is "fortress Zion," from the beginning (2 Samuel 5:7) and continuingly. In the prophetic texts to be studied below, the development of the metaphor over time will become clear.

The attitude of the prophets toward David's city was always marked by ambivalence, just as their assessment of the man David seems to have been. Jerusalem's beginnings were soberly presented by the preservers of Israel's religious heritage. The city that was in time to be viewed as the very navel of the earth ("center," Ezekiel 38:12) was once a small Canaanite town, capable of being taken by David with only a small band of supporters (2 Samuel 5). Only the late story found in Genesis 14 connects Abraham with the site, called there by the name Salem. Other locales had much the greater importance for all of David's forebears—sites such as Shechem, Hebron, Bethel. In fact, all of the institutions of Israelite religious faith have their origin elsewhere, except for the temple of Solomon. And indeed, Solomon's temple is built with the reminder that the God of Israel has no need of a house on earth (1 Kings 8).

Even so, the prophets know and accept, it seems, the development in the ideology of Zion that relates the city (and later, its temple) to the "center of the earth" tradition of the ancient Near East, a tradition that sees city-states in Sumeria "lowered from heaven," fulfilling their destiny in the purpose of the gods as they live under the shadow and protection of the heavenly city, their origin. Zion becomes for the author of Psalm 48 the "city of the Far North," the city of the Great King, a site that is and is destined to be "the joy of the whole earth." Jerusalem's beauty becomes fabled and the subject of deep longing. An exile can exclaim, "If I forget you, Jerusalem, let my right hand forget [how to play the lyre]" (Psalm 137).

The paradigmatic ideology of Israelite religion, that God is One and that every existent thing other than the one God is a creation of the one God, no doubt is responsible for this attitude of ambivalence that the prophets well display. All of Israel's institutions—covenant, law, temple, kingship, prophecy, priesthood, wisdom, even peoplehood itself—exist under the sign of divine oneness and sovereignty. The ideology of Zion comes closest of all Israel's institutions, except the Torah, to breaking through this critical principle of the divine Oneness. In later rabbinic tradition, Torah will be understood as eternally present with the deity. Wisdom too, in some Jewish circles, comes close to such identity (Proverbs 8, Sirach 24, the apocryphal Baruch; see the development and the changes present in John 1), but it does so in connection with the Torah, with which it is often identified. Zion will become, in short, the "mother of us all" (2 Esdras 10:6; see Galatians 4:28). And again, it is not the case that the significance of Zion lies in its site as the place of sacrifice. Much more important is the recognition that it is the place of God's abiding presence, the place where the LORD's name is known to dwell, the place from which peace and justice will flow out to the ends of the earth. The cultic center, of course, is religiously understood to provide cleansing and renewal for life here and now. The Zion that is coming into being is the reality that expresses one of the major strands of an Israelite universalistic faith.

The tension between these two fundamental understandings of Zion is what makes this image of such critical importance in understanding our theme, "universalist and particularist perspectives." It is not the case, however, that the picture of Zion as the navel of the earth is the universalist image and that of Zion as the City of David is the particularist image. Matters are much more complicated. It is precisely this earthly city Zion, once a Canaanite town, a city that can be called "harlot city," that shares in the universalist perspective, just as it is the "city of the Far North, the joy of all the earth" that is tied firmly to the traditions of Israel's call and of God's covenant with this distinct people. We turn now to the texts that make this assertion unmistakable.

III. Universalist and Particularist Perspectives on Zion in Eschatalogical Texts: A Typology

First, we must look at one possible objection. The texts about to be considered are a part of the picture of Zion's future that Israelite prophets, poets, and sages believe lies ahead. They do not, or at least they seem not to, describe historical realities. These texts are a part of the tapestry of Israelite self-understanding, offering a picture of who and what Israel believes itself to be. Many of these texts belong, in fact, to the realm of hope, of anticipation of what God will bring to pass in a coming time.

There is of course no way to gauge the extent of the community's belief that such things would in fact come to pass. We know that some within Israel believed that the pictures of Zion's future under God would surely find realization, and we know that a large part of the community was instrumental in preserving the texts that tell of this belief. Beyond that, we cannot go.

The fact that there is such variety in the portrayals of the future

God has in store for Zion, however, speaks for a rather widespread belief in that future. The community has not subjected the traditions to amalgamation, offering a single orthodox hope in Zion's future. Had that occurred, we might be able to say that the hopes for Zion's future had been sterilized and made safe, becoming a part of the community's standardized faith. As we shall see, in fact, there are ambiguities in these traditions, points at which options in understanding are preserved—a good sign that the texts did claim rather wide allegiance within the community, since in all likelihood, such ambiguities represent compromises between and among rival understandings.

I believe it safe to say, therefore, that the following pictures of the ways in which the Zion traditions functioned, taken together, represent a very wide community outlook, and that (in all probability) none of the four perspectives identified expressed the outlook of only a tiny minority. We will be restricting ourselves to the prophetic and prophetic-like texts that follow. Zion texts that develop directly out of the community's worship will not receive further attention here. Those texts are by nature tied to the life of the worshiping community. Only the more reflective and speculative texts such as those viewed below are likely to give us the desired clues.

Position One: Particularist A

The first position to articulate is that which is, of course, least appealing to the writer: the view that Zion will be glorified at the expense of the foreign powers and peoples who have made life miserable for the community of Israel. Two of the clearest enunciations of the position are found in Isaiah 60:4-22 and 61:5-7, texts surrounded by, or embedded within, marvelously consoling language for the suffering community. The texts, of which there are several other examples, portray God's bringing the exiles from the lands in which they have been dispersed, but it then clearly articulates the theme of the subjection of Israel's enemies to the community of the covenant. Kings shall become Israel's foster fathers, their queens Israel's nursing mothers (Isaiah 49:23). They shall become the servants of those whom they have mistreated. Like a nursing child, Israel will suck the milk of the nations, suck the breast of kings.

Clearly, such affirmations belong in the realm of God's vindication of those who have been unjustly and cruelly treated in the world. What Israel has suffered unduly at the hands of the nations, the nations shall suffer at Israel's hands. God will not forever permit such cosmic injustice to prevail. The nations must pay for their misdeeds. The remarkable fact, in my judgment, is not that there should be such texts within the prophetic literature but that the number of such texts should be so small.

Position Two: Particularist B

Alongside the above perspective there appears another. The emphasis continues to be on God's vindication of Israel and God's bringing to consummation the promises made of old. Now, however, Israel's day of vindication is brought about not by the agency of the foreign nations, but by God's own initiative alone. Glorious changes will take place at the holy center, Zion. When those changes occur, the nations will be drawn to Zion to see what is transpiring there. They will come not to bring their treasures, but to witness God's establishing of Zion as an emblem of peace and righteousness for Israel and for the nations as well. There is, however, no indication that the nations are to attach themselves to Israel; their own existence as peace-loving and righteous peoples presumably is to continue. The primary texts affirming this outlook are of course those found in Isaiah 2:2-4 and Micah 4:1-4, both of which are firmly set in a particularist frame, with Zion the "mountain of the house of the LORD," the city of David.

The imagery, even so, is close to that we will discuss below, for Zion is clearly the cosmic mountain, mysteriously rising up to dominate the world scene and to cause the nations to "flow" up to Zion, as once the waters of earth flowed from Eden to water all the earth (Genesis 2). The difference between these texts and the universalist texts below is clear. Zion stands as an emblem of God's worldwide dominion, but the nations, at their own initiative, decide what to make of that emblem. Continuing in their own ways as distinct peoples and nations, they learn the art of peace from Israel and are the better for the learning. But they do not join with Israel in the fulfilling of a destiny that binds them to the divine covenant in continuing or permanent ways.

It may well be that the "Suffering Servant" passage of Isaiah 52:13–53:12 has in view a similar situation for the nations. Assuming (as I do) that the text is speaking about Israel in personified imagery, it is the nations that are "startled" (52:15) and astonished (52:14) at Israel's deliverance from long and bitter suffering and apparent death.

It is the nations who cannot believe their eyes, when the deity acts to bring glory out of Israel's suffering and exile (53:1-6). God's abiding covenant with Israel provides a public witness for the peoples of earth. The gain for the nations is unmistakable, but that gain is not an invitation for the nations to join the covenant community.

Universalist A: Zion Provides Gifts To The Nations

In our third set of texts, the glorification of Zion means glory also for foreign nations and peoples. The establishment anew of the throne of David in Zion (see especially Isaiah 9, 11, and Micah 5) means a radical transformation of life on earth, not just for Zion and for the community of Israel. Zion is the center of God's universal sway, and thus these images differ from those addressed above. But Zion provides its gifts to the nations on the basis of God's reign in peace and righteousness through Israel's anointed king, the descendant of David whom God will raise up. These texts no doubt express a hope for an historical descendant of David to arise and claim the throne promised to endure forever. At the same time, the language of the depiction of the coming king makes it clear that no earthly descendant can fulfill the vocation there laid down. This king who sits upon the throne of David will establish peace to the ends of the earth. The bloodstained boots and garments of the warriors (Israel's and those of the other armies of earth) will become fuel for the fire. The sevenfold Spirit that rests upon this king will bring transformation of life in the natural and the historical world. This one will have the name "Peace" (Micah 5:5).

Similar texts fill out this picture. Zechariah 8 speaks of a day to come when ten men will take hold of the garments of a single (each?) Jew, saying that they will go with the Jew, for they have heard that "God is with you." Zechariah 9:9-12 addresses "Daughter Zion" with the affirmation that, when the humble king appears, he will destroy the instruments of warfare from Ephraim and from Jerusalem, establishing worldwide peace. The scourge of war comes to an end. Verses 11 and 12, which probably belong with this passage, give direct assurance to Zion that she is to continue to occupy a beloved place in God's design. Zion's "prisoners of hope" are to enjoy a double blessing as they become God's instruments of righteousness and peace "from sea to sea."

Zechariah 14:16-21 occupies a special place in this picture. It speaks about the coming Day on which the nations of earth will be compelled to worship the deity at the holy mountain, at Zion, the seat of worship for all the nations. Nor will the nations have to observe the particulars of Israelite cultic practice, for every pot will be holy on that day, and there will be no need for persons to buy from the stalls in Jerusalem the objects suitable for Jewish worship; the sellers and the stalls will be no more.[3]

The author of the Book of Revelation also offers a universal picture of Zion, but it has now been moralized to such an extent that its message is severely damaged, in my judgment. The picture of Zion in Isaiah 35, on which the presentation in Revelation 21-22 is dependent, is a much better rendering.

Universalist B: Zion Becomes the Center of Blessing for All the Earth

Several prophetic texts in the Hebrew Bible offer an unqualified perspective on Zion as the center of blessing for all the earth. Here, the claim laid down almost incidentally in Ezekiel 38:12, that Zion is the center of the earth, comes into its full import. One of the most remarkable of all these texts is found in late materials from the book of Isaiah: Isaiah 19:23-25. The passage bears quoting in full.

On that day there will be a highway from Egypt to Assyria,
and the Assyrian will come into Egypt, and Egyptian into Assyria,
and the Egyptians will worship with the Assyrians.
On that day Israel will be the third with Egypt and Assyria,
a blessing in the midst of the earth, whom the LORD of hosts has
blessed, saying, "Blessed be Egypt my people, and Assyria the work
of my hands, and Israel my heritage."

In this prose utterance found among prophecies against and for Egypt, the author (probably to be dated to the period of the return from Exile) foresees a day when the two world powers of the time of the prophet Isaiah will be covenant partners with Israel. The highway connecting Egypt and Assyria, in all probability, should be understood to pass through Jerusalem, Zion, the same highway pictured in Isaiah

---

[3]For this interpretation of the passage see my essay, "The Celebration of the Feast of Booths According to Zechariah XIV:16-21," in *Religions in Antiquity: Essays in Memory of Erwin Ramsdell Goodenough*, ed. Jacob Neusner (Leiden: Brill, 1968) 88-96.

40 and again in Isaiah 35, a text to he looked at next. Israel and Egypt and Assyria jointly will be a "blessing in the midst of the earth." There is no direct reference to Zion, and the term "in the midst" (19:24) is not the same as the "center" found in Ezekiel 38:12 to refer to Jerusalem as the center of the earth.

Even so, the picture is best understood as a promise of a day when the covenant between God and Israel will be expanded to include the other nations of earth, nations that will worship the God of Israel and will do so on terms equal with those of Israel. God's blessing reaches the other peoples of earth as it reaches Israel. Zion (if the text is rightly associated with Zion) is the center of blessing for all peoples, including Israel, but the blessing comes not through Israel's agency but through God's own direct action.

Another prophetic text from the Book of Isaiah also belongs to the time of the return from Exile, in all probability: Isaiah 35. This beautiful promise of the glorification of Zion has some lines that connect it closely to Israel the covenant people alone, but the dominant tone of the passage is universal. Zion, the wilderness will blossom like a rose. The city will bring transformation of life to all, including the blind, the lame, the deaf, and those incapable of speech. The weak hands and the feeble knees will be strengthened (the infirm and the elderly), and all will proceed to Zion on the highway that God opens up in the desert.

On that highway, no one will be barred. That, I believe, is the only sensible way to translate the critical verb in verse 8. The verse should read (I make the language inclusive by making the verbs plural):

> A highway shall be there, a way.
> It shall be called the Holy Way.
> The unclean shall not pass it by;
> it shall be for them.
> No travelers, not even the simple ones,
> shall lose their way.[4]

The text presents Zion—mother Zion, we could say—as welcoming all her children from all parts of the earth, including especially (it seems) those who have been bruised and wounded or who

---

[4] For this translation and for an extended interpretation of the chapter see my essay entitled "Isaiah 35 in Recent Research and Translation," in *Language, Theology and the Bible: Essays in Honour of James Barr*, eds. Samuel E. Balantine and John Barton (Oxford: Clarendon, 1994) 247-60.

have come into the world imperfectly formed. Zion is for all, not excluding the lepers (the "unclean"). At the holy center, all sorrow and sighing shall flee away.

A final set of texts reflects on the question of how large Zion will need to be in order to accommodate those whom God summons to the city. The first text is from Zechariah 2 (the Hebrew and English verse numbers do not correspond exactly). First, there is the vision of a man sent to measure the length and breadth of the city of Jerusalem that is being rebuilt. The man, however, is called back from this mission by an angel, at the direction of another angel. The message is that Jerusalem will be inhabited like villages without walls because of the multitude that is destined to dwell in it. No walls will be needed for protection, and no one can know where the walls would have to be built in order that the city be large enough for its destined inhabitants.

That text, clearly, has in view God's bringing of the exiles of Israel back from their places of exile throughout the earth. We learn from a prophetic oracle that follows this vision, however (Zechariah 2:6-11), that the prophet is thinking in terms larger than Israel alone. The prophet says explicitly, "Many nations shall join themselves to the LORD on that day, and shall be my people; and I will dwell in your midst" (Zechariah 2:11). The action of the nations is voluntary, it seems, just as it is in Zechariah 8:20-23. The nations take the initiative in joining with Israel, and their doing so is a part of the divine intention.

In the apocryphal (deuterocanonical) book of 2 Esdras appears a story that builds upon this vision of Zion found in Zechariah 2. Chapters 3–10 of 2 Esdras contain a long exchange between Ezra, here portrayed as a prophet and seer, and the angel Uriel. Ezra is seeking to understand how it could possibly be the will of God that most of the population of earth, including most of the members of the community of Israel, should perish because of their sins. Ezra insists to the angel that the widespread prevalence of sin and evil in the world makes it virtually sure that only the tiniest remnant of God's human creation can possibly survive. Could God not have arranged matters otherwise? Will not God not find a way to bring sinners to repentance so that they are spared on the day of God's wrath?

The angel continuingly responds to Ezra's questions by two reassurances: Ezra should focus his attention upon the righteous who in fact will be spared, and Ezra belongs among the righteous and has nothing at all to fear. Neither answer is acceptable to Ezra. He will not accept the angel's assurance that he, Ezra, truly belongs among the righteous, and he cannot help but reflect, with an almost frantic zeal, about how God will deal with the vast multitude of sinners who people the earth. The resolution of this remarkable exchange between Ezra and the angel comes in the form of a vision. Ezra, while awaiting a fourth vision promised him by the angel, sees a woman in a field who is grieving her heart out. She will not for a moment cease her lamentation. Ezra comes to her, asks what is wrong, and is told the tragic story. The woman and her husband lived for many years without children, praying to God for a child. Finally a child was given, a son. The parents reared this child, lavishing on him all possible parental care. They chose a wife for the son, the marriage day came, the two were married, and as they entered the bridal chamber, the son fell down dead. The woman, accordingly, has come into the field to weep and to die; she will never return to family and community, for her life is over.

Ezra scolds the grieving woman for her inordinate grief, at precisely the time when Zion, the mother of all, lies in ruins, her children scattered over the earth, and all hope of Israel's realizing God's promise forever dashed. How dare the woman weep so bitterly over the loss of a single child, while Zion weeps over her millions?

In a twinkling, the woman is transformed into Zion, a Zion being rebuilt[5] to accommodate the millions who are destined for Zion. The Latin text preserves the right reading, in my view: a city under construction, with massive foundations, able to receive all those whom a God of love and mercy will surely find ways to accommodate. Second Esdras comes from a period some years after Jerusalem fell to the Romans in 70 CE. The author of Ezra 3-10 has Ezra place his complaint to the angel in worldwide terms. Although Israel, God's people, is very much the center of Ezra's concern, he is constantly putting the issue of how the wicked might be spared in terms that have the peoples of the earth in view.

---

[5]See my essay "Ezra Among the Wicked in 2 Esdras 3-10," in *The Divine Helmsman: Studies on God's Control of Human Events, Presented to Lou H. Silberman*, eds. James L. Crenshaw and Samuel Sandmel (New York: KTAV, 1980) 21-40.

IV. Does the Hebrew Bible Offer a Credible Universalism?

Now we are in a position, I believe, to answer the question whether the Hebrew Scriptures offer a credible universalistic perspective still consistent with God's call of the people Israel in covenant. In the essay referred to above, Bultmann expressed the view that such a universalism was not possible for Judaism because of its understanding of the call and promise of God to an ethnic community, because of the centrality of the divine demands in the form of a divine Law, and because of the view that God's promise for Israel was to find realization geographically, on a particular land that God, according to Israelite faith, had singled out. How could the religion of Israel come to be a universal faith with such restrictions? Christianity broke with Judaism at just these points, and was thus enabled to become the universal religion that no doubt many in Israel had wished that Judaism could become.

The texts with which we have been concerned make it clear, I believe, that such a way of summing up the religion of the Hebrew Scriptures is deficient. It may be that many Jews would be pleased to have their religious faith defined in terms like those used by Bultmann, for they might well argue that the particularism of land and Torah and ethnic identity are what makes the faith of Israel worthy of consideration among the religions of earth. That, however, is not my way of understanding the matter. To my mind, three of the four positions articulated for Zion have enormous religious strength. The fourth, the one dealt with first above, is also an understandable position given the suffering to which the community of Israel, in biblical times and since, has been subjected. The other three, however, have their counterparts in Christianity and have undoubted strengths. The last of the four is the most appealing, for it leaves in the mystery of God how the consummation of God's purposes for Zion will find its realization, while it holds firmly to the conviction that the day of consummation will surely come.

As I have sought to show elsewhere, these pictures of Zion's coming glorification have the potentiality of galvanizing the community of faith to action. These visions are not merely utopian; they have to do with God's present and continuing engagements with the creation, until the day portrayed comes to realization on a transformed earth. These pictures of Zion's future are best described as prophetic, not apocalyptic; they deal with this world, though a transformed world, not with a world "lowered from heaven," along the lines found in Revelation 21:1-2. Such visions judge earthly Jerusalem for being so little like what God requires it to be (see Isaiah 1!). They offer consolation to grieving Jerusalem, for God will surely see to Zion's future. And most of all, they galvanize the human community, in particular those who can in faith share these visions, to join with the deity in the process that leads to Zion's transformation.[6]

Along such lines, I believe, we can see the connections between a covenant between God and a particular people that also is being stretched to provide a place for all peoples. In this way, Israelite faith, according to the more universalistic strains of a theology of Zion, reclaims the covenant of God with Noah (Genesis 8-9), a covenant with all peoples, with all creatures, with the creation itself.

---

[6]See the closing chapter of Randall M. Falk and Walter Harrelson, *Jews and Christians in Pursuit of Social Justice* (Nashville: Abingdon, 1996).

Difference and Reconciliation: G.E. Lessing as Partner in Ecumenical Conversation

Terry H. Foreman

*Haec omnia inde esse in quibusdam vera,
unde in quibusdam falsa sunt.* —Augustine

To invite Gotthold Ephraim Lessing (1729-81) to share in a reflection on the prospects for the reconciliation of religious communities casts him in what is in some ways a natural role, and in other ways an improbable one. On the one hand, he is noted for his advocacy and personal record of religious tolerance, as a large and growing literature on Lessing's *Toleranzbegriff* shows. Reconciling seems a natural role for him because he had "no system" (Chadwick 1957, 45), and therefore would have no investment in defending one as a theologian. In fact, to call Lessing a "theologian" is to confer on him a title he not only declined but refused with scorn, since it was, he said, the role of one bound to defend a credal position no matter what his own honest personal views.[1]

On the other hand, Lessing is also known as a subtle and energetic theological controversialist. He conducted a very public dispute with clergy in his own tradition, occasioned by his publication of some "fragments" by the Hamburg Deist Hermann Samuel Reimarus (1694-1768). Lessing, unbound from defending a credal position, played an aggressive role in one of the earliest controversies concerning scriptural authority and modernist biblical interpretation.

---

[1]He wrote: "I am a theological amateur and not a theologian. I have not had to swear allegiance to any particular theological system. Nothing binds me to use terms other than my own. I pity all honest men who are not so fortunate as to be able to say this of themselves. But such honest men mustn't also try to throw the rope fastening them to the manger around the horns of other honest men. There my sympathy ends, and I can do nothing but despise them." *Axiomata, wenn es dergleichen in solchen sachen gibt* ([Axioms, if there are any in such matters], Lessing 1989, 9:9), unpublished trans. Terry Foreman (c) 1996.

Lessing Concordant

From the very outset of his career as a writer, Lessing called into question the regnant social prejudices concerning religious, social, and gendered groups and the boundaries set in the mid-18th century German lands for religious, social, and gendered groups. In 1750, he wrote a one-act comedy, *The Jews*, dramatizing a thesis to which he returned throughout his life: in German lands, the acid test of tolerance was accepting a Jew as a fellow human. After he later met and had become a fast friend and literary collaborator with the Jewish philosopher Moses Mendelssohn, Lessing wrote a review-essay (1752) vindicating his play against reviewers' attacks on the credibility of portraying a Jew noble in spirit.[2] Lessing had proved his point.

Throughout his career as a dramatist, Lessing depicted inclusive communities, types of the unity in variety of the optimal spiritual community, as though to triangulate toward its possibility in his imagination. A simple type appears in his first theatrical hit, *The Young Scholar* (1747/50). The play opens with Damis reading Moses Maimonides's *Mishneh Torah Yod ha-hazaka* in Hebrew. In short order, rather full of himself, Damis affirms the reality of the "republic of the learned," a citizen of which "belongs to the whole world; he is a cosmopolitan; he is a sun which must give light to the whole world." In answer to his servant's question as to where this republic is, Damis exults: "The republic of the learned is everywhere," but invisibly, and admittedly coextensively with "the republic of fools," since "the learned and the ignorant are everywhere intermingled, and in such a way that the latter always compose the majority" (II. iv. Lessing 1886; 1887, 59).

Lessing provides a vision of a less intellectualistic yet cosmopolitan elite in *Ernst and Falk: Conversations for Freemasons* (1778). Falk argues that nations, religions, and *Stände* (social ranks) are collective disguises, and all are disordered. The cure is said to be the "essence" of Freemasonry. In the Second Conversation, Ernst and Falk agree that the state—read "church"—is but a mere instrumentality to promote the happiness of its members, including their spiritual associations, like Freemasonry and true Christianity. In the Fifth Conversation, the ceremony of Freemasonry is decried as ignorant and obstructive to the true spiritual Freemasonry which "at bottom does not depend on *external ties*, which so easily degenerate

---

[2]For *The Jews* and Lessing's review, see Demetz 1991, 137-172. For the issue in 1778, see *Ernst and Falk*, Fourth Conversation (Maschler 1986, 36).

into *civil ordinances*; it depends rather on the community feeling of [select] minds attuned to one another" (Maschler 1986, 41).

But for a vision of a more inclusive fellowship, we may look to the epitome of Lessing's work as a voice for religious reconciliation, his great didactic drama of 1778, *Nathan the Wise* (published in 1779), still much-performed. In it, Jews, Muslims, and Christians initially at odds with one another, are, through the action, reconciled and more. Nathan, the wise Jewish paterfamilias, retells to Saladin, Jerusalem's ruler, the "Parable of the Three Rings," versions of which had been told and retold for centuries in all three cultures (most have believed Lessing got it from Boccaccio).[3] In Nathan's parable, the Abrahamic faiths share a metaphorical kinship as heirs of the same divine Father only insofar as their deeds show they are his worthy children. In a series of disclosures, the principal characters in *Nathan the Wise* discover they share an actual kinship, part blood and part a higher spirituality than any one tradition can claim. The religions are inextricably intermingled in the very identities of Recha and the Templar. There is no way to demonstrate possession of a pre-eminent revelation since even the relation of the purported fruits of religion—moral acts—to religious adherence is historically ambiguous. This is essential: the Parable of the Rings works only if there is no need to know which is *really* the genuine heirloom ring—as though only one of them could be. Each tradition acquires truth-value by *imputation*.

Nathan is not the only agent of tolerance in the play. Saladin, too, declares: "I have never required the selfsame bark / To grow on every tree" (IV.4, Lessing 1955, 103, a scene not in Demetz 1991). It would seem that Lessing's view is plain: since no religion has an exclusive or absolute claim to truth, at the very least each religion should recognize others as potentially worthy, and amity and unity in diversity should prevail. The basis of one's ability to participate in that amity is a simple, even mute, recognition of the humanity of others. The emergence of amity from the turmoil and near-holocaust in *Nathan the Wise* is dramatically catalyzed, and from a theoretical point of view made possible, because human difference and

---

[3]For a different view, see Niewöhner 1988. His splendid specimen of Otsogery argues for a Jewish source, the Marrano Uriel da Costa, author of *De tribus Impostoribus* (1598), praised by Reimarus as a man of sound reason in the *Fragment* Lessing published in 1774. Da Costa got his tale from Maimonides, who emphasized the belief that the individual's freedom and not (the 'Pharisaic') fear of eternal punishment is the basis of morality. da Costa was known to Spinoza. On "Otsogery" see Merton 1965, 275.

complexity are stripped away and understanding transcended by a single, essentially human deed: the Templar who rescued Recha, Nathan's daughter, from a fire, "explains" his act to Saladin: "The thing I did for her I did because—/ I did it" (IV.iv, Lessing 1955, 105). Reconciliation is, of course, one of the staples of dramatic action: two contrasting characters introduced early in a play enact a dramatic conflict. One plausible outcome—the tragic one—is that one of the agents succumbs to the other or to the forces the Other represents (as in Lessing's 1772 *Emilia Galotti*). Another conceivable outcome is a continuing alternation between the two, the interesting result of which might be the emergence of a sort of irony, as Friedrich Schlegel suggested (Forstman 1977, chaps. 1-2).[4] In the most typical of Lessing's plays, the action demands of the characters a discovery and acceptance that the initial conflict rests, not on an opposition of real interests, but on a fundamental misconception that the self is easily identified by its *Stand*, ethnic identity or confessional code. In *Nathan the Wise,* the Templar laments that he, indeed like everything, is so many-sided that often he can't imagine how the aspects fit together; Saladin counsels him to "Hold always to the best, and honor God! / He knows how they fit together," and laments being himself a being "Of many sides, which often seem to fit / Each other ill" (IV.4, Lessing 1955, 105).

This kind of mutual sharing of self-discovery and inner complexity opens up antagonists to self-transcendence; and resolution and reconciliation follow as each discovers something of him or herself in the Other. This is the basic redemptive design of comedy and romantic drama, to which Lessing turned in writing *Minna von Barnhelm* (1767) and *Nathan the Wise.*

What is common to these dramatic examples of reconciliation— what makes them possible—is, again, distinguishing between the essential and the inessential. This strategy presumes that it is the accidentals that separate us as individuals and into communities of interest, and essentials that unite us. As a means of getting 'back to basics' has been the preferred meliorist strategy in modern times, as much for restorationists (e.g., the Moravians) and revanchists as for progressives (e.g., Deists). Lessing's dramas and his polemical essays played upon and also thematized the contrasts between: the person

---

[4]Such a (passing) outcome and irony are found in *The Freethinker*, when Lisidor is torn between the views of Adrast and Theophan--day and night says Adrast, from which, answers Lisidor, "an agreeable twilight" springs (1.3: Lessing 1887, 222-23).

and the persona or mask; spirit and letter; love and duty; the inner and the outer; deed and belief; the content (which might be religion, humanity, truth) and the concrete form in which it must necessarily manifest itself—in order to make a case for the liberation of the former from the latter.[5]

Lessing's location of religion in the inner life is consistent with his era—one in which religion came to be conceived by Madison and others in America as a private affair and, where established churches prevailed, religious differences found outlets in sects and in Freemasonry. Religious reconciliation would seem to require finding what is more fundamental than the concrete particulars of religious traditions. When Nathan laments having not reared Recha, a Christian orphan, in her own tradition, the Friar reminds him that he has given her love: "And children / Have need of love—and were it but the love/ Of savage beasts—much more than Christian teaching./ For Christianity there's always time" (IV.7, Demetz 1991, 255-56.).

Lessing Discordant

The irenic Lessing, author of *Nathan the Wise*, envisioned the reconciliation of the presumably irreconcilable. But in Lessing's life and work the irenic and the contentious were never far apart. This connection is illustrated in one of Lessing's favorite genres, the *Rettung* or "vindication," which he adopted from Pierre Bayle (Allison 1966, 51). In the 1750s, Lessing began a series of defenses of historical figures maligned—and sometimes executed—by orthodox religious authorities. By casting its victims in a sympathetic new light, each vindication served by implication to undermine the credibility of religious authority. But this genre was, in the end, too subtle for Lessing's purposes. When he wrote *Nathan the Wise*, he had himself just waged intra-confessional aggression so furious that it raises questions about his views on the possibility of amity in matters trans-confessional.

After entering the service of the Duke of Braunschweig as librarian in Wolfenbüttel in 1769, Lessing had largely turned from his vocation

---

[5]Lessing's exploitation of the analogies among these contrasts was unusually rich and ramified, and included additionally: reality / appearance; person / persona; humanity / role; esoteric / exoteric; self / role; agent / mask; message / rhetoric; invisible / visible; secret / manifestation; religion / adiaphora; invisible / visible; living / dead; the vital / its reification; the canon within the canon / the canon entire; Gemeinschaft / Gesellschaft; and what in the 20th century would be called the authentic and the inauthentic.

as playwright to editing and publishing manuscripts and to theological polemics. In May 1777, he had published a scathing rationalist attack in German on the credibility of the Bible (by Reimarus), disingenuously presented as "fragments" of work by an unknown author found in the Ducal Library, with some "Editor's Counter-proposals" (*Einwände*) that initially gave him cover, but which were calculatedly provocative.[6] Hamburg-area Lutheran pastors responded to the attack on the Bible in force, and in short order the elder statesman and champion of the party of Orthodoxy, Johann Melchior Goeze (1717-1786), saw through Lessing's ruse. The two then engaged in a blistering duel in print. So dodgily did Lessing conduct himself that Goeze wrote he doubted if any single sentence of what Lessing had published could be trusted as sincere (Lessing 1979, 8:23). (Lessing's characteristic willfulness and unpredictability were made the worse because, now aged 49, his first natural son and his wife had just died, in December 1777 and January 1778.)

The entire episode, now known as the *Fragmentenstreit*, evoked from Lessing some of his most seminal and interesting theological essays, but resulted in the Duke's requiring in July 1778 that Lessing thenceforth submit his writings to the Lutheran censor. Lessing, therefore, returned to his "former pulpit, the theatre" (Chadwick 1957, 26), dramatizing his ideas as he had in his university days.[7] The first result was not a stage-piece but some dialogues, the *Ernst und Falk*; but the second result was *Nathan the Wise*. An epitome of religious reconciliation was, then, the indirect offspring of religious vitriol. This pairing of *polemos* and *eirene* had been represented within the *Fragmentenstreit* itself in two essays published together in the Fall of 1777, *On the Proof of the Spirit* and *The Testament of John*.[8]

One persistent line of Lessing–interpretation has it that he was a rationalist and a Deist for whom historical revelation was but a mask

---

[6]Parts of the unpublished papers of Hermann Samuel Reimarus, Professor of Hebrew and Oriental Languages at the Hamburg *Gymnasium* and progressive civic leader, which his daughter had entrusted to Lessing to publish (Reimarus, 1970).

[7]In his Preface to the first edition of *The Jews*, Lessing had written: "My enthusiasm for the theater was so great at that time that everything I thought about turned into a comedy. I soon had the notion to see what effect would be produced on the stage if people were shown virtue where they didn't at all expect to find it" (Lessing 1989, 1:1152).

[8]The external facts of the episode are available in many places. See, e.g., Chadwick 1957, 15-26; or, more cursorily, Demetz 1991, xxiv-xxv.

for the rational truth behind it.[9] This view tempts because of Lessing's persistent attacks on Lutheran Orthodoxy and Neology (the name given the view that, in brief, Christianity's reasonableness consists in its moral value), and because of his occasional apparent experiment with rationalist philosophical theology. The relation of the "positive" (historical) religions to the rational truths of the Deists was treated graphically by Lessing in *On the Proof of the Spirit and of Power* (Oct/Nov 1777). This essay came into prominence in the 20th century under the aegis of Søren Kierkegaard, who made its focal problem the concern by which his pseudonymous author Johannes Climacus was driven in Part One of *Concluding Unscientific Postscript*, "Something about Lessing," to a desperate subjectivity from which the only escape seemed to be a "leap of faith" (Kierkegaard [1846] 1941, 59-113).

The problem in *On the Proof* seemed to be that proofs of Christianity did not work since their staple mode of argument— proceeding from historical claims to dogmatic ones—was basically flawed because "*accidental truths of history can never become the proof of necessary truths of reason*" (Chadwick 1957, 53). This is of import to an apologete for Christianity or for any religion—and certainly for modern Lutheran Orthodoxy. Such an apologete would seem to be impeded in his or her venture by "an ugly, broad ditch" (*einer grausamen, breiter Graben*) between these two kinds of truth, across which a leap cannot be made.

Lessing might seem to have stumbled onto (and nearly into) an insurmountable rationalist obstacle to securing Christian belief—unless we consider his rhetorical situation, his strategy, his broader convictions, the passage with which he introduced the text, and the text appended to it.

On the Proof was written in reply to the first published response to the "Fragments," a typical showing of the "evidence of the proof for the truth of the Christian religion" by Johann David Schumann, director of the Hanover Lyceum, which proceeded in the fashion described (Lessing 1989, 8:357-435). The mock-scholastic "*distinguo*" of Lessing's counter-attack, cutting all truths into two kinds, was a razor borrowed from §33 of Leibniz' *Monadology*. Lessing knew full well that there are more than two kinds of truth-claim. Even in a 1749 comedy, Adrast, title character in *Freethinker*, had affirmed the invisible unity yet necessary variety and inevitable variegation of truth (4.3, Lessing 1887, 227). In this light, the ditch

---

[9]Chadwick 1957, 28-29. Michalson 1985, passim.

between the accidental truths of history and the necessary truths of reason would appear to be a rhetorical device, an optical illusion created by Orthodox rationalism, and one only visible from the angle of modern apologetic. Such apologetic was not finally convincing but only appeared so, trumpeted Lessing brazenly in his prefatory note to Schumann:

> Sir, who could be more eager to read your new work than I? I hunger for conviction so much that like Erysichthon [who, in Ovid's *Metamorphoses*, was punished with a hunger so insatiable that he ate himself], I swallow everything that has even the *appearance* of nourishment. *If you do the same with this pamphlet, we are the men for one another* (Demetz, 309, my emphasis).

That is, not only Schumann's prolix piece, but also the economical *On the Proof of the Spirit and of Power* itself, has but the *appearance* of conviction. Leibniz' distinction invoked here seemed a prop to be discarded by the Lessing who, in *The Freethinker*, had lampooned those who use such excluded middles (1.3, Lessing 1887, 3:227). Lessing's skew—or critical view—of reason immunized him against the spectacle of the ditch.[10]

An anti-foundationalist in matters philosophical, Lessing differed fundamentally from Leibniz, the Enlightenment, and Reimarus (his stalking horse) over the character of both truth and reason (cf. Hannah Arendt in Demetz 1991, xvii). E.g., in the *Einwände*, Lessing repudiated a central tenet of the *Aufklärung* that "the truth of any revealed religion is to be judged, at least in part, by its conformity to a hypothesized natural religion" (Allison 1966, 99). As Peter Michelsen has pointed out, a certain skepticism about the capability of reason and a belief that human reason is limited "has long found a home in Christian orthodox tradition, but also comes to fruition--and this is a frequently overlooked sign of *Aufklärung*--as a consequence of critical thinking itself"—as Lessing and Mendelssohn had observed in their satirical 1755 "Pope a Metaphysician!" (Michelsen 1990, 61). For Lessing there are no objective, eternal, uniform standards that are in principle universally accessible. From the *Freethinker* on, Lessing inveighed against even harboring this as an ideal, since it negates the

---

[10]Gordon Michalson thinks Lessing had this immunity because he "has a secure foothold on the necessity side" (Michalson 1985, 38); but if that were the case, Lessing's major works of 1778 would be unintelligible.

individual and the temporal. Truth on the hoof is plural, and changing in aspect.[11]

Reason is not only not self-sufficient, it vitiates Christianity when it presumes to provide it its claim to truth. Modern apologetic of that sort obstructed religion itself and so any reconciliation across confessional lines. The "ugly, broad ditch" Lessing intended to suggest, perhaps, was this ditch between the rationalistic religious maximalists of the orthodox party and the religion of the simple Christian. Modern rationalist Christian apologists, Lessing held, had not strengthened religion but weakened it by depriving it of its self-sufficiency, and denying it also its very soul by pitting it against the humanity of the Other. Far from being a rationalist, then, Lessing here--as elsewhere--uses reason not only against the proofs of religion from history, but also against the proofs of religion from reason itself.[12] He consistently used rational argument to attack rationalism in religion, from his unpublished *Thoughts On the Moravians* of ca. 1752 to the final part of his *Anti-Goeze* of 1778.

On the Proof of the Spirit and of Power concludes with the wish that "all who are divided by the Gospel of John be reunited by the *Testament of John*" (Chadwick 1957, 56). In this latter "apocryphal" work, Lessing had the dying Beloved Disciple repeatedly advise his own beloved disciples that they love one another. *On the Proof and The Testament* provide more than a contrast in size. The former is written in a technical style, its logic-bound argument driving to a (desperate) conclusion. The latter is a sprightly dialogue about a simple but moving tableau that contains a parable of mimesis, inviting its reader to perform its simple lesson—a lesson the likes of which is entirely lacking in *On the Proof*—and by implication (and in fact) in the "evidence of the proof for the truth" proffered by Schumann.

In *On the Proof* and other texts in the *Fragmentenstreit* (e.g., the *Axiomata* and *Anti-Goeze* of 1778), Lessing attacked the Orthodox

---

[11]In *The Freethinker*, Adrast initially distinguishes propositions and their proposers and says he prefers the former, but he gradually changes his tune, abhorring the general as he learns to prefer the voice of his beloved. Adrast is reinforced in this by the play's voice of reconciliation, Lisador, her father, who doubts whether language can be measured with "compasses" (Lessing 1887, 2:219-287). This passage tends to support Allison's other evidence in favor of viewing Lessing as a perspectivalist in a Leibnizean sense (Allison 1966, 124ff.).

[12]Schumann's proof sprung a trap long set. In notebooks of 1768-74, Lessing identified Grotius's *Tractatus de Veritate Religionis Christianae* (1639) as having opened the way for a reinterpretation of patristic apologetic as not a defense of Christianity against heathens so much as an attempt to establish grounds (*Gründe*) for Christian faith (Schultze 1969, 72).

Lutheran insistence that Christian faith depends or ever depended on external proofs from scripture or philosophical theology. He attacked the "religion of theologians" so that the "religion of the simple Christian" could live. *Lessing the discordant was in service to Lessing the concordant.*

Lessing Errans

Although this perspective seems well and good, there remains a disquieting possibility. It is that Lessing and his antagonists did not so much disagree as they grossly failed to understand each other to such an extent that Lessing might not be of much help in reconciling those from different confessions.

There are two initial reasons to suspect that a significant *Kulturkampf* was defined in the quarrel between Lessing and the Orthodoxy party. First, on the bicentennial of the *Fragmentenstreit*, modern variants of it continued their own vigorous life in American Christianity and beyond. But second, the way the *Fragmentenstreit* was conducted and ended showed that there had been a general breakdown in communication, or at least in understanding, between its parties, and perhaps not just on the side of the Hamburg pastorate.

Certainly in his polemical writings, Lessing intentionally argued in such a way as to confuse his adversaries and *not* to be understood. In his theological writings, Lessing had naturally long drawn on the theatrical repertoire of his age, and he readily conceded to Goeze that he used a theatrical kind of logic.[13] The calculated poses and "voices" of this man of the theatre were disguises, *personae* ad hoc, which his great admirer Kierkegaard would transform into pseudonymous authorial identities. As well in dialectic as in drama, Lessing used veils not only to provoke discovery but also to hide his identity, his agenda and his true intentions, as he wrote to his brother, Karl: "I must aim my weapons at my opponent; not all that I write *gymnastikos* would I also write *dogmatikos*."[14]

Goeze and others have gone farther and claimed that Lessing argued to as to confuse the issues he raised—unintentionally.[15]   A

---

[13]In *Etwas Vorläufiges* and *Anti-Goeze, I*, Letter VI, respectively.
[14]Quoted in Chadwick 1957, 25. See ibid., 12-29, for a discussion of Lessing as an exemplary esotericist.
[15]Goeze, *Etwas Vorläufiges* (Lessing 1979, 8:23), and Michalson 1985, 31ff., who also notes that "Lessing is simply not the sort of thinker for whom technical conceptual matters prove to be decisive," but confusedly ascribes it to "Lessing's confusion" (ibid., 45).

tactfully ironic reading shows that Lessing was not confused, but spoke in a voice carefully calibrated to provoke his foils, technicians devoted to verbal univocity. The inadequacy of language to capture lived experience was part of his point, wherefore his own unambiguous, positive theological affirmations were few. Ideas, he argued, cannot always be expressed in words, nor words guarantee communication: "ERNST: 'What I understand, I can put into words.' FALK: 'Not always, and often not in such a way that the words convey to others the idea I have exactly'" (Maschler 1986, 16). Lessing conveyed a related mistrust of univocity when working out the relation between Spinoza and Leibniz: "the use of the selfsame words by both of them does not entail they are thereby bound to the selfsame concepts."[16] Ergo, any affirmation taken out of context cannot be conclusively understood, since its meaning is bound up with that of others.

When Goeze suggested that certain of Lessing's propositions in the *Einwände* functioned as dubious "axioms," Lessing seized eagerly on the notion that he had argued *more geometrico* like Spinoza. A skilled debater, Lessing used the propositions Goeze attacked to redefine the issue to his advantage and to twit the Lutheranism of the most Lutheran Reverend Mister Goeze. The resulting *Axiomata*— "Axioms, if there are any in such matters"—is an epitome of Lessing sifting essence from dross, advocating by opposing, and a handy digest of what he condemned—Wittenberg theology's "bibliolatry," which packages living tradition so it can be controlled by technicians; the pastoral yoke; and apologetics—and what he worked to vindicate— the simple Christian; and the direct, oral communication of tradition (Lessing 1989, 9:53-89).[17] Lessing dealt with the authority of the Bible first in the order of topics, as had the Reformed Confessions (and the Reverend Mr. Goeze), but in order to show the logical priority of the authority of the original confessing community, in keeping with the Augsburg Confession. Goeze, ostensibly representing the laity's concern for the Bible's integrity and sufficiency, had blundered by reproaching Lessing for having published inquiries into the authority of Scripture in German, a language available to laity, instead of in Latin, the privy language of the Lutheran magisterium in Germany. Here Lessing tartly took him to task for that and replied

---

[16]Allison 1982, 225. Quoted in German, trans. mine.
[17]Bibliolatry is a term Lessing did not coin—*contra* Chadwick 1957, 24, n.2.

that he himself had followed Luther's own example.[18]
Lessing believed and argued that much that passed for religion as
the Orthodox understood it consisted of adiaphora. But his
"Anonymous" fragmentist had argued that the Bible does not contain
what had been taught that it contains. This was perhaps not
something extraneous so far as the laity were concerned. Goeze
wished to press the issue: What is the consequence of destroying the
conventional picture of the reliability of the Bible if the laity believe
Christianity to be reliant on the Bible, especially when the
resurrection narratives are questioned, thus comforting not Christians
but Jews? Lessing retorted that Christianity was not dependent on the
truth or the authority of the Bible and, for the "simple Christian,"
whose religion was an affair of the heart, never had been.

Months before the Censor was invoked, Lessing parodied what had
passed for communication in the *Fragmentenstreit*. In *Axiomata* he
wrote "A Dialogue and No Dialogue," with 'Lessing' and 'Goeze'
talking about religion *as though* responding to each other but in fact
not doing so (Lessing 1989, 9:79-84). He called this genre a
Kanzeldialog ("Pulpit-dialogue"), to call attention to the theatrical
role of the pulpit and the great gulf between the pulpit and the pew
(see Lessing 1989, 9:859). But he does not seem to have considered
the possibility that he and Goeze had views about "religion" framed
from within such different notional paradigms that their "use of the
selfsame words [did] not entail that they were thereby bound to the
selfsame concepts."

What if there were different ideas about religion such that,
according to one "the living God lurks in detail," not just in the
Commandment to Love, and for some or many "simple Christians"
minutiae of observance and ceremony were of the essence
(Wasserstrom 1995, 9)? What if there were not just more than one
religion, but more than one *concept* of religion equally true *by
imputation?* What if—contrary to what Lessing the Lutheran
pastor's son had come to believe—the very *credulity* of the laity were
essential to the vitality of their religion, and Goeze was their true
guardian? Is this perhaps an ugly, broad ditch that Lessing could not
have imagined?

---

[18]Goeze, *Etwas Vorläufiges II*, "Eine Anmerkung" (Lessing 1979, 8:116). An
index of how control of public opinion was shifting away from the clergy to the
Mittelstand, even in Germany, is the estimate that only 12'% of all books published
in German lands in 1781 were in Latin (Holborn 1967, 309).

Lessing Quaerens

If it is possible that Lessing so little comprehended what might have been at stake in intra-confessional conversation, how might he comprehend an even more ambitious ecumenical one? He conceived reconciliation across religious lines as the working of Providence. During and after the turmoil of the *Fragmentenstreit*, Lessing drafted one scenario in which particular providence operates generally, and another in which general providence operates particularly to mitigate the divisions among humankind.[19]

In *The Education of the Human Race* (1777/1780), Lessing presented his grand vision of particular providence operating generally to reconcile humanity in an "eternal" dispensation. Henry Allison shows convincingly how a consistent Leibnizean perspectivalism connects the *Education* to Lessing's other writings (Allison 1966, chap. IV). In the *Education,* the perspectives in question are those passed through by a humankind developing in time—the model later used by Hegel, et al. Divine revelation is adapted to the condition of its recipients at each stage, and humanity outgrows the revelation fit for a prior stage (as Christians had held humankind had outgrown Judaism), and in principle humanity might outgrow revelation for a rational morality. Allison does not think Lessing took the analogy between revelation and education with ultimate seriousness, nor do I. But whereas Allison argues at length and with power that the analogy is "nothing more than an...exoteric 'hull' for a purely naturalistic conception of intellectual development" (Allison 1966, 150; ibid., 150-161), I offer briefly two reservations for regarding even that notion of human development as itself unambiguous.

Against Allison's nonreligious (future) culmination of the education of humankind stands the considerable ambiguity with which Lessing regarded reason and all of its accoutrements (univocity and the like), as we have seen. While it is true that in the later part of the *Education* Lessing envisions a humanity so highly developed that all Scriptures are dispensable (§§72, etc.), humankind even without divine direction or the guidance of reason, might achieve remarkable moral

---

[19]Lessing refused to allow either of the texts in question to be published in his own name. He could have ill-afforded it to be publicly known that he was author of the *Education of the Human Race*; and the last two Conversations between *Ernst and Falk*, deemed possibly offensive to other Berlin friends and to the authorities by Nicolai and Hamann, were orphaned by their declining author.

feats by mute, even impulsive (random?) acts of kindness, such as the one the Templar performed in rescuing Recha from the fire.

We need also ponder something Allison does not mention, the *Education*'s Augustinian Latin motto—"For the same reason, all of this is in a certain sense true, and in a certain sense false." No doubt designed to provide Lessing cover should the Censor discover the essay's author, it must also cast doubt on the author's meaning. Scriptures are "in a certain sense true" and "in a certain sense false," since they contain claims which are of a probable certitude only, or were directed to ancients in their cultural terms, as Spinoza had argued. And, adds Lessing, there is material in Scripture that doesn't pertain to religion--a point he had made in the *Einwände*, and made again even more emphatically in the *Axiomata*.[20]   But the fruits of reason fall under the same verdict.

For these reasons, then, I do not believe the grand metaphysical scenario of *The Education of the Human Race* is the model of Providence in which Lessing invested most hope. I believe he looked instead to the one we have seen before.

The scenario of general providence operating particularly to reconcile humankind is not only more characteristic of his entire oeuvre, it is also pervasively embedded in quotidian experience. In both *Nathan the Wise* and *Ernst and Falk*, Lessing reflects on the misfit between events and our language about them in relating the orders of nature and grace. Recha saved, but rhapsodizing about the "invisible angels' wings" on which her savior Templar had borne her "visibly...through the fire," Nathan reflects on the "universal miracle" that we come to regard the miraculous in our lives as "so commonplace." So invisible are the agencies of grace that the visible is causally self-sufficient—to "a thinking man" (I.ii, Demetz 1991, 180-81). Recall the similar quandary in which the Templar found himself when trying to *explain* to Saladin his spontaneous act of saving a Jewish girl (as he supposed): he could provide no reason (*Grund*) for his act.

There are some deeds and some events that seem isolate surds in the sequence of natural events. The act that defied understanding was an impulse of "the heart," which Theophan, the young Pastor in *The Freethinker*, had opposed to the "reasons" of apologists like Adrast:

---

[20]The first part of the *Axiomata* proceeds from the reaffirmation that "The Bible contains manifestly more than pertains to religion" to the accusation that Goeze had forgotten the well-known Lutheran distinction "between the Holy Scripture and the Word of God" (Lessing 1989, 9:58,63-64).

"The heart accepts no reasons (*Gründe*), and will maintain its independence of the understanding (*Verstand*) in this as in other matters" (5.3, Lessing 1887, 282). The drama in *Nathan the Wise* may be viewed as taking place within Nathan himself, where head and heart are at war for preeminence; and though he initially, somewhat scoffingly, judges Recha as governed by the latter, in the end he himself capitulates to its principle.

A similar contrast between the invisible and the visible is featured in *Ernst and Falk*. Falk introduces the subject into his First Conversation with Ernst under the topic of "the true deeds of the Freemasons." These, he says, are the most important in the world, and "aim at making most of the deeds commonly called good superfluous" (Maschler 1986, 19). Ernst, puzzled about the identity of these "true deeds," asks about the intentions of the Freemasons, which are, of course, part of the *invisible* order. In the Third Conversation, Falk suggests that the Freemasons "may...have been resorting to a familiar ruse, that of openly practicing some of their secret objectives, so as to mislead such men as, driven by suspicion, are always on the look-out for something different from what stares them in the face?" (Maschler 1986, 30). How can such deeds be talked about, even when they are not impulsive but are programmatic? The "real deeds" conducted in "plain view" pass for commonplace.

How, then, to cooperate with Providence so as to promote and foster the reconciliation among humankind? One kind of answer is given in the Fifth Conversation. Falk traces the meaning of "Masonry" to terms "in the language of the Anglosaxons, but in that of the Goths and Franks as well" that refer to older words for the table-fellowship of intimates which were still understood "in Luther's day," of which the original was a table-round in order that all might be equal, and to the ancient German custom of discussing important matters at table (Maschler 1986, 43-44). By mentioning him in this connection, Lessing brings to mind Luther's *Table Talk* in contrast to the high theology of Luther's eighteenth-century theological epigoni at Wittenberg (where Lessing had taken his M.A.), and their radicalization of *scriptura sola*. In the custom of fellowship at the human *Stammtisch*, Freemasonry and religion live without the intervention of scriptures (without "the Gospel of John"). In the equality of the round table we find what Minna von Barnhelm called "the only firm bond of love" (V.xi, Demetz 1991, 68). She may have had a different kind of love in mind (and the equal division of household labor), but we cannot exclude the possibility that even here we are permitted to understand in Lessing's text a pun pregnant with possibility. Here are occasions for the working of Providence in the commonest exchanges.

Lessing Conversant

In dialogue is the open practice of objectives that are secret because all objectives are precisely *invisible*. The presupposition for the possibility of table-fellowship is *Anerkennung*, the simple salutation, the act of recognition, exemplified by Lessing in the Masonic handshake with which Ernst and Falk begin their Fourth Conversation. The dialogues between and among Saladin and the Templar and Nathan—these supposed enemies—are not only means to reconciliation but already signs of it.

The banality of the conversation at table makes possible the "true deed" and the "miracles" hidden in plain sight. The history of the Arthurian Round Table points to the truth. The institution of the customs and rites of the table are just a "'misunderstanding,' a 'hull' under which the real form lies hidden." (Michelsen 1990, 156-57.)

In one respect, the Masonic model is defective: it is a closed, an exclusive table society. If we were to substitute "persistent" for "closed," we would probably come closer to the conditions as described by Nathan, in which wonders occur in the commonplace. It could only be closed if there were an agreement in principle that those already present at table possessed the truth. Lessing presents resounding objections to this possibility in the Fourth Conversation and in that famous passage in his *Duplik* (Rejoinder) of early 1778 in which, presented hypothetically with a choice between the truth and the search for it, he rejected the former as beyond human holding and seized the latter (Maschler 1986, 36-37; Lessing 1989, 9:508).

This is how Lessing answers my final reservation about his fitness to be a companion in interfaith dialogue. In the midst of his bitter controversy, (1) Lessing concedes that he does not possess the truth, but (2) insists it must be pursued. *And* Lessing refuses to surrender his engagement with his antagonists, persisting in his quest for truth in his works after July 1778, and so, in principle, substitutes "inclusive" for "exclusive."

Even if language fails to establish any reliable conceptual concurrence, in persistence in dialogue and in the momentary personal interpenetrations of "table-talk" are foreshadowings of self-transcendence and openness to the Other. As complex and complicated as Lessing knew human relationships to be, he also regarded them as often most eloquent in their simplicity. Lessing insisted that neither the identities of individual persons nor the boundaries that separate them are necessarily what they appear to be. Because persons can transcend themselves, in unguarded and relaxed sociability, when not wrapped up in themselves, it is possible to be available for others by being what one is not.

WORKS CITED

Allison, Henry E. 1966. *Lessing and the Enlightenment: His Philosophy of Religion and Its Relation to Eighteenth-Century Thought.* Ann Arbor: University of Michigan Press.
_____, 1982. "Lessing's Spinozistic Exercises," *Lessing Yearbook Supplement: Humanität und Dialog.* Detroit: Wayne State University Press.
Chadwick, Henry. 1957. Ed. and trans. *Lessing's Theological Writings: Selections in Translation, with an Introductory Essay,* Stanford: Stanford University Press.
Demetz, Peter. 1991. Ed. *Nathan the Wise, Minna von Barnhelm, and Other Plays and Writings.* Foreword by Hannah Arendt. The German Library 12. New York: Continuum.
Forstman, Jack. 1977. *A Romantic Triangle: Schleiermacher and Early German Romanticism.* AAR Studies in Religion 13. Missoula, MT: Scholars Press.
Holborn, Hajo. 1967. *A History of Modern Germany: 1648-1840.* New York: Alfred A. Knopf.
Kierkegaard, Søren. 1941. *Kierkegaard's Concluding Unscientific Postscript.* Trans. David F. Swenson and Walter Lowrie. (1846) Princeton: Princeton University Press.
Lessing, Gotthold Ephraim. 1886. *Gotthold Ephraim Lessings Sämtliche Werke.* Ed. Karl Lachmann, 3d rev. ed. Franz Muncker. 23 vols. in 24. Stuttgart: G. J. Goschen, 1886-1924. Vol. 1, Sinngedichte, etc.
_____. 1887. *The Dramatic Works of G.E. Lessing.* Ed. and trans. Ernest Bell. 3 vols. London: George Bell and Sons, York Street, Covent Garden. Vol. 2, Comedies.
_____. 1955. *Nathan the Wise: A Dramatic Poem in Five Acts.* Trans. Bayard Quincy Morgan. New York: Frederick Ungar Publishing Co.
_____. 1979. *Werke.* Ed. Herbert G. Göpfert with Karl Eibl, et al. München: Carl Hanser Verlag. Bd. 8: Theologiekritische Schriften

III, Philosophische Schriften. ed. Helmut Gîbel.
_____. 1989. *Werke und Briefe.* Ed. Wilfried Barner et al. Bibliothek deutscher Klassiker. Frankfurt a.m.: Deutscher Klassiker Verlag. v. 1: *Werke: 1743-1750.* Ed. Jürgen Stenzel. v. 8: *Werke: 1774-1778.* Ed. Arna Schilson. v. 9: *Werke: 1778-1780.* Ed. Klaus Bohnen and Arna Schilson.

Maschler, Chaninah. 1986. "Lessing's *Ernst and Falk, Dialogues for Freemasons*: A Translation with Notes," *Interpretation* 14.1 (January 1986): 1-49.

Merton, Robert K. 1965. *On the Shoulders of Giants: A Shandean Postscript.* Foreword by Catherine Drinker Bowen. New York: Free Press.

Michalson, Gordon E. 1985. *Lessing's 'Ugly Ditch': A Study of Theology and History.* University Park and London: Pennsylvania State University Press.

Michelsen, Peter. 1990. *Der unruhige Bürger: Studien zur Lessing und zur Literatur des achtzehnten Jahrhunderts.* Würzburg: Königshausen und Neumann.

Niewîhner, Friedrich. 1988. *Veritas sive Varietas: Lessings Toleranzparabel und das Buch von den drei Betrügern.* Veröffentlichungen der Lessing-Akademie Wolfenbüttel. Bibliothek der Aufklärung V. Heidelberg: Verlag Lambert Schneider.

Reimarus, Hermann Samuel. 1970. *Fragments.* Ed. Charles H. Talbert, trans. Ralph S. Fraser. Philadelphia: Fortress Press.

Schultze, Harald. 1969. *Lessing's Toleranzbegriff: Eine theologische Studie.* Göttingen: Vandenhoeck & Ruprecht.

Wasserstrom, Steven M. 1995. *Between Muslim and Jew: The Problem of Symbiosis under Early Islam.* Princeton: Princeton University Press.

Race, Suffering, Slavery, and Divine Providence: Some Black and White Nineteenth-Century Deists' and Theists' Voices

Riggins R. Earl, Jr.

Introduction

Did God ordain that Whites enslave Blacks for the evolutionary purpose of leading them to Christ? Or, did God permit White enslavement of Blacks as an evolutionary preparation for them to become citizens of what Whites called a "higher civilization and moral order?" No religious question that emerged out of the slave experience has been more difficult for Black Americans to answer. Some Blacks of the nineteenth century sought to answer these questions by starting with the Christian presupposition that God takes what the oppressor meant for the victim's evil and computes it for his/her higher good.[1] Other nineteenth-century Blacks presupposed that slavery, as cruel as it was, might have been God's means of exposing them to the higher moral laws of the universe. Ironically, both groups accepted the fact that slavery, even at its worse, must be viewed as an evil means to a higher good. In this sense, neither group made a radical departure from the beliefs of nineteenth-century White thinkers. Blacks of both groups appealed to the same Christian and political world views as did their White counterparts.

Contemporary Black scholars are often troubled by the fact that nineteenth-century Black leadership commonly reflected White thinkers' views of God and slavery. Unfortunately, we are tempted to impose upon the primary sources produced by these leaders our own provincial views of God and slavery. As difficult as it is, we must accept the fact that Black leaders could embrace the idea that God could permit the enslavement of their race as a means to a higher end while still affirming God as their friend. What is even more critical, as

---

[1] No prominent nineteenth-century Black leader could ignore this pervasive issue. See *Afro-American Encyclopedia Or, the Thoughts, Doings and Savings of the Race*, ed. James T. Haley (Nashville: Haley and Florida, 1896; reprint, Nashville: Winston-Derek Publishers, Inc., 1992).

I see it, is the slightly different way they interpreted God's role in the race's evolutionary struggle from slavery to freedom. The thesis here is that two types of nineteenth-century Black leadership interpretation of God's involvement in the race's suffering and enslavement are identifiable. One is what I am calling here the deistic[2] type responsive voice. The second is what I am calling the theistic[3] type responsive voice. Although influenced by the church, all

---

[2]My understanding of deism and its constitutive elements has been influenced by Roger L. Emerson's definition. He notes that "Deism is the belief that by rational methods alone men can know all the true propositions of theology which it is possible, necessary, or desirable to know. Deists have generally subscribed to most of the following propositions, and have ranged widely from the Christian rationalists or fideists to atheists:
1. One and only one God exists.
2. God has moral and intellectual virtues in perfection.
3. God's active powers are displayed in the world, created, sustained, and ordered by means of divinely sanctioned natural laws, both moral and physical.
4. The ordering of events constitutes a general providence.
5. There is no special providence; no miracles or other divine interventions violate the lawful natural order.
6. Men have been endowed with a rational nature which allows them to know truth and their duty when they think and choose in conformity with this nature.
7. The natural law requires the leading of a moral life, rendering to God, one's neighbor, and one's self what is due to each.
8. The purest form of worship and the chief religious obligation is to lead a moral life.
9. God has endowed men with immortal souls.
10. After death retributive justice is meted out to each man according to his acts. Those who fulfill the moral law and live according to nature are 'saved' to enjoy rewards; others are punished."
Philip P. Wiener, ed., *Dictionary of the History of Ideas, Studies of Selected Pivotal Ideas* (New York: Charles Scribner's Sons, 1973), 1:646b.
[3]N. H. G. Robinson has influenced my definition of theism here. "Theism has been described as a philosophical theory as distinct from a religious faith, even if the two are rarely disjoined, and it may be defined as belief in a single supreme being who is the source of everything else and who, as A.E. Taylor would have added (cf. A. E. Taylor, "Theism," in *Theologische Realenzyklopädie*, 12:261-87) being himself complete and perfect, is worthy to be worshipped." Theism fails to be distinguished, on the one hand, from deism which affirms the transcendence in theism is divorced from its immanence and which cutting off the Creator's involvement in his creation, renders the theistic themes of providence and worship highly ambiguous, and, on the other hand, from pantheism which affirming immanence at the expense of trancendence, identifies the divine with its whole of reality and destroys the distinction between Creator and creation. It also fails to be distinguished from atheism, which denies the existence of God, from agnosticism which regards the question of divine existence as

nineteenth-century Black leadership did not respond with the same type of interpretative voice to the problem of race, slavery, suffering, and divine providence. While they all condemned racism, not all nineteenth-century Black leaders started with the same presuppositions about God's involvement in the life of the race. Deistic interpretations of Christianity seemed to have been more empowering for leaders like Douglass in the protest against the evils of slavery, than conservative expressions of theism.

Frederick Douglass perfected the abolitionist protest version of Christianity to a rhetorical art. He advocated a deistic vision of a God who uncompromisingly requires that human beings take responsibility for bringing an unjust society into conformity with God's higher moral laws. Driven by this vision of moral law, Douglass was unwilling to wait on some supernatural intervention by God in human history. On the contrary, Black theists could run the danger of trying to reconcile the transcendence of God with God's immanence. This could often require that the oppressed develop a pathological tolerance level for oppression itself. Leaders of the theist persuasion were generally hard-pressed to explain how God, who was characterized as being both transcendent and immanent, could be passively present in a so-called Christian society that blessed the demonic practice of slavery. What did it mean to assume that God was suffering with those who were being oppressed? Such questions have ever haunted the consciousness of Black American Christians since their arrival in this country. They illuminate the problem that the contemporary scholar, William R. Jones, has called "divine racism." "Divine racism" is generated by ethnic suffering and vice versa. Jones notes that "by accenting the ethnic factor" we "call attention to that suffering which is maldistributed; it is not spread, as it were, more or less randomly and impartially over the total human race."[4] On the contrary, Jones observed, "Rather, it is concentrated in a particular ethnic group." Jones critically observes that "Black suffering is balanced by White non-suffering instead of White suffering." In short, "Black suffering

---

unanswerable and from logical positivism which holds the question and answer alike to be strictly meaningless. *A Dictionary of Theology*, ed. Alan Richardson (Philadelphia: Westminster Press, 1969) 334-35.

For an insightful contemporary interpretation of the notions of theism and deism as they were understood in classic times to modernity see Charles Taylor, *Sources of the Self: The Making of the Modern Identity* (Cambridge: Harvard University Press, 1989).

[4]William R. Jones, *Is God a White Racist?* (Garden City NY: Anchor Press/Doubleday, 1973).

in particular and White suffering in general raise the issue of the scandal of particularity."[5] The variable of ethnicity demands that we ask not why suffering exists. Instead, it provokes the question why it afflicts some people and not others?

Unfortunately, contemporary Black scholars of religion have treated nineteenth-century Black leaders' primary written sources as though they were all cut from a single experiential piece of religious and ethical fabric.[6] In a word, we have responded to them as though they were all one voice. In our rush to conclusive theoretical judgments, we have refused to see the intricate religious and ethical complexities of the different conceptual types of experience in the general Black experience. This allows us to see that early Black leadership was not one dimensional in its religious and ethical interpretations of race, suffering, slavery, and divine providence. Basically, the deist voice presupposed that reason takes precedence over all religious faith claims. The deist believed that the greatest call of human existence is to be in harmony with the rational process of the natural moral order of the universe. Since God is transcendent and not immanent, the deist asserted that God created these higher laws and placed them both in the cosmos and in human nature. Theists, on the other hand, claimed that God is directly involved in the daily events of human beings. Moreover, God is known through revelation. Divine revelation supersedes human beings' rational ability to understand God's actions in the world. For this reason, the theist accents faith over reason.

Nineteenth-century Black leaders' public speeches, sermons, addresses, and letters are replete with the terms "race," "suffering," "slavery," and "providence." This fact is no less noticeable in the different types of writings by slave masters and their White abolitionist counterparts. These critical concepts provoked intense discussion during and following the period of reconstruction. A critical understanding of them will illuminate how Blacks interpreted and reinterpreted themselves in a society that theologically legitimated

---

[5] Ibid, 21.

[6] Although a number of Black scholars have drawn on the primary sources produced by nineteenth-century Black leaders, most contemporary Black religious scholars have tended primarily to use the thought of DuBois and Douglass as the normative voices for theological and ethical reflections. What we fail to remember, however, is that neither of these leaders were clergy. How their thought compared with the leaders of the confessional and evangelical church is the question that we must take to the nineteenth-centy leaders' primary sources.

their affliction and exclusion. Here our query, on the one hand, will be limited to the primary writings of a single White deist voice and a collective White theist voice. Thomas Jefferson's writings on race and slavery will represent the deist voice. For a collective White theist voice, we have chosen the Methodist ministers' annual written addresses of the Freedmen's Aid Society. On the other hand, for the Black theist and deist voices, we have chosen J. W. E. Bowen and Frederick Douglass. Bowen, whose ministerial and educational leadership covers both the latter part of the nineteenth century and the first part of the twentieth century, is identified in this study as the representative Black theist voice. Frederick Douglass, the famous Black abolitionist and orator, is categorized in this discourse as the representative deistic voice.

A Single White Deist's Voice

Thomas Jefferson believed that God's active powers are displayed in the world created, sustained, and ordered by means of divinely-sanctioned natural laws—both moral and physical. His primary concern regarding those of African descent was to what extent did they reflect the mind of God. Jefferson's position is consistent with his rationalist deist voice. A member of the Episcopal church, Jefferson was in reality a deist, a rationalist, and above all, a humanitarian. He compiled, but never published, what later came to be known as *The Jefferson Bible, Being the Life and Morals of Jesus of Nazareth.* This little work, a cento of clippings from the gospels of Matthew, Mark, Luke, and John pasted in a blankbook, extols Jesus as a man for his moral teachings, omits ambiguous and controversial passages, and while rejecting many of the supernatural elements, presents the core of Christian morality and is genuinely in tone. Religion for Jefferson was essentially a utilitarian moral code[7].

While he conceded that no hypothesis could be verified until more scientific investigation had been made regarding the racial differences of Blacks and Whites, Jefferson voiced his suspicion of Blacks' possible natural and cultural inferiority: "I advance it therefore as a suspicion only, that the Blacks, whether originally a distinct race, or made distinct by time and circumstances, are inferior to Whites both

---

[7] Ernest Campbell Mossner, "Deism," in *Encyclopedia of Philosophy*, ed. Paul Edwards (New York: Collier-Macmillan Ltd., 1967) 2:333.

in body and mind."[8] Fearful of the bitterness that could exist between the races following slavery, Jefferson concluded against the policy of the two races existing in America together. He thought that it "will divide us into parties, and produce convulsions, which will probably never end but in the extermination of one or the other race."[9]

Matthew T. Mellon, a German scholar, has noted that Jefferson's "views of the Negro slave" are significantly important "because he was perhaps the one early American statesman who was best equipped to understand and appreciate the theoretical dangers inherent in the institution."[10] The German scholar has further noted: "As a political philosopher he [Jefferson] had the advantage, through education and a facility through foreign language, of being in touch with the main trends of European political thought.[11] It was Jefferson's background in political thought that drove him to defend what he termed in his day "the common people." Regarding this group, Jefferson " . . . believed in ... [their] ultimate intelligence and ability to govern themselves and he stood for the rights of the individual against the state."[12]

The concepts of God, race, reason, duty, rights, and law in Jefferson's writings demand the focus of our attention. A clearer understanding of them will illuminate such notions as suffering, slavery, and providence. As was noted above, Jefferson believed that God created higher laws to govern and maintain the world.

God, Race, and Reason

Jefferson grew up in Virginia as a planter-aristocrat. His boyhood mentors were clerics of the church. Moreover, William and Mary College, where he received a classic education, was under the strict supervision of the Church of England. Jefferson believed, as was noted above, that God governs and maintains the world through natural law. God endowed human beings with the natural law of reason to run the

---

[8] *Life and Selected Writings of Thomas Jefferson*, eds. Adrienne Koch and William Peden (New York: Modern Library, 1944) 256.

[9] Ibid.

[10] Matthew T. Mellon, *Early American Views On Negro Slavery: From the Letters and Papers of the Founders of the Republic* (Boston: Meader Publishing Co., 1934) 89.

[11] Ibid.

[12] Ibid.

world. Although an advocate of this philosophy, Jefferson was unprepared to accept Blacks as equally endowed rationally by God as Whites.

The God of Jefferson's thought was the author of natural law. Jefferson's vision of this God inspired his words for the phrasing of the Declaration of Independence. He presents God in this historical document as the creator and endower of men with certain "inherent and inalienable rights." The planter-aristocrat of Virginia noted that "among these are life, liberty and the pursuit of happiness." Observable in the remainder of the Declaration of Independence statement is the idea that God's actions in the human order are confined to that of creating and endowing human beings. Following such actions, the God of this statement is mainly an ideal observer and an ultimate judge of the behavior of individuals and institutions. Though God both creates and endows them with inherent and inalienable rights, human beings are expected to secure these rights through individual and collective means:

> that to secure these rights governments are instituted among men deriving their just powers from the consent of the governed; that whenever any government becomes destructive of these ends, it is the right of the people to alter or abolish it, and to institute new government, laying its foundation on such principles and organizing its powers in such form as to them shall seem most likely to effect their happiness.[13]

Did Jefferson's God create and endow slaves of African descent with certain inherent and inalienable rights? Or, asked another way: How could such rights be a self-evident truth for Whites only? Better still, How could Jefferson continue as a slaveholder if he really took his own words seriously?

Jefferson believed that his God had created slaves different in many ways. The differences would make it impossible, even if emancipation were to become a reality, for Blacks and Whites to co-exist together in America. Absorbing Blacks into the White population would be a mistake, Jefferson concluded, primarily because of the physical and mental differences of the inferior Blacks. Mellon's summary of Jefferson's delineation of the physical differences between Blacks and Whites is helpful:

---

[13] Quoted in Mellon, *Early American Views* , 96.

The first of these differences is that of color .... Jefferson ... attempts to show that the White race is more beautiful than the Black. He asks us whether the blushes; those 'fine mixtures of red and White' which lends to the 'expressions of every passion' in the White race, are not superior to the 'eternal monotony ... that immovable veil of black that covers the emotions of the other race.'

Further, he points out that there are other distinctions which prove a difference in the races. Among these are, 'less hair on the face and body.' 'They secrete less by the kidneys; and more by the glands of the skin, which gives them a strong and disagreeable odor.? 'They seem to require less sleep.' 'They are at least as brave, and more adventuresome than Whites. But this may proceed from a want of forethought.' 'They are more ardent after their female; but love seems with them to be more an eager desire, than a tender mixture of sentiment and sensation.' 'Their griefs are transient.'

'In general, their existence appears to participate more of equals to the Whites; in reason much inferior ... in imagination they are dull, tasteless, and anomalous.'

Jefferson then warns of the danger of forming hasty judgments and adds that it will be right to make great allowances for the difference of condition, of education, of conversation, of the sphere in which they move.[14]

Duty, Law, and Rights

Thomas Jefferson's sense of duty, law, and rights drove him to change America's public policy regarding slavery. This philosophy also motivated him to be a generous benefactor upon his death toward those he called "his faithful slaves." Motivated by a divine sense of duty to comply with natural law, Jefferson made several or more legislative attempts to emancipate the slaves. His first effort took place when he was a member of the Virginia House of Burgesses. Although it was a failure, "young Jefferson's first effort gives us an insight as to how important he considered the problem of Negro slavery as early as 1769-1775."[15] Reflecting in his senior years on his own legislative attempts as a young man in the Virginia House of

---

[14] Ibid., 106.
[15] Ibid., 92.

Burgesses, Jefferson's own autobiographical words are instructive at this point? "I made one effort in that body (the House of Burgesses) for the permission of the emancipation of slaves, which was rejected: and indeed during the regal government, nothing liberal could expect success. Our minds were circumscribed with the narrow limits, by a habitual belief that it was our duty to be subordinate to the mother country in all matters of government . . . and even to observe a bigoted intolerance of all religions but theirs. The difficulties with our representatives were of habit and despair, not of reflection and conviction.[16] Mellon cautions the reader against thinking that " . . . this effort of Jefferson's was inspired solely by a pity for the condition of the slaves, for we must remember that Virginia had too many slaves at the time and it was an increase in their numbers which not only filled their masters with terror at the thought of possible insurrection, but which also was slowly bringing many of them to economic ruin, as in the case of Washington."[17] We might conclude that Jefferson's first failure to free the slaves was a sobering lesson in political realism for him.

At a 1774 meeting in Virginia to consider the state of the colony, Jefferson, prevented by sickness from attending, presented his ideas in a pamphlet which he sent. The content of the pamphlet reflects his ideas that are deeply concerned with rights of America. He appeals to the "natural" and "inalienable rights" of man over the power of any state. Jefferson appealed to the theory of natural rights to justify the American revolution. Mellon observes about Jefferson's pamphlet that ". . . we find him pointing out to his Majesty George III, the deviations from the lines of duty with regard to the abolition of domestic slavery and the slave trade."[18]

Jefferson made a third attempt to strike at slavery in the first draft of the Declaration of Independence document:

> He (George III) has waged cruel war against human nature itself, violating its most sacred rights of life and liberty in the persons of a distant people who never offended him, captivating and carrying them into slavery in another hemisphere, or to incur miserable death in their trans-

---

[16] *Jefferson Works*, vol. I, ed. Frank Donovan (New York: Dodd Mead Publishers, 1963), 3.

[17] Mellon, *Early American Views*, 93.

[18] Ibid. 94.

portation thither. This piratical warfare, the opprobrium of infidel powers, is the warfare of the Christian king of Great Briton, determined to keep open a market where men should be brought and sold, he has prostituted his negative for suppressing every legislative attempt to prohibit or to restrain this execrable commerce. And that this assemblage of horrors might want no fact of distinguished die, he is now exciting those very people to rise in arms among us, and to purchase that liberty of which he has deprived them, by murdering the people on whom he also obtruded them; thus paying off former crimes committed against the liberties of one people, with crimes which he urges them to commit against the lives of others.[19]

This paragraph of Jefferson's document was later struck to accommodate South Carolina and Georgia, which had never attempted to restrain the importation of slaves, and wished it to continue.

Mellon reminds us that it is a mistake to conclude that Jefferson's opposition to slavery is based on altruism. The German scholar concludes that Jefferson's opposition must be based on the presupposition that slavery is degrading as much so for the master as for the slave. "Besides being bad for the morals of the people, it destroys 'their industry'."

Jefferson's sense of duty to what he called his "faithful slaves" was clearly expressed in his will where he distributed the majority of his slaves to his heirs together with his property. He made provision for freeing five of the most faithful of them in a codicil which was added to the original document a day later, i.e., on March 17, 1826.

I give to my good, affectionate, and faithful servant Burwell, his freedom, and the sum of three hundred dollars, to buy necessaries to commence his trade of glazier, or to use otherwise as he pleases.

I give to my good, affectionate, and faithful servants, John Hennings and Joe Fosset, their freedom at the end of one year after my death, and to each of them respectively, all the tools of them respectively, all the tools of their respective shops or callings; and it is my will that a comfortable log-house be built for each of the three servants so emancipated, on some part

---

[19] *Jefferson Works*, I: 19.

of my lands convenient to them with respect to the residence of their wives, and to Charlottesville and the University, where they will mostly be employed, and reasonably convenient also to the interests of the proprietor of the lands, of which houses I give the use of one, with a curtilage of an acre to each, during his life of personal occupation thereof.

I also give to John Hemings the service of his two apprentices, Madison and Eston Hemings, until their respective ages of twenty-one years, at which period respectively, I give them their freedom; and I humbly and earnestly request of the legislature of Virginia a confirmation of the bequest of freedom to these servants, with permission to remain in this state, where their families and connections are, as an additional instance of the favor, of which I have received so many other manifestations in the course of my life, and for which I now give them my last, solemn, and dutiful thanks.[20]

The Collective White Theist Voice

It seemed to have been a common consensus among both White liberal and conservative thinkers that God ordained those of African descent to be subservient to them. Themes such as God as creator, redeemer, and sustainer of the world dominated the rhetoric of nineteenth-century White theists. Phrases such as "faith in God," and "duty to God," and to the oppressed other were equally as significant. During the reconstruction era, some White theists saw themselves as codeterminists with God in both the making and re-making of Blacks for the new order. This was particularly the case following the Civil War when Whites started what came to be called the Freedmen's Aid Society of the United Methodist Church 1866-1875.[21] It came to symbolize collectively a type of Christian White consciousness for the uplift of Black Americans.

God, Creation, and Ethnicity

---

[20] Mellon, *Early American Views*, 121.

[21] *Reports of the Methodist Freedmen's Aid Society of the Methodist Episcopal Church 1865–1875*, ed. J. C. Hartzell (Cincinnati: Western Methodist Book Concern, 1893).

Although they might have been in the serious minority, many White theists invoked the biblical claim of the one-flesh creation theory. They emphatically espoused in their rhetoric that God had made of one flesh all nations on the face of the earth. These divines advocated the common brotherhood principle. They believed that this God of their common brotherhood principle created all men of every race. Subsequently, God, "has bound them together in a common humanity and a common interest."[22] Advocates of this thought taught that God does not only see men, but plans for them both individually and collectively. During an annual report to the Society, the presenter said: "God's eyes look on man—the whole broad family of man. God's plan embraces all men, and we rise and fall together."[23] The presenter further reminded the leaders of the session of their "Good Samaritan duty to the victimized of the one-family regardless of his/her race." Theists of this type advocated that God so created the human family that the common duty of human beings toward each other grows out of their common need to belong to each other. By doing this, they preserved the interlinking of transracial brotherhood while affirming ethnic differences. In short, they celebrated God as the author of ethnic differences: "And God seems to have written it from the very beginning that every people shall be its own regenerator, that every people shall work out its own peculiar work, unfold its own peculiar character in the world."[24]

White theists of the Society rhetorically denounced discriminating against a people because of their race, class, or nationality. Speaking of Blacks, they taught that "God is still on the side of this poor people. He will be partial to them until there is no need for partiality." [25] A clear indicator of God's partiality was heard in God's voice as God spoke through the Black man from the bottom of the society. The primary lesson being taught by this providential indicator was that God "is on the [the colored man's] side; that even the colored man is our brother, and that our destiny is closely associated with his; . . . "[26] Divines of this persuasion also believed

---

[22]"Anniversary of the Freedmen's Aid Society," October 6, 1870, reprinted in *Reports of the Methodist Freedmen's Aid Society of the Methodist Episcopal Church 1865–1875*, .23.

[23]Ibid.

[24]Ibid., 29.

[25]Ibid., 21.

[26]Ibid., 24.

that because of this interlinking of brotherhood that existed between White oppressors and the Black oppressed, God had given Whites "the duty and responsibility to take care of him, educate him, and lift him up into a higher life, that he may be a brother on whom we shall look with satisfaction and with pride."[27] To do no less was to risk the welfare of the nation.

Confession of Guilt

Some White theists confessed publicly before God the sins of slavery. They dared counter those public voices who claimed that God used slavery to bring Blacks to Christ. A few White theists had the courage to admit openly that slavery originated more out of the selfish wills of enslavers rather than the will of God: "We brought them here because we needed them; . . . .." This was quite a contrast to those who would say that Africans were brought to be enslaved because they needed a God who could save their benighted souls. Some Whites publicly confessed, even after the Civil War, that the need was still there for Blacks to cultivate the soil of White landowners. The most radical confession of the White theists admitted that they were debtors to those of African descent for the wrong that they had heaped upon them. Moreover, they even believed that God had used the Civil War to punish Whites for this corporate sin against this helpless race of people.

The following is an unusually classic confession:

We tore them from their sunny home; we gave them to know the horrors of the middle passage, in which they perished by the thousands; we brought them to a strange and bleak land, and there we made them to groan under heavy burdens; we lashed them to their tasks till the blood trickled from their backs; we trifled with their affections, parting husbands and wives, parents and children; we consumed their beauty upon our lusts; we did not spare for their tears; nor regard their groans or prayers; we shut them as by a flaming sword from the Eden of reading God's precious promises to the poor, afflicted and downtrodden—if they fled from their woes, we hounded them back to the most inhumane barbarities; we denied them humanity and counted them as

---

[27] Ibid.

chattels, which portions of their rights for an hour were held sacred by us. The indictment against us might be written in blood, and we should have to plead guilty to 'the sum of all villanies. We owe them pay for their toil and redress for their wrongs. He that keepeth the books and knoweth all things, has strict account with us in this matter. He has said 'For the oppression of the poor, for the sighting of the needy will I arise,' 'for the Lord will plead the cause, and the spoil of the soul of those who spoiled'. He has been busy at this work. Our desolated homes and bleeding hearts declare it, and so does our burden of taxation that generations can not liquidate.[28]

These unusual confessors of the sins of slavery conceded that this tragic episode of history had made the White race a debtor to the Black race. Countering those who argued for sending Blacks back to some part of Africa or South America, the corporate leadership voice of the Freedmen's Aid Society emphatically warned other Whites regarding the future of Blacks? "We brought them here, and they are here, and here they will remain."[29] Not only will they remain, but one speaker said? "Their dusky faces will be seen in every assembly, from the Senate to the caucus, from the General Conference to the class-meeting.[30] It is for this reason that a leadership voice of the Freedmen's Aid Society could say that God, not only works in human events on behalf of the victimized, but also holds oppressors responsible for aiding those they have wronged. As one report to the Freedmen's Aid Society said: "If the books of heaven are kept by double entry, so that what is charged to us is credited to those we have wronged, the freedmen may have yet an immense claim upon us that the Sovereign Ruler will enforce if we do not voluntarily pay it." Cautioning those who would take the sluggard's posture on this serious matter, the corporate voice of the Society said: "Let us delay and litigation will come with God on the side of the freedmen, and we must lose the case with careful accumulated costs."[31]

Duty to An Oppressed Race

---

[28] Ibid., 16-17.
[29] Ibid., October 6, 1870.
[30] Ibid.
[31] Ibid., October 6, 1870, 16-17.

Whites of the Freedmen's Aid Society reminded critics of their work on behalf of Blacks that it was in keeping with: ". . . God's movement; it is God's work, his benevolent impress is stamped upon every page of it; his benedictions fall like a flower upon it; ...."[32] They taught that their ultimate responsibility to benighted Blacks was "to help them help themselves." This would be done by training select Blacks to lead and uplift their race. Supplying necessary clothing was but a part of that work. The intellectual education of people these Whites saw as another part of their moral duty. These corporate leaders summarized the objective this way: "The grand work is the elevation of the people, fitting them for the duties and the responsibilities of their new position, making them better men and citizens, winning them to Christ, and preparing them for eternal life." How would such be accomplished? Corporate leaders proposed that they would use "the highest motives that God has furnished—the best means that he, in his wisdom, has provided—the gospel in the hands, and with the example of living Christians."[33]

Field missionaries of the Society interpreted Blacks' insatiable desire for an education as "the unmistakable evidence that God was preparing them by his Spirit for the freedom to which he had led them by his providence."[34] This was consistent with the philosophy that religion and education alone could make freedom a blessing to the freedmen. These missionaries characterized freedmen as "anxious to have the Gospel preached to them . . . and to have churches planted among them."[35] They reported that they were "preparing the thousands of ignorant and degraded children for usefulness on earth and happiness in heaven."[36] Through education and the gospel of Jesus Christ, field missionaries reported that thousands of ignorant and degraded children were being converted into intelligent and promising youth for the American society; and, ultimately, for the kingdom of heaven.

Church leaders who published their reports to the Society seemed clear that it was their duty to represent God to Blacks and vice versa

---

[32] Ibid., 18.
[33] "Organization Convention (Official Report)," August 7, 1866, in *Reports of the Freedmen's Aid Society of the Methodist Episcopal Church 1860--1875*, 8.
[34] Ibid., 2.
[35] "Anniversary of the Freedmen's Aid Society, "February 8, 1872," in *The Freedmen's Aid Society of the Methodist Episcopal Church 1868—1875*, 6.
[36] Ibid., 11.

until the latter could do for themselves. In short, these leaders had to keep in mind that they were not merely working to help the freedmen. Whites were to see it as an avenue for helping themselves. This meant that field missionaries had to approach the work in the proper attitude: "If we would benefit the freedmen, we must go down to them with our hearts of sympathy and our hands of strength." They were told to do the work in the manner and spirit of Christ: "As the savior came down to us, and lived and died for us, that we might be raised in glory with him, so must we labor for the needy ones, his spirit; and with his blessing, we can not fail."[37]

Teaching and converting Blacks to Christ would prepare them to lift their own people. Sensible leaders of the Freedmen's Aid Society warned that it was impossible to lift the race without training indigenous leaders: "The Southern colored people will be lifted up and made great only by the agency of men of their own race and locality, and our race among them, in order to succeed, must be manned by colored men of the South."[38] Their leaders would be expected to teach the love of Jesus to a ruined race. This only would make for a "useful life, a happy death, and a glorious immortality."[39] White leaders took as their challenge "to put (Blacks) on their feet; to give them a fair start; to help them over the disabilities of the hour. This done, the rest will depend on themselves."[40] Whites of the Freedmen's Aid Society believed that the educated freedmen would be capable of spreading the Christian faith over the dark places that can scarcely be reached by others.

Finally, these Whites believed that teaching and converting the Black race to Christianity would make their own race the beneficiaries of Black people's special spiritual gifts:

> But what of the Negro's heart? Is he capable of loving God? Then has he the highest attribute of humanity? The ideal of greatness which the Gospel presents is the perfection of love; the qualities which it most extol are patience, humility, and meekness. The character of Christ is one in which goodness subordinates superhuman power and wisdom to its own ends,

---

[37] Ibid., 8.

[38] "Comments by Dr. Curry," *The Freedmen's Aid Society of the Methodist Episcopal Church 1868–1875*, 10.

[39] Ibid.7.

[40] "Anniversary of the Freedmen's Aid Society," October 6, 1870, *The Freedmen's Aid Society of the Methodist Episcopal Church*, 20.

and eclipses both by its surpassing splendor; as mind is superior to matter, so love to mind. May not the African Churches of the South pay for the knowledge they receive from us by inspiring a higher faith and a brighter hope in our more cold and philosophic communities?"[41]

A Black Theist's Voice

The poem below was intended as a response to the questions about God and the purpose of enslaving those of African descent. This anonymous "African Servant's Prayer" was intended to give voice to every African who was brought to this country as a slave. It was to counter those abolitionist voices that condemned slavery. The main lesson of this poem was that the "African Servant" of the prayer was suppose to value having received Jesus Christ in slavery over being left free back in his African country. His ultimate desire was to have this gospel taken to all relatives back in Africa:

The African Servant's Prayer

I was a helpless Negro boy,
And wandered on the shore;
Men took me from my parents' arms,
I never saw them more.
But yet my lot, which seemed so hard,
Quite otherwise did prove;
For I was carried far from home,
To learn a savior's love.
Poor and despised though I was,
Yet Thou, O God, was nigh;
And when Thy mercy first I saw,
sure none so glad as I.
And if Thy Son had made me free,
Then am I free indeed;
My soul is rescued from its chains;
For this did Jesus bleed.
Oh, send Thy word to that far land
Where none but Negroes live;
Teach them the way, the truth, the life;

---

[41]Ibid., 19.

> Thy grace, Thy blessing give.
> Oh, that my father, mother, dear,
> Might there your mercy see;
> Tell them what Christ has for them,
> What Christ has done for me.
> Whose God is like the Christian's God?
> Who can with him compare?
> He has compassion on my soul,
> And hears a Negro's prayer.[42]

Nineteenth-century Black clerics confidently believed that the Christian God, whom they first encountered in slavery, was without equal. They held strong to this belief despite the fact that Whites had enslaved their race in the names of the Christian God and Jesus Christ. None better articulated such belief than the erudite J. W. E. Bowen. Mr. Bowen was a highly trained scholar, with an earned Ph.D. from Boston University, who pastored the Asbury Methodist Church of Washington, D.C. During his pastorate at the Asbury Church, Bowen formally articulated, in a series of sermons, his critical views on the compound dilemma of being Black and Christian. The Christian God's involvement in the Black race's past, present, and future was one dominant issue that shaped Bowen's reflective theological and ethical explorations. Pastor Bowen called a published collection of his sermons *A Series of Plain Talks To The Colored People of America On Their Problems.*[43]   In these well-written reflective narrations, Bowen judiciously addressed the very practical aspects of the race, slavery, suffering, and Divine Providence conundrum.

Bowen refused to believe "that God had created the world and had wound it up like a clock, and that he had receded to some celestial attic to let things go as they pleased without his interference or even concern."[44]   Instead, the Methodist minister subscribed to Jesus' teaching about God's particular care for the least of the creation? "Not a sparrow shall fall to the ground," and "the very hairs of your head are numbered."[45]   He warned his congregation against constructing a theodicy, however. He noted that such task might

---

[42] Quoted in *Narratives of Colored Americans* (New York: William Wood and Co., 1875), 100-101.
[43] J. W. Bowen, *What Shall the Harvest Be? National Sermons or, A Series of Plain Talks to the Colored People of America on Their Problems* (n.p., 1991).
[44] Ibid., 31.
[45] Ibid.

presume to "vindicate the ways of God to man." "This," he observed, "is not only a difficult but a dangerous undertaking? for 'his way is in the sea and his path in the great waters, and his footsteps are not known'."[46]

The Methodist cleric claimed no pretense to have "sounded the depths or to have given the final word upon the vital question" of Christianity's message for the suffering Black race. Bowen claimed that he was interested primarily in both what his generation called "the Manhood Problem" . . . and the "Negro Problem."[47] Unequivocally, for Bowen, the former problem took precedence over the latter. In Bowen's mind, what was called "the Negro Problem" was solvable only when it could be deemed that the race had developmentally reached its manhood stage of the civilizing process. Speaking of the two problems, Bowen said? "I believe that the solution to the first ('the Manhood Problem') will dissipate the second ('the Negro Problem') as the sun scatters the morning dew."[48]

Faith in God and Christ

Bowen confessed a stern belief in the gospel of Jesus Christ. He named it as the solution to his race's problems. It was for this reason that he deemed that "New Testament ethics is clearly apprehended, sharply defined, and vigorously applied to every phase of our complex life."[49] Bowen's generous references to God and Jesus Christ demands, on our part, a close scrutiny of his philosophy of God and Jesus' role in Black people's progressive developmental history.

The minister characterized God as "the highest good essential for the progress of individuals and nations." He noted that "Nothing permanently good can be established without His assistance."[50] Pastor Bowen subscribed to the belief that faith in God is essential for all nations and persons to do well in the world. Nations or individuals who "tampered with the idea of God have paid a terrible consequence." No nation ought "forget the rock from which it was hewn, or the pit from which it was dug." Never should it substitute "aesthetic culture for religious culture and genuine piety." Bowen told

---

[46] Ibid., 32.
[47] Ibid., 13.
[48] Ibid.
[49] Ibid.
[50] Ibid., 16.

the worshippers of the Asbury Church that were this to happen, "the lamp in the temple of our prosperity will go out; and I will chisel in deep Black letters above its door posts 'Ichabod'; for the glory is departed."[51]

Bowen expressed an unwavering faith in God's existence, even in the face of the ugliest expressions of social evil. He was certain in every situation that "the voice of God so speaks and the hand of Providence so directs." Bowen prescribed the following credo for his race:

We must and fully believe that there is a 'divinity that shapes our lives, rough hew them how we may'; and that he presides and directs in the destinies of nations, races and individuals; and that, in our particular history, the hand of Providence is as manifest as it was in that of Ancient Hebrews. Moreover, if we will purge ourselves of the evil that is among us, and return or destroy the golden wedge and the Babylonish garment, that same Hand will ever be our—guide and protector."[52]

Note in the statement above that Bowen's belief is that God forges a great people out of the crucibles of affliction. He really appeals to Deutero-Isaiah's vision of God rather than that vision of God portrayed in the Book of Exodus. This is the prophet's vision of God that comes from the Babylonian captivity/liberation paradigm, rather than the Exodus vision, that starts with Israel's enslavement/ liberation from Egypt.[53] These two rather similar, and yet dissimilar, visions of the deity's expectations of the people's role in their own liberation are critical for theological reflection. Bowen's statement above identifies self-purging as one of God's liberation perquisites that the oppressed Black race must meet. His call for it, however, implies that the oppressed share some responsibility for their oppression and liberation. A future study comparing and contrasting the liberation expectations of the biblical God of the Exodus with those of the biblical God of the Babylonian exile would serve to deepen our understanding of the notions of race, slavery, and Divine Providence.

---

[51] Ibid., 17.

[52] Ibid., 32.

[53] The primary difference in these two captivity/liberation paradigms is that God makes it explicitly clear through Second Isaiah that the Israelites are in Babylonian captivity because of their sins against God. However, in the Exodus enslavement/liberation paradigm ,Moses' God of liberation makes no mention of the people's sins. The unspoken assumption is that the Israelites have been innocent victims of an ungodly people.

An even further study would be to compare and contrast nineteenth-century Black leadership's interpretative use of these biblical captivity/liberation paradigms with that of Black leadership following the mid-twentieth century.

Bowen implies in the quote above that Israel's visualized God of the Babylonian captivity makes radical confessional expectations, both verbal and demonstrative, upon the captives. The captives are expected to purge themselves of their sins. Their God prescribes the ritualistic means for the Israelites to cleanse themselves. Driven by this presupposition, Bowen calls for his oppressed race to remove itself from all the signs of idolatrous Babylonian culture: " . . . destroy the golden wedge and the Babylonian garment." His theological premise is that his race must purge itself of evil and remove itself from its oppressor's idolatrous culture. Bowen's teaching here is consistent with the teachings of many nineteenth-century Black clerics.

J. W. E. Bowen concludes that Scripture is the authoritative source through which God is disclosed to the oppressed. Scripture provides both the theological and ethical principles for the progressive developmental process of both nations and individuals. He reasoned that "the Scriptures are rationally and scientifically true; and though the language used is that of common-sense, the truth conveyed is the bedrock." He subscribes to Jesus' good-tree/good-fruit principle rather than Jesus' bad-tree/bad-fruit principle for constructively exhorting his race: "A good tree cannot bring forth evil fruit, neither can a corrupt tree bring forth good fruit." Bowen also subscribed with equal commitment and intensity to the scriptural principle that "All have sinned and come short of the glory of God!"[54]

Race and Duty

Although he advocated the belief that God was in charge of the destiny of Blacks in America, Bowen was emphatic in his assertion that Blacks must be co-determinists with God in their collective and individual developmental process. Faith in God and race shaped his sense of ethnic duty.

Responding to the contemporary critical voices of his day regarding the evil fruits of slavery, Bowen summarized the problem cogently:

---

[54] Bowen, *What Shall the Harvest Be?*, 20-21.

I am one that believes that there are two problems in which we are specially interested to-day, viz, 'The Negro Problem' and 'The Manhood Problem.' 'The Negro Problem' is the Nation's problem, but it must be borne in mind that the Negro is the major term of the major premises. What is it? It is whether the nation will incorporate the Negro into its life, so that he shall become a contributing and a determining factor in the body politic; and whether he shall share in all the rights and privileges, fruits, and blessings and protections of American Citizenship.[55]

Bowen reasoned that the 'Negro Problem' was of second importance to what he termed the "Manhood Problem." What did he mean by the latter? In this problem, he defined what he termed "the Negro" as being both the "major term" and the "minor also; nay, he, himself is the problem." In the "Manhood problem" the "Negro is the problem." This problem had to do with the Black man's willingness to "vindicate for himself a right to stand among the thinking nations of the world, and to claim citizenship by contributing to the thoughtful and material products of civilization in the republic of thought." What Bowen called "The Manhood Problem" had what he termed developmental implication. Speaking rather emphatically of this problem, Bowen said of the Black man: "It is whether he will develop those manly and Christian virtues which are essentials of a worthy character and conclusively prove that the color of his skin is only skin deep and that it does not reach his brain and heart!" He notes the second premise to be " . . . whether he [the Black man] will regain in an educated Christian civilization his pristine position in arts and sciences, in literature and history, in architecture and philosophy; the position that he held in his original home. ...." For Bowen, the critical issue for the "Negro" is "whether he will come back to the heights from which he had fallen; to a civilization second only to this Christian civilization in that it lacked the touch of a divine afflatus."[56]

Although he could posit the premise "that God has hidden somewhere in the unrevealed future the solution of all these problems, ..." Bowen concluded that those of his race would have to accomplish it through self-actualization. He noted that: "History has not a single

[55] Ibid., 22-23.

[56] Ibid., 23-24.

illustration of any race that has ever come up to be counted, that did
not do so by force of character and by its own internal exertion."[57]
Bowen concluded that it was for this reason that those of his race
must ask the question? "What shall we do for ourselves?" He called
for his race to "give up the unreasonable and unhistorical basis of
expecting to have its future made for it, and begin with might and
main to write its own history and make its own future." Moreover, he
told them that "in your hand is your future, and you can make it
whatever you chose."[58]

Suffering and Equality

Using the biblical paradigms of personal and collective suffering,
and forgiveness and political power, Bowen told his hearers: "We
have to suffer yet more before we are thoroughly purged and made
equal of our White Brother." He could say this and simultaneously
denounce slavery and oppression of Black people: "I could not if I
would, and I would not if I could, justify the slavery and oppression of
my people."[59] However, he could concede that God was purging the
race for the day of full equality with White Americans. With the
realization of that day, Bowen envisioned that his race shall expect
the following metamorphosis of its character:

its virtues shall sparkle like burnished silver; when it shall
reveal the elements of character that God can trust; and when
it shall have divested itself of the filthy rages of that black
civilization, whose noxious stench is an offense in the nostrils
of God and of good men; yea a thousand times, when carcasses
of those who have come up from the land of slavery, and
upon which may be found the marks of the curse, and even
when this present generation, so worthless, helpless, godless in
so many cases, have all rotted in the wilderness of
forgetfulness, and a new generation shall spring forth whose
feet shall keep pace with the electric strides of this new
civilization, whose face shall catch the first rays of yon rising
sun, and whose God shall be the 'Lord of Lords' and the 'King
of Kings'; then, and not until then, will the crown of honor,

---

[57] Ibid, 26-27.
[58] Ibid., 27-28.
[59] Ibid., 42.

glory, power, and victory adorn his sable brow.[60]

Like most Blacks of his generation, Bowen invoked the Israelite's experience of suffering and destiny, found in Hebrew scripture, as the hermeneutical paradigm for interpreting how his race of people ought to understand their own affliction. He reasoned conclusively that "the history of Israel fully illustrates the same truth, viz., that discipline and affliction are necessary to the production of serviceable manhood." He went on to say: "That all these afflictions were for some great purpose their subsequent history puts beyond dispute. These were the cleansing fires to purge them that they might rise to great and heroic King David, the man after God's own heart, and the magnificence and splendor of Solomon. Moreover, these fires were necessary to purify them, and to make them fit depository for the Incarnate God, to give him to the world of mankind that he might bring it back to God. Out of this race was to come the law-givers, prophet, teachers, and the Great Teacher for all other people upon divine truths."[61] Bowen concluded: "The Wilderness was then, a great and necessary school to prepare the Hebrews in their youth for the glories of their manhood in Canaan." Consistent with his philosophy of the developmental process of history, Bowen said, "It seems to be in the very constitution of affairs that affliction is necessary to bring out our virtues. All races before us that have made a history worth reading, have had to suffer and to write it with the crimson ink that came from their veins."[62]

Bowen's thesis was that "all have had to suffer and endure hardships, privations, slavery in some form, and afflictions and death, that they might be prepared for the sober duties in the manhood of their race." He warned his race: "We have failed to grasp the lesson that Providence designed to teach us if we have brought with us from that past only bitterness and prejudice." The cleric thought it imperative that Blacks "must rise to that elevation where we will be able to examine ourselves with malice toward none." By this, he does not mean that Blacks should forget slavery. Acknowledging the difficulty of trying to convince his race that slavery had some positive value, Bowen dared say:

---

[60] Ibid., 43-44.
[61] Ibid., 36.
[62] Ibid., 39.

I am possessed of the opinion that God was in all of it, and under his hand some mighty results will be brought out which could not have come had not this experience been ours. I am not such an historical optimist as to justify all the events of history, disregarding the agencies that brought them to pass, but I can discover, through all acts of history, a Providence working out his plans over and above and in spite of man's wrath or "inhumanity to man."[63]

Although a highly-trained theologian, Bowen stakes his faith claim in a God who brings an oppressed people through the fires of persecution.

A Black Deist's Voice

Premier Black leaders near the end of the nineteenth century all seemed inclined to the deist perspective. Frederick Douglass, Booker T. Washington, and W. E. B. DuBois are three prominent leaders of this era whose writings reflect some of the fundamental elements of the deist philosophy. Interestingly enough, none of these leaders were professional clergy. The self-imposed constraints of this discourse will only allow me to focus on Frederick Douglass' deistic perspective. Frederick Douglass was a Black abolitionist who became the dominant Black voice on the complex issues of race, slavery, suffering, and divine providence for almost a half century.

Douglass's confessed belief in the one and only transcendent God is a repetitive theme in his public speeches and writings. The cornerstone of that belief, however, seems to have been in his notion that? God's active powers are displayed in the world—created, sustained, and ordered by means of divinely-sanctioned natural laws, both moral and physical. The ordering of events constitutes a general providence. Douglass, moreover, believed that all men have been endowed with a rational nature which allows them to know truth and their duty when they think and choose in conformity with this nature. This natural law requires the leading of a moral life, rendering to God, one's neighbor, and one's self what is due to each. In short, it requires a sacred sense of duty. For Douglass, the purest form of worship and the chief religious obligation is to lead a moral life. God has endowed even Blacks with immortal souls. While Douglass saw signs of it being

---

[63] Ibid., 40-41.

done in this life, he was convinced that retributive justice would be meted out primarily after death.

God, Creation, and Moral Law

Douglass quoted Theodore Parker, who noted: "All the space between man's mind and God's mind is crowded with truth that wants to be discovered and organized into law, for the government and happiness of mankind."[64] Countering the teachings of those Southern preachers and slave masters who taught that God had made those of African descent to be the slaves of Whites, Douglass forcefully asserted his convictions in natural law philosophy, which stated that God had created all men equal and in his image. Defenders of slavery, even Southern preachers, espoused the notion that God created those of African descent to be hewers of wood and drawers of water. They taught that all Blacks ought to be grateful to God for having blessed them with this place in society. Being obedient to their White superiors would assure them happiness in this world and that to come:

Oh! if you wish to be happy in time, happy in eternity, you must be obedient to your masters; their interest is yours; God made one portion of men to do the working, and another to do the thinking; How good God is![65]

Southern Preachers celebrated what they characterized to be the aesthetics of this oppressive class structure. They exclaimed to their slaves "How beautiful are the arrangements of Providence!"

Frederick Douglass noted in his writings that White slave preachers played a pivotal role in portraying God as the endorser of slavery. He recalled White slave preachers theologizing about the role and nature of slaves' suffering status. These preachers majored in accenting the compensatory aspect of Christian salvation. White slave preachers, when speaking specifically to the slaves in the balcony of the church, would say: "And you too, my friends, have souls of infinite value— souls that will live through endless happiness or misery in eternity." Capitalizing on the slaves' undivided attention, the White preacher would then say what the masters desired most: "Servants, be obedient

[64] *The Frederick Douglass Papers*, ed. James W. Blassingame, Series One: Speeches, Debates, and Interviews, 1881-95 (New Haven: Yale University Press, 1992) 5:139.
[65] Ibid., 1:12.

unto your masters."[66]

The abolitionist Douglass was clearly convinced that a God who approved of one race subjugating the other did not merit his loyalty. He emphatically stated that: "I do not believe that Christ and his Apostles approved of slave-holding, nor of slave-catching." Vowing his loyalty to a God who was pro-emancipation of Blacks, Douglass concluded in the face of majority opinion: " I will continue to look to God and to Christ for support in my humble efforts for the emancipation of my race." The Black abolitionist made it clear that his commitment was clearly conditional to the point:

> that should doctors of divinity ever convince me that the Bible sanctions American slavery, that Christ and his apostles justify returning men to bondage, then I will give the Bible to the flames, and no more worship God in the name of Christ. For of what value to men would a religion be which not only permitted, but enjoined upon men the enslavement of each other, and which would leave them to the sway of physical force would permit the strong to enslave the weak? What better would such a religion be than black atheism, which knows no God? To defend slavery in the name of God, is simply to reduce mankind absolutely to the law of brute force.[67]

Douglass' radical opposition to slavery is forcefully heard in his conclusion about God's actions and nature: "God had no attribute that could take sides with the oppressor in such contest." He has reference to the debate contests between slave abolitionists and enslavers. Quoting from Thomas Jefferson, Douglass appealed to the transcendent attribute of God and confessed his apprehension of its ultimate consequences: "I tremble for my country when I reflect that God is just, and that his justice can not sleep forever." Proceeding with a commentary on the Jefferson's confessional warning, Douglass observed: "Such is the warning voice of Thomas Jefferson and every day's experience since its utterance until now, confirms the wisdom, and commends its truth.[68]

While he reasoned that the Bible, the Constitution, and the

---

[66] Ibid., 17.
[67] Ibid., 2:284-85.
[68] Ibid., 272.

Declaration of Independence mirror the principles of the higher mind of the universe, Douglass was unwilling to concede that God's governing principles were limited to such man-made documents or institutions. When the legal blows of systematic White racism all but numbed his senses, Douglass never lost faith in God's transcendent power ultimately to govern the created order. His conviction of this is clearly expressed following the United States Supreme Court decision under Judge Tawney. That decision said in essence that the Black man had no rights that the White man was bound to respect. Douglass countered in almost platonic rhetoric when he said:

The Supreme Court of the United States is high, but the Supreme Court of God is higher. It cannot undo what God Almighty has done, he has made all men free, and has made their freedom self-evident. . . . The very moment that God said "let us make man in our own image," that moment freedom became inherent in man.[69]

The celebrated Black abolitionist taught that God was Moral Governor of the universe. Individuals, nations, and nature were all subject to the natural-law workings of this God's divine government. For Douglass, flagrant violators of these "laws of this Divine government will certainly bring national sorrow, shame, suffering and death."[70] Slavery was the ultimate violation of these laws. Employing a fluid metaphor to characterize it, Douglass spoke of God's governance as "(t)he moral chemistry of the universe." He noted that "the moral chemistry of the universe made peace between Liberty and Slavery impossible."[71] Douglass dared remind his White adversaries that the constitution of human nature would speak the truth for God when the human-made document was distorted by misguided men: "The existence of the right is self-evident. It is written upon all powers and faculties of man."[72] It is what I would call the self-evidentiary right-for-liberty principle.

Duty, Rights, Truth, and Citizenship

Douglass, like all deists, espoused the idea that all authentic religion must be "based upon that broad, that world-embracing principle, 'That whatever you would that men should do to you, do even so to

---

[69]Ibid., 3:147.

[70]Ibid., 475.

[71]Ibid., 554.

[72]Ibid., 1:261.

them'."[73] For Douglass, this natural law required that the leading of a moral life—"rendering to God, one's neighbor, and one's self what is due to each"—is universal.[74] Slave masters' disregard for this law robbed them of their conscience and their freedom of will. Douglass's advocacy of mutual respect for this do-right-unto-each-other-law was as crucial for the building of a great republic as it was for a Christian body of believers in the church. Interestingly enough, Douglass was not so pious in his religious belief that he would be manipulated by this doctrine of mutual respect for each other in the social encounter. This is classically demonstrated in his story of fighting to defend himself against the tyranny of his slave overseer, Covey. Douglass' inevitable violent confrontation with Covey helped him to see that the do-right-unto-each-other-law taught by slave masters only worked when it was held in mutual respect by both parties in the confrontation. In this case, the theology of the slave society had predetermined Douglass as having been created by God to be subservient in any relationship with Whites. Only through a violent confrontation with Covey was Douglass able to forge out a new social space for declaring his God-given right to self-dignity.[75]

The celebrated abolitionist's violent encounter as a slave drove him early to a political awareness that human beings have to fight for their natural right of self-dignity. Physically resisting Covey's assumed right to attack him, Douglass forced his attacker to the mutual consensus that they both stood within the special context that affirmed the right of each to self-defense. In this struggle, Covey was confronted by a Douglass who dared invoke the natural law of self-defense. Douglass's microcosmic experience of self-defense became the framework by which he would affirm everyone's universal natural right to this law. Both in America and Europe, the great orator untiringly recalled for his audience the drama of how he defended himself from being beaten physically by the bully Covey. It became the driving force behind Douglass's conclusion that "there is no freedom without a struggle." Those who will not defend themselves against their evil attackers stand in violation of their natural-law right.

Douglass was clear in his convictions that self-defense was a sacred

---

[73] Ibid., 44.
[74] Ibid.
[75] See my article "The Genesis of Douglass' Moral Understanding While a Slave: A Methodological Approach to Freedom," *Journal of the Interdenominational Theological Center* 9 (Fall 1981): 19-29.

duty to oneself, to the attacker, and to God. Calling it a sacred duty was another way of characterizing the natural right. He expounded upon that sacred duty in this way: "Every man is the original, natural, rightful, and absolute owner of his own body; or in other words, every man is himself, is his self, if you please, and belongs to himself, and can only part from his self ownership, by the commission of crime."[76] This understanding of natural-right law drove Douglass to demand fair play from the American people.[77] The provocative question for Douglass's era and following has been, "Will the colored man be as good a servant to himself as he was to his master?" The aging conservative Douglass thought that this could only be accomplished by the nation and his race accenting character rather than race. With the nation in mind, Douglass said: "We must be truthful and honest. We are religious and want to shun the wrath to come, but what we need is absolute truthfulness and character."

Conclusion

These theistic and deistic voices illuminate the nuances of nineteenth-century Black leaders' interpretation of race, suffering, slavery, and Divine Providence. This study ought show that there is much scholarly work to be done with the primary sources produced by Black nineteenth-century leaders. It shows, too, that Black leadership did not struggle with these issues in a vacuum. They were, however, greatly influenced by the dominant theistic and deistic voices of the epoch. Despite the illiteracy caused by racism, the historical fact is that the latter part of the nineteenth century produced some very provocative clerics such as J. W. E. Bowen. A critical understanding of his thought gives us a new perspective on such Black leaders as Washington, Douglass, and DuBois.

---

[76] *Frederick Douglass Papers*, 4: 42.
[77] Ibid., 420.

A Theologian's Reflection on General Education

Steve R. Gordy

Like every other colleague in a small liberal arts and sciences college, the theologian must attend to many matters of the mind that lie beyond his or her certified intellectual region. Theological training, in my judgment, is excellent preparation for these extra-disciplinary responsibilities. In the first place, theology is a field-encompassing discipline. Not only do we want to know about a variety of other disciplines, but we must know about them. In the second place, many of us are sufficiently prideful to insist that every substantive issue is a moral issue and, therefore, each of these issues is also a theological issue. This is the whence and the necessity of our interest in other disciplines. Finally, and at a practical level most decisively, our discipline is uniquely put upon. At institutions like Moravian College, the pervasive secularity of contemporary culture manifests itself as colleagues' uncertainty over-verging on suspicion about: the utility of theological studies in the curriculum (not to mention the resources necessary to support such studies). Stating the matter generously, the students' mirror their teachers' ambivalence about theology. With relatively few students majoring in religion, we find ourselves in the role of "service department." Typically, such departments are particularly anxious over the prospect of curriculum revision. Theologians, then, have especially good cause to ponder higher education as such, and their own place within it. The public's mounting dissatisfaction with baccalaureate education provides an atmosphere of urgency to the pondering.

When I talk with prospective students and their parents about college education, I point out to them that there are three components of that education to be concerned about: the major, electives, and general education requirements. The order of those components is intentional—it reflects the typical student's priorities from first to last, from his or her sense of what is important to what is sheer hurdle. During the past several years I have been increasingly preoccupied with that third component. I am convinced that general education is the essence of a liberal arts and sciences curriculum, and that what a college chooses to do with general education speaks loudly about its sense of mission. What follows, then, is my counsel about general education. Although it is not patently biased by theological commitments, it is the result of a trained theologian's experience as instructor and colleague. The reader will quickly identify my philosophical debt to the existential-phenomenological tradition.

Basic Considerations

Nothing is exceptional about the claim that well-educated persons ought to be language-competent. For a long time now, a substantial portion of education at every level has been given over to the mastery of one's own language. We learn to speak and to write well, to listen attentively and to comprehend. Educators continue to insist that students be exposed to classical *cum* canonical testaments to the power of their native language—we read great literature. Tradition's conviction is also clear that facility in a second language, for a variety of compelling reasons, is beneficial. Required experience with a second language, if not quite normative for secondary and post-secondary education, is at least very widespread. In the last generation, especially, educators have become quite intentional about acting upon the insight that self- awareness and self-esteem are intimately related to the freedom of personal voice—listening, speaking, and writing are carried over into the realms of identity, personal and social authenticity, the therapeutic. In the sphere of the political, where matters of justice, responsibility and accountability, problem-solving, and public decision-making are at stake, "communication" is currently an outstanding theme.

There is very little serious and substantive dispute about the importance of language skills among educators as such, including college and university professors. I am certainly not inclined to challenge the wisdom of this consensus. To the contrary, I judge that the matter of language ought to be at the very center of our enterprise as students and educators. I also judge that we should differently, and with more success, disclose to our students the very complex matter of language. This essay, then, has two foci: conviction about the centrality in education of the subject matter "language," and the implications of this conviction for the design of a general education curriculum. With regard to the first focus, I write with considerable confidence and with the plain intention to convince the reader about particular matters. My intention in the second focus is heuristic: the suggested curriculum in the second part of the essay, while not merely a kite-flying expedition, is certainly only one possible implementation of my convictions about language in education. I conclude the essay by commenting upon some of the practical impediments to serious revision of liberal arts and sciences curricula.

I take it as a given that human beings, in our very sophisticated capacity to "speak," are distinctive among creatures. This capacity "to speak," of course, is construed very broadly. We can begin with the remarkable ability to name the multitude of things and persons that we encounter, and to hold these names in common with our closest fellows. Indeed, we must recognize that the barest meaning of "encounter" is that we exercise the power to name the things and others that constitute the world of our experience. Experience as such does not occur apart from the act of naming. Well beyond that remarkable power there is another, viz. our ability to represent things in diverse and highly complex interpretive articulations (recognizing, of course, that the "mere" naming in the first place is a significant act of interpretation). We utter declarative sentences, ask questions, spontaneously exclaim. We make music. We craft for practical purpose. We paint or sculpt or photograph. We quantify and calculate. We decide upon and act. We go about our daily affairs. In all of these endeavors, we accomplish relationship: relation to things, relation to others, self-relation. To persist along this obvious line, these three modes of relation are always simultaneous and interdependent, and they are always rooted primordially in our linguisticality. We know ourselves (or not), we are social (or alone), we freely participate in a world (or are largely determined by it) always and only because we "speak" interpretively.

The very primordiality of language, its sheer givenness, has the effect of making the phenomenon of "speaking" opaque to us. This endowment is so commonplace that, by and large, we take it for granted and do not seek to really understand it. "Speaking" as such is not a typical subject matter for inquiry, despite the fact that it is the singularly unique thing about us as creatures; it is the utter foundation of the human, the *sine qua non* of anything uniquely human that occurs. Educators are not simply indifferent to language, to be sure. I have already acknowledged what everyone knows well enough: curricula from preschools through graduate and professional degree programs pay homage to language. We should assume that, within the range of what these curricula intend, educational institutions deal sufficiently, more or less, with the matter of language.

Problematical, in my judgment, is "the range of what is intended" at the level of postsecondary education. We err in relation to two paths. On the one hand, we parse the matter of language departmentally. This is the path we routinely walk, and it is a path that most of us, apparently, would not agree is errant. I want to make the case for the contrary. Language, that most central of all human phenomena, is radically decentralized in the course of education. Students are not brought to language as a subject matter simply as such. At best, we facilitate their mastery of language as it functions in one or another, perhaps a few, intellectual regions. One student speaks well within the range of music, another of art, another of economics and business, another of mathematics, another of biology, and so forth.

I am reminded at this point of a statement made by a former colleague during debate about Moravian College's decision to institute an "Information Systems" track in the Computer Science Department. When queried about the field of information systems, my colleague responded that specialists in this area facilitate the efficient transformation of data into relevant, usable information. I was so struck by the off-handedness of his comment that I laughed out loud in spite of myself. It still strikes me that neither "data" nor "information" (relevant, usable, or otherwise) are univocal concepts. The process of transforming the former into the latter can only be more question-begging than the concepts themselves. In this era of technologically-induced intellectual "big bang," I can well understand the utility of persons skilled at retrieving and organizing discrete quanta of stuff from out of the mental soup, but to toss the terms "data" and "information" about so blithely should really strike us as bizarre, if not a little frightening.

What constitutes data depends upon prior decisions about how to interpret some region of the world. In the first place, the acquisition of data presumes the adequacy of quantitative interpretation of subject matters. Are the following items all "data" in the same univocal sense: scrupulously inscribed figures of daily arrivals and deaths at Auschwitz, plant closings during 1995 calculated as a percentage gain or loss to the GNP, the number of times that the word *blespein* is used in the Gospel according to John, the average number of ozone molecules per cubic meter of atmosphere over Britain during January 1996, the average minimum birth-weight as an indicator of survival rates among premature infants?

The figures in each case are data, but what do we really mean when we say that? At the very least, each data set represents a way of interpreting discrete phenomena. Moving from a statistical interpretation of the phenomena to information about them obviously entails additional interpretive acts. I worry whether or not we are sufficiently conscious of the implications of our choices for or against possible interpretive acts. There is a palpable difference, for example, between understanding (another famously controversial concept) lost jobs as an insignificant portion of GNP and understanding lost jobs as specific effects upon formerly employed workers and their families. Either interpretation tends to cover over the other, i.e. the language we choose determines the reality we have in view. People my own age or older, for example, are far too close to the Vietnam War and the routine reporting of "favorable kill-ratios" to simply ignore the point that "data," and the "information" that it becomes, doesn't always tell the entire story. I am inclined to think that it simply never "tells the story" in an adequate way.

Educators need to be clear about their effect upon students at just this point. To facilitate mastery of a particular interpretive scheme (a language specialty, if you will) is to contribute substantially to the formation of a student at the level of the moral life. How the student chooses to act in the world is directed by what reality and possibilities with which the student is familiar. The reality and the possibilities are simultaneously opened up and limited by the language that is primarily in play for that student. John Updike's interpretation of marital relationship in the late twentieth century, for example, is not quite the same thing as the varieties of social science interpretations of contemporary marriage. My point, of course, is that language is never neutral. Even the purported objectivity of quantification is not neutral. Quantification's "objectivity" resides solely in the capacity of numbers to be widely shared (something now approaching a universal language) with relatively little controversy. Numbers might not lie, but they are easily manipulated, their meaning is subject to interpretation in many different directions and, above all, as a chosen mode for disclosing a particular reality numbers can cover over more of the world than they open up. When we teach language we are teaching a way of having "the world." Each of us is a "professor" precisely in this sense, and whether we intend to be or not. When we instruct about a particular way to articulate "the world," we contribute toward "the world" being as the mode of articulation requires of it.

The language issue, broadly conceived as it must be, resides at the heart of a lot of the disagreements that faculty have among themselves. When my colleagues in the Political Science Department protest the degree to which students are exposed to the essential tenets of *The Wealth Of Nations* in its most contemporary mathematical instantiations, they are resisting the formation that accrues in company with mastery over one particular language rather than another. They have caught sight of the problem that, all too often, mastery over a discrete interpretive schema entails being mastered by that schema. We lose our ear, so to speak, for other languages—which is to say that important dimensions of the world become closed to us. When my colleagues in the Religion Department insist upon the importance of students seriously encountering the biblical tradition, they are emphasizing the significance of that symbolic universe for shaping our experience of the world. While the issues are greatly more complex than the following observations imply, the point gets made nonetheless: it makes a difference whether the world is conceived in terms of consumable resources available to our selfinterested manipulation or as "creation" to which we are obliged as "stewards"; it makes a difference whether we conceive ourselves as creatures naturally seeking to improve our lot in life or as sinners constantly tempted to love self more than neighbor; it makes a difference whether one is subject to an "invisible hand" or to the hand of God.

This brings me to the second path in relation to which we err. In this case, however, the erring occurs as a path not taken. We are not intentional about locating our students within pedagogical settings that bring them firmly before the problem of language. For example, we do not offer (let alone require) a course that the tradition calls "anthropology," the interpretation of human being as such. We get at theological anthropologies in some religion courses. Our philosophers worry the problem of anthropology in several courses. Anthropology as a social science is routinely taught. Courses in the biological sciences and in psychology are clearly anthropological by orientation. As ever, we are very explicit, within a certain range of intentions, about dividing responsibility for the important matter of learning about human being. I am convinced, however, that this regionalizing—convenient as it appears to be, and so seemingly intractable in the polity of higher education—is problematical. Except by sheer dint of will (and an unhealthy amount of denial), a person's experience in the everyday world is not disciplinary. Still more problematical about our collective endeavor as faculty are the implicit anthropological assumptions at work within the academic disciplines, i.e. in the majors where the primary formation of our students tends to occur. The respective world-interpreting texts of Isaac Newton, John Locke, Adam Smith, William Wordsworth, Karl

Marx, and Richard Wagner were guided by identifiable assumptions (frequently divergent) about human being. Does this ever become sufficiently clear to our students? In what contexts do they have opportunity to sort through and evaluate these foundational anthropological assumptions? When, if ever, do we help them toward clarity about the relation between these assumptions and the diverse languages by means of which we have "a world" together?

John Reynolds, my colleague in the Political Science Department, renders his students a tremendous service in just this regard. In his own courses and in the College's experimental core curriculum of interdisciplinary courses, Reynolds explores the relationships among economy (emergent capitalism and industrialization), political theory (the formation of the U.S. Constitution), and Enlightenment anthropology. In thus exemplifying Marx's analysis of the relation between the sub- and super-structure of a society, Reynolds also demonstrates in very practical terms that an operative language, with its attendant perspective, makes a difference in how one comprehends the particular "world" that he or she inhabits. Along the way, Reynolds facilitated my own recognition that anthropological convictions shared by Hobbes, Locke, Rousseau, Montesquieu, and Madison are Augustinian with one remarkable qualification—finitude, passion, self-interest, and reason were no longer understood to be marked by fallenness and sin. My point is this: It makes a difference whether a student's formation is centered upon "self-interest" interpreted as a neutral and given condition of human being (biology), a biologically-based condition that founds individuation and sociality (psychology and sociology), a condition that grounds relations of power and productivity (political science and economics), or a condition that articulates the human will *coram deo*. We err as educators when we leave it to the students to worry over this diversity of anthropological convictions that found our respective disciplines— or, worse, not to worry over them at all.

General Education Centered Upon
The Problem Of "Language"

I continue with the most obvious implication of my argument to this point. If the current disciplines must remain decisive for the academic specialization of both students and faculty then, nevertheless, something other than discipline-based learning ought to be at the heart of general education. Moreover, we must present the matters of general education as the context from which the meaning of our specializations is derived. A bare majority of the faculty at Moravian College, at least, has already conceded that discipline-based general education is problematical. Therefore, we offer a modestly interdisciplinary core curriculum for up to twenty-five per cent of our students. It is not at all clear that we share a common understanding of the substantive relationship between general education and the majors. I am convinced that the quality of specialized learning can only be enhanced by rooting it firmly and coherently in a larger vision of experience than we currently offer our students. In my judgment, I am not proposing something that denigrates the major. This perception, if it arises at all, is founded upon the unexamined assumption that how we currently handle the majors is necessary and fully sufficient to accomplish our mission as educators. My assumption is that the quality of general education enhances the quality of the major but that the opposite is not necessarily the case at all.

Colleges and universities must revise their general education curricula. I strongly urge that the problematic "language" be taken as the most important signpost as we seek a new direction. I am guided in the specific proposals that follow by at least four resources: my participation in Moravian's core curriculum for most of its pre-history and for the full six years of its execution; the constellation of discrete collegial forums on liberal education that have tapped my colleagues' energy during the last dozen years; the now-perennial dialogues about the College's mission and identity as we enter upon a new millennium; the trajectory in philosophy that places the fundamental matter of hermeneutics at the center of human experience and, necessarily, of academic inquiry. The first three of those resources, the multiplicity of institutional differences notwithstanding, I take to be common ground for a large number of college and university professors. My particular philosophical commitments, of course, are obviously open to challenge. I don't pretend that the courses that follow ought to constitute a universally acceptable general education curriculum—happy as I might be if something akin to my proposal were to be adopted. These suggestions are really subject matters rather than courses, and they are offered as a demonstration of what a practical, coherent, and interdisciplinary education might look like. For the sake of expediency, I frame my proposals as semester courses. The proposals are readily adaptable to other academic calendars.

I remain convinced that familiarity with a foreign language is very important. Consistently with that conviction, I urge that two semesters' study in a foreign language be required for general education purposes. This should occur during the Freshmen year. We should articulate this conviction with some new emphases, however. Motivation for rethinking how foreign language is offered in colleges and universities resides in the commonplace of three phenomena: a majority of students (to understate the matter) resent a foreign language requirement, they recognize the requirement as essentially a matter of "time served" and, if they are mentally acute, they recognize that the requirement serves to justify large and tenured foreign language departments servicing small numbers of majors. My own experience has been that, within a restricted curricular framework, more language can be learned if the emphasis is placed upon reading—rather than conversation—skills. I learned far more Koine Greek (exclusively reading emphasis) than Spanish (primarily speaking emphasis) during two semesters' work in each. As with so many other Ph.D. candidates, I found that acquiring the necessary reading competency in German and French (in my case) was significantly more useful, and an easier matter, than speaking two semesters' worth of a second language. Reading courses have the advantage of allowing students to work with contemporary texts (daily newspapers, for example) at a very early stage in the learning process. The advantage resides in the exposure to another culture's perspective on both common issues (press coverage in France of peace-keeping procedures in Bosnia or of U.S. presidential candidates) and also culture-specific issues (agricultural conditions in the wine-growing regions of France). These two semesters ought to be the occasion for introducing students to the traditions of creative expression specific to the language they are studying. Folklore, lyrics, poetry, drama, and literature are obvious texts to be utilized, but there is no reason to slight relevant traditions of architecture, dance, instrumental music, painting, and sculpture. We cannot be exhaustive here, and we don't need to be. We only need to make the point that creativity and conceptions of the beautiful, for example, take different forms among peoples of diverse language traditions. The foreign language courses, at the level of general education, should also attend to the foundational matter of how language as such tends to work, and how different languages work differently. I am not proposing a mini-course in linguistics. I only mean that we might explore, at an introductory level, in what respects the German language is different than English. How are common purposes of language as such accomplished differently in German than in English? Students should learn that every language has a history, that each language belongs to one or another family of language, that languages continue to develop. Students should experience that languages are living, subtle, complex, and marvelous—and not simply hard work in the mastering. It is worth noting that the proposed strategy for foreign language in general education does not preclude a place for conversation courses sufficient to meet the demands of students, particularly students who continue study of a language in which they have advanced during their secondary education.

During the fall semester of the freshman year, students should also be introduced to the diversity of "anthropologies" as a problem. This course ought to focus upon similarities and differences among paradigmatic interpretations of human being selected from both Western and non-Western cultures. Since the subject matter is the problem of "anthropology," and the paradigms are only examples in service to disclosure of the problem, we need not be exhaustive in our selection of, or attention to, the paradigms. Diversity of paradigms among the syllabi for the several sections of the course would be inevitable and legitimate. I can imagine a course in which students discover Aristotle and Augustine; Sophocles and Shakespeare; Hesiod, Lucretius, and Newton; Milton and Marx; Michelangelo and Picasso; Lina Wertmueller and Spike Lee. A crucial point intended with these examples is that we need not limit ourselves to the more or less scientific anthropologizing that are the hallmark of theological and philosophical texts. Our interest lies in interpretations of human being, in the irreducible problematics of understanding and articulation. For our purpose in this course, Sophocles and Picasso speak as powerfully as Aristotle and Marx; the lyrics of Coolio or the tales of the Sioux are as poignant and disclosive as the soliloquies of Hamlet, and so forth. If students complete this course even with only a dawning awareness that they have their being as interpreters within a complex historical nexus of interpretations, then we have made a good beginning in our task as educators.

During the spring semester, freshmen should attend to the matter of imagination and creativity. In contemplating a specific plan for this course, I drift ever further from safe harbor. I do have confidence, however, about the substance of the claim that underlies the course, i.e., about the importance of the subject matter in view. The ordering of human experience, and the decisive accomplishments that drive us toward reordering, are founded upon the exercise of imagination and creativity. While we accomplish nothing *de novo*, new orderings of experience continue to arise from among the possibilities latent in the past and present. We are far more submissive before the givenness of "the world" than we are assertive about creative re-imagining of it. This reason is the plainest, I suppose, that we so readily acknowledge and admire creativity and at the same time tend to anxiously recoil in the face of new possibilities. Our students should be confronted by imagination and creativity in all of its manifoldness. If imagination and creativity is the subject matter at stake then, once again, the range of potential examples proves to be extraordinarily broad. Why not study the singular brilliance of an Einstein alongside the accomplishment of a Mozart? Why not admire the construction of Egyptian and Mayan pyramids, the Chartres Cathedral, and the Brooklyn Bridge as instances of imagination and creativity? The popular Western prejudice that creativity is the purview of the varieties of visionary fine arts ought to be set over against the physical sciences as "art" (the imaginative construal of a phenomenon, or an implication of data, that yields a theory) and the practicality of creativity (the everyday ingenuity of a traditional society in reconciling itself to its environment, for example). We should attend to historical currents that carried forward the possibilities that qualified Galileo's choices about experiments, for example, or shaped the insights of Simone de Beauvoir. In just this way we can explore the inherent limits upon "the new." We should also attend to any discrete "world's" constraints upon imagination and creativity, whether it be the "givenness" of the Ptolemaic universe, the presumed fragility of female affections, the "order of creation" status of gender relations, the canonical status of particular art forms, and so forth.

The fifth course, taken during the fall of the sophomore year, is a course that explores the meaning of numbers, mathematization as interpretation, and the possibilities and limitations resident in statistical information. Surely, students will benefit from an introduction to current research regarding numbers and cognitive processes (psychology), a historical overview of numbering and calculation in relation to cultural conditions and accomplishments (history), the perceived social utility of numbering and calculation in diverse cultures (cultural anthropology), mathematizing as a philosophical *cum* hermeneutical problem (philosophy), and current strategies in quantitative problem solving (mathematics and the social sciences). Certainly this course would be an appropriate place to ensure that every student is familiar with the foundational role played by mathematization for the modern physical sciences and, more gradually, the social sciences. In this course, if nowhere else, students should become familiar with the strengths and weaknesses of the modernist tradition of positivism, with special attention paid to both "cost-benefit analysis" and the "fact-value distinction" as problematical.

The sixth course in the general education sequence, taken during spring semester of the sophomore year, will locus upon issues of language and politics. The adequacy of two claims should guide us at this point: the human being is a political animal, i.e., a creature whose potentials are maximized within a highly developed social order; everything is political, i.e. all social relations entail claims upon and concessions about power. It is our responsibility as educators to facilitate each student's understanding of language as power, and his or her self-understanding as a political being. Toward this end, students should become familiar with the classical principles of rhetoric, the nature of propaganda, the role of the arts in persuasion and in social-moral formation, the business of creating market demand through advertising, alienation; as a phenomenon of language, and so forth. Discrete topics for study are plentiful and, once again, the following are intended only as suggestions. Our own century is ripe with examples of contest over language as essential to empowerment. Students should explore the interplay of language and power in the context of the American civil rights movement and contemporary feminism. The rhetorical and propagandistic strategies of German National Socialism and Italian and Spanish fascisms are tragic paradigms for study of willful deformation and manipulation of societies. Students can be critically introduced to the role of the news media, as matters both of principle and practice, in shaping their understanding of individuals and groups, issues, events, political platforms, etc. Faculty can facilitate students' analysis of the role of language in contemporary moral and political conundrums: how the very complex matter of clinical abortion is variously conceived and publicly articulated, for example. Whatever the syllabi might contain by way of case studies, the function of this course in general education is to enhance, perhaps provoke for the first time, the students' awareness of the play of language in ordering relations of power in their society.

The general education course suggested for fall semester of the junior year focuses on issues of race, ethnicity, and gender. I strongly encourage that this course be literature-based. The professors should rely upon the rich literature produced by women and minorities to disclose the experience of alienation and the social practices rooted in race- and gender-bias. I am convinced of several advantages to this pedagogical strategy. In the first place, such an approach to the subject matter ensures that students (and faculty) become better acquainted with a literature that is, at least historically, neglected. In the second place, this approach offers a possibility to transcend an all-to-common phenomenon: the majority of our traditional-age students (especially males) are largely unaffected by "objective" treatments of gender and racial- ethnic alienation. My own experience as a teacher inclines me to think that students are more likely to be moved by narrative disclosure of the routinized alienation in which they participate than they are by social-scientific analysis. This claim is closely related to another. The observation by James Gustafson is accurate enough: literature discloses the depths of injustice, moral confusion, and the exercises of a bad will far more compellingly than detached analysis. All matters of the moral life, among which we must certainly number racial-ethnic and gender alienation, are profoundly affective matters. We should take advantage of a rich and constantly expanding literature that discloses such alienation in a way that existentially involves rather than detaches readers. This is not to say, of course, that second-order reflection on prejudice isn't important for our purposes in this course. It is only to say that objectively analytical texts ought to supplement the autobiography and fiction that, by design, makes the relevance of such analysis transparent for the students.

The general education subject matter for spring semester of the junior year is religion. In particular, students should become acquainted with the role of symbol, myth-making and cultus, tradition, canon, and theology in the ordering of human experience. Necessarily, this course must also raise fundamental issues about the transcendence that is the referent of religious language, including the issue whether or not this language has any referent at all beyond the immanence of human experience which this language, at a minimum, articulates. In this context, students should continue to explore the problem of the possibility of truth as more than sheerly measurable immanence (the positivist option). In this context, again, students should examine the effects upon the religions of interrelated modernisms, viz. the presuppositions and judgments of methodically articulated historical consciousness, the assumptions and conclusions of the sciences (both physical and social), the assumptions and social implications of classical liberalism (in both its political and economic modes). At this point, the meaning of atheism, and its social implications, should be considered. Since religious experience is inherently discrete, students ought to grapple with particular pieties and texts drawn from particular religious communities. While Judaism and Christianity ought to provide the larger share of these texts, and receive the larger share of students' attention, this course should also be an opportunity to explore both the particularities of a third religion (at least) and also the possibility of universals among the religions. Therefore, paradigmatic texts from other religious traditions should be prominent in the course. It is not sufficient if students gain some insight into "the world" conceived from within a Christian symbolic universe but have no substantial appreciation for an Islamic "world," for example. Students should leave this course with an understanding of the historical capacity of religions to construct diverse "worlds," and also with an initial sense for the possibilities of religious "world-construction" now and in their future.

A final course is reserved for fall semester of the senior year. I urge the location of this course, and its subject matter, for the senior year for two reasons: (1) opportunity to build upon prior accomplishments both in general education and the student's major and (2) to ensure the highest level of maturity among the greatest number of the students involved in the course. The subject matter for this final course in general education is "truth and the moral life." By this point in the undergraduate's career, he or she will have had ample opportunity to inquire a bout the human being as moral decision-maker, including the varieties of interpretive schemes by which we conceive moral problems and seek to resolve them. I recommend the following features for this course. The course should be oriented toward case study. Its several sections should explore, in considerable detail and from a variety of perspectives, various contemporary moral conundrums—one conundrum per course section and professor(s). The set of cases, then, will certainly vary (slightly or a lot) from year to year. If such a course was currently in play, then students might choose to enroll in one among the following sections: the abortion debate, regulation of nuclear energy, basic research in physics as a national priority, private and public responsibility for peace in Bosnia, Palestinian and Israeli rights and responsibilities, the moral responsibilities of multinational corporations, the role of the federal government in health care, gay and lesbian rights, moral accountability with regard to the outcomes of genome research, response to public violence, public education and political process, federal support for the arts, and so forth. Sad to say, we do not lack for problems worthy of our inquiry; these are only examples quickly taken. Colleagues can readily suggest many other and better possibilities. The purpose of the final course, however, is clear. We ought to bring students to the task of careful, well-informed reflection upon a real moral dilemma. This focus is good practice for the adult life they are about to enter upon, and it provides the occasion for each student to utilize the broadest possible range of their learning to that point in their education.

Concluding Comments

Over the course of a several-years debate about general education at my own college, colleagues have accumulated considerable experience with various environmental, institutional, and "philosophical" constraints upon new directions for the curriculum. I won't attempt to address every one of these constraints in this conclusion. Some of them, of course, are peculiar to Moravian College. These, in particular, are not relevant to a general readership. On the other hand, at least a modest account of problems common to institutions of higher education is in order since it is commonly acknowledged that general education at colleges and universities is in a sorry condition.

One obvious constraint upon revisioning of general education is the divided judgment of faculty about freedom and students' rights. What I have suggested as a curriculum clearly eschews the value of a student's right to choose courses in the general education component of his or her education. By this point in time, this will come as no surprise to my colleagues at Moravian. I will simply reiterate my concerns over the issue. In the first place, free choice of courses is more fiction than fact at most institutions, as most students at registration time will attest. In the second place, left entirely to their own devices the students will exercise their right to choose general education courses under the influence of less than noble motives: time of day, days of the week, oral tradition regarding course and instructor, perceived relevance of the course to major and/or vocational interest, and so forth. In the third place, I do not comprehend the logic which suggests that students will discern coherency in general education when, to date, their instructors have no agreement about how the knowledge imparted in these courses holds together. At this point, the plea for students' right to choose seems transparently ideological: unable to see a clear way ourselves, we glorify the students' right to wander about among discipline-based courses. That the buffet of courses that we offer as general education might be seasoned with individual and departmental self-interest supports the inclination to interpret the principle of free choice as a piece of ideology. This problem is endemic to higher education as such. The commonplace of foolishness, however, is no justification for persisting in it. I cannot imagine how a college would put itself at risk through the initiative to reach beyond the academic status quo at a time when higher education is, quite rightly, under close public scrutiny.

In this very competitive and critical higher education marketplace, it is clearly important to be outstanding. Revision of the curriculum holds out the promise that risk-taking institutions can become superior in the marketplace. It strikes me that too few colleges and universities hold the problematics of truth and value at the core of what they do. Truth and value (the essence of general education in the liberal arts and sciences tradition) have been superseded by "competency" (arguably the legitimate goal of the major) as the *sine qua non* of the Bachelor's degree programs. Truth, value, and specialized competency are hardly incompatible. What is crucial to acknowledge, however, is that the latter is a function of the former two and not vice versa. Eichmann and Himmler were competent enough; so are Buchanan and Perot. Clearly competency is, in itself, not sufficient for the general weal of humankind. Why should colleges and universities not stand out as institutions that require of their constituency that they coherently worry the problematics of truth and value as foundational for whatever else they do? The fact that many corporate employers will dissent from that perspective only begs questions about the mission colleges and universities and the ideological tendencies of the professoriate.

Until faculty learn to do it very well, an integrated and interdisciplinary general education curriculum of the sort envisioned here might well be a problem for many students. They will need to read, hear, behold, discourse, and compose with greater thoughtfulness than is currently required of them. They will need more self-discipline and a higher sense of personal expectation than is currently demanded. In the first place, this is our problem as their instructors, not their problem. One promise that inevitably attends serious curriculum revision is the renewal of minimum standards for each student's effort. In a very close second place, this becomes a matter of enhanced learning environment. A new program of general education will no doubt require a new institutional self-understanding that finds articulation in programming for students beyond the classroom. Unfortunately, that is the subject for another essay altogether.

An obvious problem that resides in the sort of curriculum proposed here is the conflict that arises between general education and the majors that, to date, regularly claim an unusually large share of the student's course load according to a largely inflexible sequencing of those courses. Education, premedical, and an expanding variety of vocational track programs will have to yield the current degree of control they exercise over their students' course selection. This problem will test the faculty's will about the priority of general education, and also its ingenuity in dealing with externally imposed requirements governing certain degree programs. If general education is the top priority at a college, then "the tail cannot wag the dog" in the matter of curriculum design. The same principle is applicable in our proper and inevitable concern for the needs and circumstances of non-traditional and transfer students.

Finally, radically revising general education along an interdisciplinary line will test the openness of diverse faculty specialists toward new learning and teaching possibilities. A broad challenge to higher education, possibly even a profound one, presents itself at just this point. Academic specialization *cum* intellectual regionalism, nurtured in doctoral programs, resides at the heart of colleges and universities. We are twenty-one in number within discrete disciplines; we are hired according to departmental needs; we are recognized within our institutions, academic guilds, public and private funding sources on the basis of contributions to our particular fields of expertise. In short, the polity of higher education is firmly set against interdisciplinary general education. If serious curricular innovation occurs at all, it is inevitably experimental. It is limited by departmental self-interest, the influence of speciality-centered colleagues, and the professional risk that accrues to junior faculty who are otherwise open to new direction-taking. The tenacity of the polity problem ensures that curriculum revision must become a matter of concern to the whole community of scholars, and not only the problem of individual colleges and universities.

I cannot identify an impediment to new directions in general education that is insurmountable if the will to innovate is present. Many actual problems exist that impede an easy transition to a more fruitful general education. After these many years of debate, trial innovation, plan-making, legislating, and mounting frustration, it is hard not to draw the conclusion that we have moved very little, because genuine conversion of the will has not occurred. In the face of hardened wills on all sides, practical impediments loom as irresolvable problems (more ideology in play). When we don't like a proposal that is offered, our tendency is to claim that the proposal in question cannot be enacted under the institution's existing conditions. Logistical problems are, by now, largely convenient devices for avoiding both an uncomfortable disagreement on substantive issues and the risk that each individual might lose what he or she currently holds dear in the pursuit of something better for all of us together.

PART TWO

"THE NEW REFORMATION" OF THE
DISCIPLES OF CHRIST,
ALWAYS REFORMING

The Nineteenth Century Reformation in Historical-Theological Perspective: The First One Hundred Years

by James O. Duke

The "nineteenth-century reformation" is one of several names for a movement that, born on America's early nineteenth-century trans-Appalachian frontier, advocated the unity of all Christians on the basis of what was variously called biblical, New Testament, ancient, primitive, original, apostolic, common, and at times "simple evangelical" Christianity. Joint meetings in Kentucky (1831-32) signaled the coalescence of two initially distinct groups of such reformers, the western branch of "the Christians" under the aegis of Barton Warren Stone and "the Disciples of Christ" led by Thomas Campbell and Alexander, his son. Growth thereafter made proponents of "the current Reformation" or "the Restoration movement" one of the larger religious groups in the United States at the dawn of the twentieth century. Two major schisms long in the making—the first ratified by 1906 census data, the other by a 1968 church yearbook— have led today to three sizable and separate bodies, the Christian Church (Disciples of Christ), the Churches of Christ, and the Christian Churches.

The church-historical story of this reformation has been often told before, variously and at length in denominational histories. It receives brief coverage in surveys of American Christianity, and references to Disciples (using now standard shorthand for the movement's participants except where greater precision is necessary) appear at times in specialized studies of American religious history.[1] Found here, it has been said at one time or another, is an apt illustration of God's wondrous providence, the frontier thesis, a passage from sect to church, millennarian dreams and experiments of the antebellum era, the democratization of American Christianity,

---

[1] See, e.g., the recent integration of the Disciples within the context of "populist" trends in American Christianity by Nathan Hatch, *The Democratization of American Christianity* (New Haven: Yale University Press, 1989).

and the rise and fall of erstwhile mainstream Protestantism. The conflict of interpretations confirms that efforts to understand this movement's institutional and social history in the context of American religious history are simply historiographical business as usual.

The same can hardly be said of the history of Disciples theology per se. With rare exception the topic has been left to the denominational historians alone, who have dutifully recorded the movement's leading thinkers, ideas, and controversies.[2] Some of them (more and more in recent decades) set these developments in their wider intellectual context. Yet searching studies of the character and course of Disciples theology are few. Fewer still are those that examine the matter in expressly historical-theological terms, that is, as though it were an integral component of Christianity's theological tradition in toto and as such neither more nor less than than yet another episode in the on-going story of attempts to discern the nature and meaning Christian faith to the best of human understanding at some given time and place. One result to date is that the movement's theological identity is less controverted than indistinct.

I offer here, then, a few exploratory historical-theological soundings of the theology of the Campbell-Stone movement during its first one hundred years in hopes of ascertaining its place within the history of Christian thought. The centennial celebration of the Disciples at Pittsburgh (1909) is a serviceable cutoff date, even though, strictly speaking, it represented a church-historical rather than a theological milestone and granted first honors to Thomas Campbell's *Declaration and Address* (1809) rather than Stone's leadership in the Cane Ridge, Kentucky revival (1801) and *The Last Will and Testament of the Springfield Presbytery* (1804).[3] Yet coming so soon after public notice of the movement's first great schism, it attested that an era as well as a century had passed. At the same time, acrimony over featuring the Disciples Old Testament scholar Herbert L. Willett as a speaker portended a second schism to come in due course. Willett, a protégé of William Rainey Harper first at Yale and

---

[2]An orientation to and bibliographical survey of the history of Disciples "theology" are offered in James O. Duke, "Scholarship in the Disciples Tradition," *Disciples Theological Digest* 1 (1986): 5-40 and the notes there.

[3]*Declaration and Address by Thomas Campbell; Last Will and Testament of the Springfield Presbytery by Barton W. Stone and Others* (St. Louis: Bethany Press, 1955).

then Chicago, where in 1894 he helped found the Disciples Divinity House, symbolized the rising tide of evangelical liberalism (along with ripples of scientific modernism) among the Disciples, who had entered the ecumenical associations, theological schools, and diverse enterprises of the Protestant establishment in increasing numbers from the 1880s on.[4] After 1909, the liberal, moderate, and conservative camps of the divided and dividing movement come to look ever more akin to those pervasive throughout American Protestantism at large, and thus readily tagged as denomination-specific variations on common theological themes.

Where to place the theology of this reformation before and apart from this late-date liaison with Protestant liberalism(s) on a large-scale map of the history of Christian theology is another question altogether. Denominational studies detect before the 1890s several controversial figures, distinguished from the crowd by drifting toward evangelical liberalism a bit beyond the standard deviation from the Disciples' mean, who might be called proto-liberals.[5] What is striking, however, is the lack of a historical-theological brand-name for the theological mean itself. During the last half of the nineteenth-century Disciples routinely termed their distinctive position their "plea"[6] and proclaimed that their aims, teachings, and practices were distinctive precisely, and only, by virtue of their total conformity to biblical Christianity. The unwary might well suspect that Disciples thought was sui generis, so singular and isolated from the overall sweep of Christian theology that no standard historical-theological differentiations applied to it.

---

[4]On Willett, see M. Eugene Boring, "The Disciples and Higher Criticism: The Crucial Third Generation" and Leo G. Perdue, "The Disciples and Higher Criticism: The Formation of an Intellectual Tradition," in *A Case Study of Mainstream Protestantism: The Disciples Relation to American Culture, 1880-1989*, ed. D. Newell Williams (Grand Rapids: William B. Eerdman's Publishing Co.; St. Louis: Chalice Press, 1991) 29-70, 71-106.

[5]Perhaps the earliest leading candidate would be L. L. Pinkerton (1812-75). See *The Life, Letters, and Addresses of Dr. L. L. Pinkerton*, ed. John S. Schackleford (Cincinnati: Chase and Hall, 1876); and Frank Gardner, "The Heretic—L. L. Pinkerton," *Scroll* 40 (1943): 235-43.

[6]The term was in use early on, as e.g., in the title of Alexander Campbell's "biblical theology," *The Christian System in Reference to the Union of Christians and A Restoration of Primitive Christianity as Plead by the Current Reformation*, 2d ed. (Pittsburg: Forrester and Campbell, 1839). As a genre of literature, however, accounts of "the plea" flourished from the early 1860s to the early 1920s. A long but only partial listing of such titles is given in Duke, "Scholarship," 33, n. 31.

The movement's founders did much to foster such suspicions by their insistence on certain modifications of the rules of the grammar of faith. Stone and the two Campbells were agreed that the historical-theological labels Christians used to differentiate themselves from one another were indicative of flawed if not false witness to the gospel set forth in the New Testament. Therefore the only labels applicable to the mean struck by those in genuine continuity with the Christianity founded by Christ and his apostles were biblical, Christian, and true. They agreed as well to reject the authority of any historic (viz., "human") creeds and confessions, catechisms, directories of worship, and books of order or discipline in favor of taking "the Bible alone" as the sole test of Christian faith, fellowship, and unity. Bereft of explicit biblical sanction and a symptom of sectarian division, the term "theology" itself was in effect retired from use except as a cuss word.

According to church lore, then, the nineteenth-century Reformation was sui generis indeed in its plea for a unity of all disciples of Christ in a once (New Testament) and future (millennial) church, truly traditionless and theology-free. What began as a theological protest against post-Reformation dogmatism took on a life of its own: pride in being biblical *instead of* theological has been a staple of the movement throughout its history. Late nineteenth-century liberalizers seem the first Disciples to call the thought of the movement's founders "theology," hastily adding that it was neither so rigid nor so binding as to hinder free, open, and fresh inquiry or devotion to the simple, practical truths of biblical Christianity.[7] In due time (1945) none other than Edward Scribner Ames, the first member of the movement to achieve world-class fame (as a theologian/philosopher of religion and a self-avowed modernist), praised his heritage for having long ago discarded not only Catholicism and its scholastic theology, creeds, and ecclesiasticisms but "protestant theology" as well.[8] The Reformation by then had become a divided movement which at its rightwing and leftwing extremes agreed on little other than that the phrase "Disciples theology" was oxymoronic.

In historical-theological perspective, this view of theology and the

---

[7]The most notable example is Winfred E. Garrison, *The Theology of Alexander Campbell: Its Sources and Historical Setting* (St. Louis: Christian Publishing Co., 1900).

[8]Edward Scribner Ames, "The Disciples Are Modernists," *The Scroll* 42 (1945): 289-98.

church is of course nonsense, differing in content but not in kind from that found among other churches because of inadvertent or willful misreadings of their own theological traditions. This Reformation arose because—in addition to its social sources—Stone, the Campbells, and their co-workers engaged in the task of "faith seeking understanding" and urged everyone else to go and do likewise. It sought to discern and then confess, preach, and teach the faith of the church of Jesus Christ responsibly and thoughtfully. None of its nineteenth-century thinkers rank on historical theology's short lists of "the great" theologians and scholars, and precious few of them vie for position on theology's historic junior varsity teams. Even so, their writings are, to judge by their genre, content, aim, and effect, what historical theologians call theological. Indeed, the output en masse looks—once one moves on from theology's masterpieces to its standard literature—very much like that circulating in other Protestant churches of the day.

It also looks, to judge by its mode of reasoning and even its conclusions, far less sui generis than the first generation reformers themselves and their heirs have customarily, namely, traditionally, taken it to be. It is, contra Ames, genotypically Protestant theology, as Roman Catholics, Eastern Orthodox, and Enlightenment pagans of Peter Gay fame would attest. Of the major theological traditions stemming from the sixteenth-century Protestant Reformation, it belongs to the extended Reformed family whose varied members have on occasion, usually in times of historic stress, roiled their home churches as well as others by actually pursuing rather than merely giving lip-service to an *ecclesia reformata sed semper reformanda.* In brief, the theology of "the current Reformation" is classifiable as a species of the genus the Reformed tradition in transit.

This historical-theological classification will doubtless strike many Disciples (and countless Reformed tradition loyalists) as a woeful misreading of history. Much can be said against it. Stone for his part and the Campbells with their ally Walter Scott for theirs left Presbyterianism to become Bible-believing reformers instead of Reformed theologians. The partings were so distinctly unpleasant that no one involved seemed to look back with regret then or later. Nineteenth-century Disciples delighted in assailing "Calvinism." In addition, their reform platform included certain "catholic" as well as various free church or radical features. On these grounds alone, and apart from others in ready reserve, a dutiful historical theologian seeking to do justice to the unity and diversity of Disciples theology ought to know better than to categorize it as "Reformed."

It must suffice here to explain what my curious claim means rather than fend off objections to it. A theologically normative definition of "Reformed Christianity" is a matter for others, say, the World Alliance of Reformed Churches, to debate and decide. My thesis turns on a (more or less strictly) descriptive construal of the Reformed tradition, taking that label to be a historical-theological category of relatively high-level analytical abstraction for genetic connections and family resemblances among many different and at times mutually hostile particular churches. The high status this tradition regularly accords John Calvin and Calvinism is no excuse to forget that these two "objects" are themselves moving targets and disputed questions of research or to overlook the influence of many others (Zwingli, Bucer, Beza, and Bullinger, just to start). By 1800 the Reformed tradition was certainly dispersed and diversified, and even more so by 1900. The situation on the ground and in theology was never as clean and simple as the convention, and convenience, of using the terms Reformed and Calvinist as synonyms would seem to indicate.

Archibald Alexander Hodge, for example, sought to acknowledge as much when he spoke of the Reformed tradition in the sense of "the general class" rather than in that of strict usage. The class, he stated, extends from the usual suspects to the Congregationalists, to the Baptists (Regular or Particular) of England and America, to the Anglican-Episcopal churches as a subdivision, and with them by lineage although farther removed from the "normal type," Wesleyan Methodists. Hodge, Princeton guardian of Reformed orthodoxy, there ended his list, attributing Anglo-American Unitarianism to a lapse into Ebionite-Socinian heresy on the part of "degenerate" English Presbyterians and New England Congregationalists and making no mention of Disciples of Christ at all. Even so, the expansiveness of this inventory is instructive precisely because Hodge was no impartial observer of the state of church(es). The Reformed tradition was, and is, not one thing.[9] Its identity as a class encompasses a certain range of bands along a spectrum, and within that range (the precise boundary lines of which are at times tough or close calls) appear not only various standard combinations of coloration but scattered evidences of anomalous and even aberrant trace elements.

If description is as "thick" as it is broad, the metaphor of a spectrum will not alone serve to capture the complex of features formative of this tradition's typicality, for the many elements of the

---

[9]A. A. Hodge, *Outlines of Theology,* rev. and enlarged ed. of 1879 (Edinburgh and Carlisle, PA: Banner of Truth Trust, 1972) 101-4.

tradition are laterally multilayered and in constant, albeit often sluggish, motion. The range of diversity apparent at the surface rests on subterranean masses, tectonic plates so to speak, bonded together large and small by manifold connections, some rigid, others supple, and still others fragile indeed. Fault lines run throughout the structure, and pressures within push and pull materials—frequently in contrary directions. At levels of greater depth, for example, are grand thematic paradoxes of faith such as God hidden and revealed, divine sovereignty and human responsibility, the gospel as gift and calling, and the church universal in unsteady relationship to particular churches. Generations of Reformed theologians have undertaken to expound and if possible "resolve" these tensions in light and in terms of changing views of theology's intelligibility.

The nineteenth-century Reformation took its rise (call it uplift or slippage, according to taste) along the fault lines of this tradition. When, where, and how shifts of this sort are triggered are determined by what Lessing called "accidental truths of history." So it was that Stone's role in the Cane Ridge revival and Thomas Campbell's laxity in fencing the Lord's Table led first to church court, then schism, then two reformatory movements, and at length to a coalescence of the two. The initial disputes were for Presbyterians (and other Reformed churches in the United States) minor incidents, each in its own way symptomatic of stress-and-strain in an age of Pietism, Enlightenment, national expansion, and disestablishment of church from state. The defendants replied to the charges against them with stock Reformed arguments, and finally justified going off on their own by appeal to the *norma normans sed non normata* their home church had set: "The Supreme Judge, by which all controversies of religion are to be determined . . . can be no other but the Holy Spirit speaking in the Scripture."[10]

Ruptures of church fellowship along the fault line of *sola scriptura* versus tradition are of course by no means uniquely Reformed. Nonetheless, these two were quite traditional Reformed protests against the Reformed tradition, which not only occupies territory through which that line runs but grants the line itself confessional status. In both cases the way-station between intramural discord and total independence was an effort to negotiate waivers from total conformity to the books of faith and order. In this respect, the

---

[10]*The Westminster Confession* 1.1, in *The Creeds of Christendom, with a History and Critical Notes,* 3. vols., 4th ed., rev. and enl.(New York: Harper and Brothers, 1877; reprint, Grand Rapids: Baker Book House, 1966) 605-6.

Springfield Presbytery of Stone's group, on the one hand, and a renewed but unsuccessful overture to the Presbyterians and then the stormy alliance with Baptists on the part of the Campbellites, on the other, were patent replays of the "subscription controversies" familiar to Britain's Reformed churches. This claim is not to deny that, once underway, both of these original reformatory streams exhibited patently "radical" tendencies. Although the formation of the Springfield Presbytery was no more contra-Reformed than the rise of Cumberland Presbyterianism or the schism of New Lights and Old Lights some decades after, its early suicidal death was its theologically decisive action: for a season Stone's New Light Christians were revivalists virtually without doctrinal or organizational cohesion.[11] What emerged in time under Stone's titular leadership, however, was a form of congregationalism (in non-juridical association) whose stress on Scripture alone amounted to Christocentric theological latitudinarianism. Stone's writings on the Trinity, Christology, and atonement led defenders of Protestant orthodoxy to lump him with other "liberal Christians," referring at the time to latitudinarians, emergent Unitarians, and others suspected of leaning more toward "rationalism" than "sound reason." In historical-theological retrospect, these polemics conceal as much or more than they reveal about the state of the Reformed tradition at the time. Stone's views on these doctrinal controversies stopped at least one step short of classical turn-of-the century Unitarianism and Universalism. But their "heterodoxy" and certainly his was altogether in keeping with notable trends *within* Anglo-American Reformed theology during this era, A. A. Hodge's censures of "degeneracy" notwithstanding.

The Campbellite movement, a "reformed" party among Regular Baptists from 1813 until about 1830, fixed during that time on what it called the "ancient order" and "ancient gospel" of the New Testament church. Its initial quest to "restore unity, peace, and purity to the whole Church of God"[12] became in the pages of Alexander Campbell's *The Christian Baptist* (1823-30) a reform program which, by denouncing as divisive, sectarian, or apostate every feature of the church lacking biblical sanction by express precept and/or approved

---

[11] See, e.g., Paul K. Conkin, *Cane Ridge: America's Pentecost* (Madison: University of Wisconsin Press, 1990); and Richard T. Hughes, *Reviving the Ancient Faith: The Story of the Church of Christ in America* (Grand Rapids: William B. Eerdman's Publishing Co., 1996).

[12] Thomas Campbell's phrase in the *Declaration and Address,* 24

precedent, could be read as a mandate for either maximal toleration or narrow exclusivism. Campbell later adopted, in his *Millennial Harbinger* and other works a tone and a stance toward evangelical Protestantism that was irenic if not lax by comparison with his earlier writings.[13] Hence, he became for his followers and their followers the equivalent of Luther and Melanchthon rolled into one—a powerful combined force during his lifetime but a source of contrary impulses free to express themselves thereafter.

The "current Reformation" emerging in the middle third of the century was, then, a blended family, in the main far more domesticated than before. Stone, both Campbells, and a critical mass of their associates turned to the task of consolidating hard won gains, and the movement sought to organize itself for evangelistic, educational, benevolent, and assorted ventures in home and foreign missions. Conflicts over introducing "innovations" along the lines of the ways and sects of the world arose before the Civil War, grew thereafter into charges and counter-charges of betrayal, and finally spelled division. Yet despite its discord within, the movement prized its distinctiveness. The Stone-Campbell movement had come far from its (mainly Presbyterian) origins and absorbed large numbers of people who had chosen its "plea" over inter-denominational rivalry. The result was an *ensemble* of features that formed something of a historical-theological sphinx: *sola scriptura* as the rule of faith, order, and practice; no creed except a—"the simple"—biblical confession of faith in Jesus as Messiah, Son of God, and Savior; baptism by immersion for the remission of sins; corporate "free church" worship on Sunday (the day of the Lord's resurrection, but not a Christian Sabbath) with observance of the Lord's Supper *sine qua non;* self-governing congregations in cooperative but non-juridical connection, and emphasis on the priesthood of all believers, led by a putatively non-hierarchical public ministry of evangelists at large and a cadre of elected congregational elders (who both taught and ruled) and deacons, working in ever-more cases alongside and in uncertain connection with settled preacher-ministers.

---

[13] Alexander Campbell's explicit assertion in 1837 that there were "Christians" in paedobaptist churches was alarming to some of his followers. But he had long before that date shifted from his aggressive warfare against the "sects" of evangelical Protestantism: see Richard Hughes, "From Primitive Church to Civil Religion: The Millennial Odyssey of Alexander Campbell," *Journal of the American Academy of Religion* 44 (1974): 87-103, and Richard T. Hughes and C. Leonard Allen, *Illusions of Innocence, Protestant Primitivism in America, 1630-1675* (Chicago: University of Chicago Press, 1988) chap. 8.

Multiple social factors intersected, and clashed, in the making of this Reformation and the form of church it advocated and represented. Theologically, the rhetorical slogan of "the Bible alone" cannot conceal how many and varied elements of catholic, evangelical, and free church tradition were rewoven into a new pattern. And it is not the pattern as a whole but the selection of *these* particular strands rather than others that sets the character and course of this Reformation in the context of the Reformed tradition in transit. The catholic impulses and features of the movement extended no farther than points at issue among the Reformed churches with regard to that tradition's *catholicity*; likewise, the only free church or radical reforming impulses and features of the movement were intra-Reformed points at issue with regard to the tradition's *apostolicity* and *purity*.

A return *(restitutio)* to the standards of "primitive" faith and order was as appealing to Puritans and Enlightenment moderates, Anglicans and Calvinist dissenters alike, as it was to divers radicals of the sixteenth-century Reformation, although each case led to quite different outcomes.[14] The movement's core Christological creed was beholden at once to the generic Reformation theme *solus Christus* and Locke's attempt to reconcile if not unite Anglicans and Reformed in comprehensiveness. Calvinist Congregationalists and Baptists demonstrate that congregational polity was as truly Reformed as Presbyterianism was. They also demonstrate that in referring to baptism and the Lord's Supper as ordinances, Disciples followed a convention permitted by the Westminster Confession and favored by various Reformed bodies. Stress on believers' baptism by immersion was common to Particular and General Baptists alike. Observance of weekly communion had been Calvin's preference, and along with (Zwinglian) memorialism one finds among Disciples instrumentalist language regarding Christ's "spiritual presence."[15] Here, and in emphasizing baptism for (assurance) of remission of sins, Disciples harkened back to catholic Reformed themes eclipsed by what

---

[14]The *restitutio* ideal within Puritanism is the theme of *To Live Ancient Lives: The Primitivist Dimension of Puritanism* by Theodore Dwight Bozeman (Chapel Hill: University of North Carolina Press, 1988).

[15]James O. Duke, "The Disciples and the Lord's Supper: A Historical Perspective," *Encounter* 50, 1 (Winter 1989): 1-28; Richard Leigh Harrison, Jr., "Early Disciples Sacramental Theology: Catholic, Reformed, and Free," in *Classic Themes of Disciples Theology: Rethinking the Traditional Affirmations of the Christian Church (Disciples of Christ)*, ed. Kenneth T. Lawrence (Fort Worth, Texas Christian University Press, 1986) 49-100.

Mercersburg theologians called "modern Puritanism." The striking anti-clericalism and (re)ordering(s) of ordained ministries in this Reformation reflect renewal of Reformed rhetoric on the one hand and modification of Reformed practice on the other.[16] Illustrations such as these of the Reformed traditionality of Disciples's ecclesiology are soundings of tradition in Gadamer's sense of that word. We deal, that is, in this case first with a view of scripture as *norma normans* so traditional that it neither prompts second thoughts nor brooks objections and second with traditional judgments of Scripture's material content which pre-qualifies only a limited number (or range) of alternatives as worth serious consideration. For example, faith as an ellipse with two foci, justification and sanctification, was so taken-for-granted as "biblical fact" that Disciples considered appeals to *theology*—whether Calvinism, Wesleyanism, or (in the fullness of time) Ritschlianism— of no weight at all. Those "isms" were, after all, sectarian.

By the same token, the literature other than the Bible that Disciples read, discussed, and cited was overwhelmingly of English-Scots-American provenance. Continental thinkers came within their purview hardly at all except by passing through this funnel. Wycliff, Hus, and sixteenth-century magisterial reformers were honored rather than studied with care, and Protestant scholastics were generally considered to have undermined the cause of reformation from within.[17] What received their serious, and more favorable, attention was the long line of thought extending from the new learning of the early seventeenth century (Francis Bacon et alia) to Chillingworth and his circle, to latitudinarians and Baxterians, to Locke and Newton and their schools, to Scottish common sense thought, and at length to

---

[16]The most up-to-date studies of the ordering of ministries among the Disciples are those of D. Newell Williams: "Historical Development of Ministry among Disciples," *Mid-Stream* 14 (1985): 293-315; *Ministry among Disciples: Past, Present, and Future,* Nature of the Church Study Series, No. 3 (St. Louis: Christian Board of Publication for the Council on Christian Unity, 1985).

[17]Early on, occasional appeals were made to Johann Lorenzo Mosheim's description of the fixed system of apostolic Christianity, the apostasy of the church, the Reformation, and its aftermath, as told in his *Ecclesiastical History.* Later, and not surprisingly, the histories of Neander, J. H. Merle D'Aubigne, and Schaff became popular among Disciples as surveys of the history of the church and its theology. Yet in 1847, S. K. Hoshour, a Disciples "scholarly" pastor, published an edition of the Maclaine translation of Mosheim: *Mosheim's Church History of the First Two Centuries* (Cambridge City, IN: Published by S.K. Hoshour; Milton, IN: Printed by C. B. Bentley.)

the nineteenth-century scholars of the pan-national evangelical movement.

This Reformation was anything but intellectually isolated, for this body of literature was taught in the academies and colleges of Anglo-American Protestantism, read by those seeking self-education, and widely diffused in American culture. The first generation leaders of the Disciples were like many other Reformed thinkers negotiating their tradition's passage through cross-currents of scholastic, pietistic, and enlightened thought. Even as settlement was being concluded on these fronts, however, new forces and new challenges had appeared on the scene. Later nineteenth-century Disciples found themselves, like other evangelical Protestants, confronted with the paradigm shift triggered by Kant's Copernican revolution of philosophy, which gained uneven but wide currency in manifold guises of Romanticism. In sum, nineteenth-century Disciples theology in historical-theological perspective represents a lagging indicator of Britain's diverse Reformed tradition (transplanted in post-colonial America) attempting to weather two transitions over time: the first an antebellum-era sifting of traditional themes through the grid of theology's eighteenth-century developments, the other a resifting—and eventual separation—of the earlier product after the Civil War under the impact of theology's post-Kantian cutting edges.

The first transition or sifting took place through the efforts of the founders of the Stone-Campbell movement, coming to fruition in a tensive equipoise of theological impulses during the 1830s and 1840s. The linchpin of the reform was a proposed resolution to the confused, and fractious, Protestant disputes over "the true church" rife after the formation and during the frontier expansion of the new nation. The proposal involved breaking inter-confessional deadlock: let all agree to look afresh *ad fontes*, retesting each church tradition against its own self-avowed *norma normans* and thereafter requiring of churches and their members nothing other than that required of first generation Christians.

Formulating the Reformation's originary plea in these terms discloses its theological intent and substance as neither appeals to "pure Biblicism" nor attacks on "the sects," two beloved themes of Disciples rhetoric, were—or are—capable of doing. The church is, like the gospel it proclaims, a gift of God. Christians are free to rework and even discard historic traditions precisely because Christian freedom is not license to define the faith of the church as one pleases. The *notae* of the church universal are not to be confused with those of the church divided and parochial, i.e., sectarian), for the latter demand tests of fellowship and unity that in effect retroactively expel Christianity's earliest churches from the church of Jesus Christ. It also discloses this plea's historic fragility, and far more aptly I suspect and wager than commonplace references to the incompatibility of dual commitment to "restoration and unity." It explains, for example, why Disciples might state their case at times irenically, claiming their Reformation asked of churches nothing other than to be true to their avowed continuity with original, common, and "simple" evangelical Christianity and yet at another moment polemically, railing against sectarianism and apostasy as though there were no post-apostolic churches except their own. It explains too why the movement shifted readily and often from appeals to the Bible in toto to the essentials of Christianity's ancient gospel and ancient order to the person and work of Jesus Christ himself. During the antebellum era at least, Disciples profited from their ability to argue that all three appeals were connected and mutually reinforcing. This "achievement," however, endured only for a time, and though it did not break down all at once like the Deacon's One Hoss' Shay, the connections loosened over time with the result that strains at any one point took their toll on the other two as well.

Witness to the character of the church as "gift of God" found expression early on in Thomas Campbell's dictum, "the church is essentially, intentionally, and constitutionally one."[18] Constitutional oneness proved to be the most striking, controversial, and (as Disciples history, recapitulating ecumenical history, shows) problematic element of early Disciples ecclesiology. The magisterial Reformation's two classic marks of the church, word and sacrament, were carried over as word and ordinances (baptism and the Lord's Supper). As Alexander Campbell specified the "ancient order" in the 1820s, constitutionality included the forms used for confession, baptism (of believers by immersion), and the Lord's Supper (weekly), as well as the church's governance structure (congregationalism). With Walter Scott Campbell included in the church's constitutional schema adherence to "the ancient gospel," i.e., an *ordo salutis* in six consecutive steps: faith, repentance, baptism for the remission of sins, the gift of the Holy Spirit, and eternal life. Its advocacy of a "gathered church" under a God-given constitution made the movement seem to aspire for a time at mid-century to become what a historian might call either the highest low church or the lowest high

---

[18]*Declaration and Address by Thomas Campbell*, p. 44.

church on the American scene. Emphasis on the permanency of the church's divinely-ordained primitive constitution prompted numerous Disciples to put a decidedly sectarian, triumphalist spin on their plea for the recovery of the church from the sects. Their internal debates—questioning whether there are any Christians at all among the sects, open communion, the establishment of missionary societies, the use of instrumental music in worship, the "hiring" of settled congregational ministers, and others—leave the impression of an isolated community indeed. The *historical-theological* matrix of these phenomena, however, is neither a revival of the sixteenth-century "Anabaptist vision" nor "freedom's ferment" but the Reformed tradition's own undecidability with regard to the theological status of church structure.

The Reformed tradition had resisted making discipline, and with it governance structures requisite for disciplined faithfulness, a third confessionally defining mark of the church *in addition to* word and sacrament. In a word, "polity" was shifted from the *esse* to the *bene esse* of the church. But this decision was made with considerable misgivings and had to be remade over and over again thereafter. Calvin's church ordinances for Geneva were, like their prototype in Bucer's Strassbourg, the results of an effort to reestablish the permanent order of apostolic Christianity. Assertions of divine right presbyterianism and divine right congregationalism were as much part and parcel of later Reformed theology as divine right episcopacy was among "catholic-type" churches. The disputes of Reformed Christians over polity, both with one another and with outsiders, were typically driven by high anxiety over disciplinary laxity or ecclesiastical tyranny. At any rate, whether anything injurious to the *bene esse* of the church could or should be regarded as adiaphora was an open, and touchy, issue.

In the case of the Disciples, what appears in terms of social history to be expressive of frontier counter-culturalism is equally expressive, in terms of historical theology, of a Reformed subculture. By the same token, the willingness of so many Disciples over time to accommodate to the patterns and mores of "evangelical Protestantism" is a sign not only of growing prosperity but of growing concern to promote spiritual-moral development within the church and "righteousness" throughout the nation and the world. Transformist urges for the sanctification by the third use of the law such as these arose as naturally from Reformed roots as did misgivings over any compromise with worldliness.

Regarding issues of polity, discipline, and the Christian life, as well as word and ordinance, Disciples followed the Reformed tradition in preferring (if at all possible) to take *sola scriptura* to mean "in accord with" rather than "not contrary" to express precepts and approved precedents set forth in the Bible. This preference, which Disciples exercised without the constraints of church-wide confessional or catechetical guidelines, opened the doors to a good deal of ill-informed exegesis and tendentious argument. Even so, under the circumstances, the consistency of basic viewpoints achieved among the movement's far-flung congregations is remarkable. So too is the predictability of points of disagreement, starting with questions regarding the interpretation of the silences of scripture, proceeding to those about "the letter and the spirit" of its texts, and then on to disputes about sound versus destructive criticism.

The overall construal of the authority of Scripture was an (unstable) combination of precritical and Enlightenment-era elements, taking precritical in the expert if rather idealized sense of Hans Frei's description of it.[19] The Scriptures are a canonical whole whose diverse parts form a totalizing narrative of the divine-human relationship from first (in the beginning, God) to last things (the Book of Revelation). This "story" is God's word of law and gospel to humanity, coming by way of mediation and accommodation through the words of humans whose witness is inspired by God the Spirit. This frame of reference was not distinctively Reformed, but it came to first-generation Disciples by way of English, Scots, and Scots-Irish heritage.

This "old Protestant" construal of the canon appeared in Disciples literature already modified by its long journey through scholasticism, puritanism, pietism (viz., the evangelical awakening), and the enlightenment. The version that came to dominate the movement was first most clearly and fully articulated by Alexander Campbell. The totalizing narrative of the Bible was a sequenced story of God's covenantal dealings with humanity, set forth in history and in literature as successive dispensations from Eden and the fall to Patriarchal religion, to Mosaic Judaism, and to Christianity. This covenantal schematization of the Bible is a telltale sign of Reformed provenance. The accented dispensational motif, which focuses on covenant and recasts that motif from a *topos* and a (scholastic) rubric into the terms of a story-shaped *Heilsgeschichte*, is an inheritance

---

[19]Hans W. Frei, *The Eclipse of Biblical Narrative: A Study in Eighteenth and Nineteenth Century Hermeneutics* (New Haven: Yale University Press, 1974), chaps. 1-2.

174   *Christian Faith Seeking Historical Understanding*

from Cocceius and his school[20] and, more distantly, from Zurich, Heidelberg, Herborn, and the Reformed wing(s) of the early English reformation.

One hardly need search long and hard for the historical-theological label to pin on the sort of thinking that early emerged as the nineteenth-century Reformation's theological mean: it is federal theology. This was heritage common to Stone, both Campbells, Scott, and legions of their followers. In keeping with the Westminster Confession (along with the Congregationalist and Baptist traditions beholden to the Westminster divines), they focused on the conditionality of the covenant, though never altogether unaware of an unconditional or testamentary option ready at hand. Alexander Campbell's sharp distinction between the era of the law and that of the church, combined with Scott's *ordo salutis*, so rankled "Calvinists" of the day that Disciples might almost be forgiven for claiming that their views were drawn from fresh reading of the Scriptures alone. In fact, of course, the federalist line itself was by 1800 multi-branched—at once so widespread yet diversified among Hodge's general class of the Reformed—that it easily passed for "simple evangelical Christianity," and for that matter "true Biblism" as well. The federalism of the current Reformation was one of many, distinct from the rest mainly by its *norma normans* appeal to the covenant-conditions specified for the church of the "Christian dispensation," which began "after the gospels" at the creation of the church at Pentecost. The biblical books that recorded the acts and (epistolary) instructions of "the apostles" were therefore regarded as both deposit of faith and enabling legislation for the Christian-

---

[20]The "Cocceian" background of Disciples covenantal-dispensational construal of Scripture was recognized, in the case of Alexander Campbell's thought particularly, by a few Disciples scholars at the turn of the twentieth century: Garrison, *Theology of Alexander Campbell,* 129-58; Hiram Van Kirk, *The Rise of the Current Reformation, or a Study in a History of the Theology of the Disciples of Christ* (St. Louis: Christian Publishing Co., 1907) 30-51. Garrison, much in harmony with "liberal" Reformed scholarship of the day, saw Cocceius as a "deviation" from "strict Calvinism," but regularly drops the qualifier "strict" and so leaves the impression that Campbell continues—or completes—a line of progress leading beyond the "Calvinist" (Reformed?) tradition as a whole. Yet to their credit these denominational scholars acknowledged connections between Disciples and the Reformed heritage as few thereafter chose to do. By and large, accounts of the origins of the Campbell-Scott group stress ties with Scots dissenters (Glas, Sandemann, the Haldanes, e.g.) and treat those movements as though these divisions within the Scottish Reformed church were due to repudiations of rather than internecine conflicts over "Calvinist" theology.

specific conditional covenant.

With apologies to Bultmann,[21] it can be said that for first generation Disciples the life and message of Jesus as well as the entire Old Testament were presuppositions of New Testament Christianity. They were ineradicable parts of the church of Jesus Christ ever after only because and insofar as they *were* already presupposed at the time of its origins. To require of Christians more or less than the covenantal conditions of "the apostolic church" would be to proclaim another gospel than the one given by God in Jesus Christ and by the power of the Spirit. That God covenants (at all) with humanity, and indeed even with sinful humans, attests to God's sovereign, free, and unconditional love and mercy for the world; that these covenants, whether of faith through grace or works of obedience in fulfillment of the law, impose certain conditions upon humanity attests to God's holiness, righteousness, and justice.

The current Reformation's first century represented relatively late-date federalism, one (like others of the time) reshaped by Pietism and the Enlightenment. And here again a historical-theological label is applicable to the type, rather than specific content, of Disciples thought: rational supernaturalism. Varieties of rational supernaturalism had emerged in the Anglican, Lutheran, and Reformed traditions at the end of seventeenth century and rose to prominence during the 1700s and 1800s, peaking first in Germany, then England, and lastly America. As an ideal type, rational supernaturalists used reasoned arguments formulated in terms of "modern," namely, enlightenment, philosophy and science to support Christian claims to truths above but not contrary to confirmation by natural human reason.

This model of argumentation was the trademark of Enlightenment moderates who sought to come to terms with critical inquiry and its "new learning" without surrendering anything deemed of essential Christian substance over to it.[22] In Germany, *Übergangstheologie*, neology, and Wolffianism fall into this category. In the English-speaking world, the line runs along mainly empiricist tracks set down by the likes of Bacon, Newton, and Locke and their schools, and then Paley as well as Scottish Common Sense thinkers. Apart from the creative alliance of Turretin, Westminster confessionalism, and Scots Common Sense struck by Princetonians, rational supernaturalists

---

[21]Rudolf Bultmann, *Theology of the New Testament,* trans. Kendrick Grobel (London: SCM Press Ltd., 1952) 1:3.

[22]On the "moderate Enlightenment" in America, see Henry E. May, *The Enlightenment in America* (Oxford: Oxford University Press, 1976).

pressed for a distinctly post- and anti-scholastic presentation of theology. They fought on multiple fronts, reproving sheer dogmatism, enthusiast fanaticism, and rationalist radicalism. Accepting the method(s) and worldview of Newtonian science, they countered its materialistic interpreters by physico-cosmological and teleological proofs of divine governance. Accepting empiricist epistemology, they distinguished their "healthy" appreciation for knowledge derived from sense-data and reflection from deistic arrogance and Humean skepticism.

In the United States, where the lingua franca for intelligent discussion was first Lockeanism and then Common Sense thought, rational supernaturalism flourished among the general class of the Reformed. The model's popularity was surely due at least in part to its virtually limitless adaptability. Appeals to truths in accord with human reason might serve to establish the "supernatural" origin and hence the authority of Christianity per se as revealed religion, or its biblical canon in toto (rather than church traditions), or its New Testament particularly, or the person and work of Christ, or minimally the life-teachings of Jesus. With evidence in place for one or another of these claims, unbelief and fanaticism alike were ipso facto unmasked as willful, irrational hubris even while confessional disputes over the scope and specific content(s) of divinely-revealed truth "above but not contrary to reason" continued apace.

The nineteenth-century Reformation's understanding of biblical-Christian faith took its place within this broader arena of theological discussion. Enlightenment influences, that of Locke above all, on the founders of the movement have been too often noted to demand long discussion here. These notations, however, are of greater import than commonly recognized. It is not enough to say that various Enlightenment themes appear in their writings, that some or much of their discontent with theological tradition generally and "Calvinism" in particular was due to "reasonable, empirical, and pragmatic thinking,"[23] or that despite their encounter with Enlightenment thought they sought to hold fast to the Bible alone. Instead, the situation was that they viewed Scripture and traditions alike through the lens of the English-Scots-American Enlightenment.

One index of their rational supernaturalism was the reinterpretation of the language of biblical faith and historic doctrine

---

[23]W. B. Blakemore, "Reasonable, Empirical, Pragmatic: The Mind of Disciples of Christ," in *The Reformation of Tradition,* ed. Ronald E. Osborn, The Panel of Scholars Reports, vol. 1. St. Louis: Bethany Press, 1963) 161-83.

in light of empiricist epistemology and Newtonianism. A case in point was the use of the term "supernatural" for what was once referred to by such phrases as the transcendence, otherness, mystery, or objectivity of God. The supernatural is defined as that which is "above" nature and nature's laws in the sense of a principle and power that "makes" the natural realm an intelligible, lawfully-ordered system of sensory "facts" and their interrelationships. Supernatural revelation refers to a communication of information about the supernatural and its "architectural" design of the natural world coming from above through the introduction or adaptation of facts *in* nature. Religious knowledge is what results from firsthand encounter with these facts; religious faith is assent to (and trust in and action taken in response to) testimony to such matters of fact offered by credible eye-witnesses. Religious opinions are inferences, deductions, speculations, theories, guesses, or even fantasies that lack solid evidentiary grounding.

Thus, for example, the Pauline phrase "faith comes by hearing" was carried over in Disciples teaching as assent to, trust in, and conformity with the testimony of scripture, and focused especially on the testimony of the original (eye-witness) apostles and disciples of Christ. These testimonies have as their subject matter "facts" regarding God's will for and relationship to humanity, including acts in history, commands, promises, and "institutions" ordained by God, which together form "the Christian system," "the scheme of redemption," or the "plan of salvation."

A second index is Disciples's preoccupation with issues relating to the evidences of Christianity. In spite of—or at least along with— what appears to be sheer biblical fideism, the Stone-Campbell movement shared with other representatives of rational supernaturalism the concern to demonstrate on rational grounds the authenticity and credibility of Christianity as revealed religion. In so doing, they consulted and added to the evidentiary literature that circulated widely among Protestants, adducing internal and external evidences of the unique authority of Jesus Christ, the Bible, and the Christian religion as a whole.[24]

---

[24]Alexander Campbell's debate with Robert Owen is routinely noted in denominational histories, and several times reprinted: Alexander Campbell and Robert Owen, *Debate on the Evidences of Christianity: A Debate between Robert Owen, of New Lanark, Scotland and Alexander Campbell, President of Bethany College, Virginia, containing an examination of the "Social Systems" and all the Systems of Skepticism of Ancient and Modern Times* (Bethany, Virginia: Alexander

Yet another index of rational supernaturalism is the adoption of empiricism's account of the relationship between word, thoughts, and things as well as reliance on grammatico-historical hermeneutics. Behind the insistence on using only "Bible words for Bible things" lay not only a correspondence theory of truth but a correspondence theory of language, paradigms that were post-Lockean but pre-Kantian and pre-Romantic, and largely taken for granted by Reformed theologians and many others of the day.[25] Alexander Campbell warmly welcomed Moses Stuart's translation of Ernesti's hermeneutics, claiming that those rules of interpretation had long been his own, and consulted the philologically-oriented text critics up to Griesbach in preparing his own revision of the McKnight-Campbell-Doddridge translation of the Bible.[26] Even as German scholarship ventured far beyond Ernesti in the direction of a more thoroughly historical criticism (Semler, Keil, Gabler) and then on to a historical-genetic paradigm (Schleiermacher et al.), grammatico-historical principles gained ascendancy in England and the United States as "inductive hermeneutics."

At mid-century, not only Moses Stuart at Andover and other Reformed Trinitarians including Charles Hodge, but also their pre- and anti-Transcendentalist Unitarian opponents relied on grammatico-historical method. It is ironic that J. S. Lamar, one of the second generation Disciples who fits into what denominational historians

---

Campbell, 1829). Walter Scott also followed, used, and wrote on Christian evidences, as did many Disciples at the middle of the nineteenth century: e.g., Robert Richardson's ten part series entitled "Thoughts on Evidence" in the *Millennial Harbinger* (1839-1840); and James Challen, *Christian Evidences* (Philadelphia: J. Challen and Sons, 1857 (©1856). A partial list of later Disciples literature on the topic appears in Duke, "Scholarship," 34, nn. 33 and 35.

[25]On the post-Kantain paradigm shift in language theory , see Jerry Wayne Brown, *The Rise of Biblical Criticism in America, 1800-1870: The New England Tradition* (Middletown, CT: Wesleyan University Press, 1969); Donald A. Crosby, *Horace Bushnell's Theory of Languagae: In the Context of Other Nineteenth-Century Philosophies of Language* (The Hague: Mouton, 1975); James O. Duke, *Horace Bushnell: On the Vitality of Biblical Language*, SBL Cenntennial Publication Series (Chico, CA: SBL/Scholars Press, 1984).

[26]Campbell's revision of the translation by George Campbell, James Macknight, and Phillip Doddridge appeared as *The Sacred Writings of the Apostles and Evangelists of Jesus Christ, Commonly Styled the New Testament* (Buffalo, Virginia: A. Campbell, 1826. See also M. Eugene Boring, "The Formation of a Tradition: Alexander Campbell and the New Testament," *Disciples Theological Digest* 2 (1987): 5-62; Cecil K. Thomas, *Alexander Campbell and His New Version* (St. Louis: Bethany Press, 1968).

term the "scholastic" (and provincially isolated) era of Disciples thought would feature significantly in Theodore Dwight Bozeman's study of antebellum Presbyterianism as a prime exemplar of the widespread popularity of inductive hermeneutics within the Reformed tradition at the eve of the Civil War.[27] It was not adherence to grammatico-historical principles per se but the determination to hold to them long after so many theologians in other churches "followed" the Germans into higher criticism and romantic hermeneutics that has clouded denominational judgments about the parochialism (or contrariwise, the biblical fidelity) of late nineteenth-century Disciples thought. The sort of scholarship which was in Ernesti's day "pioneering" and eminently respectable though not avant-garde when Campbell, Stuart, and even Lamar first wrote, had become at the end of the century—when J. W. McGarvey (the Disciples Moses Stuart) clashed with Herbert L. Willett over the "new" higher criticism—an embarrassment to "progressive" thinkers within the current Reformation.

To these few and sketchy historical-theological remarks about the first one hundred years Disciples "theology" many others might be added. The longevity of the Reformed tradition's *triplex munus* formula "prophet, priest, and king" in Disciples' Christology might be noted, to allude to just one possibility. Also relevant would be the hold of penal substitutionary and governmental accounts of the atonement despite Stone's preference for a moral influence view. This view would gain new-found currency among Disciples at the end of the century—yet this time in the context of post-Kantian classical liberalism rather than that of the Great Western Revival. Enough has been shown here, I trust, to explain my curious claim that the nineteenth-century Reformation was an effort at "faith seeking understanding" that belongs to the Reformed tradition in transit from seventeenth-century scholasticism and puritanism to early nineteenth-century English, Scots, and post-colonial American

---

[27]Theodore Dwight Bozeman, *Protestantism in an Age of Science: The Baconian Ideal and Antebellum Religious Thought* (Chapel Hill: University of North Carolina Press, 1977). James Sanford Lamar apparently considered his own work pioneering: *The Organon of Scripture; or the Inductive Method of Biblical Interpretation* (Philadelphia: Lippincott, 1860 [©1859]). Later Disciples literature along these lines, e.g., David Roberts Dungan, *Hermeneutics: A Textbook* (Cincinnati, 1885) and Clinton Lockhart, *Principles of Interpretation: The Laws of Scripture Treated as a Science, Derived Inductively from an Exegesis of Many Important Scripture Passages* (Des Moines, IA: Christian Index Publishing Co., 1901), looks ever more outdated in context.

modernity. Its message was a rational-supernaturalist federalism, and although its "plea" was certainly distinctive, it was at root and aim a reformation of the Reformed tradition under the banner *semper reformanda*. To know even this much of its historical-theological identity affords Disciples, as well as those who have dealings with them, a historical-theological framework within which to place them.

Two other planks must go into the framework, however, if it is even to make any sense, much less sound at all convincing. The one concerns this Reformation's broadside and relentless attacks on "Calvinism." The *fides quae creditur* of the Reformed tradition is not, strictly speaking or "ultimately," the Reformed book of confessions but the objects ("the realities") of God and things of God which "reformed" Christians are prompted to confess as faith's meaning to the best of their common understanding. The objection to the *authority* of the church's historic creeds, confessions, and catechisms that the Stoneite Christians and the Campbellite Disciples made, first independently and then in concert, was not in and of itself objection to that to which those texts sought to witness. Thus the question remains of what historians of Christian thought are to make of the material content of Disciples theology with respect to and salvation vis-á-vis Reformed theology.

The confessional standards of the Calvinist churches camouflage the swirl of grass roots controversy on just these points within Reformed churches during the first half of the nineteenth century. The lack of any explicit confessional standard—other than "the Bible"—does the same with regard to Disciples. Nonetheless, the most persistent complaints that Disciples lodged against Calvinism had to do with its predestinarianism and its requirement of tests of religious knowledge and experimental conversion "by the power of the Spirit" for church fellowship. The counter-charges against the Disciples were, of course, arminanism and then (here evangelical Arminians join the chorus) even worse—neo-pelagianism, salvation by works rather than grace, baptismal regeneration, denial of the work of the Holy Spirit, and laxity unbecoming a self-avowed reforming "gathered church." The polemics of the day, on every side, cast more heat than light on the true historical-theological stakes at issue. It is surely only just to grant that this Reformation was safe haven for anti-predestinarians per se and, beyond that, for vast numbers of people unable to stand— or withstand!—the tests of doctrine and experiential conversion that most other churches put before them.

Even so, it pays to be circumspect. A strong case has been made to the effect that Stone's piety was far more "Calvinistic" than his theological articulation of it, meaning by the phrase "Calvinist piety" not a set of doctrinal reformulations but the heightened awareness of human sinfulness and a "falling in love with God" by the power of grace in Jesus Christ.[28] Biographers of the elder Campbell note he retained his "Calvinist opinions" without denying fellowship to those with differing views. Though Scott allied with the two Campbell's after finding that eastcoast Scot Baptists, unlike his small Pittsburgh congregation, were "mired in Calvinism," he nonetheless viewed the human condition after the fall to be so depraved and ruined that nothing less than the "gospel restored" offered hope of salvation. Alexander Campbell's view differed not at all from Scott's on these points. Indeed, this "simple" view was the doctrinal mean set early on and held basically in place throughout the movement's first century. It represented, Disciples liked to claim, "the biblical" position, as distant from Arminianism as it was from Calvinism, each of which was one-sided theoretical extremism.

Taking supralapsarian double predestination as the norm, the Disciples were patently off the Reformed reservation. But this view had never attained widespread normative status among Reformed churches, and "high" as well as "hyper" Calvinists now and again risked suspicion of antinomian tendencies.[29] The account of salvation by grace in terms of divine decrees in Dort and the Westminster, London, Cambridge, and Philadelphia confessions were chief among the standards of orthodoxy Disciples called "speculative," or as one might put the same point today, doctrinal over-determinations of Christianity's symbolic tradition. Their difficulties with Calvinism's efforts to set sin and salvation within a predestinarian framework were no different than those which lead generations of Reformed theologians to revisit and recast these doctrines: the need to witness to the benevolence of God, the salvific power of the person and work of Christ, the importance of human accountability, and the value of the divinely-ordained means of grace. In discarding the framework of divine decrees, Disciples did not thereby automatically or necessarily seek recourse in a God without wrath, a Christ without the cross, and a world without sin. That was

---

[28] See D. Newell Williams, "The Theology of the Great Revival in the West as seen through the Life and Thought of Barton W. Stone," Ph.D. diss., Vanderbilt University, 1979; and "Barton W. Stone's Calvinist Piety," *Encounter* 42 (Autumn 1981): 409-17.

[29] See, e.g., Peter Toon, *The Emergence of Hyper-Calvinism in English Nonconformity* (London: Olive Tree, 1967).

not to happen until later in the nineteenth century, after multitudes of Reformed theologians had led the way.

Throughout the extended middle third of Reformation's first century its "theology of the Spirit" was commonly considered by Protestantism's evangelical caucus generally and Reformed theologians in particular to be proof positive of neo-pelagianism. Stoneites arose as New Light revivalists who required no more of converts than response to the gospel preached but whose techniques, including the use of the anxious bench, marked a stage of development in the revivalistic tradition between the evangelical awakening of the eighteenth century and that of Finneyite "new measures." Their alliance with the Campbell-Scott group brought that group, so denominational history often says, a jolt of fresh evangelistic zeal to what was in most respects a staid, biblically-based, and rationally-oriented faith and order movement. In any case, the coalesced Reformation made its peace with revivalism in much the same way as Presbyterians and Congregationalists who feared but could not totally resist it—accepting it guardedly as an extension of the church's ordinary means of grace, beneficial yet fraught with dangers of excess.

The *theological* point common among Disciples was that the Spirit was imparted only after "conversion," i.e., as a gift to those who had become believers by responding to the gospel by their faith, repentance, and baptism. Evangelical Protestants generally took this point to mean that Disciples understood conversion—and faith—to be an act of human "free will" instead of a divine gift brought about by the power of the Spirit. Entering into the great debate over reliance on ordinary means of grace versus the employment of new measures by which to trigger outpourings of the Spirit to work conversion by immediate, convulsive power upon sinners, Disciples took the stand that conversion was effected by the power of God *mediated* through the proclamation and hearing of the inspired Word in Scripture and that (forensic) justificatory forgiveness of sin was completed and assured through the act of baptism. The receipt of imparted grace of the Spirit followed, and aided the Christian's efforts along the path of faithful, sanctified living.

In certain respects, then, the Reformation plea took positions akin to those prevalent among Old School Reformed theologians on the hand and various newly-emerging Reformed romantics like Nevin and Schaff at Mercersburg and Horace Bushnell on the other. Resort to extraordinary means of conversion was considered a de facto denial of the church constituted by word and sacrament (ordinances) that

God provided for effecting the salvation of sinners. This stress on *mediated* grace was one of the very few traits the Reformation's antebellum leaders, rational supernaturalists that they were, shared with the Reformed tradition's early representatives of post-Kantian and romantic theology.[30]

Finally, then, a brief word must be said of the Reformed tradition's second great transition, from rational supernaturalistic confessionalism to classical liberalism. By the 1909 Pittsburgh assembly, every observer of religious affairs was aware of the push-and-pull between "conservative" and "liberal" opinion that cut across evangelical Protestantism as a whole and threatened to divide each of its churches. Liberal scholars in other denominations had already written histories of the fitful but inexorable advance of "modern" theological thought over the course of the nineteenth century. Its parallel tracks ran in Germany from Schleiermacher to *Vermittlungstheologie* and on to Ritschl, Hermann, and Troeltsch, in England from Coleridge to Maurice and *Essays and Reviews*, and in America from the Transcendentalists, Mercersburg theology, and Bushnell to Andover's new or progressive orthodoxy, the Chicago school, the social gospel, and ecumenical movement. These individuals and movements, in the view of liberal historiography, helped emancipate the churches from confessional dogmatism, to prepare them to address the intellectual and social challenges of changing times, and to direct them to higher goals on behalf of Christianity and civilization.

Certainly they represented a turn not only from Protestant scholasticism but also from the empiricist-common sense framework of rational supernaturalism to a post-Kantian, romantic paradigm focused on the mediation of the infinite through finite historical forms of life. This turn involved a reordering the task and method(s) of theology, conceived now as a critico-constructive reflection upon and then symbolic reexpression of religious experience. By religious experience was meant feelings, sensings, motions, inspirations, and moral impulses of the divine at the depths of the self rather than biblical sense-data or born-again conversion. Scripture, the creeds, and traditions alike were viewed in developmental terms, and serious

---

[30]Essential in this regard is W. Clark Gilpin, "The Doctrine and Thought of Alexander Campbell and John W. Nevin," *Mid-Stream* 19,4 (October 1980): 417-27. On Nevin's critique of Campbell's "restorationist" program, see James Hastings Nichols, ed., *The Mercersburg Theology* (New York: Oxford University Press, 1966), 93-119 and the notes there.

biblical study turned from strictly grammatico-historical to historical-genetic hermeneutics and higher (source) criticism in search of historically original religious experiences of God that gave rise to the scriptures and the spiritual-moral ideals of biblical faith. The message of the prophets and the teachings and life example of the historical Jesus reconstructed from the Gospels was regarded of greater canonical force than the Pauline (and/or pseudo-Pauline) kergymata favored by *Altprotestantismus* and its "conservative" heirs.

What writers such as these praised, others viewed with alarm as an ongoing erosion of commitment to scripture and historic church doctrine. In this situation, what to make of the nineteenth-century Reformation remained an open question, though one of little interest, it seems, to anyone except members of the movement. And they by that time had divided into Churches of Christ and Disciples of Christ, the former branch dedicating itself to New Testament Christianity free of any modern innovations or entanglements with the sects, and the latter devoted to contributing its fair share to the varied tasks of educational, evangelistic, ecumenical, missionary, and social witness underway among mainline Protestantism. This is not the place to discuss the complex, and still controverted, causes of division, which was by no means an early example of fundamentalist-modernist schism despite the fact that the drift to theological liberalism was one bone of contention. Of immediate interest here instead is the question of what, if anything, the transit to liberalism(s) within the Reformed tradition as a class has to do with identifying the current Reformation's theological mean at the end of its first century in historical-theological terms.

The theological mean in 1909 was not (quite yet) that of Willett and his associates at Chicago or like-minded liberals sporting advanced degrees from Yale and other Protestant theological seminaries. They had made the paradigm shift from rational supernaturalism, and their church as a whole—as distinct from en masse—was well along in the process of making common cause with "the liberal" churches. Even so, they were a significant, capable, and well-placed minority, movers and shakers rather than the dominant powers. The next two decades were to test their rise to institutional ascendancy—heresy trials at the College of the Bible in Lexington, Kentucky, the formation of an International Convention and a United Christian Missionary Society, and from the 1920s on conflicts with "restorationists." A thorough-going classical liberal reinterpretation of the Disciples plea was already underway in 1909, but at the time it still labored under the handicap of sounding uncomfortably radical, and foreign.

The theological position that laid claim to the broad center of Disciples thought at the time was, as one might expect, a mediating view which sought with considerable skill—and ultimately failed—to comprehend both paradigms within one body or, alternatively, to forge a compromise between them. Two "centennial histories" of the movement reflected ambitions of this sort, the one by J. H. Garrison and the other by W. T. Moore. Each in its own way told the story of a Reformation committed to "progressive" understandings of the meaning of discipleship and comprehensive in its toleration of diverse theological opinions while adamant on certain basic points of biblical faith and wise in its wariness of extremist views.[31] It was of interest to Disciples "centrists" that groups of Protestants who had once scorned Stone, the Campbells, and Scott were in the process of discarding theological dogmatism and revising theological doctrines for the sake of a more truly biblical and practical Christianity in many ways akin to that which Disciples had advocated from the start.

These accounts of the nineteenth-century Reformation, roughly equivalent to "Whig historiography," have not withstood serious cross-examination. For Disciples of Christ, they were transitional histories, as one would expect, since the Reformation movement itself was in transition. The movement's intellectual leaders were not pioneering *Neuprotestanten*, but Reformed theologians who, like so many of their day, were constrained by tradition, Pietism, and the Enlightenment to recast a "biblical" covenant theology in rational supernaturalist terms and in so doing reassess the nature and purpose of the church. Even as they sought to do this, however, numerous churches of the Reformed tradition "as a class" were entering a much-disputed transition to post-Kantian liberalism. The Disciples underwent this transition too, but not until the closing decades of the nineteenth century, and even then first in very small (albeit vocal and influential) numbers.

This essay is not the place to attempt an evaluation of the strengths and weaknesses of the way Disciples made the transition. One loss incurred, however, deserves mention: those who remained Disciples of Christ after the first great schism felt justified in ignoring

---

[31] J. H. Garrison, *The Story of a Century: A Brief Historical Sketch and Exposition of the Religious Movement Inaugurated by Thomas and Alexander Campbell, 1809-1906* (St. Louis: Christian Publishing Co., 1909); W. T. Moore, *A Comprehensive History of the Disciples of Christ: Being an Account of a Century's Effort to Restore Primitive Christianity in its Faith, Doctrine, and Life* (New York: Fleming H. Revell, 1909).

their Reformed theological heritage not only because they were "biblical" but also because they were now "liberal." Comforting and energizing as that feeling must have seemed to them at the time, its longterm after-effects have included mass confusion about "the theological identity" of the Christian Church (Disciples of Christ). Historical-theological studies are not themselves "the one thing needful in life and death," but they may nevertheless serve the church as hardly anything else can: in this case set the scripture principle, the liberalism, and even the confusion of Disciples today in the context of Christianity's theological tradition.

Faith and Learning Among African American Disciples of Christ

by Kenneth E. Henry

African American Disciples of Christ have relied heavily upon religion and education to clarify and maintain their place in church and society. The strong link between faith and learning has roots within the African holistic view of life. The two elements became part of the survival strategy of Africans enslaved at the time of the earliest congregations of Disciples of Christ. This combination has been basic to the liberation struggle in every period. It is the most enduring answer to the American dilemma—racism—in church and society.

This article will seek to explore how this dynamic was operative within the Christian Church (Disciples of Christ). Selected centers of early Disciples witness among African Americans will be reviewed, focusing on the initiative, activity and results of black and white Disciples. Vignettes of key individuals, churches, and educational institutions will be incorporated.

It is not by accident that several writings on African American Disciples history bear such titles as *The Untold Story: A Short History of Black Disciples* or "Unknown Prophets: Black Disciples Ministry in Historical Perspective." Equally revealing are the titles, *Two Races in One Fellowship* and *Journey Toward Wholeness: A History of Black Disciples of Christ in the Mission of the Christian Church*[1] Obviously there is a clear perception that the story of African American Disciples is not well known but also that it is an integral part of the total witness of the Disciples of Christ.

---

[1]William K. Fox, ed., *The Untold Story: A Short History of Black Disciples* (St. Louis: Christian Board of Publication, 1976); Kenneth E Henry, "Unknown Prophets: Black Disciple Ministry in Historical Perspective," *Discipliana* 46 (Spring 1986); R. L. Jordan, *Two Races in One Fellowship* (Detroit: United Christian Church, 1944); Brenda Caldwell and William K. Fox, Sr., *Journey Toward Wholeness: A History of Black Disciples of Christ in the Mission of the Christian Church* (Indianapolis: National Convocation of the Christian Church, 1990).

Given these conditions, Vincent Harding's analysis of history provides a helpful interpretive framework.[2] He identifies three historiographical postures or overlapping emphases in the study of American history. There is first "American" or "standard" history that makes the Euro-American perspective normative, absolute and ideal. The romanticized exploits of Europeans in this country are seen as fulfillment of God's plan: an errand into the wilderness to establish the righteous empire with a covenant theology to justify it.[3]

With this scenario the contribution of Africans, imported as slaves, is generally ignored or greatly distorted. They are portrayed as docile, happy, superstitious, lazy, uncivilized, immoral, and natural subjects for enslavement. There were pro-slavery advocates among the early Disciples who shared these views (as well as abolitionists who did not).

The second approach Harding defines allows for the introduction of "Negro History." The fundamental premises of American history remain, but African American achievements are added whenever they conform to the prevailing pattern. This was an attempt to say African Americans have paid their dues and can play the game successfully even by Euro-American rules if given equal opportunity. Merle Eppse, an African American historian, wrote a book with the provocative title: *The Negro, Too, in American History*.[4] This era was one of a few paragraphs or a chapter on "Our Negro Work" in standard Disciples histories.[5]

The third approach is that of "Black History." This method questions the fundamental assumptions of standard history and declares some are distortions and some are deliberate lies that must be

[2]Vincent Harding, *American History, Negro History, Black History*, cassette, (Atlanta: Institute of the Black World).

[3]Currently, most historians tend to identify this tendency without subscribing to it, e g., Sidney E. Ahlstrom, *A Religious History of the American People* (New Haven: Yale University Press, 1972); Robert T. Handy, *A Christian America: Protestant Hopes and Historical Realities*, rev. ed. (New York: Oxford, 1984); Martin E. Marty, *Righteous Empire: The Protestant Experience in America*, 2d ed. (New York: Harper and Row, 1977); Perry Miller, *Errand into the Wilderness* (Cambridge: Belknap Press of the Harvard University Press, 1956; reprint, New York: Harper and Row, Harper Torchbooks, 1964).

[4]Merle Eppse, *The Negro, Too, in American History* (Nashville: National Publication Co., 1943).

[5]Recent Disciples histories have tended to integrate the African American contribution within the period and logical topic under discussion. Cf. Lester McAllister and William E. Tucker, *Journey in Faith* (St. Louis: CBP, 1989).

destroyed. It is a call to recognize the validity of the African heritage throughout history and give credit for the indispensable role Africans played in making America the powerful nation it became. While it is becoming more generally admitted that the material success of America north and south was made possible by slave labor,[6] we still have trouble admitting the practical, intellectual, social, and spiritual contributions of African Americans absorbed by the dominant culture.

All of the above is an attempt to say this article cannot rewrite history in the sense of changing publicly verifiable data. The third approach will be used to affirm the distinctive insights born of a unique heritage touched by the witness of the Disciples.[7] Within the designated geographical areas the development will be chronological.

A personal experience of the writer may clarify "the distinctive insights born of a unique heritage" as implied in the writing. As a seminary student many years ago, I wrote one of the fairly standard term papers most students write at one time or another, "A Socio-Religious Study of _____" and you fill in the name of the selected congregation. The selected congregation was a Freewill Baptist Church in New Haven, Connecticut. It was a small congregation, worshiping in a dilapidated building.

My method of investigation was participant observation. I shared in the rather spontaneous Sunday worship, dominated by the part-time pastor, a person short of stature with one stiff leg. His preaching style seemed to include at least 30 minutes of scolding the congregation and almost equal time devoted to the blessings and joy of obedience. There was no youth program other than a Sunday school class, and the women met occasionally to sponsor special money-raising projects. On the basis of what I observed I surmised that it was only a matter of time before the building collapsed, the congregation drifted away, or urban renewal required relocation. My paper received a grade of "A."

Almost ten years later, I returned to New Haven and often walked to churches near the Divinity School campus. When I arrived at one church that ten years before had housed a white congregation and saw two black girls entering, I noted to myself, "They have integrated." As I entered the sanctuary I saw wall-to-wall black people! A team of uniformed ushers were finding seats and doing other important things.

---

[6]Lester P. Scherer, *Slavery and the Churches in Early America, 1619-1819* (Grand Rapids: Eerdmans Publishing Co., 1975) 106-107.
[7]Caldwell and Fox, *Journey Toward Wholeness* is a creative use of this perspective.

A men's chorus and youth choir were in place. At about 11:00 A.M., onto the platform came, yes, that short minister with the stiff leg; this time with three or four assistants. To the sound of organ and piano music, a third choir was moving down the center aisle. Beautifully attired in peach-colored robes, they moved with syncopated rhythm as they sang to me, and perhaps the others present, "We've Come This Far by Faith, Leaning on the Lord." Many African American Disciples congregations sing a similar song, and that is the story that must be told.

Beginnings in Black and White: The Piedmont Region

The area of Virginia, North Carolina, and West Virginia has been referred to as the Piedmont Tri-State area for the organization of African American churches. This area was an early center for reformation- and restoration-minded church leaders. The conditions of a young and expanding nation created a climate of adventure that often meant abandoning old patterns and seeking new ways of meeting the necessities of life. Natural resources were bountiful but persistence and hard work were necessary to sustain the growth of the young nation. The dominant culture was transplanted from England, purged of what was regarded as negative elements.

In religious circles, this purge meant taking the English Protestant tradition and freeing it from the corruptions and restrictions of the past. A popular formula was to seek to restore New Testament Christianity and eliminate the creeds, structures and practices that tended to obscure the biblical model. Out of the Anglican Church emerged the Methodists, and by 1792, James O'Kelly led a movement that objected to the authority and life tenure of the superintendents of the Methodists. When the General Conference did not support his views, he led a secession that formed the Republican Methodists who adopted the name the Christian Church. By 1795 the Methodists reported "decreases of 4,673 among white and 1,644 among the colored" with the assumption that most of these were claimed by the O'Kelly Movement.[8]

Out of the Baptist tradition, another reform movement was taking shape. The spirit of freedom and independence, and a warm and

---

[8]W. E. Garrison and Alfred T. DeGroot, *The Disciples of Christ: A History* (St. Louis: CBP, 1945).

simple faith had gained momentum. One stream, the Freewill Baptists, became Arminian rather than Calvinist and championed a non-creedal, clearly autonomous expression of the church. The movement was strong in North Carolina and many of these congregations became Churches of Christ. Baptist and Methodist traditions had great impact upon African Americans in this area even before the Campbell-Stone Movement was established.

The element seldom recognized was the influence of traditional African religion or spirituality. There is no agreement relative to the amount of African culture transplanted to America. On the one hand, some scholars are convinced that little or nothing of African culture was preserved due to the conditions under which Africans were brought to this country. Captured and enslaved, there was no provision for perpetuating social, economic, political, or even family ties.

On the other hand, other scholars perceive Africanisms that were not only retained by Africans, but also had their impact on the dominant culture. These scholars embrace the wider realms of music, dance, medicine, language, folkways, oral tradition, and others. Religion provided the vehicle for passing on the essence of the African way of life, not simply duplication of forms.

> African style of worship, forms of ritual, systems of belief and fundamental perspectives have remained vital on this side of the Atlantic, not because they were preserved in a 'Pure' orthodoxy but because they were transformed. Adaptability, based upon respect for spiritual power wherever it originated, accounted for the openness of African religion to syncretism with other religious traditions and for the continuity of a distinctly African religious consciousness.[9]

All of the components mentioned above may be seen in the history of African American Disciples of Christ. Among the earliest Disciple congregations at Cane Ridge, Kentucky, and at Washington, Pennsylvania, there were black members before the Civil War.[10] Most of the blacks were slaves on hand to render whatever services were needed. Upon hearing the gospel they were permitted to become

---

[9]Albert J. Raboteau, *Slave Religion* (New York: Oxford University Press 1978) 4-5.

[10]Robert L. Jordon, *Two Races in One Fellowship* and William J. Barber, *Disciple Assemblies of Eastern North Carolina*; all accounts attest to the slave presence.

members of the church without any change in their status as slaves. Some of the gifted ones were ordained to preach.[11]

We have no records of the sermons by these first black preachers but they exhibited talent for exhortation and leadership. E. Franklin Frazier has suggested that the earliest black preachers may have continued a leadership tradition with roots in Africa. These preachers were the persons who kept alive hope for a better day. The African traditional religion belief in a most high God manifest in various forms in the universe and whose spirit may possess the believer was accommodated to the Christian teaching of a God of love and power. This God liberated Israel and has shown his love and power through prophets, priests, and his own son. Knowledge of this God was indeed good news to an oppressed people.

Evidently they were effective in communicating to other slaves as congregations developed in Kentucky, North Carolina, and beyond. A former slave named Alexander Campbell led a congregation at Midway, Kentucky, as early as 1834. There were churches that included free blacks as well as whites, Indians, and slaves. Among the Black Disciples in Eastern North Carolina, the oldest church on the northeast side of the Tar River (known as the Mother Church in the Washington-Norfolk District) is the Uniontown Church.[12] William Barber has noted that traditional accounts indicate this church was at first a Freewill Baptist Church but became Disciple before the Civil War. Churches developed in free states also, occasionally with integrated congregations.[13]

The churches became the focal points for improving the condition of the African Americans with evangelism and education their major strategy. Denominations established before the Disciples had pioneered in this role. Anglicans, Congregationalists, Presbyterians, Baptists, and Methodists were the most prominent Churches, became the first schools, and the Bible was the first textbook. Here was laid the foundation for a new orientation to the world so greatly different for the African American.

This story is customarily told in terms of what whites did for blacks who passively received according to standard history. Black history informs us that many Africans were rebelling at every point. They were not all anxious to adapt a version of Christianity that

---

[11]Hap Lyda, "Black Disciples in the 19th Century," in *The Untold Story*," ed. William K. Fox (St. Louis: CBP, 1976) 9.

[12]Barber, *Disciples Assemblies in Eastern North Carolina*, 2.

[13]Lyda, "Black Disciples," 9.

served to reinforce slavery. In many instances, the "Invisible Institution" was alive and well. Slaves took the Christian teachings and fused them with their African heritage and gave expression to their spirituality in their own way. In the cabins late at night, in the woods and fields away from the masters, they expressed themselves in song and dance, prayer and exhortation.

More specifically, after emancipation, struggling black congregations often launched efforts to organize schools and were joined by white Disciples. Schools were thought to be the best answer to the question of what to do with the Negro. Increasingly, there was awareness that the Negro should be a party to answering the question.

A Board of Education and Evangelism was established to coordinate the program. An example of local Black Church initiative and cooperative response was the Piedmont Christian Institute. A report in a comprehensive study of Disciple service institutions gives the following:

> The Piedmont Christian Institute had its inception in the minds of a group of Negro Disciples in the Piedmont section of Virginia and North Carolina. They were eager to provide educational advantages for their children and youth, and especially that these advantages should be afforded under the influence and in the atmosphere of their own religious communion.[14]

The small one-room building of the Fayette Street Christian Church, a Negro congregation in Martinsville, Virginia, was the place of beginning in 1900. The person called to head the school was James H. Thomas who was born in 1877.[15] His father had been a slave, and after emancipation mastered the art of brick masonry. The father and mother were charter members of the Church of Christ in Chatham, Virginia. Consequently, James felt born into that communion! His parents were strongly committed to seeing that he received every opportunity for an education. He attended State College at Petersburg and taught at Chatham before accepting the position at Martinsville. His ties with the church remained strong. The founder and pastor at Fayette Street, Elder R. A. Spencer, encouraged him to enter the

---

[14]*Survey of Service* (St. Louis: CBP, 1928).

[15]James H. Thomas, *Those Recurring Memories*, unpublished autobiography (United Christian Missionary Society), selected materials.

ministry. Eventually, he did, and this helped supplement his small salary at the school.

The history of the school is one of heroic efforts by Thomas and the churches with some assistance from the Christian Women's Board of Missions. They acquired property, built facilities, and served many students more than thirty years before the economic depression forced them to close in 1932.[16]

This account illustrates the great commitment of Black Disciples to faith and learning. The church provided the vision, rallying point, and resources. Education, in turn, would empower its students with knowledge for the uplift of the race and witness of the church to black and white. The realistic, hard-working, holistic approach gained tangible results far beyond the relatively brief period the school existed.

From this general region may be drawn another example of faith and learning in action. Among the colored Disciples of Christ, as they were described in the early history of the movement, there was a hunger and thirst for knowledge and the betterment of the Negro race and the 'Brotherhood.' So in the 40th session of the Colored Disciples of Christ in Eastern North Carolina which convened at Broad Creek, North Carolina with Elder I. Darken, chief, presiding, a report was received from the newly appointed School Work Committee.[17]

The essence of the report was the election of E. S. L. Whitfield as president of their school work and granting him power "to lay such plans as he thought wise for the success of the work."[18]

In recognition of Whitfield's scholarship, business principles, energy, forethought, and determination, he was granted all the powers regularly possessed by the president of the recognized colleges of the state. The action is not to ask permission or guidance or funds (at this point). Their confidence was in themselves as servants of God's people.

With great energy, Whitfield began his work as the assembly purchased land north of Goldsboro, with the intention of developing a

---

[16]John C. Long, "The Disciples of Christ and Negro Education" (Ph.D. diss., University of Southern California, 1960) 191.

[17]J. O. Williams, "Goldsboro Christian Institute," unpublished manuscript, 1.

[18]Ibid.

training center for both clergy and laity. After completion of a two-story seventeen-room building, the Goldsboro Christian Institute (G.C.I.) formally opened in 1911. Whitfield reflects much of the history of initiative and achievement on the part of black Disciples in the area. He was one of a family that gave several persons to the ministry. They stand beside many others who sought to use their education and commitment to reach many others in need.[19] In all fairness, the story of G.C.I. reflects the challenges and opportunities, strengths and weaknesses, achievements and failures of cooperative enterprises. Over the years, many types of programs drawing upon varied resources have been tried. The challenge remains.[20]

Kentucky and Tennessee

The witness of Disciples among Negroes in Kentucky embraces all the stages and patterns that would be duplicated elsewhere. Not only were there African American converts at Cane Ridge as noted earlier—Alexander Campbell, Samuel Buckner, and Charles Spencer—but other congregations listed African American members before the Civil War.[21] The slave members of white congregations became the core groups of independent black congregations. After the formation of the Midway Congregation congregations were developed at East Second Street in Lexington, Hancock Hill at Louisville, and Little Rock in Bourbon County organized by Samuel Buckner. After the Civil War, nearly 70 more were organized before 1900. During this time a state organization of Negro churches came into being in 1872-73.[22] At the point of statewide cooperation, the passion of the black churches for tangible enhancement of faith and learning is made clear. In 1865, the convention hired an evangelist, W. P. Richards, and voiced its interest in education of men for ministry. This interest gave rise to the establishment of a Bible School in the Hancock Street

---

[19]Barber, *Disciples Assemblies*, following page 244.
[20]Williams, "Goldsboro Education Institute,"17.
[21]Claude Walker, "Negro Disciples in Kentucky" (B.D. thesis, College of the Bible, 1969) 8.
[22]Ibid., 14.

Church in Louisville,[23] where there were twenty-five student preachers in 1875. An earlier school at Louisville had operated about four years. John Long has gathered data suggesting there was a P. H. Marse who headed the school rather than the more widely known P. H. Moss.[24]

A number of schools were started that lasted for brief periods: Christian Bible College, Louisville Bible School, Central Christian Institute. Some of the most prominent leaders of black Disciples were involved as leaders or students with these schools, including Preston Taylor, Thomas B. Frost, and Jason Cowan.[25] Preston Taylor was hired as a National Evangelist about 1900 by the American Christian Missionary Society. He was given the responsibility of organizing churches and raising funds for the establishment of Louisville Bible School.[26]

The Preston Taylor story truly belongs to the whole church but may be appropriately introduced here. Born in slavery in Shreveport, Louisiana, in 1849, his life story reflects the dramatic changes of the period. Taylor resolved to become a minister after hearing a sermon by Samuel Buckner in Lexington, Kentucky.[27] Taylor became an outstanding example of the multi-vocational black Disciple minister. He was a stone cutter, railroad work contractor, manager of a funeral home, cemetery, and recreational park in addition to becoming minister of High Street Christian Church in Mt. Sterling, Kentucky.

Every aspect of the work among black Disciples received attention from Preston Taylor. He served as a local pastor, state and national evangelist, fund raiser for churches and schools, founder and guiding spirit of the National Christian Missionary Convention. A major emphasis at the founding of the convention was to help bring into existence a college-level institution for the training of black church leaders. His impact is most pronounced in Tennessee and Kentucky.

A final microcosm of the total witness was the development in Tennessee. The white congregation at Nashville had the largest number of African American members prior to the Civil War and organized two Sunday Schools for them as early as 1849. Ten years

---

[23]Ibid., 6.

[24]Long, "Disciples of Christ and Negro Education," 137.

[25]Ibid.

[26]James Blair, "The National Convention Facing Integration" (B.D. thesis, Butler University, 1958).

[27]James Blair, "Preston Taylor: A Doer of the Word" in *The Untold Story*, ed. William K. Fox (St. Louis: CBP, 1976) 30-34.

later, one was constituted a church and led by a free Negro, Peter Lowery. The independent congregation was called the Grapevine Church, which some scholars have labeled the first independent Negro congregation in the South.[28] After emancipation, several congregations were organized. From these congregations came representatives to form the American Evangelical and Education Association in 1867.[29] An annual Missionary Convention was organized in 1880. Tennessee also claims one of the early, though short-lived, schools for Negroes. John Long asserts that the School known as Central Christian Institute opened first as Warner Christian Institute in 1908. When Disciples began negotiating for the purchase, "a committee from the Negro churches had raised the first payment of $400.00."[30]

Christian and industrial training was the dominant educational model of the age for equipping African Americans for a better life. The school was relocated at Shelbyville and known as Tennessee Christian Institute. The World War aborted the plan for opening the school. Eventually the property was sold and the proceeds spent on work among Negro churches.

New Challenges in the South:
Alabama to Texas

From the end of the Civil War to the present is a period of dramatic change in the history of the United States. During this period the churches have been challenged to radically transform their programs to keep abreast of changes in the social, economic, educational, and political spheres. The scope and intensity of change for African Americans has few parallels in modern history. Faith and learning appear to be the only guidelines, the only principles on which the African Americans find agreement within and support beyond their immediate community. At this stage of the history, we now discover that the words of Benjamin E. Mays still ring true. The Negro church, in harmony with the larger church in doctrine and structure, emerges as a sociological necessity.[31] Faith and learning

---

[28]Herman A. Norton, *Tennessee Christians* (Nashville: Reed and Co., 1971) 129.
[29]Ibid., 134-35.
[30]Long, "Disciples of Christ and Negro Education," 195.
[31]Benjamin E. Mays and J. W. Nicholson, *The Negro's Church* (n.p.: Institute of

must be regularly appraised from the African American perspective for the most effective strategies to serve the present age. The new challenges in the South were, of course, the rapid changes following the Civil War. It is important to clarify how these changes affected the lives of African Americans. The end of the war and adoption of the 13th, 14th, and 15th constitutional amendments (abolishing slavery, establishing citizenship, and [male] voting rights) are at the heart of the changes.[32] For the implementation of these changes, federal agents and troops were dispersed throughout the South for a period of about twelve years, the Era of Reconstruction. Among the changes were the following:

1. Blacks began to work for pay, however minimal and irregular it might be.
2. The acquisition of land on their own terms became a possibility for more African Americans.
3. African Americans were free to travel at the time and place of their choosing.
4. Families could reunite without the fear of being sold apart at the convenience of a slave master.
5. Participation in the political process was protected as state constitutions were rewritten and state and national leaders were chosen.[33]

While these changes may not sound extraordinary to us today, they were radical changes to the social, economic, political, and religious order of the South with implications for the North as well. Working for pay meant some control over one's labor, time, energy, and what goals one might set. Freedom to acquire property began to put former house servants (overwhelmingly mulatto) and former field hands on level footing. The former were often given property by their slave master fathers, while the latter were denied ownership of land.

Social and Religious Research, 1933) was the earliest comprehensive study of the black church using social science methodology. The most recent and comprehensive is C. Eric Lincoln and Lawrence H. Mamiya, *The Black Church in the African American Experience* (Durham: Duke University Press, 1990).

[32]Benjamin Quarles, *The Negro in the Making of America*, 3d ed. (New York: Collier Macmillan, 1987) 109-155.

[33]Ibid., 132.

Freedom to travel opened the door to major population shifts: from the plantations and rural areas to the growing population centers, from the South to the North and West, from former slave territory to the open frontier. Black males could assume responsibility for their families as they worked to provide food, clothing, and shelter, perhaps to restore the patterns of apprenticeship so much a part of maturation within African society. Participation in the political process resulted in the election of two black senators—Hiram Revels and Blanch K. Bruce—and 20 congressmen from eight southern states.[34]

This period of change came to a dramatic halt when white males cut deals for their best interest at the expense of the freedom of the African American. In order to resolve a contested presidential election and avoid the uncertainty of a congressional resolution, northerners (Republicans) agreed to withdraw the federal troops from the South in return for the southerners' agreement to allow the Republican candidate, Rutherford B. Hayes, to assume the presidency uncontested. This Compromise of 1877 set the stage for the rise of white supremacy in the South. Through intimidation and violence, economic pressure, and political maneuverings, African Americans were essentially disenfranchised and the rigid patterns of segregation were put in place.

Now just in case there is the impression that this is a mere recital of irrelevant, distant history, I share with you this personal note. I never knew my paternal grandfather, because he was shot to death around 1915 as he returned in a wagon from paying his poll taxes. My father was only 21 at the time. Although it was generally known that the perpetrators were white men, no formal charges were brought against anyone. My maternal grandfather, clearly a mulatto from the one photograph I have seen, never formally knew his father, although he recalled having seen his mother beaten on many occasions by her slave master.[35]

This is the context within which African Americans had to make sense of the fellowship of the church, empowerment of the Holy Spirit, the justice of God, theodicy, and eschatology. From this background, my father, older brother, five uncles, and myself have

---

[34]Ibid., 135.
[35]Personal reflections of my mother, Ophelia Henry (age 95), Summer 1993.

given collectively more than 350 years to the ministry of the Christian Church.[36]

Let us sharpen the focus on the challenge of these conditions to the church and what response was made by the churches. The most obvious and significant response was the evangelism of black and white northern churches in the South. Frazier suggests the institutionalized churches of the North joined ranks with the invisible institution alive and well among blacks in the South. The only leader permitted among the slaves—the slave preacher—and the only semblance of an organization—the church—could now surface and receive a little help from the North.

Church membership statistics are impressive. All of the predominantly black denominations greatly increased their memberships immediately after the Civil War. Among Disciples of Christ, the number of independent black churches dramatically increased due to separation of blacks from white congregations as well as the formation of new congregations. A summary statement from Hap Lyda in *The Untold Story* gives the picture clearly:

In 1861 there were known black churches in the states of Kentucky, Ohio, North Carolina, Georgia, and Tennessee. By the end of 1876 congregations were organized in the additional states of Indiana, Texas, Virginia, Mississippi, South Carolina, Michigan, Alabama, Kansas, Missouri and Louisiana.

During the era of 1861-1876 there were marked gains in the numbers of black churches and members; from churches in five states to churches in 15 states; from about 7,000 to approximately 20,000 members.[37]

Robert L. Jordan has preserved an impressive list of the pioneer preachers evangelists of this era. Among them are outstanding women as well as men.[38]

The churches offered a model for the reconstruction of the black family. The patriarchal society of the Old Testament came close to the conditioning received in America with all the promises of rewards for obedience and punishment for disobedience intact. The New Testament community of sharing and caring inspired not only the

---

[36]A plaque noting these facts was awarded the Henry family by the National Convocation of the Christian Church.

[37]Lyda, "Black Disciples," 14-15.

[38]R. L. Jordan, *Two Races in One Fellowship* (Detroit: United Christian Church, 1944) 35-42.

church and families but also the fraternal orders, insurance, and burial associations.

Although the churches held sway in the rural areas, they were slow to adjust to the urban migration.[39] This situation claimed the attention of leaders for many years to come. The height of this concern was eventually expressed in a study, *Design for Renewal and Growth*.[40] It was noted that in the 15 cities showing black population growth of over 58 percent between 1940 and 1960, black Disciples claimed less than one-half of 1 percent of the total. New lifestyles and the lack of community structure left the churches out of touch with thousands who clustered around the places of work. Other community services were equally slow: schools, medical services, recreational facilities all experienced overload.

The basic discomfort of the black Disciples lay in the fact that the church seemed to have no effective comprehensive church-wide strategy. R. H. Peoples reported in a study, "Historical Development of Negro Work and its Relation to Organized Brotherhood Life":

Between 1860 and 1880 much work was done in Negro churches by individuals, both Negro and white. Many of the white leaders made repeated requests each year in the General Convention for the American Missionary Society to do something for the Negro work. Each year for a number of years the Convention appointed a committee to study this problem and bring in recommendations. This was done many, many times but that was as far as the action went until 1890 when the Board of Negro Education and Evangelism was set up. In the meantime, some individuals were stimulated to do something for the freedmen because of some of these recommendations, all of which emphasized education and evangelization as the only way to help the Negro.[41]

Coordination at the national level moved slowly with limited attention from the American Christian Missionary Society until C. C. Smith was elected as secretary for the Board of Education and Evangelization. Raising money for the Negro churches and educational institutions was his major responsibility. The key role of Southern Christian Institute is discussed below.

---

[39]Franklin Frazier, *The Negro Church in America* (New York: Schocken Books, 1974) 54-57.

[40]Paul A. Sims, "Church Development," in *Design for Renewal and Growth* (Indianapolis: National Christian Missionary Convention, 1966), 26.

[41]Robert H. Peoples, "Historical Development of Negro Work and Its Relation to Organized Brotherhood Life," unpublished, n.d.

The next shift in the national strategy was for the Negro work to be lodged with the Christian Woman's Board of Mission (CWBM). While many were convinced that the church manifested a rather cavalier attitude toward the work among Negroes,[42] C. C. Smith felt this was a constructive move. Peoples affirmed C. C. Smith's analysis of the need.

For development of the Negro church:we need: first, an educated ministry, and the church needs to be taught to appreciate and support such a ministry. Second, they need a well trained general evangelist who would be in touch and sympathy with his people and yet by his training would be able to organize and give the work unity and cohesion. Third, they need a competent woman who can organize and lead the women in each state.[43]

C. C. Smith was succeeded by J. B. Lehman which brought together the interest of our oldest education venture for African Americans— the Southern Christian Institute—of which Lehman was president, and the structured direction of the CWBM. In response to the growing unrest concerning lack of participation in decisions regarding black people, two black national staff persons were named: Rosa B. Bracey to work with women's organizations and P. H. Moss as church school and young people's worker. State and regional structures were developing among the African American churches. Before the end of the nineteenth-century there were state or regional conventions or assemblies in North Carolina, South Carolina, Kentucky, Alabama, Texas, Virginia (in the Piedmont Tri-State Convention), and Mississippi. With the twentieth-century came expansion along the east coast of the Assembly Churches into the northeast.

The stage is set for a national voice of the black churches. The most concrete, though not the only, expression of this concern was the development of the National Christian Missionary Convention. Both "pushing" and "pulling" forces were at work in the formation of the Convention.

From the address delivered by Preston Taylor, the most prominent leader in the organization, and the views expressed by many at the historic meeting on August 5-9, 1917 in Nashville, Tennessee, these pushing and pulling forces may be characterized in the following way:

---

[42]Caldwell and Fox, *Journey Toward Wholeness*, 13-14.
[43]Peoples, "Historical Development."

1. Black Disciples were pushed in the direction of forming the convention by a general attitude of many Whites that the Negro was a ward, pet, or second-class human being, not a full equal partner in the family of Disciples.
2. The question of race was addressed in moving speeches at the General Convention occasionally, but little application was made to how Blacks were treated in terms of accommodations at the meetings, or even as they traveled in the interest of the church program.
3. A lack of communication and misunderstanding of how Blacks were served by the agencies of the church was another pushing force.

The formation of the convention was not just a negative reaction, but also an affirmation of basic beliefs that may be regarded as pulling forces.

1. Black Disciples were seeking a mechanism for discussion and decision-making about their own needs. Nurturing the faith, strengthening the witness among Black Americans needed the regular and systematic input of Black Disciples.
2. Recognizing immediately their need for prepared leadership, they affirmed a desire for a school of higher education, particularly for ministerial training. Preston Taylor charged that there was no first-rate, four-year college for Negroes in 1917. As recently as 1940, *The Christian Plea* reported that while there were twenty-one Disciples related colleges for Whites to study for the ministry, only Drake, Eureka, and Butler would accept Negroes. Chapman was later added to this list.
3. The need for a medium of communication was identified for continued nurture of Black church life.[44]

Many of the challenges of the period are clearly focused in the complementary emphasis on education. A few examples from the period must serve our purpose.

About thirty-five miles southwest of Montgomery, Alabama in Lowndes County, Robert D. Brooks opened a school in a miserable

---

[44]Henry, "Unknown Prophets," 6.

shanty on October 15, 1894. The community was called Lum and C. C. Smith referred to it as one of the blackest parts of the Black Belt.[45] No public schools were in existence for more than 1000 Negroes in the area. From this community, Robert D. Brooks and J. E. Bowie had attended Southern Christian Institute (SCI) and returned with the determination to establish a school. H. J. Brayboy, who had attended the Louisville Bible School, was a landowner who returned to Lum to lead the movement for a school. They sought to generate support from whites and blacks. A white woman donated five acres of land and the blacks raised funds among themselves to start the school. They began work in a little old church, hanging cloth to divide it into classrooms. They started with three teachers and a lot of determination. Mr. Brayboy mortgaged his property to buy lumber to build a school.

C. C. Smith visited on several occasions and shared the story of the struggling school. Long cites his statement in *Missionary Tidings*:

Negroes in Alabama have put up a school building which will be large enough for their school for years to come, ... it is not ceiled [*sic*] on the outside, hence, quite incomplete. They have insufficient stoves and their blackboards are not worthy of the name and they have no maps or other school furniture. In this building they have a fine school of 110 pupils.[46]

Eventually, the school included 70 acres and several buildings, including a church, dormitory, classroom building, and various shops. Support and actual labor on the buildings came primarily from the black churches of the area. C. C. Smith praised them for their sacrificial giving for the uplift of their people. The campus became the meeting place for the state convention of Negro churches. The convention voted to change the name from the Lum Grade School to the Alabama Christian Institute.[47]

As the county school system improved and the cost of operation increased, United Christian Missionary Society (UCMS) officials decided to discontinue support and decided to close the school in 1924. Still, the larger question remains in regards to criteria for

[45]Long, "Disciples of Christ and Negro Education," 167.
[46]Ibid., 171.
[47]Ibid., 177.

decisions and policy that relate to the service of institutions and lives of persons.

Southern Christian Institute

Southern Christian Institute (SCI) may be regarded as the prototype of Disciples efforts to serve the educational needs of the black constituency of the church. In an age when the Booker T. Washington philosophy of education for the Negro received such overwhelming support from blacks and whites, North and South, it is not surprising that many supporters would visualize SCI as "Our Tuskegee."

The school had many spurts of life with the American Christian Missionary Society taking the initiative in 1874. Randall and Letitia Faurot were called into service, but all of the support system was not in place.[48] R. L. Jordan reports that a Negro, A. I. Williams, made a second attempt to continue SCI after the school closed the first time.[49]

The coming of J. B. Lehman in 1890 provided stability and direction for the program. He was able to deal effectively with southern whites as well as blacks. Beginning at grade school level, SCI upgraded its program until it reached junior college level under the administration of John Long. Lehman conducted workers' conferences for the training of black church leadership. He seemed convinced that this was the appropriate and adequate level of training for black church ministry. When he succeeded C. C. Smith as secretary of the Board of Education and Evangelism, he wielded great influence in the development of black schools and black church life.

This was an age of segregation as underscored by the Supreme Court decision, Plessey vs. Ferguson. SCI for years provided separate dining and living areas for all its white faculty and all black students and other workers.[50] This policy was eliminated during the administration of John Long who succeeded John Lehman. Many traditional customs were defied as SCI tried to develop a more relevant, quality curriculum. The faculty became almost evenly divided, black and white. Curriculum innovations included a traveling

---

[48]Caldwell and Fox, *Journey Toward Wholeness*, 13-14.
[49]Jordan, *Two Races in One Fellowship*.
[50]Long, "Disciples of Christ and Negro Education," 122.

library, health workshops, and other programs taken into the community. By 1949, the enrollment reached 597.[51]

Once again, as the public education system improved, the need for SCI seemed less urgent. There was some opposition to the school among accrediting association personnel as SCI continued to advocate a more racially inclusive program. The dual issues of cost and changing times led the UCMS to propose closing SCI and joining forces with Tougaloo College in Mississippi in 1953.

No other school had educated as many black church leaders as SCI. Many who continued their education at senior colleges and graduate schools received their early education at SCI. The list would include such notables as Cleo Blackburn, W. K. Fox, P. H. Moss, S. S. Myers, and many others.

Northeast Texas Christian Theological and Industrial College

Near Palestine, Texas, there is a historic marker noting the site where the Northeast Texas Theological and industrial College once stood. In November 1900, the Northeast Christian Missionary Convention, located in Dangerfield, Texas, with A. J. Hurdle as president, took action toward the goal of a college. This action was supported by the Christian College Building Association, organized by a group of dedicated women. Over $10,000 was accumulated to begin the college.

In 1904, forty-nine acres were purchased. In 1910, a contract was let by H. D. Dartie and others to J. L. Randolph, contractor. On May 26, 1911, the cornerstone was placed and on January 2, 1912 the school opened with D. T. Cleaver as president and about eight faculty and staff. One of the college's first students was Ophelia Henry (she is my mother, age ninety-six, and still lives in Palestine, Texas). A fire destroyed the main building in 1920, and the school was never rebuilt.

Jarvis Christian College

The only institution to achieve fully accredited senior college status is Jarvis College at Hawkins, Texas. Its pattern of growth is perhaps more clearly reflected in the outstanding black leaders who have guided the institution throughout its existence.

---

[51]Ibid.

Black Disciples of East Texas were determined to have a school and began a fund toward that end before the idea was taken seriously by white Disciples. Colby Hall quotes Mrs. Mary Alphin, the organizer of the Negro Women's Work in these terms:

> Among the Negro churches of Texas there had been for years a silently growing fund for a Negro college. This came mostly from small country churches, there being few city churches .... When it came to the attention of some white friends in Texas, it was between four hundred and five hundred dollars ... a large sum to have been secured noiselessly and without effort.[52]

Much of the pioneering spirit and determination noted earlier comes to full expression in the story of Jarvis College. The Jarvis Bulletin for 1929-30 offered the following description of the school:

> Jarvis Christian College was founded in 1912 under the leadership of the Christian Women's Board of Missions of the Christian Church. The institution was made possible by Mayor and Mrs. J. J. Jarvis of Ft. Worth, Texas who gave the tract of land and designated that it be used specifically for Negro education. The college, by the action and repeated expression of its founders and benefactors, is independent of ecclesiastical control, but under special auspices and fostering care of the Disciples of Christ a democratic religious communion.[53]

Onto the scene at Hawkins came persons who had already demonstrated their capacity to build. Professor T. B. Frost began the initial clearing of the land, fencing the property and producing crops. He was joined by C. A. Berry, a SCI graduate, who helped build the first dormitory which contained classrooms, dining facilities, and living quarters. All of this was accomplished in about the span of a year and an opening date of January 1913 was announced. Professors Frost and Berry began with 14 pupils and had 34 by the next June.

J. N. Ervin was called as the first president of the Institute. He was born May 6, 1873 in Johnson City, Tennessee. His formal education was received at Knoxville College, Columbia University, and Leland

---

[52]Colby D. Hall, *Texas Disciples* (Fort Worth: T.C.U. Press, 1953) 332.

[53]*Bulletin*, Junior College, High and Elementary Schools of Jarvis Christian College (Hawkins, Texas: 1929-1930) 3.

Stanford University. He was a high school principal prior to coming to Jarvis.

Ervin initiated a philosophy at Jarvis of training the head, heart, and hand. Students could work for a year to pay their school expenses. There developed a family atmosphere with faculty, administration, and students in elementary through high school work.[54] There was a close working relationship between Jarvis and SCI. With Jarvis's accredited status, it had to require SCI students to receive additional training before they were qualified to teach at Jarvis. Under Ervin's leadership, the junior college program was added and the way cleared for a senior college in 1937 before his death in 1938.

Ervin was succeeded by Peter C. Washington in 1938. Born in Alabama, Washington was a graduate of SCI. He was also a graduate of Eureka College and University of Illinois. He held pastorates in St. Louis while serving as a high school principal before coming to Jarvis; he served from 1938 to 1949.

During Washington's tenure, the college received state senior college recognition. Substantial improvements to the physical plant were made possible by discovery of oil on the property. The pressure to receive Southern Association accreditation also marked the period of growth. Jarvis grew in stature with the churches as the number of alumni serving at all levels of the church increased.[55]

Washington was succeeded by Dr. John Eubanks. "Vigorous and forward-looking administration characterize the third college president." A native of Baton Rouge, Louisiana, his formal education includes the B.Th. and A.B. from Howard University, the M.A. and Ph.D. from the University of Chicago, specializing in history of cultures. He was head of the Division of Social Science at Morris Brown College before becoming president of Jarvis.[56] His vigorous academic leadership resulted in the accreditation of the college by the Southern Association in 1950. At the time, this was the only accreditation available to Negro institutions.

Dr. Cleo W. Blackburn brought to the presidency of Jarvis the vision of a broader educational enterprise identified as Fundamental Education. With a major concern for addressing the problems of the poor, it is a comprehensive approach to the use of human and material resources to improve the quality of life. Dr. Blackburn was

---

[54]"Charles C. Mosley, Sr.," James Nelson Ervin," Archives, Jarvis Christian College.

[55]"Peter C. Washington," Archives, Jarvis Christian College.

[56]"John B. Eubanks," Archives, Jarvis Christian College.

born in Port Gibson, Mississippi and was educated at Butler and Fisk Universities. He had served as director of research at Tuskegee and director of Flanner House in Indianapolis before becoming president. The Board of Fundamental Education was the only such board founded by an African American to receive a federal charter. A truly modern campus building program was begun during the Blackburn administration.[57]

Space does not permit completing the profiles of presidential leadership to the present, but it is clear that this latest educational institution has made the transition from mission status to independent church-related institution. It has continued the preparation of leaders for church and society. The number of graduates continuing graduate and professional schools grows each year, and the curriculum is updated.

There have been notable achievements during the successive administrations of Dr. J. O. Perpener, Dr. John Paul Jones, Dr. E. W. Rand, Dr. Charles A. Berry, Dr. Julius Nemmons, and currently, Dr. Sabetha Jenkins, the first woman to become president. A new chapter is needed for the full account through the dramatic changes of the 1970s through the 1990s.

Conclusions

Examples could be multiplied of the churches, pioneer preachers/ teachers, missionaries and other leaders. The picture drawn suggests the following:

1. Disciples witness is strengthened by recognition of the rich diversity of our roots. We spring not from Scotch, Irish, and European alone, but African American also.
2. The most profound testing of the inclusive, New Testament, egalitarian posture of our pioneers has come with the need to deal with the African American.
3. African Americans have taken initiative and used their meager resources to begin churches, schools, and programs. They have not been merely passive recipients of the resources of white people.

---

[57]"Cleo W. Blackburn," *Indianapolis Star*, 7 June 1978; Progress Report on the Board for Fundamental Education, 1965.

4. Black spirituality has been a positive, creative force within the church though subject to misunderstanding and abuse.
5. African Americans could never afford to ignore the significant theme of God's liberating and sustaining love for all God's people.

We have come into a period of renewed awareness of the African American cultural heritage. High technology, global economics, the capacity to annihilate humankind through nuclear war, and the massive problems of hunger, disease, and poverty are undeniable realities of our age. Are education and evangelization still appropriate emphases for Disciples witness among African Americans? Narrowly conceived, no! Attuned to a culturally pluralistic society, hungering for guiding principles, personal fulfillment, and ultimate purpose, we may do well to revisit what the principles have taught us about abundant life.

Reformed Roots of Disciples Worship

Richard L. Harrison, Jr.

In the common memory of the Christian Church (Disciples of Christ), there has been an assumption that the founders of the church not only left their former Reformed—specifically Presbyterian— heritage behind, but that they created a new, or restored, expression of the Christian faith based on the New Testament. This included a new way to worship—forms of worship adapted and adopted from Scripture, not "human tradition."

In recent years, historians have shown that many of the theological and ecclesiastical forms of the early Disciples were, in fact, only modifications of Presbyterian traditions. This is as true of the understanding of worship and the liturgical structure of worship as it is true of theology and polity.[1]

This is not to deny that there were changes, significant changes, in worship from the beginning. It is, rather, to argue that the basic outline of worship changed little from late eighteenth-century and early nineteenth-century Presbyterian worship. In fact, it can be argued that liturgy in Disciples churches changed only modestly from the early nineteenth century until the middle of the twentieth century. Even now, at the end of the twentieth century, many small, rural churches follow a worship pattern that is remarkably similar to that of Presbyterian churches in the 1820s.

---

[1]James O. Duke, "The Disciples and the Lord's Supper: A Historical Perspective," *Encounter* 50, 1 (Winter 1989): 1-28; James O. Duke and Richard L. Harrison, Jr., *The Lord's Supper* (St. Louis: Christian Board of Publication, published for the Council on Christian Unity, 1993); Richard L. Harrison, Jr., "Early Disciples Sacramental Theology: Catholic, Reformed, and Free," in *Classic Themes of Disciples Theology: Rethinking the Traditional Affirmations of the Christian Church (Disciples of Christ)*, ed. Kenneth Lawrence (Fort Worth: Texas Christian University Press, 1986) 49-100; Richard L. Harrison, Jr., "Nailed to the Church Door: How Protestant was Alexander Campbell's Reform?," in *Lectures in Honor of the Alexander Campbell Bicentennial, 1788-1988*, ed. James M. Seale (Nashville: Disciples of Christ Historical Society, 1988) 47-63; Mark G. Toulouse, *Joined in Discipleship: The Maturing of an American Religious Movement* (St. Louis: Chalice Press, 1992) 108; Clark M. Williamson, "The Lord's Supper: A Systematic Theological View," *Encounter* 50,1 (Winter 1989): 47-67.

Presbyterian worship forms underwent a major change in the second half of the nineteenth century and the early twentieth century. These were shaped largely by the work of the Mercersburg theologians, particularly John Williamson Nevin, and the impact of the Anglican Oxford movement on much of mainline Protestant liturgy.[2]

The founders of the Disciples came primarily out of the Presbyterian tradition, both the main Presbyterian body and the Seceder Presbyterians represented in the United States by the Associate Reformed Synod. The second major tradition formative of the early Disciples was Baptist—a congregationalist, free church form of the Reformed tradition, with roots in English Calvinism.

The major first step in the development of the Disciples occurred around and through the leadership of Barton Warren Stone. Stone was the minister of the Concord and Cane Ridge Presbyterian Churches in Bourbon and Nicholas Counties, Kentucky. He was the host pastor of the famous Cane Ridge Revival in August 1801. Stone was clearly a part of the pro-revival, New Light Presbyterians.[3]

After two years of revival fever sweeping across the Bluegrass of Kentucky, some of the Presbyterian leaders were concerned about the dilution of theological orthodoxy, and the emphasis on experiential, highly emotional religious activities that characterized much revival worship. When charges were brought against a group of New Light Presbyterians by some clergy in the Transylvania Presbytery, Stone and four other ministers resigned from the Presbytery and established the Springfield Presbytery in the fall of 1803. The next few months were charged with religious controversy. Then, on June 28, during a meeting of the Springfield Presbytery at Cane Ridge, Stone and his colleagues dissolved their presbytery, and proclaimed their wish to "sink into union with the Body of Christ at large." They prepared a highly satirical document, "The Last Will and Testament of the Springfield Presbytery," which expressed some of their concerns and defended their decision to be called "Christians only."[4] This, along with a supporting piece called the "Apology for the Last Will and

---

[2]Julius Melton, *Presbyterian Worship in America: Changing Patterns Since 1787* (Richmond: John Knox Press, 1967) 59-118.

[3]See D. Newell Williams, "The Theology of the Great Revival in the West as Seen Through the Life and Thought of Barton Warren Stone," (Ph.D. diss., Vanderbilt University, 1979).

[4]"Last Will and Testament of the Springfield Presbytery," in Lester G. McAllister and William E. Tucker, *Journey in Faith: A History of the Christian Church (Disciples of Christ)* (St. Louis: Bethany Press, 1975) 77-79.

Testament," stated their intention to leave the Presbyterian church and create a church based as closely as possible on the simple teachings of the New Testament. Over the next few years, of the five original signers of the "Last Will and Testament," only Stone remained with the new Christian Churches.[5]

Soon after the separation of the Christians from the Presbyterians, representatives from the Shakers, "The United Society of Believers in Christ's Second Appearing," a highly revivalistic, communal church, moved into the revival fields of Kentucky. Many of those whose spiritual lives had found new birth in the fires of the emotional revival services found encouragement and support from the Shakers. Two of the signers of the "Last Will and Testament" joined the Shakers.[6]

Barton Stone at first responded positively to the message of the Shakers. He was moved by their fervor and sincerity. When the only recently married Stone learned of their teachings about celibacy for all members, Stone moved away from the Shakers, and began to denounce their movement. He never again supported what he later called the "fanaticism" of the revivals, though he did support the legitimacy of revivals that were warm, so long as they did not boil over emotionally. He believed that the conditions of the people and the times required strong, experiential religion, but his dealings with the Shakers left him fearful of extremism.

Unfortunately, very little is known about the worship practices of the Christians prior to their union with the Disciples in the 1830s. It is clear that some Reformed elements continued. Specifically, there was a conflict between the Christians and the Disciples over the issue of presidency at the Lord's Supper. Stone's Christians followed the Reformed practice of requiring an ordained minister to lead the communion service.[7]

The Disciples side of the Christian Church (Disciples of Christ) came from the leadership of Thomas Campbell and his son, Alexander. The Campbells were immigrants from Ulster, the heavily Scots-Irish region of Northern Ireland. Thomas Campbell had been raised Church of Ireland (Anglican) but as a young man he joined the church of some friends, a church that became known as the Old Light,

---

[5]"Apology of the Springfield Presbytery," in Barton Warren Stone, *The Biography of Eld. Barton Warren Stone, Written by Himself: With Additions and Reflections. By Elder John Rogers* (Cincinnati: J. A. and U. P. James, 1847) 147-247.

[6]Richard L. Harrison, Jr., *From Camp Meeting to Church: A History of the Christian Church (Disciples of Christ) In Kentucky* (St. Louis: Christian Board of Publication, published for the Christian Church in Kentucky, 1992) 16-18.

[7]Barton Warren Stone, *Christian Messenger* 9 (September 1835): 205-207.

Anti-Burgher, Seceder Presbyterians. This was a particularly contentious bump on the body of Christ.[8]

Thomas Campbell developed friendships and relationships with Christians of several sorts, including a range of Independents who represented a form of Presbyterian primitivism or restorationism. These individuals were looking increasingly at the New Testament for a model church and theology. This perspective undermined Campbell's participation in his Old Light church. The Old Light, Anti-Burgher, Seceder Presbyterians were defined by issues that were mostly a reaction to church-state issues in Scotland.

Campbell grew increasingly frustrated with the divisions in the Irish church, and urged his church to set aside some of their differences with other Anti-Burgher churches. His views were rejected,[9] and soon thereafter he sailed to America to begin a ministry with the Seceder Presbyterians in Western Pennsylvania. Here Campbell once again became embroiled in a controversy over divisions among Presbyterians, this time centered on the observance of the Lord's Supper. As Campbell moved up and down the valleys of the Allegheny Mountains, he found many regular Presbyterians who had not had opportunity—because of a shortage of ministers in the frontier area—to share the Lord's Supper. As he found them to be worthy recipients of the Supper, he opened the Table to them.

As a result, Thomas Campbell was charged with a number of improper actions and beliefs. Before he could be disciplined by the Chartiers Presbytery, he resigned and accepted leadership of a grassroots evangelical missionary society, the Christian Association of Washington, Pennsylvania.

About this time, Campbell's family joined him. They had remained in Ireland after his 1807 emigration to America. He had sent for them in the summer of 1808. By the time they were ready to set sail it was October, and a severe storm caught up their ship soon after departure from Londonderry. They were shipwrecked against a small island off Scotland, and decided to delay their trip until the next summer. The Campbell family, headed by Jane Corneigle Campbell, moved inland to Glasgow. There the six children were able to continue their studies.

---

[8]Still the best work on Thomas Campbell is Lester G. McAllister, *Thomas Campbell: Man of the Book* (St. Louis: Bethany Press, 1954). Most of the references to Thomas Campbell's life are based on McAllister.

[9] Fifteen years later, however, the Presbyterians of Northern Ireland, as well as in Scotland, began overcoming many of their divisions so that by the middle of the century most Presbyterians were in one of only two or three Presbyterian denominations.

Twenty-year old Alexander attended the University of Glasgow, and participated in the worshiping life of a church related to their Northern Ireland churches.[10] Without knowing what controversies were swirling around his father's head, Alexander became engaged in his own ecclesiastical problems. Shortly before sailing for America, Alexander chose not to participate in an observance of the Lord's Supper because of his distress over the barriers placed between many people and the Table. He walked out of the church, effectively excommunicating himself from a church of which his father—so he thought—was an ordained minister.

Then the family traveled to meet father. Father and son had much to tell each other. Alexander enthusiastically joined with his father in the Christian Association, and began preparing himself for ministry through a rigorous study of theology, Bible, biblical languages, and church history. In May of 1811 the Campbells established the Brush Run Church, made up primarily of supporters of the Christian Association. The next year, Alexander was ordained to ministry.

We know little of the early worship of the Brush Run Church, with one major exception. On the occasion of the congregation's founding, the members decided that they would try to base all that they did on the model of the New Testament. Thus, they celebrated Holy Communion that first Sunday, and every Sunday thereafter.

Presbyterian observance of the Lord's Supper tended to be quite infrequent—almost never more often than quarterly. More commonly, they followed a semi-annual schedule. This was also the practice of most other churches of the day. Methodists, Baptists, Congregationalists, even Episcopalians, celebrated the Lord's Supper infrequently. In many places, this practice was in part affected by a severe shortage of clergy. For Episcopalians, who had no American bishops until after the American Revolution, there had been no way for them to receive confirmation without a trip to England. Without confirmation, Anglicans were not permitted to receive the bread and wine. Thus, even though Anglican bishops had been present in the United States for twenty years prior to the arrival of the Campbells, the common practice of the Episcopal Church was infrequent Communion. At the same time, the Book of Common Prayer made it clear that regular communing should be the norm.

---

[10]Jane Corneigle Campbell was the granddaughter of Reformed French Huguenot refugees who settled in Ireland after French King Louis XIV began a severe persecution of Protestants in France.

The Campbells' church adopted believer's immersion as the proper form of baptism and congregational polity as the proper form for governance. This adoption led them into a relationship with the Baptists. This relationship was troubled from the beginning by both theological and sociological issues. The Campbells and their followers were well-educated middle-class elites. Baptists during the early nineteenth century were largely working class people with limited formal education. Many of their ministers had some education, and a few talented individuals were able to move beyond their modest formal training. These sociological differences only accentuated the theological differences to be found in the more traditionally Reformed Campbells. Further, the Campbells were significantly influenced by the ideas of the Enlightenment and its rationalistic approach to all areas of understanding. Alexander Campbell often referred to John Locke as "the Christian philosopher," about whom he had learned in his father's school.[11]

It is not surprising, therefore, that by the late 1820s the Campbells were in a process of separation from the Baptists. This found the backdrop for their union with the Christians of Barton W. Stone during the 1830s.

It is not until this period of union between Disciples and Christians that we begin to have some clear evidence of the structure and character of early Disciples worship. Their views on the nature and purpose of worship were classically Protestant: the purpose of worship is to give praise and gratitude to a gracious God and a beloved savior. When the community gathers, all elements of worship are to focus on God and the community's relationship with God. As Alexander Campbell reminded his readers,

> Every one that speaks or acts must feel himself specially in the presence of the Lord, not as on other days or in other places. Not a thought must be entertained, not a word spoken, not an action performed, that would make the disciple blush, if the Lord Jesus was personally present. The Lord, indeed, "is in the midst of them" if they have met in his name and according to his word.[12]

---

[11]Samuel C. Pearson, "Faith and Reason in Disciples Theology," in *Classic Themes of Disciples Theology*, ed. Lawrence, 101-29.
[12]Alexander Campbell, "Order," *Millennial Harbinger*, 1835: 508. See also Campbell's comments in "Reformation—no. X," *Millennial Harbinger*, 1836: 179.

In his *The Christian System*, Alexander Campbell describes a model worship service. He notes that it is a service in which there is no one present capable of preaching—probably more common than not in the 1830s. He thus describes a service without clergy as most would understand clergy. (It is certain that Campbell was employing a literary device here. He never shied away from volunteering to speak, whether there was a preacher present or not.)[13]

The role and place of clergy in early Disciples thought is a rather complex matter. Briefly, as noted above, the followers of Barton Stone practiced the Presbyterian tradition that word and sacrament were to be led by clergy. For the Campbell churches, however, the congregation was seen as competent to determine who was worthy to lead in pulpit and at the Table. While it was not required, their practice was to have ordained elders preach and pray at the Lord's Supper. These ordained elders were neither laypersons nor traditionally ordained clergy. Their ordination was seen as valid only in the congregation where they were ordained.

Well within the first generation of Disciples, however, the churches themselves began making a distinction between elders who had the gift to preach and those who did not have such a gift. In the search for able ministers, the churches quickly moved to recognize the validity of the ministers' local ordinations beyond individual Disciples congregations. It continued to be the practice to have locally ordained elders preside at the Table. Thus evolved a distinction between elders of word and elders of sacrament. By the turn of the twentieth century, the former were clearly understood as clergy and the latter were seen as lay leaders, much like lay elders in the Presbyterian tradition. The one major difference was the right of Disciples elders to preside at Communion rites.[14]

Campbell's model service, therefore, was a typical service led by elders—though in this instance, elders meant simply senior members of the congregation because no one with the formal qualifications for eldership was present. There was, thus, no preaching, though there was an invitation to Communion and a period for commentary on Scripture. Both occasions provide for a Reformed "Word" as well as sacrament. Campbell noted that since his visit to the church occurred

---

[13]Alexander Campbell, *The Christian System* (Cincinnati: Bosworth, Chase, and Hall, 1871) 272.

[14]See D. Newell Williams, *Ministry Among Disciples: Past, Present, and Future* (St. Louis: Christian Board of Publication, published for the Council on Christian Unity, 1985).

during the winter, the service began at 11:00 a.m. and dismissed about 2:00 p.m. Had the season been warmer, and the days longer, the service would have begun earlier in the day.
The order of service was as follows:

Call to worship
Hymn of Praise ("Christ the Lord is risen today!")
Gospel reading
Prayer
Congregational Amen
Epistle reading
Communion Hymn
Communion
Invitation to Communion, including a paraphrase or quotation of the Words of Institution
Prayer of Thanksgiving for the loaf
Fraction
Distribution
Prayer of Thanksgiving for the cup
Distribution of the cup—common cup, apparently each one serving the person next to them
Post Communion hymn
Prayer of intercession
Offering
Open sharing of Scripture readings and commentary
"Several spiritual songs"
Apostolic benediction[15]

Campbell's co-worker, and later his biographer, Robert Richardson, also described a typical Disciples order of worship in the mid–1830s. He first listed the basic elements of worship in order:

Reading the Scriptures
Teaching
Exhorting
Presiding
Praying
Singing
Giving thanks
Breaking the loaf

[15]Alexander Campbell, *The Christian System*, 290-292.

Contributing for the poor[16]

This listing is of a general sort of the elements of worship in a commonly observed order. Richardson then offers his own version of a visit to a specific congregation and how their worship was structured:

Call to worship
Intercessory prayers, including for all in authority
Readings from the New Testament
  Prophets
  Psalms
  Law ("Proceeding regularly through the book, with the omission of genealogies and sundry matters relating to the civil polity of the Jews which do not tend to general edification")
Teaching/interpretation of readings
Breaking of the Loaf
The Fellowship (offering)
Exhortation
Benediction[17]

Richardson adds that "appropriate psalms, hymns, and songs are interspersed through the worship between the other exercises." He then compares this order of worship with that presented by Justin Martyr, as recorded by Eusebius, noting that the basic outline was the same as that of a second-century Christian service. Nevertheless, the specific order of worship is seen to be a matter of indifference so long as the church obeys Paul's admonition to "Let all things be done to edification." The differences to be noted in the two services, such as the variation in placement of scripture readings, fall clearly within the area of "indifference" or freedom as understood by Richardson.[18]

While Campbell's experience of the Presbyterians had been Irish and Scottish Presbyterianism, there was great similarity between the worship practices of the American Presbyterians and their homeland. Even the appearance of revival supporting New Light Presbyterianism had strong roots in Scotland. However, the Scottish worship forms that translated into the frontier setting in which the Disciples were born and flourished were most likely rooted in the rural

[16]Robert Richardson, "Order—No. 4," *Millennial Harbinger*, 1836: 562.
[17]Richardson, *Millennial Harbinger*, 1836: 563.
[18]I Corinthians 14:26. Richardson, *Millennial Harbinger*, 1836: 563-564.

and small town worship of the old world.[19]

Early Disciples worship came out of both the pro-revival New Light styles favored by Barton Warren Stone, and the more traditional, if not Old Light, approaches of the Campbells. While Alexander Campbell was distinctly anti-revival, he nevertheless challenged the traditional forms of church out of which he had come. He thus urged a form of worship that was simple, rational, and true to the model of the New Testament.

Thus, he emphasized strongly a distinction between those parts of worship which are clearly laid out in the New Testament and those areas of worship which are not so clear. For him, the design of Christian worship could be found most fully in Acts 2:42, where the early Christian community is described as following a regimen of gathering on the first day of the week where "they devoted themselves to the apostles' teaching and fellowship, to the breaking of bread and the prayers." These were the essential elements. Questions of time and place, arrangement of the worship setting, even the order of worship, were all matters of *adiaphora*. They were issues not clearly addressed in Scripture and so they were left to the judgment of the community.

Like Robert Richardson, Campbell had little patience with those who wanted to find a detailed order of worship in the New Testament.

> As the Lord has left it discretionary with us whether we shall meet at sun rise, noon, or sun-set—under an oak, in a garret, or in a synagogue—whether we shall begin with singing, praying, reading, teaching &c.—whether we shall stand or sit in singing—whether we shall kneel or stand in praying— whether we shall sit around one table or in our pews while we partake of the loaf—whether we should have a chest fixed in some part of the house called "the Lord's treasury," or whether we should have reserved a plate or book, &c. &c.—I say, while it is obviously left without a single precept or precedent in all the New Testament wholly discretionary with us, why should we seek to impose any form upon all the churches as essential to the acceptability of their worship—as

---

[19]Leigh Eric Schmidt, *Holy Fairs: Scottish Communion and American Revivals in the Early Modern Period* (Princeton: Princeton University Press, 1989) 59-68. See also Paul K. Conkin, *Cane Ridge: America's Pentecost* (Madison, WI: University of Wisconsin Press, 1990).

of divine authority.[20]

Presbyterian worship in the early decades of the Republic shared exactly these values upheld by the Disciples. For them, worship was to follow the teaching of the New Testament. This had been the heart of Reformed teaching about worship from the days of the purifying of the cathedral in Zurich under Zwingli's leadership, and certainly was the teaching of both Martin Bucer in Strasbourg and John Calvin in Geneva.[21] Indeed, Bucer's critique of the first Book of Common Prayer was based on his evaluation of its fidelity to scripture.[22]

For Calvin, all that is central to the Christian faith must be based on the clear testimony of scripture. This is as true of worship as anything else. Yet, contrary to the common view that Calvin was a rigid and unbending church leader, the Genevan reformer recognized that many questions about worship cannot be directly or clearly answered in scripture. Thus, there is latitude for how Christians conduct many of the elements of worship.[23]

The American Presbyterian churches followed Calvin's direction here, and had long felt free to alter elements of worship as needed, so long as the primary concerns of the Word rightly preached and the sacraments rightly administered were met. The proposed American Directory of Worship (1787-88), while not fully adopted, did reflect the common practices of the leading eastern seaboard churches in the first days of the Republic. The outline of worship advocated is quite similar to that followed by the early Disciples. Parts of the proposed Directory were not approved, namely those that offered outlines for prayers and anything else that might give the appearance of liturgical norms or a devaluing of extemporaneity in public prayer.[24]

The specific order of worship would change little through the nineteenth century (though actual practice would be quite another story by later in the century):

1787 Directory   1821 Directory

Prayer of adoration, invocation,   Short prayer of adoration,

---

[20]Alexander Campbell, *Millennial Harbinger*, 1838: 250.

[21]H. Jackson Forstman, *Word and Spirit: Calvin's Doctrine of Biblical Authority* (Stanford, CA: Stanford University Press, 1962) 29.

[22]Martin Bucer, *Censura*, in E. C. Whitaker, *Martin Bucer and the Book of Common Prayer* (Great Wakering, England: The Alcuin Club, 1974) 12-13.

[23]John Calvin, *Institutes of the Christian Religion*, 4.10:31-32.

[24]Melton, *Presbyterian Worship*, 17-21.

and preparation	recognition of unworthiness, invocation, plea for acceptance through Jesus Christ Psalm or Hymn "Full and comprehensive Prayer," similar to the Long Prayer of 1787
Reading of Scripture	Sermon
Singing of Praise	Prayer after sermon
Long prayer of adoration, confession, thanksgiving, supplication and intercession, followed by Lord's Prayer	
Sermon	
(Lord's Supper, when celebrated)	(Lord's Supper, when celebrated)
Prayer	
Singing of a Psalm	Offering
Offering	Psalm or hymn
Blessing	Benediction[25]

The 1821 Directory makes it clear that readings from both the Old and New Testament are to be a part of the service, placed as deemed reasonable by the minister along with other Psalms and hymns. By 1821 more direction is given to the character of prayers, even to the point of presenting prayers that might be used or seen as models. The minister, however, still had the full right to use or not those suggestions. Like Disciples worship of about the same period, the Presbyterian worship service was modeled on the fourfold precedent cited in Acts 2:42: Scripture and preaching/teaching, prayer, Lord's Supper, offering (fellowship).

Given the acceptance of appropriate variation in the order of worship, the basic outline of the two Disciples services and the two Presbyterian orders of service are very similar. There is nothing in

---

[25]Melton, *Presbyterian Worship*, 21-22; *Directory for Worship in A Draught of the Form of Government and Discipline of the Presbyterian Church in the United States of America* (New York: S. and J. Loudon, 1787); *The Directory for the Worship of God in The Presbyterian Church in the United States of America, 1821*, 424-28.

the Presbyterian order that would not be acceptable to the Disciples at worship except for the matter of frequency of communion. (Ironically, the regular observance of the Lord's Supper was encouraged by the Presbyterians, and Calvin had called for weekly communion.) Matters that would have been problematic for Disciples, such as the regular use of one of the historic creeds, were not in regular use in the Presbyterian churches of the early nineteenth century.

The outline of the observance of the Lord's Supper changed among the Presbyterians between the 1787 and 1821 orders of worship. The traditional Action sermon that had been included in 1787 had been reduced to a kind of invitation to communion for those who were worthy. Both warned unworthy recipients. Both recognized the possibility and value of an extended sacramental season lasting several days, but neither required it.[26]

Although the Disciples design of the Lord's Supper was markedly simpler in design, it did present essentially the framework of the Presbyterian service.

Campbell's 1835 version of Communion Liturgy	Presbyterian 1821 version
Communion Hymn	Invitation [my word], including a warning
Communion	to those who should not commune, and a
Invitation to Communion, including a paraphrase or quotation of the Words of Institution	statement on the meaning of the Supper
Prayer of Thanksgiving for the loaf	Prayer of thanksgiving for bread and wine
Fraction	Fraction
Distribution	Words of Institution
Prayer of Thanksgiving for the cup	Distribution (communicants gathered before or around Table, common cup)
Distribution of the cup—common	

---

[26]Melton, *Presbyterian Worship*, 22-27; *Directory for Worship, 1787; Directory for the Worship of God ... 1821*, 432-36.

cup, apparently each one serving the person next to him or her	Minister may give post-communion word to communicants and non-communicants
Post Communion hymn	about the meaning of Communion
	Post-communion prayer[27]

The striking similarity in orders of worship, both for the Lord's Supper and for the whole service, shows a strong likelihood that the former Presbyterian Campbells and Stone relied on their Reformed heritage perhaps far more than they realized. Of greater importance, however, is that in the interpretation both of the meaning of worship (see above) and the interpretation of the Lord's Supper, the Disciples retained a strong Reformed perspective. It is telling that in all of the debates Campbell held with Presbyterians—in person and in print—over a variety of topics, there seems to have been no controversy over the meaning of the Lord's Supper. While it is risky to argue from silence, that alone could be cited as evidence that the early Disciples retained a Reformed theology of the Lord's Supper.[28]

However, a study of Disciples understanding of the Lord's Supper, focusing on the fundamental issues of the nature of the presence of Christ, the value or import of the Supper, and the sacramental character of the Supper, shows that there is little distinction to be made between the Disciples and the classic Reformed positions. Robert Milligan, student and co-worker with Alexander Campbell, interpreted the Communion in a manner not at all different from Calvin. Milligan said that the Supper is far more than a mere memorial service:

> It is also the medium of spiritual food to the hungry and thirsty soul. We are required to *eat* the bread, and to *drink* the wine. Why? Not because they are converted into the body, blood, and divinity of the Son of God. . . . They are still of the meat that perishes. But there is here present a beautiful analogy between the wants of the body and the wants of the soul. To supply the former, it is not enough to remember that there is bread sufficient and to spare; it is not enough that we

---

[27]Alexander Campbell, *The Christian System,* 290-292; *Directory for the Worship of God . . . 1821,* 432-435.
[28]Harrison, "Early Disciples Sacramental Theology," 49-100.

even look upon the rich provision that has been bountifully supplied. We must *eat* it. We must masticate and digest it. We must appropriate it to the nourishment of our bodies, or our physical existence will soon terminate.

Just so it is with the soul. It needs its regular supplies of food as well as the body. And this food must be spiritually eaten, spiritually digested, and spiritually appropriated, or the soul will languish and perish forever.[29]

Milligan's views on this crucial issue of theological interpretation of the Lord's Supper closely parallel those of Calvin. Where Calvin could say:

As bread nourishes, sustains, and keeps the life of our body, so Christ's body is the only food to invigorate and enliven our soul. When we see wine set forth as a symbol of blood, we must reflect on the benefits which wine imparts to the body, and so realize that the same are spiritually imparted to us by Christ's blood. These benefits are to nourish, refresh, strengthen, and gladden.[30]

Robert Milligan makes a similar affirmation of the value of the Supper for the soul:

We must, therefore, simultaneously eat of the commemoration loaf and of the bread of life; and while we literally drink of the symbolic cup, we must also, at the same time, drink spiritually of that blood which alone can supply the wants of the thirsty soul. *Unless we do this, the bread that we eat, can in no sense be to us the body of the Son of God; nor can the wine that we drink be in any sense he blood of the new covenant, which was shed for the remission of sins of many.*[31]

During the period of rapid development of the Disciples, from the union of the Stone and Campbell groups in 1832 to the Civil War, American Protestantism was dominated by the rise of a new form of evangelicalism. Charles G. Finney was the most prominent leader, and

---

[29]Robert Milligan, *Millennial Harbinger*, 1859: 603-604.
[30]Calvin, *Institutes*, 4.17:3.
[31]Milligan, *Millennial Harbinger*, 1859: 603-604.

under his guidance worship was turned over in large respect to the evangelistic task of the church. Eveiything from order of worship to music and sermons was considered and shaped by a desire to "win souls." Presbyterian worship was affected by this trend in significant ways.[32]

Disciples worship was also heavily evangelical, especially given the revival origins of the Stone churches. The more moderate evangelicalism of Campbell, however, shaped the development of Disciples worship, with a combination of evangelical fervor and Enlightenment rationalism. Like the Presbyterians, Disciples preferred extemporaneous prayers and sermons preached without notes, though not without preparation!

The Presbyterians also had a countermovement at work. It began in the Old School resistance to some evangelical emphases, and then received strong support in the return to romanticism in the nineteenth century. Nowhere among the Reformed in America was this more obvious than the Mercersburg theology developed by German Reformed theologians Philip Schaff and John Williamson Nevin. This renewal of liturgical worship created severe controversy among Presbyterians for the rest of the century and well into the twentieth century. By the 1906 Book of Common Worship the Presbyterians were well on their way to a form of worship that was quite different, far more liturgical in nature, than it had been in the early nineteenth century.[33]

The Disciples have followed the same route, only they have followed a slower schedule. The Disciples in the 1960s were beginning to concern themselves with the kind of liturgical renewal hotly debated by Presbyterians in 1900. Even so, in rural Disciples and Presbyterian churches at the end of the twentieth century, it is not unusual to find a pattern of worship that is closer to that of the 1820s and 1830s than the more liturgical twentieth-century directions.

Disciples, as rebellious children of the Reformed tradition, have far more of the parent in them than they are likely to admit. But with age and maturity often come both an awareness and an appreciation of heritage. For the Disciples, the richness of Reformed worship helps provide a basis for self-critique. Worship that is an appropriate expression of thankful praise before the majesty of God still focuses on the Word rightly preached, and the sacraments rightly administered.

---

[32]Melton, *Presbyterian Worship*, 43-58.
[33]Melton, *Presbyterian Worship*, 59-134.

Disciples at Worship:
From "Ancient Order" to *Thankful Praise*

Paul H. Jones

Worship characterizes the fundamental posture of the Christian life. It is grounded in Paul's admonition that "whatever you do, in word or deed, do everything in the name of the Lord Jesus, giving thanks to God the Father through him" (Colossians 3:17), and it expresses the grateful response of humans to the Creator's initial gift of life and continued self-giving.

Although all of life may be understood as "thankful praise" to God's initiating grace, specific times and specific places are usually set aside deliberately and corporately to honor God.[1] These communal expressions of gratitude and praise are the traditional referent of the term "Christian worship." This essay examines the particular corporate pattern of worship in the Christian Church (Disciples of Christ) in three movements. The first section examines the restoration concept of "the ancient order of things" with particular attention to the centrality of the Lord's Supper and the reestablishment of Word and Sacrament in the Sunday worship service. The second part examines G. Edwin Osborn's *Christian Worship: A Service Book* in the context of the psychology of worship movement and its emphasis on the individual worshiper's inner states. The third movement examines the newest worship resource book, *Thankful Praise*, edited by Keith Watkins, with specific focus on situating Disciples worship practice within the broader framework of eucharistic worship.

The "Ancient Order"

Echoing the voices of his Reformed forebears[2] who claimed that

---

[1] Frank Burch Brown, "Worship—Style and Substance in Christian Worship," in *Interpreting Disciples: Practical Theology in the Disciples of Christ*, eds. L. Dale Richesin and Larry D. Bouchard, (Fort Worth: Texas Christian University Press, 1987) 50.

[2] Disciples theologians as well as liturgical scholars place the Christian Church

the chief purpose of humanity is to glorify God,[3] Alexander Campbell, seminal thinker of the Stone-Campbell movement, affirmed the essential role of worship in the Christian life.

> It is not discretionary with disciples . . . whether Christian societies shall regard the first day of the week to the Lord; whether they shall show forth the Lord's death at the Lord's table till he come to raise the dead; whether they shall continue in the fellowship for the saints and the Lord's poor; whether they shall sing psalms, hymns, and spiritual songs; unite in social prayers, and in reading the sacred writings in their regular meetings. These are the traditions of the Holy Apostles who were commanded to teach the disciples to observe all things which the King in his own person had commanded them.[4]

Convinced that Christian unity would be achieved by the restoration of the New Testament church, Campbell and other Disciples founders presumed that the Bible supplied a blueprint for worship practices. Thomas Campbell, father of Alexander, typified the attitude of the movement when he wrote that the Scriptures provided the "perfect ... constitution for the worship, discipline and government of the New Testament church."[5] Because the Bible contained the "constitution" for the restoration of the church in general and the church's worship pattern in particular, Disciples founders read Scripture to determine "the ancient order of things."[6]

(Disciples of Christ) within the Reformed tradition. See especially James F. White, *Protestant Worship: Traditions in Transition* (Louisville: Westminster/John Knox Press, 1989) 172, 174.

[3]*Westminster Shorter Catechism.*

[4]Alexander Campbell, *Christian Baptist* 5 (1831): 656.

[5]Colbert S. Cartwright, "Disciples Worship on the American Frontier," essay provided by the Disciples of Christ Historical Society, Nashville, Tennessee, 2.

[6]The Disciples emphasis on the scriptural basics of worship has fostered not only a suspicion of liturgical forms, but also a lack of interest in the liturgical developments in the life of the church. According to Harry B. Adams in "Worship Among Disciples of Christ, 1865-1920," *Mid-Stream* 7 (Summer 1968): 42: "In the eyes of many Disciples, every change in the church after the New Testament period was by definition an apostasy. Although Disciple worship itself stands in a broad Reformed tradition, the Disciples were not interested in traditions or historical heritage. They proposed to leap over the centuries to return to the 'purity' of the New Testament practice."

From 1824 to 1828, in a series of six essays in the *Christian Baptist*, Alexander Campbell sought "to demonstrate from rational principles that there is a divinely instituted worship" for congregations and, furthermore, that this "divinely authorized order of Christian worship" is uniform.[7]

By the phrase, 'order of Christian worship,' we do not mean the position of the bodies of the worshippers, nor the hour of the day in which certain things are to be done, nor whether one action shall always be performed first, another always second, and another always third, &c. &c. though in these there is an order which is comely, apposite, or congruous with the genius of the religion, ... but that there are certain social acts of Christian worship, all of which are to be attended to in the Christian assembly, and each of which is essential to the perfection of the whole as every member to the human body is essential to the perfect man—is that which we wish to convey by the phrase 'order of Christian worship.'[8]

This explication identified the "order of Christian worship" as the essential, communal acts of corporate worship. Because the Bible did not mandate a precise order of service, individual churches were free to arrange the elements. Circumstantials, such as standing, kneeling, furniture, time, and the set order of service were "matters left to the discretion of the brotherhood."[9]

However, variability in Christian worship meant neither an indifference to order nor an inordinate reliance on the Holy Spirit. Alexander Campbell expressed confidence in local congregations to study Scripture, discern a pattern (as suggested in Acts 2:42) and, more important, live under the authority of the living Lord. Since worship was constrained by both scripture[10] and the presence of the living Lord,[11] for Disciples founders it was fundamentally "free." The style or manner of the service reflected the purpose and nature of

---

[7]Walter W. Sikes, "Worship Among Disciples of Christ, 1809-1865," *Mid-Stream* 7 (Summer 1968): 6-7.

[8]Johnny Miles, "The Origins of Alexander Campbell's Eclectic Theology of Worship," *Discipliana* 55 (Summer 1995): 35.

[9]Fred B. Craddock, "Worship Among Disciples: Literature and Practice," *Disciples Theological Digest* 3 (1988): 16.

[10]Colbert S. Cartwright, *Candles of Grace* (St. Louis: Chalice Press, 1992) 100.

[11]Craddock, "Worship," 17.

worship itself; "decency and order," "dignity and simplicity" denoted its marks.

Campbell's phrase, "order of Christian worship," referred then to Christ's orders or ordinances. An ordinance for Campbell conveyed "the indispensable moral means of spiritual life and health."[12] Like the word sacrament in many church traditions, the word ordinance signified the availability of God's grace to the community of faith.

Because all ordinances for the Christian life are grounded in God's initiating grace and boundless love, obedience to Christ's orders springs from a "thankful heart." Campbell wrote: "*God never commanded a being to do any thing, but the power and motive were derived from something God had done for him.*"[13]

As to the means by which Christians enjoy God's gracious love, Campbell refused to finalize the number of ordinances. Yet study of the apostolic epistles revealed ordinances that were delivered to the church and, therefore, were expected to be observed in all her meetings.[14] Campbell cited five categories required for Christian public worship:

1. Hymns of praise
2. Reading of Scripture
3. Prayers, including Thanksgiving for each element at the table
4. Lord's Supper, with all members partaking of both elements
5. 'Fellowship' or contribution of money.[15]

Thus, the restoration movement's stress on flexibility in the sequence of public worship precluded the emergence of a normative pattern.

Although these five categories were, in theory, of equal importance to the founders, in practice the supremacy of the Lord's Supper was universally acclaimed by them. From his reading of Scripture in general and the Book of Acts in particular, Alexander Campbell concluded that "the primary intention of the meeting of the disciples on the first day of the week was to break bread."[16]

---

[12]Mark G. Toulouse, *Joined in Discipleship: The Maturing of an American Religious Movement* (St. Louis: Chalice Press, 1992) 123.

[13]Cartwright, "Disciples Worship," 6.

[14]Ibid., 6 and 18-19 for two separate lists of ordinances.

[15]Sikes, "Worship," 9.

[16]Cartwright, *Candles*, 4.

Because Campbell practiced the Reformation partiality for "calling biblical things by biblical names,"[17] he rejected the terms "eucharist" and "sacrament," and called the Lord's Supper "the breaking of the bread" (Acts 2:42, 20:7).

Significant for current Disciples theology of the Lord's Supper, Alexander Campbell's elevation of this ordinance above the others was not based solely on the frequency of celebration. More important, the supper identified the heart of corporate worship. By retrieving the ordinance of the Lord's Supper as the central act of public worship, Campbell refocused the "very nature of what it means to worship God" and also corrected the infrequent observance of the meal in his day.[18]

The centrality of the Lord's Supper and its normative weekly observance for Disciples worship were grounded in Scripture and ordained by Christ. On this matter, Alexander Campbell insisted:

It was the design of the Savior that his disciples should not be deprived of this joyful festival when they meet in one place to worship God. It will appear (if it does not already) to the candid reader of these numbers, that the New Testament teaches that every time they met in honor of the resurrection of the Prince of Life, or, when they assembled in one place, it was a principal part of their entertainment, in his liberal house, to eat and drink with him. He keeps no dry lodgings for the saints—no empty house for his friends. He never made his house assemble but to eat and drink with him.[19]

As the divinely sanctioned memorial of Christ's death, the Lord's Supper gained greater and greater prominence in the constellation of Disciples worship categories. Consequently, the relationship of the Lord's Supper to the other ordinances became more and more tenuous. The table soon eclipsed the importance of the other ordinances and evolved independently of them.

The ascendancy of the Lord's Supper as the central act of corporate worship inaugurated nothing less than a revolution in the liturgical practice of the restoration movement. Heretofore, frontier

---

[17]Gerard Francis Moore, "The Eucharistic Theology of the Prayers for the Communion Service of the Lord's Supper of the Christian Church (Disciples of Christ), 1953-1987" (Ph.D. diss., Catholic University of America, 1989) 40.

[18]Cartwright, *Candles*, 5.

[19]Ibid.

worship focused almost exclusively on the proclamation of the Word. The great contribution of the Disciples founders was the re-establishment of the proper balance between Word and Sacrament, the sacrament being the ordinance of the weekly "breaking of the bread."

Though it is possible to read the founders' emphasis on the Lord's Supper as a depreciation of preaching, such a conclusion would be mistaken. Rather, the paucity of trained ministers on the frontier precluded weekly sermons for many small congregations. Elders would read from scripture and then celebrate "the breaking of the bread." Liturgical equality as articulated in the Reformation principle of the "priesthood of all believers" applied to the table but not to the pulpit. In cultural terms, Jacksonian democracy applied to the observance of communion and not to preaching.[20]

Yet Alexander Campbell, a "prince of the pulpit" himself, fervently reminded preachers of their supreme task "to impress the moral image of God upon the moral nature of man."[21] When the proclamation of the gospel is interpreted in the light of apostolic doctrine, Campbell presumed, "there is written upon the understanding, and engraved upon the heart, the will, or law, or character, of our Father who is in heaven."[22]

Preaching the gospel and partaking of the supper were, for the early Disciples, interdependent and mutually interpretive. Preaching without communion minimized the experiential presence of the living Lord, while the Lord's Supper without preaching limited the theological horizon of communion.[23] Frank Burch Brown said it well: "If the Lord's Supper is the heart of [Disciples] worship, then the Word is its mind; it is the union of heart and mind that comprises the soul of the worshiping community of Disciples."[24] For this reason, the liturgical scholar James F. White has observed that among Prot-estants, the Disciples were the first people to recover the normative practice of including both Word and Sacrament in the Sunday worship service.[25]

---

[20]White, *Protestant Worship*, 175.

[21]Cartwright, *Candles*, 105.

[22]Ibid., 106.

[23]Ibid.

[24]Brown, "Worship," 59.

[25]James F. White, *Christian Worship in Transition* (Nashville: Abingdon, 1976) 68.

Christian Worship: A Service Book

Although Disciples founders agreed that the New Testament
authorized ordinances for the worship life of the church, the Bible, for
them, did not sanction a fixed form or liturgy. Second-generation
Disciples also identified the basic elements of worship and were
equally loathe to prescribe a set order.[26] Beginning with the latter two
decades of the nineteenth century and continuing into this century,
this reluctance gradually disappeared with the introduction of worship
manuals. Widespread use of the mimeograph machine in the 1920s
provided the final impetus for the stabilization and development of a
worship order. Fixed items—like the Doxology, the Gloria Patri,
offertory sentences, prayer responses, calls to worship, invocations,
benedictions, and other antiphonal responses—appeared.[27] As the
demand for worship materials increased, publishing houses printed
more and more manuals.[28]

The most influential idea introduced into American Protestant
worship during the twenties, which would give particular shape to
Disciples manuals, was the pioneering work in the psychology of
worship by Von Ogden Vogt, a Unitarian minister in Chicago. Vogt,
along with Disciples W. S. Lockhart and E. S. Ames, recognized
Isaiah's vision in the Temple as normative for Christian worship.
Beneath the variety of all religious worship, they argued, lay a
sequence of inner states.

Their studies into the subjective state of the worshiper provided
ministers who were hungry for worship materials new criteria by
which they could plan the Sunday worship service. For Disciples, the
psychology of worship movement culminated in G. Edwin Osborn's
Christian Worship: A Service Book, published by the Christian Board
of Publication in 1953. Then a professor at Phillips University,
whose doctoral dissertation had been entitled, *The Psychology of
Christian Public Worship*, Osborn's monumental work was described

---

[26]According to Adams, "Worship Among the Disciples, 1865-1920," 36, these
elements were song, prayer, Scripture, sermon, invitation, Lord's Supper, and
offering.

[27]W. B. Blakemore, "Worship Among Disciples of Christ, 1920-1966," *Mid-
Stream* 7 (Summer 1968): 57-58.

[28]For a detailed examination of selective manuals from Joseph H. Foy's *The
Christian Worker* in 1889 to B. A. Abbott's *At the Master's Table* in 1925, see
Moore, "Prayers," 51-78.

by W. B. Blakemore as:

catholic in its garnering of items for inclusion in services of worship, biblically rich, indicating a psychological basis for the ordering of worship, [it] none the less perpetuated the 'liberal' attitude that a service of worship is something to be planned. This liberal point of view did believe that a service should have unity—but the unity was provided by the theme chosen by the minister for his sermon. And that theme was *chosen*, not given.[29]

Osborn invoked the use of themes to unify the service because neither Campbell's idea of ordinances nor the psychology of worship movement's emphasis on the worshiper's inner states offered a way to integrate the elements of worship.

For Osborn, the elements of worship that comprised the order of service followed a general pattern. This pattern, in turn, corresponded to a definitive cycle that is repeated each time in the consciousness of the worshiper. The four major movements in the cycle that find expression in the order of worship are: an Act of Reverence, an Act of Fellowship, an Act of Dedication, and an Act of Renewal. This cycle reflected an alternating pattern. An attitude of reverence by the worshiper is answered by God who brings the worshiper a sense of fellowship. In turn, this sense of fellowship engenders an attitude of devotion in the worshiper that God subsequently answers by bringing a sense of empowerment.[30] The sample order for Sunday morning worship, found in the front of *Christian Worship: A Service Book*, recommended this fourfold pattern:

An Act of Reverence
    Organ Prelude
    A Choral Call to Worship
    A Period of Silent Prayer
    The Processional Hymn
    An Introit
    The Gloria Patri or The Sanctus
    A Unison Prayer of Invocation
    The Lord's Prayer (or as part of the Communion Service)

---

[29]Blakemore, "Worship," 61.

[30]G. Edwin Osborn, ed., *Christian Worship: A Service Book* (St. Louis: Christian Board of Publication, 1953) 3.

An Act of Fellowship
A Period of Silent Prayer
An Anthem, or a Solo
Announcements
The Scripture Lesson
Choral Response of Praise
The Pastoral Prayer
A Choral Prayer Response
An Act of Dedication
A Hymn of Affirmation, or, of Consecration
The Offering
The Offertory Sentences
The Offertory
The Doxology
All Things Come of Thee
The Offertory Prayer of Dedication
An Act of Renewal
Musical Interlude, or Hymn
The Sermon
An Invitation To Christian Discipleship
A Hymn of Invitation and Consecration
The Communion of the Lord's Supper
The Benediction
A Choral Response, or Amen
The Recessional Hymn
The Organ Postlude

Echoing Campbell, Osborn agreed that scriptural ordinances governed the selection of the elements of worship but not their exact order. Although ordinances were valid and essential, since they were part of "the ancient order of things," a separate integrating factor was necessary. For the psychology of worship movement, the "form of worship" more than the content determined a satisfactory experience of worship.[31] Thus, the four movements in the cycle followed by the consciousness of the worshiper provided a pattern but not a unifying factor. It was left to the discretion of the local minister to import that theme. Therefore, *Christian Worship: A Service Book* offered 105 different themes by which a service could be planned.[32]

---

[31]Moore, "Prayers," 107-108.
[32]See Osborn, *Worship*, vi.

According to Fred Craddock, "Dr. Osborn's single most significant contribution" was broadening the liturgical context of Disciples worship.[33] By invoking the Disciples's commitment to the unity of the church, Osborn included materials from the ancient, ecumenical, and contemporary church.[34] As a result, the service book introduced the Disciples to the "Christian Year."[35] Although the calendar found at the front of the book mixed cultural and denominational topics with the traditional liturgical year, it nonetheless contained a two-page statement on "Holy Week" and a list of the dates on which Easter would fall through the millennium.

Osborn's greatest legacy to Disciples worship was the introduction of a definite pattern for worship as followed by the consciousness of the worshiper. Sunday morning worship services no longer resembled a liturgical kaleidoscope of independent ordinances. Rather, *Christian Worship* provided a pattern and a theme.

Osborn's greatest accomplishment also located the manual's Achilles' heel. By theologically grounding worship in the consciousness of the worshiper, the service became predominantly subjective and individualistic. Despite Osborn's forceful argument against human-centered worship in his *magnum opus*, *The Glory of Christian Worship*,[36] and his insistence in the same work that the charge of subjectivism ignored his theological norms,[37] the service book committed the fateful error of reversing the priority by making the individual worshiper the center of worship, rather than God.[38] Throughout *The Glory of Christian Worship*, Osborn endorsed an encounter model of worship that views worship as the meeting place between God and humanity that results from the initiating presence of God.[39] The manual, however, failed to incorporate consistently this theological conviction into the practical application of the pattern of worship.

The charge of inconsistency also applied to Osborn's declaration in *The Glory of Christian Worship* that worship consists of more than

---

[33]Craddock, "Worship," 8.

[34]Osborn, *Worship*, vii.

[35]Ibid., x-xiii, 568-572.

[36]G. Edwin Osborn, *The Glory of Christian Worship* (Indianapolis: Christian Theological Seminary Press, 1960) 25.

[37]Ibid., 48-50.

[38]Ibid., 25.

[39]Ibid., 16, 51, 66.

a group of individuals. The use of unison prayers, litanies, responsive introits, antiphons, and collects may advance communal consciousness[40] as well as offer vehicles by which the Reformation concept of the priesthood of all believers may be fulfilled; however, *Christian Worship: A Service Book* failed to realize this potential. In three of the four acts of service, individualism displaced any and all efforts at communal consciousness.[41] In the opening Act of Reverence, individual worshipers are to engage in a "period of silent prayer" before the processional hymn and remain bowed in prayer during the first stanza which is "sung by the choir only." The Act of Fellowship begins with devotional organ music and a "period of silent prayer." Only the Act of Dedication excludes a directive to silent meditation. The final Act of Renewal repeatedly admonishes worshipers to pray and meditate silently during the Lord's Supper:

> During the Communion and for a few moments following let the People bow in silent Prayer and Meditation. It may be suggested that preceding their participation their devotions should be of self-examination and penitence, and that following their participation they should engage in *silent thanksgiving* and intercessions. Throughout the service devotional music may be quietly played by the Organist (my italics).[42]

Although Osborn's *Christian Worship: A Service Book* filled a liturgical void in the worship life of the Christian Church (Disciples of Christ), it unintentionally shifted the focus of Disciples worship from what Campbell called the "social acts of Christian worship" to a service fixated on the individual worshiper's inner states.

Thankful Praise

In 1961, less than ten years after the publication of Osborn's service book, collaborators Josh Wilson and Keith Watkins, future editor of *Thankful Praise*,[43] condemned the inordinate stress on the

---

[40]Ibid., 46.

[41]Osborn, *Worship*, 14-19.

[42]Ibid., 27-28; also see 30.

[43]Keith Watkins, ed., *Thankful Praise: A Resource for Christian Worship* (St. Louis, CBP Press, 1987).

psychological character of worship. To them it was the great heresy of contemporary worship: *The motivation for our worship ought not to be what we get out of it.* Rather, worship must always be the grateful response of God's people to what he has done in history, and especially in Jesus Christ.[44]

Although the preface of *Thankful Praise*, published by CBP Press in 1987, acknowledges Disciples' indebtedness to G. Edwin Osborn in general and *Christian Worship: A Service Book* in particular,[45] *Thankful Praise* nonetheless serves as a corrective to Osborn's overemphasis on the subjective and individualistic dimensions of worship. The opening sentence sets the tone: "Thankful praise is the theme of the Christian life."[46]

This assertion directly challenges Osborn's notion of subjectivism. Praise is first and foremost a response to the prior gifts of God. Like the individual's response, the church's corporate expression of thankful praise is also grounded in the initiating grace of God. According to *Thankful Praise*, "worship is essentially corporate thanksgiving and praise offered by sinful and redeemed human beings in response to God's saving revelation."[47]

Two activities characterize Christian worship: coming together and sharing food. The gathering of the people of God identifies the locus of Christ's presence in the world and their gathering around the table actualizes communion with Christ and one another. Most important, the emphasis on corporate celebrations of the Lord's Supper, not only reinforces the uniqueness of Disciples of Christ worship, but also provides a vehicle by which the service can be unified. Because Campbell's emphasis on the independence of ordinances fragmented rather than unified the service, Disciples have always been searching for an integrating principle for worship. For *Thankful Praise*, this principle is the "eucharistic service, including both proclamation of the Word and sharing of the sacred meal."[48] Thus, the distinctive feature of Disciples frontier and contemporary worship practice—the balance of Word and Sacrament (the ordinance

---

[44]Harold Keith Watkins and Josh L. Wilson, Jr., eds., *Hear the Word of the Lord and O, Taste, See that the Lord is Good!* (Berkeley: Christian Churches (Disciples of Christ) of Northern California-Western Nevada, 1961) 3.

[45]Watkins, *Thankful Praise*, 9.

[46]Ibid., 7.

[47]Ibid., 20.

[48]Ibid., 14.

of the weekly "breaking of the bread")—provides the church universal with a viable pattern for renewal.

The Disciples, however, have not been immune to historical distortion and spiritual lethargy. In an effort to "provoke dialogue and renewal," as well as to rediscover "authentic Christian worship," *Thankful Praise* identifies five principle sources for its worship materials:

1. The great tradition of Christian worship.
2. The ecumenical church, especially *Baptism, Eucharist and Ministry* and *COCU Consensus* resources.
3. Traditional Disciples worship, particularly lay leadership, new prayers at the Table, and preeminence of the Lord's Supper.
4. Contemporary life, with awareness to issues of social justice, anti-Jewish teachings in the church, and sex inclusive language.
5. Vivid language and variety in the ordering of the service to enhance the beauty and diversity of worship.[49]

Six principles of renewal are also noted:
1. Authentic worship is rooted in the church's experience of the gospel, especially as it is expressed in the Bible and in the church's living experience through history.
2. Worship is deeply and inevitably theological.
3. The church encompasses significant diversity in the theological positions on which its worship is based.
4. Worship is intimately connected with the church's mission, including its struggles for peace and justice in the world.
5. While worship involves ideas that are timeless and universal, it should be expressed through the culture of the local worshiping community.
6. Worship should be both open to creative transformation and conformed to enduring standards in its meaning and patterns.[50]

Convinced that renewal of worship is the key to Disciples creative growth, Watkins expressed hopes that this volume would strengthen Disciples public worship in general and the celebration of the Lord's

---

[49]Paraphrased from *Thankful Praise*, 8-9.
[50]Ibid., 17-19.

Supper in particular. Toward that objective, the manual recommends an order of service that contains five headings and displays the essential elements with emphasis.

The Community Comes Together To Serve God In Worship
Gathering of the Community

Opening Music
Greeting
Hymn
Opening Prayer(s)
The Community Proclaims The Word Of God
First Reading from the Bible
Psalm or Other Response
Second Reading from the Bible
Anthem or Other Response
Reading from the Gospel
Sermon
The Community Responds To The Word Of God
Call To Discipleship
Hymn
Affirmation of Faith
Prayers of the People
The Community Comes Together Around The Lord's Table
Invitation to the Lord's Table
Offering
Prayers at the Table
Words of Institution and Breaking of the Bread
Lord's Prayer
Peace
Communion
Prayer After Communion
The Community Goes Forth To Serve God In Mission
Hymn
Closing Words
Closing Music[51]

By situating Disciples of Christ worship practice within the broader framework of eucharistic worship, *Thankful Praise* corrects the

---

[51]Ibid., 24-27.

individualist and subjectivist bias of Osborn's *Christian Worship: A Service Book*. Just as important, Watkins' model reintroduces into Disciples congregational worship life the larger liturgical tradition while preserving the distinctive Disciples worship heritage.

Osborn's overemphasis on individualism and subjectivism is countered by a stress on the corporate and God-centered nature of worship. According to *Thankful Praise*, "worship is essentially *corporate* thanksgiving and praise offered by sinful and redeemed human beings in *response to God's saving revelation*" (my italics). Throughout the service book, Christian worship is expressed in collective terms. The five headings for the movements of worship "deliberately emphasize the corporate character of worship." Moreover, the commentary repeatedly encourages "fuller participation" of the congregation and, at one point, extols "the congregation's role as co-celebrants of communion."[52] In turn, this theological principle is incorporated into numerous examples of different prayer forms and responses.

Subjectivism is redressed by understanding the gathering or opening act of worship to be the congregation's deliberate response to God's prior activity. Watkins writes: "The content of the greeting may change with the liturgical season . . . but the purpose of this part of the service remains constant: to acknowledge and express that our worship is a *God-centered activity* (my italics)." Furthermore, by interpreting worship as eucharistic worship, *Thankful Praise* views the Sunday service as an integrated action of Word and Sacrament: "While [the] Word addresses the world in many ways, it customarily finds expression during worship in the readings from the Bible and in the sermon, and it is enacted in the meal at the Lord's table.[53]

The Lord's Supper is no longer an independent ordinance that can be placed either before or after the sermon, depending on ministerial or congregational preference. Instead, the table is the central act of worship. The manual declares: "The response of thankful praise reaches its climax in the Lord's Supper."[54] By situating worship within a eucharistic framework, *Thankful Praise* affirms the early Disciples emphasis on the centrality of the Lord's Supper and the normative practice of including both Word and Sacrament in the Sunday morning service. It also affirms the ecumenical desire to place the Lord's

---

[52]Ibid., 20, 25, 51-52.
[53]Ibid., 31, 34.
[54]Ibid., 44.

Supper after the sermon in the "shape" or structure of the service. Here early Disciples practice and the ecumenical convergence agree that worship features the proclamation of the Word of God, *followed* by the enacting and embodying of that Word in Holy Communion, all in a setting rich with hymnody and prayer. This shape is presupposed throughout *Thankful Praise* and is elaborated in the following commentary.[55]

The reassertion of the Word and Sacrament pattern for the Sunday service has numerous implications for the ordering of the service. For Disciples, the pastoral prayer traditionally precedes the sermon. In this resource it is renamed the "Prayers of the People" and is understood as a response to the Word.[56] As "a thankful response to the proclamation [of] the Word of God and an act of preparation for the Lord's Supper,"[57] the offering is deliberately located after the sermon and before communion. Creeds or affirmations of faith (witnesses to Christian faith and not guardians of orthodoxy) are introduced as a corporate response to the preached Word. The term "invocation," usually associated with the opening prayer of a service, is reserved for the *epiclesis* at communion. The role of the Holy Spirit at the Lord's Supper, as well as *anamnesis,* is expanded. Multiple readings of the Bible, preferably selected from the lectionary, are suggested as a means for congregational life to participate more fully in salvation history. To facilitate the "continuity of God's work from Abraham through Christ," *Thankful Praise* uses the term "Hebrew Scriptures" instead of Old Testament and "Apostolic Writings" instead of New Testament.[58] Finally, this manual recommends Trinitarian language and responses for congregational worship.[59]

Although to many Disciples the appropriation by *Thankful Praise* of so-called "Catholic" or "high church" practices may appear to violate Disciples worship sensibilities, the opposite is true. This service book remains faithful to Disciples heritage precisely because it incorporates the insights and practices of the larger tradition into the worship life of the church. In contrast to *Christian Worship: A Service Book*, where individual items from the Christian worship tradition

---

[55] Ibid., 20.
[56] Ibid., 41.
[57] Ibid., 45.
[58] Ibid., 56, n. 3.
[59] Ibid., 37.

were sprinkled throughout the volume, *Thankful Praise* integrates practices from the universal church into the very shape of worship.[60] Yet the distinctive Disciples worship heritage is preserved and enhanced. The centrality of the Lord's Supper[61] remains the cornerstone of *Thankful Praise* while concurrently repositioning Disciples worship into the broader stream of eucharistic worship. Typical of the Disciples, this manual affirms the roles of the minister and elder(s) at the table. To "signify the unity and continuity of Christ's church" in general, and to comply with our ecumenical partners in particular, *Thankful Praise* recommends, however, that an ordained minister preside at the Lord's Supper and say the Words of Institution.[62]

Perhaps *Thankful Praise*'s greatest accomplishment is the seriousness with which it takes the Disciples ecumenical imperative. It is no longer possible that we can affirm the unity of the church without at least dialoguing with the larger church on matters of worship. Toward this end, the volume is a teaching book. From its five principle sources to its six convictions for renewal and its rich commentary on the order of the service, *Thankful Praise* epitomizes the interdependence of theology and practice. Because this service manual neither prescribes how Disciples should worship nor reinforces current Disciples practice (but rather seeks "to stimulate reflection about worship and to provide models" of worship for local development), this book must be judged an overwhelming success.

Although *Thankful Praise* can be enthusiastically endorsed for its accomplishments, it can be improved. It is inconsistent, for example. A subtle, yet persistent, theme of "correctness" throughout the volume undermines the claim of *Thankful Praise* to respect different theologies within the church. In particular, the editor insists that "one of the greatest needs in churches today" is the "rediscovery of authentic Christian worship."[63] This wording implies that current worship practices are invalid and this statement is simply too judgmental.

More important, the commentary repeatedly[64] employs the word "Gospel," without ever defining it. This omission diminishes the

---

[60]Moore, "Prayers," 93.
[61]Watkins, *Thankful Praise*, 44-55.
[62]Ibid., 58, n. 8.
[63]Ibid., 18, 12.
[64]Ibid., 17, 28, 38-39.

teaching function of *Thankful Praise*. Also frustrating is the manual's announced practice of highlighting in bold type the essential elements of the order for the Sunday service without stating the reasons. Why, for example, are the Lord's Prayer (prayed in most liturgical traditions) and hymns (cited by Campbell as one of the five categories required for Christian public worship) judged to be nonessentials? After all, users of this worship book deserve to know the selection criteria as well as the theological rationale employed by the editor.

Even more regrettable is the exclusion of a prayer of confession from the order of service.[65] Because the stated definition of worship for this resource book includes the phrase "offered by sinful and redeemed human beings in response to God's saving revelation," confession and absolution are implied. Yet the Lutheran concept of *simul iustus et peccator* (simultaneously justified and sinner) cannot be found in the shape of the service. Although it could be argued that the typically optimistic Disciples view of humanity precludes the need for confession, this volume counters any sanguine anthropology with a strong dose of post-Holocaust realism.[66] Moreover, Disciples emphasis on self-examination at the Lord's Supper and most Christian communities' use of a confession argue for its inclusion in this service book.

A theological inconsistency also occurs during *Thankful Praise*'s discussion of the enlarged role of the minister and the corresponding reduced role of the elder at communion. This whole conversation is erroneously set within the context of the Lord's Supper as an independent ordinance and not within the more encompassing context of Word and Sacrament. Consistency requires that the role of the elder, like all the other elements and participants in worship, be interpreted within the larger Word and Sacrament framework. Hence, the person who presides at the table must have some prior relation to the Word in order to preserve the continuity of Word enacted in Sacrament.[67]

This brief discussion of the role of the elder at the table and the omission of a prayer of confession from the order of the Sunday service suggests that *Thankful Praise* has accomplished its purpose of stimulating reflection about worship. This volume represents one more invaluable step in the Disciples continuing effort to define

---

[65]Ibid., 27.

[66]Ibid., 56, n. 3.

[67]I am indebted to Moore, "Prayers," 136.

theologically its worship practice. However, the relationship between "the emerging ecumenical consensus" in worship and the distinctive Disciples pattern of worship needs further study.

Since the vitality and authenticity of the church's life and its creative growth are inextricably tied to its worship life, I second Ron Allen's call in *The Disciples Theological Digest* "to commission a definitive study of the fundamental issues in the history, theology, and practice of Disciples worship and of how this life of worship compares with the lives of other Christian communities."[68] In its worship patterns, the Christian Church (Disciples of Christ) has journeyed from "ancient order" to *Thankful Praise*. It is time to determine the next move.

---

[68]Ronald J. Allen, "'Worship Among Disciples: Literature and Practice'—Some Further Considerations," *Disciples Theological Digest* 3 (1988): 25.

Overcoming A Liberal-Conservative Divide: The Commission on Restudy of the Disciples of Christ

D. Newell Williams

Introduction

The Commission on Restudy of the Disciples of Christ was established in 1935 to overcome divisive tendencies within the Disciples of Christ. The Commission did not reverse the tendencies that ultimately produced the "moderate" Christian Church (Disciples of Christ) and the "conservative" Christian Churches and Churches of Christ (often referred to as the Independent Christian Churches).[1] Nevertheless, the Commission, composed of prominent Disciples representing a wide range of positions, identified a theological basis for Christian unity and, after 1949, became an "invisible fellowship of prayer" that nurtured and developed ties among individuals from the two groups. The story of the Commission, an important chapter in the history of the Stone-Campbell Movement,[2] sheds light on the theological challenge of overcoming a liberal-conservative divide.

---

[1]Wade Clark Roof and William McKinney classify religious groups along a liberal to conservative spectrum according to religious, social, and political views. On the left is the Jewish community. Just to the right of the Jewish community are liberal Protestants, identified as Episcopalians, Presbyterians, and the United Church of Christ. In the center are Catholics and moderate Protestants, identified as the Methodists, Lutherans, Northern Baptists, the Reformed churches and the Christian Church (Disciples of Christ). To the right of center are Black Protestant denominations. To their right are conservative Protestants, including Southern Baptists, Churches of Christ, Nazarenes, Assemblies of God, Churches of God. Roof and McKinney do not name the Christian Churches and Churches of Christ. See Roof and McKinney, *American Mainline Religion: Its Changing Shape and Future* (New Brunswick, NJ: Rutgers University Press, 1987) 223-28.

[2]The term Stone-Campbell Movement recognizes the importance of the leadership of Barton W. Stone and Thomas and Alexander Campbell in the formation of the movement now represented by three bodies: the Christian Church (Disciples of Christ), the Christian Churches and Churches of Christ, and the Churches of Christ. The history of the Commission has received attention from two Christian Churches

Background

The nineteenth-century founders of the Stone-Campbell Movement pled for the union of Christians by the rejection of human creeds as tests of fellowship and by the restoration of New Testament Christianity. By 1906, the Movement had divided over the use of instrumental music in worship and over the support of missionary societies to fund and oversee the work of missionaries. The larger of the two groups, identified as the Disciples of Christ, affirmed the employment of both instrumental music and missionary societies as acceptable means toward fulfilling the church's mission, while the Churches of Christ rejected both as violations of the New Testament church order.[3] By the second decade of the twentieth century, a new conflict had emerged within the Disciples segment of the Movement. The *Christian Standard*, one of the most widely read Disciples journals, charged that some Disciples had abandoned the "plea" by accepting the higher criticism of the Bible (which the *Standard* asserted undermined the authority of the New Testament), by participating in the Federal Council of Churches (which the *Standard* claimed *condoned* denominationalism), and by advocating "open membership"—the practice of receiving into membership Christians who had not received believer's immersion (which the *Standard* charged violated New Testament teaching). In July of 1919, the *Standard* called a "congress" to meet at Cincinnati, in advance of the October Cincinnati International Convention of the Disciples of Christ, to rally "loyal advocates of the Restoration cause" against "the propagandists who are endeavoring to swing the Restoration movement away from its mission."[4] The Cincinnati congress, which drew over 2,000 participants, was the beginning of *organized*

---

and Churches of Christ historians: James DeForest Murch, *Christians Only: A History of the Restoration Movement* (Cincinnati: Standard Publishing, 1962) 263-71; and Henry E. Webb, *In Search of Christian Unity: A History of the Restoration Movement* (Cincinnati: Standard Publishing, 1990) 339-58.

[3]The division had actually occurred by the 1890s, but was officially recognized by the U.S. Religious Census of 1906. See D. Newell Williams, ed., *A Case Study of Mainstream Protestantism: The Disciples' Relation to American Culture, 1880-1989*, (Grand Rapids: William B. Eerdmans Publishing Company, 1991) 3-10.

[4]"The Challenge of the Cincinnati Convention," *Christian Standard*, August 2, 1919, p. 9 quoted in Webb, 288. "Restoration movement," is one of several names that has been used for the movement led by Stone and the Campbells. It was the term favored by the leadership of the *Standard*.

opposition to the developments that the *Standard* had identified as "disloyal to the plea." The ensuing battle, waged over the next seven years, resulted in divisions that led to the establishment of the Commission.[5]The battle, though related to other issues, focused on open membership. Beginning in 1920, supporters of the *Standard* sought to recall missionaries who favored open membership by a series of resolutions presented to the International Convention and the Board of Managers of the United Christian Missionary Society. The convention and the board of the society both declared their opposition to open membership, but refused to recall missionaries who, according to the society, did not *practice* open membership or make their views "an occasion of strife."[6]

Matters came to a head at the October 1925 Oklahoma City convention. The *Standard* had campaigned hard to ensure a large showing of its supporters. A "Peace Commission" headed by Tulsa pastor Claude E. Hill proposed a resolution including the following provisions:

1. That no person be employed by the United Christian Missionary Society as its representative who has committed himself or herself to belief in or practice of the reception of unimmersed persons into the membership of Churches of Christ.
2. That if any person is now in the employment of the United Christian Missionary Society as representative who has committed himself or herself to belief in or practice of the reception of unimmersed persons into the membership of Churches of Christ, the relationship of that person to the United Christian Missionary Society be severed as an employee.[7]

---

[5]The following sketch of the conflict that led to the formation of the Commission follows Henry E. Webb, *In Search of Christian Unity*, 287-338. For alternative accounts of the conflict see Stephen J. Corey, *Fifty Years of Attack and Controversy* (St. Louis: The Committee on Publication of the Corey Manuscript, 1953) and William E. Tucker and Lester G. McAllister, *Journey in Faith: A History of the Christian Church (Disciples of Christ)* (St. Louis: The Bethany Press, 1975) 380-85.

[6]"'Sweeney's Resolution with Higdon Interpretation, as Endorsed by the Winona Convention," *Christian Standard*, September 30, 1922, p. 8, quoted in Webb, *In Search of Christian Unity*, 299.

[7]"Report of the Peace Conference Committee," *Christian Standard*, October 24, 1925, p. 9, quoted in Webb, *In Search of Christian Unity*, 305.

A. E. Cory, pastor at Kinston, North Carolina, argued before the Committee on Recommendations that adoption of the resolution would be approval of a creed (hence, disloyal to the plea). After a long discussion, the committee recommended to the convention that the clause calling for the discharge of all employees of the UCMS who were "committed ... to belief in" open membership be stricken from the resolution.[8] The convention rejected the recommendation of the Committee on Recommendations and voted overwhelmingly in favor of the original resolution!

Supporters of the *Standard* who thought the issue was settled were mistaken. At the UCMS board meeting in St. Louis, December 2-3, 1925, discussion focused on the meaning of the phrase "committed to belief in" the practice of open membership. At length, the board adopted the following statement: "The Board of Managers interprets the expression 'committed to belief in' as not intended to invade the private judgment, but only to apply to such as open agitations would prove divisive."[9] Little wonder that supporters of the *Standard* came to believe that UCMS was beyond democratic control!

The UCMS board also appointed a Commission to the Orient to investigate the *Standard*'s charges that missionaries were practicing open membership in the Philippines and China. The Commission to the Orient reported to the 1926 Memphis International Convention that there *had* been some "irregularities" in membership practices in the Philippines and China, but that they had been rectified. Former UCMS missionary Leslie Wolfe, who claimed that he had been recalled by UCMS because of his opposition to the open membership practices of other UCMS missionaries, and Filipino Juan L. Baronia disputed the report, but to little effect. Young people attending separate sessions were brought in for the vote and the convention sustained the report of the Commission. Edwin R. Errett, reporting the convention for the *Standard*, dubbed it "A Convention of Bad Faith" and noted that "Many devout disciples of the simple Nazarene went away declaring it the last International Convention they would attend; at least, until they could see evidence of a genuine 'clean up.'"[10]

---

[8]Corey, *Fifty Years*, 102-103.

[9]"Peace Resolution Policy Adopted," *United Society News*, December, 3, 1925, 2, quoted in Webb, *In Search of Christian Unity*, 306.

[10]Edwin R. Errett, "A Convention of Bad Faith," *Christian Standard*, November 27, 1926, 8, quoted in Webb, *In Search of Christian Unity*, 309.

Following the Memphis convention, many Disciples dissatisfied with the convention and UCMS directed their energies to developing new channels for fellowship and mission. These included the North American Christian Convention, a preaching and fellowship gathering that held its first meeting at Indianapolis in 1927. Though initially intended to provide a forum to advance the unity of the Disciples, it quickly became an alternative to the International Convention (called "International" because it included Disciples from both the United States and Canada). Support was also given to missions independent of UCMS. Newly organized Bible colleges to train "loyal" preachers, a summer camping program to prepare youth for Christian service, and associations for evangelism and new church development, all independent of existing Disciples organizations, also received support.

Study

The idea of a commission to restudy the Disciples as a means of responding to the division that had begun in the 1920s began with William F. Rothenburger, pastor of the 2,300 member Third Christian Church of Indianapolis. Rothenburger, who was president of the 1934 Des Moines International Convention, later wrote that his attempt to build a convention program representative of the various types of thought among Disciples had made him aware of the "paradox" in the Disciples use of the term "brotherhood" for their movement.[11] Upon Rothenburger's recommendation, the 1934 convention passed a resolution calling for the appointment of a commission to "restudy the origin, history, slogans, methods, successes and failures of the. . .Disciples ... with the purpose of a more effective and a more united program ...." Rothenburger's resolution specified that the commission be composed of persons "proportionately representing the varied phases and schools of thought and the institutional life among us."[12]

Nineteen commissioners were appointed by the president of the 1935 Convention, president of Drake University D. W. Morehouse. In following years, additional commissioners were appointed by the convention, upon nomination by the Commission. Morehouse designated Frederick D. Kershner, Dean of the College of Religion at Butler University (now Christian Theological Seminary), as chair and

[11]Rothenburger, Commission on Restudy of the Disciples. (A review from 1934 to 1945 inclusive.), Archives, Christian Theological Seminary Library, Indianapolis, Indiana, F. D. Kershner Collection MC 55 XVI:2.
[12]Ibid.

Rothenburger as secretary of the Commission.[13] Kershner and Rothenburger were later elected to their offices by the Commissioners themselves, Kershner serving as chair for nine years and Rothenburger as secretary throughout the fourteen year history of the Commission. Attendance at meetings of the Commission was irregular. In addition to Kershner and Rothenburger, the following eleven men (there were no women appointed to the Commission) provided continuity and direction to the Commission's work: E. S. Ames, pastor of University Church of Disciples and dean of the Disciples Divinity House at the University of Chicago; George W. Buckner, Jr., editor of *World Call* (a forerunner of the *Disciple*) and later Secretary of the Association for the Promotion of Christian Unity (now the Council on Christian Unity); F. W. Burnham, pastor of the Seventh Street Christian Church of Richmond and former president of UCMS; A. E. Cory, head of the Pension Fund and later adjunct professor of Missions at the College of Religion (who as pastor from Kinston, North Carolina had argued before the Committee on Recommendations of the 1926 convention that adoption of resolutions of the Peace Commission would be the approval of a creed); Homer L. Carpenter, pastor of First Christian Church, Louisville; Edwin R. Errett, editor of the *Christian Standard* since 1929; W. E. Garrison, Professor of Church History at the University of Chicago (elected to the Commission in 1937); C. C. Morrison, editor of the *Christian Century*; T. K. Smith, pastor of the Tabernacle (now First) Christian Church of Columbus, Indiana (elected to the Commission in 1937); O. L. Shelton, who followed Kershner as dean of the College of Religion (elected to the Commission in 1944); and Dean E. Walker, Professor of Church History at the College of Religion (elected to the Commission in 1936).[14]

---

[13]Morehouse's appointment of Kershner as chair of the commission accords with Dean E. Walker's claim that Rothenburger got the idea of a commission to respond to the division among Disciples from being a member of a discussion group led by Kershner that addressed issues related to the mission of the church. The group, which Kershner dubbed "Intelligentia," included a Methodist bishop, a Presbyterian pastor and a rabbi, in addition to Rothenburger and Disciples associated with the state and general work of the Disciples. William J. Richardson, Notes taken from class presentations (1985) by Dean E. Walker and Joseph H. Dampier giving their reflections on the Commission on Restudy, private collection of D. Newell Williams, Indianapolis, Indiana.

[14]Other commissioners appointed by Morehouse were: C. E. Lemmon, First Christian Church, Columbia Missouri; R. H. Miller, National City Christian Church, Washington D.C.; George A. Campbell, Union Avenue Christian Church, St. Louis, Missouri; Graham Frank, Central Christian Church, Dallas, Texas; P. H. Welshimer,

Discussion meetings of the Commission were initially held twice a year, alternately at Indianapolis and Chicago.[15] At most of the discussion meetings two or more papers were presented, followed by discussion.[16] Topics included the origins of the Disciples, sources of schism, possibilities for union with other Christians, and Disciples "methods" or polity. Worship was included at every discussion

---

First Christian Church, Canton, Ohio; C.M. Chilton, First Christian Church, St. Joseph, Missouri; A.W. Fortune, Central Christian Church and the College of the Bible, Lexington, Kentucky; W. E. Sweeney, Broadway Christian Church, Lexington, Kentucky; L. D. Anderson, First Christian Church, Fort Worth; Edgar DeWitt Jones, Central-Woodward Christian Church, Detroit, Michigan; L. N. D. Wells, East Dallas Christian Church. See Christian Church, Disciples of Christ *Year Book*, July 1, 1936–June 30, 1937, 155. At the Commission meeting, held July 6-9, 1936 at the Gladstone Hotel, Chicago, it was voted that four candidates for membership on the Commission should be recommended to the International Convention. The four candidates recommended were Willard E. Shelton, editor of the *Christian-Evangelist* (one of the journals continued in the *Disciple*), St. Louis; Henry C. Armstrong, First Christian Church, Anderson, Indiana and President of the Association for the Promotion of Christian Unity; George W. Buckner, Jr.; and Dean E. Walker. The minutes identified the four nominees as "younger men" and reported the conviction that "younger men would not only make a fresh contribution to our studies but would also perpetuate the results in the future." See Third Meeting of the Commission, Archives, Christian Theological Seminary Library, F. D. Kershner Collection MC 55 Series XVI:3. Of the thirteen commissioners who provided continuity and direction to the work of the Commission, more than half were over sixty years of age when appointed to the Commission: Kershner, Rothenburger, Ames, Burnham, Garrison, and Morrison.

[15]Expenses for the first three discussion meetings were covered by The Association for the Promotion of Christian Unity (now the Council on Christian Unity). *Year Book* 1936, p. 99. Costs for all other discussion meetings in the fourteen-year history of the Commission were covered through a travel expenses equalization fund provided by the Commissioners themselves. See Minutes, Columbus, Ohio Meeting, Deshler-Wallick Hotel, October 27, 1937; see also Wm. F. Rothenburger to Friends of the Commission on Restudy, Nov. 14, 1936, Archives, Christian Theological Seminary Library, F. D. Kershner Collection MC 55 XVI:3.

[16]At the Commission meeting, held July 6-9, 1936, at the Gladstone Hotel, Chicago, it was agreed that no paper presented to the Commission should be published, except with the approval of both the Executive Committee of the Commission and the author. Several of the papers presented at the Chicago meeting were later published in a special April-July, 1941 issue of the College of Religion's *Shane Quarterly* (now *Encounter*). At least two papers, one by Kershner and the other by C.E. Lemmon, pastor of the First Christian Church of Columbia, Missouri, were edited by the Executive Committee. See Archives, Christian Theological Seminary Library, F. D. Kershner Collection MC 55 XVI:3.

meeting. The Commission also met for business sessions, usually over lunch, during meetings of the International Convention.[17] The commission made its first response to the division among Disciples in 1937. In May of 1937, Kershner and Rothenburger learned that T. K. Smith, immediate past president of the North American Christian Convention, preferred that there be no more meetings of the North American Convention.[18] Smith, who was not at that time a member of the Commission, was invited to attend the Commission's discussion meeting, June 21-23, 1937, at the Gladstone, Hotel, Chicago. Smith reported that a growing number of the leaders of the North American Convention were in favor of discontinuing the convention, provided that the International Convention would include a wider range of preaching and doctrinal messages. In response to his report, it was suggested that the Commission on Structure and Function of the Convention might include in a projected study the work of the North American Convention and also the National

---

[17]The Commission made its first substantive report to the 1937 Columbus Convention. The report was titled, "Report on Agreements Reached, To The U.S.A. Convention 1937." Though the report makes no mention of the 1937 World Conference on Faith and Order, it addresses the subjects discussed at the 1937 conference and was intended to provide guidance to Disciples delegates attending the Conference. The report consists of a preamble and seven sections. Each of the sections began as a 500 to 750 word statement prepared by a member of the Commission: Walker, "The Call to Unity"; Burnham, "The Nature of the Church"; Lemmon, "The Message of the Church"; Errett, "The Church's Common Confession of Faith"; A. W. Fortune, "The Ministry of the Church"; P. H. Welshimer, "The Christian Ordinances" (original title, "The Sacraments of the Church"); R. H. Miller, "The Unity of Christendom in Relation to Existing Churches." The statements were first presented at the third discussion meeting, January 19-20, 1937 at the Lincoln Hotel, Indianapolis. Following discussion of the statements, the manuscripts were returned to their authors for revision. The revised statements were discussed and revised further at the fourth discussion meeting, June 21-23, 1937 at the Gladstone Hotel, Chicago. See Rothenburger to Friends of the Commission on Restudy, November 14, 1936; Minutes of the Meeting at the Lincoln Hotel, Indianapolis, Indiana, January 19-20, 1937, and Minutes of the Meeting at the Gladstone Hotel, Chicago, Illinois, June 21-23, 1937, Archives, Christian Theological Seminary Library, F. D. Kershner Collection MC 55 Series XVI. The preamble contains the classic Disciples theological commission disclaimer: "These studies are the report of the Commission as a whole and are presented after its careful consideration, but not in any sense as an official pronouncement or as exhaustive treatments of the selected topics." There is no mention of the issue of open membership. See *Year Book* 1939, 188.

[18]Rothenburger to Kershner, May 6, 1937 and Kershner to Rothenburger, May 8, 1937, Archives, Christian Theological Seminary Library, F. D. Kershner Collection MC 55 Series XVI.

Evangelistic Association (which also held conventions) with a view to
building a general convention program sufficiently inclusive to satisfy
all three constituencies. The commission voted to approach the
Commission on Structure and Function, the Continuation Committee
of the North American Convention and the executive of the National
Evangelistic Association regarding a meeting to explore possible
integration of the three organizations.[19]

A meeting of the Commission with representatives of the three
organizations took place at the Deshler-Wallick Hotel in Columbus,
Ohio, October 27, 1937, during the Columbus International
Convention. W. R. Walker, father of commissioner Dean E. Walker,
spoke in behalf of the North American Convention, explaining that
the gathering had grown out of the feeling of many Disciples that the
International Convention had been introducing "organizational
matters" and discussing current church and world conditions to the
neglect of the basic tenets of the Disciples. He stated, however, that
the programs of recent conventions had given greater attention to
the basic tenets of the Disciples. Charles Reign Scoville, of the
National Evangelistic Association, stated that his organization had
come into existence to provide an annual discussion of problems of
evangelism. He indicated, however, that the N.E.A. would be willing
to disband if such action would promote the "unity of the
Brotherhood." H. B. McCormick, pastor at Lakewood, Ohio,
represented the Commission on Structure and Function of the
Convention.[20] No action was taken, the meeting having been viewed
as strictly informational.

The commission's next two discussion meetings, held at the
Marott Hotel, Indianapolis, July 26-27,1938, and July 13-14, 1939,
continued the Commission's consideration of sources of schism
among Disciples, the possibilities of Disciples union with other
Christians, and Disciples "methods."[21] At the business session
conducted at the Jefferson Hotel during the Richmond Convention,
October 21, 1939, the Commissioners agreed to discuss fewer subjects

[19]Minutes of the Meeting at the Gladstone Hotel, Chicago, Illinois, June 21-23,
1937, Archives, Christian Theological Seminary Library, F. D. Kershner Collection
MC 55 Series XVI.

[20]Minutes, Columbus, Ohio Meeting, Deshler-Wallick Hotel, October 27, 1937,
Archives, Christian Theological Seminary Library, F. D. Kershner Collection MC 55
Series XVI.

[21]Tuesday, July 26 1938 and Minutes of July 13, 14 1939, Marott Hotel,
Indianapolis, Indiana, Archives, Christian Theological Seminary Library, F. D.
Kershner Collection MC 55 Series XVI.

and focus on those "most vital to the unity of the Brotherhood." Three subjects were identified as particularly pressing: the general convention, missionary policies, and evangelism, with priority given to the general convention.[22]

The next meeting of the Commission was held January 14-15, 1941, at the Spink-Arms Hotel, Indianapolis. The purpose of the meeting was succinctly stated by Rothenburger: "to find a basis for unity within the Brotherhood." On the first day of the meeting, Cory read a paper titled "The Cooperative Life and Convention of the Disciples of Christ." Walker presented a review of Cory's paper. Discussion produced agreement (1) that the Disciples were in a divided state, (2) that closer unity was possible, and (3) that the Commission should attempt to recommend to the Convention a plan for greater cooperation. Smith, Buckner, Burnham, and Errett were appointed to draft a recommendation to the executive committee of the International Convention outlining a plan for greater cooperation. The recommendation drafted by Smith, Buckner, Burnham, and Errett, and approved by the Commission, advised "That the president of the International Convention and the president of the Continuation Committee of the North American Christian Convention present each to the other a list of names from which there shall be selected a joint committee (the number to be agreed upon by these two leaders) to serve as the program committee for the succeeding International Convention."

On the second day of the meeting, Rothenburger read a paper titled "Missions Among the Disciples." It was followed by a paper from Errett on the same subject. After lengthy discussion of both papers, Errett, Rothenburger, and Walker were appointed to draft proposals for consideration by the Commission. The proposals drafted by Errett, Rothenburger, and Walker contained the relatively benign recommendations that Disciples recognize the right of each local church to select its own channels of missionary endeavor and that unfounded accusations regarding missionary organizations and independent missionaries be avoided. Their final proposal, however, was that "confidence in organized efforts would readily be regained by a policy of action and of selection of representatives, in which any given society would disavow endorsement or support of open membership." This proposal required that the Commission face

---

[22]Minutes of Business Session, October 21, 1939, Jefferson Hotel, Richmond, Virginia, Archives, Christian Theological Seminary Library, F. D. Kershner Collection MC 55 Series XVI.

squarely the issue of open membership. Taking one of the only actions that would allow advocates of open membership to remain on the Commission, the Commissioners voted to table the Errett, Rothenburger, and Walker proposals until the next discussion meeting.[23]

The next discussion meeting, held July 8-9, 1941 at the Stevens Hotel, Chicago continued the discussion of issues raised in the previous meeting. Cory and Walker reviewed their papers from the January meeting. Smith stated that if there was any hope that the next International Convention would make room for the people he represented, he would oppose the holding of a North American Convention in 1942. W. A. Shullenberger, pastor of Central Christian Church, Indianapolis and President of the 1942 International Convention indicated that he could not speak for the Executive Committee of the Convention, but that he would attempt to carry out the Commission's recommendation that the Executive Committee of the International Convention invite representatives of the North American Christian Convention to collaborate in preparing the program for a unitary convention in 1942. Commissioner Walker, who was also President of the Continuation Committee of the North American Convention, responded that he was "in the same boat" as Shullenberger as to binding the actions of the Continuation Committee, but that he, too, would support the Commission's recommendation of a unitary convention in 1942.

---

[23]On the back of his copy of the minutes of the July 13-14, 1939, meeting, Kershner plotted the membership of the Commission along a left to right continuum: on the right he listed Smith, Welshimer, Errett, Sweeney, Walker, and Robert S. Tuck of Wooster Ohio (who had been added to the Commission in 1939). In the center leaning toward the right, he listed himself, Anderson, Miller, and Claude E. Hill, First Christian Church, Tulsa (who had been added to the Commission in 1939). In the center leaning toward the left he placed Rothenburger, Frank, Cory, Wells, and George W. Stewart, Winnipeg (who had been added to the Commission in 1937 in response to a request that Canadians be represented on the Commission). On the left he placed Burnham, Carpenter, Lemmon, Fortune, Campbell, Ames, Chilton, Jones, Armstrong, W. E. Shelton, Morrison, Buckner, and Garrison. See Minutes of July 13-14, 1939, Marott Hotel, Indianapolis, Indiana, Archives, Christian Theological Seminary Library, F. D. Kershner Collection MC 55 Series XVI:3. Present at the January 14-15, 1941, meeting, according to Kershner's classification of the Commissioners, were four conservatives: Errett, Smith, Sweeney, and Walker; one from center right: Kershner; six liberals: Ames, Buckner, Burnham, Chilton, Garrison, and Fortune; and two from center left: Cory and Rothenburger. Minutes of Meeting Held at Spink Arms Hotel, Indianapolis, Indiana, January 14-15, 1914, Archives, Christian Theological Seminary Library, F. D. Kershner Collection MC 55 Series XVI.

Rothenburger and Errett next reviewed their papers from the January meeting. The resolution on missionary policies was returned to the floor for further discussion. Participants voted to consider the resolution item by item. The items recognizing the right of congregations to fund the missions of their choosing and calling for a halt to the making of unfounded charges were approved. Participants rejected the recommendation that confidence in organized efforts could be regained by a policy of action and of selection of representatives that would disavow endorsement or support of open membership.[24]

The next discussion meeting of the Commission was July 6-7, 1942, at the Marott Hotel, Indianapolis. The executive committee of the International Convention had rejected the Commission's recommendation that representatives of the North American Convention be invited to collaborate in preparing a program for a unitary convention in 1942. Shullenberger explained the process by which the program committee of the convention was appointed. Errett, still active on the Commission despite the vote on missionary policies at the last meeting, stated that he did not want the president of the convention to select a program committee from the North American Convention as such, but rather as "brethren." Buckner remarked that the Commission might well intercede with the executive committee of the convention regarding the appointment of the program committee for the next convention. Regarding the future of the North American Convention, Tulsa pastor Claude Hill (added to the Commission in 1939) declared that if half a dozen of the Commissioners would use their influence to stop the passage of a motion in the North American Convention to perpetuate itself, it would be stopped. Smith disagreed, stating that there could be no assurance that the convention would not demand fixing the time and place of another meeting. Walker added that there would have to be some recognition of independent missions at a unitary convention.

The commissioners voted to arrange a meeting in the near future with the president of the International Convention, the chair of the

---

[24]Using Kershner's classification, of the fourteen members present, three were conservatives, Errett, Smith, and Walker; two were in the middle leaning to the right: Kershner and Miller; two were in the middle leaning to the left: Cory and Rothenburger; seven were liberals: Lemmon, Buckner, Burnham, Jones, Morrison, Ames, and Garrison. Even with the support of all of the "middle of the roaders," the conservatives would not have been able to pass a resolution opposed by the liberals. Minutes July 8 and 9, 1941, Stevens Hotel, Chicago, Illinois, Archives, Christian Theological Seminary Library, F. D. Kershner Collection MC 55 XVI.

Continuation Committee of the North American Christian Convention, and one representative from each of the Disciples agencies to discuss the program of the 1943 convention before plans crystallized.[25] There is no record that this meeting took place, and given events that were just on the horizon, it is unlikely that the meeting was held. At the July 1942 Grand Rapids International Convention, a forthright advocate of open membership, Columbia, Missouri, pastor C. E. Lemmon was elected president.[26] Supporters of the *Standard* interpreted Lemmon's election as a clear indication that the International Convention was not interested in conciliation with opponents of open membership.[27]

Due to the Second World War (which the United States entered in December of 1941), there was no meeting of the Commission in 1943. Neither was there a meeting of the Convention. Nevertheless, events occurred that affected the Commission. In the fall of 1943, rallies were held at the Cincinnati Bible Seminary resulting in the publication in the *Standard* of a "Call for Enlistment" to oppose further efforts at conciliation with the International Convention and the United Christian Missionary Society. Burris Butler, minister of the South Side Christian Church, Kokomo, Indiana was appointed chair of a "Committee of Fifty."[28] On December 4, 1943, W. H. Mohorter, Secretary of the Standard Publishing Company, announced a change in the character of the *Standard*, stating that the journal would cease to be a publication of "general religious information and instruction" and become "a rallying center for all who believe implicitly in the authority of Christ as revealed to us in the divinely inspired New Testament Scriptures."[29]

Errett expressed his disappointment with conciliatory efforts in a December 25, 1943, editorial: "Restudy commissions are so much insincerity and, therefore, so much futility insofar as brotherhood is concerned as long as some agencies continue to claim to be and are acknowledged as 'official,' 'recognized,' etc., especially when they violate the basic doctrines of the Scriptures and, consequently, of our

---

[25]Minutes July 6 and 7, 1942, Marott Hotel, Indianapolis, Indiana, Archives, Christian Theological Seminary Library, F. D. Kershner Collection MC 55 Series XIV.

[26]Lemmon was a fairly inactive member of the Commission but had attended the last two discussion meetings.

[27]Webb, *In Search of Christian Unity*, 352.

[28]Ibid., 355.

[29]Ibid., 355.

people." Expressing a position that seemingly could only support division, Errett added:

Moreover, we had as well recognize it now as later: there is no chance of unity between those, on the one hand, who accept the Scriptures as uniquely inspired and the commands of Jesus and His apostles as binding and those, on the other hand, who do not accept the Scriptures as uniquely inspired and, therefore, can, without compunction, introduce such practices as open membership in the congregations and missionary and educational institutions. . . . It is not merely that we do not believe such unity feasible; we do not desire it.[30]

Nevertheless, Errett—who had remained active on the Commission even after the proposal regarding open membership had been voted down—was not ready to disfellowship all supporters of UCMS and the International Convention. Hence, he believed that his dismissal as editor of the *Standard* was imminent. Preparing for this event, he spoke with directors of the Christian Foundation of Columbus, Indiana, regarding the establishment of a more moderate journal.[31] Before anything could come of such efforts, Errett died of a heart attack, January 29, 1944.[32]

A month earlier, Kershner, assuming that the Commission would not meet due to wartime conditions, had written to the Commissioners regarding several concerns, requesting that they send him their suggestions as to what ought to be done, and promising that he would prepare a redaction of their responses to be mailed to the entire membership. Kershner's concerns were (1) the declining growth rate of the Disciples ("we have made far less numerical progress than appeared certain in our youthful dreams of four or five decades ago"), (2) the declining social influence of the Disciples ("forty years ago many of the leading figures in the social, intellectual and political life of our community were Disciples"), (3) the loss of enthusiasm and confidence among Disciples regarding their mission ("There is a note of defeatism on the lips of most of us even when we are consciously

---

[30]*Christian Standard*, 78:1091-1092.
[31]The Christian Foundation had been organized by Kershner and Columbus, Indiana industrialist William G. Irwin to fund the College of Religion and other projects.
[32]*Webb, In Search of Christian Unity*, 356.

trying to preserve our optimism"), and (4) the increase of internal strife ("a resurgence of schismatica and unbrotherly contentions, which almost inevitably accompanies a loss of vital enthusiasm").[33]

Kershner received eight responses to his December letter. Burnham and Edgar DeWitt Jones, a Detroit pastor who had been appointed to the Commission by Morehouse, indicated that commercial competition between rival publishing companies was responsible for much of the internal strife.[34] Buckner and Carpenter pointed to the need for passion and a sense of purpose.[35] W. E. Sweeney, of Lexington, Kentucky, appointed to the Commission by Morehouse and a staunch opponent of open membership, stated that the principle cause of dissension among Disciples was the fact that some had departed from the traditional Disciples position while others adhered to it. He charged that the Commission had refused to face this problem.[36]

The two lengthiest responses were from Hill and P.H. Welshimer of Canton, Ohio, pastor of the Disciples' largest congregation, whose name had appeared in support of the "Call to Enlistment." The content of their responses was remarkably similar, though a kinder, gentler spirit was expressed in the letter from Hill than in the letter from Welshimer. Both stated that Disciples had suffered lamentable decreases in their evangelistic passion and their enthusiasm for uniting the contemporary church by restoring the New Testament church. Hence, in the view of both respondents, the Disciples had largely lost their distinctive mission and message and had become merely another denomination. Hill blamed the preachers for not preaching the gospel and the distinctive Disciples mission. Welshimer laid the blame at the door of certain unnamed educational institutions. Welshimer admitted, as well, that some preachers had injured the cause both within and outside the movement by an "unkind" preaching of the truth. Hill suggested that dissension among Disciples was to be credited

---

[33]Kershner to the members of the Commission to Restudy the Disciples of Christ, December 12, 1943, Archives, Christian Theological Seminary Library, F. D. Kershner Collection MC 55 Series XVI.

[34]Burnham to Kershner January 18, 1944, and Jones to Kershner, January 20, 1944, Archives, Christian Theological Seminary Library, F. D. Kershner Collection MC 55 Series XVI.

[35]Carpenter to Kershner, January 25, 1944, and Buckner To Kershner, January 5, 1944, Archives, Christian Theological Seminary Library, F. D. Kershner Collection MC 55 Series XVI.

[36]Sweeney to Kershner, February 29, 1944; see also Sweeney to Kershner, January 11, 1944, Archives, Christian Theological Seminary Library, F. D. Kershner Collection MC 55 Series XVI.

not to any one group, but to individuals "on all sides and in all quarters" who cared more for personal desires and programs than for the Disciples mission of uniting the church for the purpose of evangelism. Hill also suggested that the Commission should meet, pray and, in an obvious reference to the "Call to Enlistment," issue a "call to our Brotherhood—a call to repentance—a call to unity—a call to evangelism."[37]

A different spin on the Disciples loss of their distinctive mission and message was offered by Burnham. Burnham suggested that some Disciples had lost enthusiasm for certain elements of the Disciples "plea," not because of a sense of defeat, but (1) because they saw that major forces of Christendom had taken up the call to unity through the ecumenical movement and (2) because they discovered that Disciples lacked a definite program for unity, other than "absorption," which no longer seemed as workable to them as it once had. Burnham also observed that American Protestants had lost interest in denominational distinctions. "If they are inclined to religion, except for Roman Catholics, any convenient—or fashionable—church will do."[38]

Disappointed at the small number of responses received, Kershner resigned as chair of the Commission March 9, 1944.[39] In response to an appeal from W. E. Sweeney that he withdraw his resignation as chair of the Commission, Kershner wrote to Sweeney March 24, 1944:

> The situation in the Commission is such that it does not seem to me that I am able to do anything …. As you know, I have been anxious to retain the responsibilities involved in the chairmanship of the Commission. Up until this year, however, it appeared to me that I could render some service by continuing in the position. Everything is different now …. I am always glad to meet with any of my brethren who are

---

[37]Hill to Kershner, January 14, 1944, and Welshimer to Kershner, January 25, 1944, Archives, Christian Theological Seminary Library, F. D. Kershner MC 55 Series XVI.

[38]See Burnham to Kershner, January 18, 1944, Archives, Christian Theological Seminary Library, F. D. Kershner Collection MC 55 Series XVI.

[39]Kershner to Fortune, March 9, 1944, Archives, Christian Theological Seminary Library, F. D. Kershner Collection MC 55 Series XVI:4; see also Kershner to Will [Sweeney] January 15, 1944 and Kershner to Sweeney March 2, 1944, Archives, Christian Theological Seminary Library, O. L. Shelton Collection MC 65 Series I:4.

willing to meet with me, but you can't get people together
unless they are willing to come.[40]

Kershner's resignation as chair automatically made the vice-chair,
R. H. Miller, chair of the Commission.[41] Formerly pastor of National
City Christian Church in Washington, D.C., Miller had become editor
of the *Christian-Evangelist* (a forerunner of the *Disciple* magazine) in
1941. In response to Kershner's December 1943 letter, Miller, in a
spirit akin to that of Hill, had suggested that the Commission should
meet in the near future, discuss Kershner's letter, and take a stand for
"freedom in unity" in response to the "Call to Enlistment."[42]

The commission met at the Marott Hotel, Indianapolis June 22-
23, 1944. Individual commissioners had been selected to initiate
discussions on the following topics: Burnham, "Our Plea;" Walker,
"Things That Divide Us;" Welsheimer, "A Unitary Convention;"
Miller, "Well-Defined Groups Among Us;" and Kershner,
"Fellowship, The Neglected Phase of Our Plea." Burnham identified
five elements of the plea: the unity of all believers, the right of
private interpretation, unity in diversity, the historical approach to
the Bible (to whom, by whom, and for what purpose was a particular
book written?), and Jesus Christ as the Son of God as the church's
confession. Walker indicated that Disciples were divided by such
organizations as the Campbell Institute (headed by Ames) among
"liberals" and the Fellowship of Ministers in Indiana among
"conservatives," by the two conventions (International and North
American), and by journals. Welsheimer stated that tolerance and
kindness would be essential to a unitary convention. Miller declared
that classifying preachers as loyal and disloyal (a long standing
practice of the *Christian Standard*) had never been wholesome.
Kershner argued that baptism is both individual and social: it puts the
individual right with God and associates the individual with other
believers. He asserted that if Disciples had the full measure of love in
their hearts, they would not be divided—a sentiment with which,

---

[40]Kershner to Will [Sweeney], Archives, Christian Theological Seminary Library, O. L. Shelton Collection MC 65 Series I:4.
[41]Kershner to Fortune, March 9, 1944, Archives, Christian Theological Seminary Library, F. D. Kershner Collection MC 55 Series XVI:4.
[42]Miller to Kershner, January 6, 1944, Archives, Christian Theological Seminary Library, F. D. Kershner Collection MC 55 Series XVI: 4.

according to the minutes, all of the Commissioners present concurred.[43]

In accord with Miller's recommendation that the Commission take a stand for "freedom in unity" in response to the "Call to Enlistment," the Commission approved resolutions (1) recommending that the International Convention appoint a committee to restudy the constitution of the convention in order to insure access to all and (2) recommending that future conventions devote three half-days to programs for the discussion of current issues with a view to the promotion of greater unity.[44] The Convention also nominated to the Commission eight persons. Two of that number were members of the Committee of Fifty: Orville Morgan, pastor of Broadway Christian Church, Lexington, Kentucky and J. J. Whitehouse, pastor at Angola, Indiana.[45] At their business meeting during the October, 1944 Columbus Convention, the Commission added two more members of the Committee of Fifty to their slate, J. H. Dampier, of Milligan College, Johnson City, Tennessee and Burris Butler, chair of the Committee of Fifty.[46]

The next discussion meeting of the Commission was held January 16-17, 1945 at the Marott Hotel, Indianapolis. The program featured

---

[43]Commission on Restudy of Disciples Minutes, Archives, Christian Theological Seminary Library, F. D. Kershner Collection MC 55 Series XVI.

[44]A committee to restudy the constitution of the convention to insure access to all was not appointed and, apparently, was not needed. A year later the Commission instructed the secretary to send a letter to President M. E. Sadler of Texas Christian University, president of the 1946 International Convention, requesting (1) that the convention be made representative of the "brotherhood" as a whole and not merely of the cooperative agencies and (2) *that it be made clear that according to the constitution of the Convention, both cooperative and independent agencies submitting their records for auditing may participate in the convention.* See Commission on Restudy of the Disciples. (A review from 1934 to 1946 inclusive.), Archives, Christian Theological Seminary Library, F. D. Kershner Collection MC 55 Series XVI.

[45]The other six nominees were Eugene Beach, Youngstown, Ohio; Hugh B. Kilgore, Toronto, Canada; James DeForest Murch, Cincinnati; O. L. Shelton, Indianapolis; Gerald Sias, Ponca City, Oklahoma; and R. M. Bell, Kimberlin Heights, Tennessee. See Commission on Restudy of Disciples Minutes, Archives, Christian Theological Seminary Library, F. D. Kershner Collection MC 55 Series XVI: 4. Murch identified Beach as on the "left," Kilgore, Shelton, and Sias as in the "middle," and himself and Bell on the "right." See James DeForest Murch, *Adventuring for Christ in Changing Times: An Autobiography of James DeForest Murch* (Louisville: Restoration Press, 1973) 133.

[46] Commission on Restudy of the Disciples. (A review from 1934 to 1945 inclusive.), Archives, Christian Theological Seminary Library, F. D. Kershner Collection MC 55 Series XVI:4.

both old and new members of the Commission in the leadership of the meeting. Responsibility for initiating discussion on selected topics had been assigned as follows: Stephen A. England, Phillips University, Enid, Oklahoma (elected by the 1942 Grand Rapids Convention), "Can the Disciples have a Comprehensive Convention?"; Garrison, "Is the Restoration Movement a Workable Approach to the Unity of the Church?"; Cory, "How Can the Divergencies already Discovered Best be Reconciled or Made Non-Divisive?"; and James DeForest Murch (elected by the 1944 Convention), "The Autonomy of the Local Church."[47]

One newly nominated member was notably absent from the 1945 meeting. Burris Butler, who had become editor of the *Standard* following Errett's death, declined nomination to the Commission. Rather, he requested that he be permitted to attend sessions of the Commission as a visitor. This request was denied. The Commission renewed its invitation to Butler to become a member. Butler, again, refused.

Among the 1944 nominees present was O. L. Shelton.[48] Formerly pastor of the Independence Boulevard Christian Church of Kansas City, Missouri, Shelton had been appointed dean of the School of Religion in April, 1944, succeeding Kershner who, in failing health and blind, had resigned the deanship to devote his full energies to teaching. In July of 1945, the Commissioners elected Shelton to follow Kershner as chair of the Commission.[49]

Under Shelton's leadership, the Commission published reports that aimed at extending to a broader constituency the Christian unity that had developed through the Commission. The first of the reports published under Shelton's leadership was submitted to the August 6-11, 1946 Columbus International Convention. It was a compilation of

[47]Minutes of Meeting, Marott Hotel, Indianapolis, January 16, 17, 1945, Archives, Christian Theological Seminary Library, F. D. Kershner Collection MC 55 Series XVI:4. Much, a member of the editorial staff of the Standard Publishing Company, had refused to endorse the policy opposing conciliation with UCMS and the International Convention. In February, 1945, Much was relieved of his duties with Standard Publishing. See Much, *Adventuring*, 147-151.

[48]Minutes of Meeting, Marott Hotel, Indianapolis, January 16, 17, 1945, Archives, Christian Theological Seminary Library, F. D. Kershner Collection MC 55 Series XVI:4. Other newly elected members present in addition to Much (who presented a paper) were Dampier, Whitehouse, and R. M. Bell, President of Johnson Bible College, Kimberlin Heights, Tennessee.

[49]Commission on Restudy of the Disciples. (A review from 1934 to 1946 inclusive.), Archives, Christian Theological Seminary Library, F. D. Kershner Collection MC 55 Series XVI:4.

papers on "Causes of Unrest and Dissension Among the Disciples of Christ" presented July 9-11, 1946 at the Marott Hotel by Morrison, an outspoken advocate of open membership, and Walker, who following Errett's death, was viewed as the champion of the opponents of open membership on the Commission.[50]

Regarding baptism, the 1946 report stated that "Our churches have from the beginning administered the ordinance of baptism by the immersion in water of a penitent believer." The report further stated that "It has also been our practice, in the case of unimmersed members of other churches who sought membership with us, to receive them only on condition of their acceptance of immersion." Divergent viewpoints were stated as follows:

> Some hold that, under the authority of Christ we have no right to receive any who have not been scripturally baptized, and that we are bound to apply this principle to the penitent believer and the unimmersed Christian without discrimination. It is maintained that any such discrimination is a surrender of the witness which we have been called to bear with respect to the scriptural action of baptism.
>
> Others hold that in making the distinction between a penitent believer and one who brings credentials from a sister church of Christ, they are acting under the authority of Christ. They believe that inasmuch as Christ has received such a person into the membership of his church, they would be disloyal to Christ in not recognizing the full status of such a person as a Christian, a member of the Church of Christ, and receiving him as such without re-baptism, unless he desire to be re-baptized.

The commission identified two other issues as also being "causes of tension among us." One was the development of the North American Convention as an expression of dissatisfaction with the International Convention. The commissioners stated: "We are . . . agreed that our people have not yet found a type of convention which fully satisfies their tradition, their convictions and their sense of obligation to give united expression to the interests of Christ's kingdom." Noting that conventions have served "to enlarge the vision of the local churches

---

[50]Minutes of Meeting Indianapolis, Indiana, Marott Hotel, July 9-11, 1946, Archives, Christian Theological Seminary Library, A. E. Cory Collection MC 1 Series III:1.

by exchange of views and experiences and by keeping the churches conscious of belonging to one another," they asserted that it is evident "that the brotherhood has a clear call to provide itself with a convention that will unite our people. . ."

The other cause of tension identified by the Commissioners were "challenges" to the "simple, scriptural and truly catholic creed, namely faith in Jesus Christ as the Son of God and man's Savior" endorsed by the Disciples founders. These challenges were identified as follows:

> Some among us seem to have abandoned the theological implications in the simple confession of Christ, and have come to regard His Lordship chiefly and essentially in ethical terms. He is the supreme moral and spiritual leader of mankind, and the confession of faith in Him is essentially a decision to follow His way of life.
>
> Others go to the other extreme and seem to confound faith with doctrine. They insist that the Lordship of Christ must be interpreted theologically, and that their particular interpretation must be made explicit in the confession as the basis of our fellowship and unity.

The commissioners asserted that for the Disciples founders, "faith represented not a belief about Him in terms of the historic creeds, but was simple acceptance of the fact of His divinity and a spiritual and moral attitude toward Him."

In addition to causes of tension, the Commission identified differences regarding four issues that had emerged by the 1940s: *denominational status* ("Some ... hold that we must ... refuse to accept any denominational status, and rather seek to occupy non-partisan and ultimate ground in all points of faith and order"/"Others hold that we are compelled by the existing order ... to be a denomination, while at the same time testifying against denominationalism and exploring all possibilities of finding common ground on which all Christians may stand"), *local church autonomy* ("Some ... hold that there is a tendency on the part of agencies and conventions to assume and to exercise authority over the local churches"/"Others interpret the utterances and policies of the agencies and conventions as . . . the exercise of . . . leadership which the churches desire" and to which they respond "voluntarily"), *the New Testament church* ("Some ... find in the New Testament the divinely authoritative pattern for the form and organization of the local church"/"Others ... recognize in the New Testament certain *principles* which inherently belong to any local church that calls itself Christian, but they do not find any evidence that forms of organization or procedure prevailing in the primitive church, were authoritatively prescribed as a pattern"), *connexional relationship* (Some believe that since the New Testament "gives no clear evidence of an organization of local churches in a general or connexional relationship," our churches would deviate from the New Testament norm should they create an agency as their "exclusive" instrument for mission or create a "single" convention for the formation and expression of their convictions/"Others believe that the absence of an authoritative pattern leaves the churches free, and their relation to each other in the Church renders it their duty ... to create such agencies ... as may be needed ... to carry on their ... enterprises and their plea for Christian unity in the most adequate and responsible manner").

The commissioners also asserted that "a principle cause of the major dissensions which disturb us" was that for many Disciples "the ideals of union and restoration have tended to fall apart as two concepts that are not coordinate or mutually dependent (Some affirm "that Christian unity is possible only on the basis of the restoration of the primitive church"/Others "are content to abandon the concept of the restoration of the primitive church and center our emphasis upon union"/Yet others "believe that a new synthesis of these two concepts of unity and restoration is possible").

The report recommended "a general and open discussion in our press, on our convention platforms and in the boards of our agencies, of the questions indicated in our present report, and any other questions relevant to our unity." The commissioners also stated that "the spirit of mutual consideration, respect and brotherly trust has drawn the members of our commission, representing the diversities of opinion existing among us, into an exceedingly precious fellowship." They declared that it was their highest desire and prayer that the same spirit would spread through "the brotherhood" as it pursued the discussion of issues outlined in the report.[51]

Far from encouraging discussion of the issues outlined in the report, the *Christian Standard* refused to publish it. However, Burris Butler drafted a response to the report that was sent to the Commission. Butler charged that the report assumed that "the brotherhood" consisted of "any who wish association in any way." He

---

[51]*Year Book* 1946, 116-20.

noted that when the Commission admits that open membership is a
"cause of tension" among Disciples it "acknowledges that it occupies
a legitimate place '*within the brotherhood*.'" According to Butler, the
Commission had confused the New Testament bond of fellowship
(requiring obedience to Christ) with an artificial or "denominational"
unity. In other words, the Commission had "placed matters of faith in
the category of opinion." Butler was especially sorry to see the names
of opponents of open membership associated with the report.
Referring to those members of the Commission, Butler asked, "In
their 'exceedingly precious fellowship' with men of *every shade of
unbelief* have these men, hitherto concerned about New Testament
teaching, come to place human friendships and social amenities above
loyalty to the direct commands of Christ?" From Butler's
perspective, what the Commission had failed to realize was that "what
they present as 'causes of tension' are really irreconcilable principles
that no amount of restudy can harmonize."[52]

The Commission's report to the 1947 Buffalo Convention was
largely the work of Buckner (who, in 1941 had become head of the
Association for the Promotion of Christian Unity) and Walker.[53]
Revised at a May 6-7 discussion meeting at the Marott Hotel with
significant help from Cory,[54] it appears to have been designed to
answer Butler's charge that the Commission was confused regarding
the true basis of Christian fellowship. The introduction to the report
declared the Commission's belief that "unity does not demand
uniformity in all things." Then followed six items upon which, the
Commission declared, Disciples agreed:

---

[52]"Commission on Restudy's Report Assumes Brotherhood To Be a
Denomination," Editorial Proof Sheet, Archives, Christian Theological Seminary
Library, F. D. Kershner Collection MC 55 Series XVI:4. The January 2-3, 1947,
discussion meeting at the Marott Hotel, Indianapolis was devoted to further
discussion of topics addressed in the 1946 Columbus Convention report. Orville
Morgan's resignation was accepted with regret. See Minutes of Meeting, Marott
Hotel, January 2nd and 3rd, 1947, MC 55. It is evident from correspondence with
Shelton that Morgan wanted to disassociate himself from the 1946 Convention
report. See Shelton to Morgan, February 10, 1947, MC 65 Series I:4 and Morgan to
Shelton, March 27, 1947, Archives, Christian Theological Seminary Library, O. L.
Shelton Collection MC 65 Series I:4.

[53]First two paragraphs of Buckner-Walker statement. Then —, Archives, Christian
Theological Seminary Library, A. E. Cory Collection MC 1 Series III:1.

[54]Shelton to Morrison, July 22, 1947, Archives, Christian Theological Seminary
Library, O. L. Shelton Collection MC 65 I:4 and hand written copy of final version,
Archives, Christian Theological Seminary Library, A. E. Cory Collection MC 1
Series III:1.

(1) "The acknowledgment of Jesus Christ as Lord and Savior is the sole affirmation of faith necessary to the fellowship of Christians."

(2) "The New Testament is the primary source of our knowledge concerning the will of God and the revelation of God in Christ. . ."

(3) "Each local church is, under Christ, a self-governing unit; that organization and agencies are in no sense governing bodies but may be useful instruments in carrying on Christian work and in fostering and expressing fellowship; that likewise congregations and individuals have the inherent right to initiate and carry on Christian work through directly supported enterprises without breach of the wider fellowship; and that the unity of the whole church in faith, fellowship and service is to be earnestly sought."

(4) "In the proclamation of the gospel of Christ as the message of salvation to the affection and intelligence of men, we have found our largest unity."

(5) "The Unity of Christians according to the program and prayer of our Lord, with Christ Himself the center of that unity, by the restoration of New Testament Christianity, is necessary to the realization of God's program for human redemption."

(6) "Their historical position has given them practical insight into the New Testament fellowship which they desire to share with the whole divided body of Christ."

As if responding to Butler's charge that the Commission was trying to maintain the unity of a "denomination" rather than the church, the Commissioners stated that their efforts were not only for their immediate fellowship, but for the whole church. "Solution of our problems in these matters," they averred, may contribute to "the ultimate triumph of the church over the ills of division."[55]

The commission's 1948 report was largely the work of Walker.[56] Approved at a discussion meeting held May 4-5, 1948 at the Marott,

---

[55]*Year Book*, 1947, 117.

[56]Shelton to Dear Commissioner, May 12, 1948; Minutes of Meeting at Marott Hotel, Indianapolis, Indiana, May 4 and 5, 1948, Archives, Christian Theological Seminary Library, F. D. Kershner Collection MC 55 Series XVI:4.

it stated that to preserve and develop their unity, Disciples must give attention to three major problems: *(1) The problem of distinguishing the nature of their agreements and differences.* The Commission asserted that differences were "in the realm of history, of theology, of application of principles to the problems of the church, of methods in labor and cooperation," while the agreements were "in the area of fact, of faith, and of doctrine." *(2) The problem of discovering, maintaining and enjoying fellowship.* The Commission declared that "Fellowship among Christians is based on the relation they sustain to Christ." Therefore, it is "personal, not organizational; religious—personal commitment to Christ—not theological; moral, not legal." The commission noted that among the means of expressing this fellowship were various agencies for Christian work, including direct participation by a congregation in work beyond its community and the Ecumenical Movement. *(3) The problem of educating Disciples to the realization, intellectually and practically, of the nature of their movement.* The commission urged Disciples not to think of their "brotherhood" as a sect, but as "a demonstration of that unity to which Christ has called his whole Church." The plea for unity upon the Good Confession of Christ was not merely for the sake of unity, and neither was it merely to abolish human creeds, but rather that "Christ may be unobscured and that the world may believe in him, and be saved."[57]

The final discussion meeting, held at the Marott July 5-6, 1949 revised and approved a preface and conclusion to the 1946, 1947, and 1948 reports prepared by Shelton, Walker, and Garrison.[58] As if to answer Butler's charge that opponents of open membership on the Commission had been blinded by the fellowship of the Commission, the Commissioners observed that "close fellowship" had not blunted, but sharpened their understanding of each other, their convictions, and the problems facing Disciples. They encouraged all Disciples to engage in similar studies, meeting in groups small enough to allow for full exchange of information and conviction, and disciplined enough to require careful preparation by the participants. Declaring that "our agreements are larger than our differences," they admonished that

---

[57]*Year Book* 1948, 121-22.
[58]Minutes of Study Meeting, Marott Hotel, Indianapolis, Indiana, July 5th and 6th, 1949, Archives, Christian Theological Seminary Library, F. D. Kershner Collection MC Series XVI:4.

"truth is found not in reiteration of our understandings in friendly audiences, so much as in submission to mutual criticism."[59]

At its final discussion meeting, the Commission also drafted four recommendations that were approved by the 1949 Cincinnati Convention. One of these recommendations concerned the continuing need for disciplined and informed theological discussion among Disciples. Observing that it would appear to be of great value to Disciples to have a "representative Commission for reference and resource concerning phases of faith and doctrine in the various proposals looking toward unity among Christians," the Commission called on the convention to establish a Commission on Christian Doctrine composed of theologically informed and interested persons representative of both the geographical and theological diversity of Disciples. It was further resolved that this commission be organized in "convenient regional sections" to ensure the participation of members and that terms of service be staggered so as to provide continuity in each section. It was also resolved that this body should study the significance of various statements of faith and doctrine and Christian practice in relation to New Testament Christianity, pursue as it should deem advisable joint studies with similar bodies, serve as a body of reference and resource for those who desire to avail themselves of its labors, and issue from time to time findings and statements in Reports to the Convention and in such other forms as the Convention may advise.[60]

The remaining recommendations had to do with the Commission's dismissal and the dissemination of its work. A final action of the Commission at their October 26, 1949 business meeting, held during the Cincinnati International Convention, was a vote not to dissolve the Commission, but to become an invisible fellowship of prayer.[61]

---

[59]The Report of the Commission on Restudy of the Disciples of Christ Authorized by the International Convention of the Disciples of Christ, San Francisco, 1948, Archives, Christian Theological Seminary Library, O. L. Shelton Collection MC 65 Series I:3.

[60]*Year Book* 1949 pp. 124-25.

[61]Minutes of the Business Session. Y.M.C.A., Cincinnati, Ohio, Centennial Convention October 26, 1949, Archives, Christian Theological Seminary Library, O. L. Shelton Collection MC 65 I:3. Much indicated that he gave the final devotional at the final discussion meeting (at Indianapolis) from Colossians 3:1-15, elaborating on what is involved in continuing in the oneness of Christ. "Above all, I said in the words of the text, it is imperative that 'forbearing one another and forgiving one another,' we 'put on love, which is the bond of perfectness and let the peace of God rule in our hearts'." Much reported that some years later (1960), Morrison has stopped him at an International Convention to tell him how much he had appreciated

Accomplishments

The literature of the Commission abounds in statements regarding the fellowship that developed within the Commission. This is not to suggest that the Commissioners came to one mind. In 1949, responding to the question of whether the Commission would be able to arrest trends toward disunity, Miller declared that "The differences of opinion within the Commission itself as to what may be done to arrest trends toward disunity I think are probably irreconcilable both as to the authority of the local church, the value of organizations in promoting co-operative endeavors, the place of conventions and conferences within the brotherhood, and the principle matter which has been up at every meeting of the Commission—that of open membership."[62] Nevertheless, the Commissioners, as Burris Butler had observed, had affirmed a theological basis of Christian fellowship broad enough to embrace supporters and opponents of open membership. Members of the Commission, notably W. E. Garrison, O. L. Shelton and Dean E. Walker remained faithful to that theological basis of fellowship.[63] The slender ties that bind Disciples and Independents today are often most evident in organizations that commissioners supported and helped to shape: the Disciples of Christ Historical Society, The European Evangelistic Society, and the World Convention of Churches of Christ.[64]

---

that devotional: "It spoke the feelings of my heart then, and still does." See Murch, *Adventuring*, 136-37.

[62]Miller to Shelton, January 23, 1948 , Archives, Christian Theological Seminary Library, O. L. Shelton Collection MC 65 Series I:4.

[63]As late as 1961, Garrison declared in a speech at the International Convention "I refuse to admit that those Disciples who do not cooperate with the agencies represented in this convention do not, on that account, belong to 'us'." Quoted in James DeForest Murch, *The Free Church: A Treatise on Church Polity with Special Relevance to Doctrine and Practice in Christian Churches and Churches of Christ* (n.p.: Restoration Press, 1966) 110-11.

[64]Garrison served on the board of the Historical Society from its inception in 1941 until his death in 1969. From 1948-1952 he served as chair. See James M. Seale, *Forward From The Past: The First Fifty Years of the Disciples of Christ Historical Society* (Nashville: Disciples of Christ Historical Society, 1991) 76-79, 176-77, 179. O. L. Shelton was chair of the Program Committee of the World Convention for two successive assemblies, 1947 and 1952. At the 1952 assembly he was appointed to chair a newly organized Study Committee charged with coordinating study between assemblies, an office he held until his death in 1959. Walker was president of the European Evangelistic Society from its founding in 1946 until 1974, remaining a supporter of the organization until his death in 1988. See Robert W.

The commission also succeeded, far more than has been previously recognized, in furthering theological discussion. To be sure, the Commission's recommendation of a Commission on Doctrine, though approved by the 1949 International Convention, was never implemented by the International Convention. Nevertheless, aspects of the recommendation were implemented by the World Convention and the Council on Christian Unity.

A program to encourage study between meetings of the World Convention was authorized by the 1952 Melbourne convention.[65] Between Melbourne and the 1955 Toronto assembly, six subjects were studied by twenty-five study committees located in fourteen countries. From Toronto to the 1960 Edinburgh assembly, another six subjects were reviewed by thirty-four study committees located in nineteen countries. From Edinburgh to the 1965 San Juan assembly, six more subjects were examined by forty-one study committees located in 17 countries. Manuscripts produced by the study committees were printed and commended to the churches for their study and consideration. By 1965, the following titles were available from the office of the World Convention and the Christian Board of Publication: *The Nature of the Unity We Seek, The Theology of Evangelism, The Authority in Revelation, Who is Jesus Christ?, The Congregation and the Body of Christ, The Ethical Demands of the Gospel, The Nature of the Church, The Place of Theology in the Church, The Lord's Supper, The Christian Ministry, The Christian Hope, Christian Baptism, Christianity in a Revolutionary Age, Churches of Christ within Ecumenical Christianity, The Nature and Work of the Holy Spirit, The Nature and Place of Worship in the Church, Biblical Authority Today,* and *The Ministry of Believers.* The founding chair of the World Convention committee that coordinated the studies was O. L. Shelton. Following Shelton's death in 1959, Stephen J. England (who had joined the Restudy commission in 1942) assumed leadership of the Study Committee.

In 1955, the Council on Christian Unity (previously known as the Association for the Promotion of Christian Unity) established a Department of Ecumenical Study to "relate Disciples in a responsible way to official ecumenical studies, to maintain a program of serious

---

Shaw, "Thus It Began" in *Faith In Practice: Studies in the Book of Acts: A Festschrift in Honor of Earl and Ottie Mearl Stuckenbruck,* eds. David A. Fiensy and William D. Howden (Atlanta: European Evangelistic Society, 1995) 9-41.

[65]The World Convention was organized in 1930 through the leadership of Jesse Bader, Edwin Errett, and other U.S. Disciples for the purpose of world fellowship among the churches of the Stone-Campbell tradition.

study among Disciples, and to prepare Disciples for competent participation in world-wide ecumenical study."[66] The connection to the Commission was Buckner, who was Executive Secretary of the Council. One of the study commissions of the Department of Ecumenical Study—the Commission on Biblical Theology— eventually became the Commission on Theology. A series of study documents on the Nature of the Church produced by the Commission are currently available from the Council on Christian Unity.

As late as 1945, Claude Hill expressed confidence that the Commission would prevent an "open, down-right split" in the movement. He indicated that as a result of the Commission "the radicals are not quite so radical, and some of the conservatives are not so conservative."[67] A hopeful soul, Hill gets no points for prophecy. Despite the work of the Commission, the divisions among Disciples evident in the 1930s and 1940s only hardened during the 1950s and 1960s, leading to the division of congregations. In 1968, after a plan for restructuring the International Convention and related agencies was approved by the convention, more than a third of the congregations listed in the Disciples *Year Book* formally withdrew from the Christian Church (Disciples of Christ). Many of these congregations had not supported the "cooperative" program of the Disciples for many years. Over the next few years, many other congregations that had earlier stopped support for the Disciples cooperative program also formally withdrew from the Christian Church (Disciples of Christ). In 1971, the Christian Churches and Churches of Christ asked to be listed as a separate body in the *Year Book of American Churches*.

Given the Commission's success both in identifying a theological basis for Christian unity and promoting theological discussion, why was the Commission unable to extend its "precious fellowship" to the larger Disciples movement? The answer is that persons on each side of the division simply did not desire fellowship with persons on the other side. With keen insight, the Commission noted in the preface to its final report that "tensions" regarding the mission and witness of the church were detrimental to continued relationship: "What seems very important to some, seems unimportant to others. What some consider essential to this Mission and Witness, others deem of minor

---

[66]*Year Book* 1956, 48-49.
[67]Hill to Shelton, November 6, 1945, Archives, Christian Theological Seminary Library, O. L. Shelton Collection MC 65 Series I:4.

importance or irrelevant."[68] Persons who believe that they have little in common rarely desire continued fellowship.

The problem of discovering, maintaining, and enjoying fellowship, as the Commissioners had described it in their 1948 report, points to the theological failure of the Commission. The commission asserted in its 1947 report that Disciples were agreed that "The acknowledgment of Jesus Christ as Lord and Savior is the sole affirmation of faith necessary to the fellowship of Christians." They further asserted in the 1947 report that, "In the proclamation of the gospel of Christ as the message of salvation to the affection and intelligence of men, we have found our largest unity." In their 1948 report they declared that "Fellowship among Christians is based on the relation they sustain to Christ." However, in none of their reports did they discuss "the gospel of Christ," what it means to "acknowledge Jesus Christ as Lord and Savior," or what they meant by "salvation," beyond the statement that for the Disciples founders "faith represented not a belief about Him in terms of the historic creeds, but was a simple acceptance of the fact of His divinity and a spiritual and moral attitude toward Him."

The absence of any further development of what the Commissioners understood to be the content of the confession of Jesus Christ as Lord and Savior is all the more striking in light of the Commission's acknowledgment in the 1946 report that a cause of tension among Disciples were "challenges" regarding the meaning of the confession. As the Commissioners reported in 1946, some had "abandoned the theological implications" in the confession of Christ and had "come to regard his Lordship chiefly and essentially in ethical terms . . . and the confession of faith in Him is essentially a decision to follow His way of life," while others had confused "faith with doctrine" and "insist that the Lordship of Christ must be interpreted theologically, and that their particular interpretation must be made explicit in the confession as the basis of our fellowship and unity." What the Commission failed to recognize was that the bare statement of the confession of Christ that they affirmed was not sufficient to maintain the fellowship of the Disciples. What Disciples needed was a description of the meaning of confession of Jesus as Lord and Savior that would allow persons who differed over such issues as the character of biblical authority, the proper relationship of the Disciples to the "denominations," and open membership, to recognize and claim a

---

[68]Typescript of report, Archives, Christian Theological Seminary Library, O. L. Shelton Collection MC 65 Series I.

common identity and task. Hence, despite its achievements in identifying a basis of Christian unity and promoting theological discussion, the Commission did not provide a description of the content of that basis of unity sufficient to empower the larger body of Disciples to reverse the divisive tendencies evident among them since the 1920s.

Conclusion

The story of the Commission is an important chapter in the history of the Stone-Campbell movement. Though the Commission failed to avert the Disciples-Independent division, it identified a basis for Christian unity, fostered disciplined and informed theological discussion, and was a force for unity within the divided Stone-Campbell Movement. Its institutional legacy runs from the European Evangelistic Society and the World Convention of Churches of Christ to the Disciples of Christ Historical Society and the Theology Commission of the Council on Christian Unity. The story of the Commission also sheds light on the theological challenge of overcoming a liberal-conservative division. The commission asserted rightly that "Fellowship among Christians is based on the relation they sustain to Christ." The failure of the Commission was to describe adequately the content of personal confession of Christ that overcomes division.

Seeking Triumphant Union and Being Found In Schism: Historical Patterns and Recent Polarities Among Disciples[1]

Anthony L. Dunnavant

Visitors to the Disciples of Christ Historical Society in Nashville, Tennessee, are greeted with a brief sign that points to the chief irony of Disciples history. Provided by the Historical Commission of Metropolitan Nashville and Davidson County, the sign begins "Disciples of Christ Historical Society: Library and archives of the 19th c. American religious unity movement which became: the Christian Church (Disciples of Christ); Christian Churches; and Churches of Christ." This "unity movement" added three significant new religious communities to the already divided and subdivided Church.

For Disciples, Christian division has been the sin that has particularly troubled their historical memory. Division was, after all, the epidemic that Disciples had seen raging in the history of "Old World" Christianity and wished to cure in the new American situation. Neither the Disciples' commitment to Christian unity nor their experience of division, however, has emerged without contexts. These must be briefly sketched.

The Stone-Campbell movement (in which the Disciples are rooted) arose in the United States in the early national period. This tradition subsumed several other rivulets into its stream, but it identifies the ministries of Barton W. Stone in central Kentucky and Thomas and Alexander Campbell in northwestern Virginia (now West Virginia) and Pennsylvania as its main sources.

In the historical literature of the Christian Church (Disciples of Christ), the interpretation that became conventional was a focus upon the Stone-Campbell movement's pursuit of Christian unity through

---

[1]This paper was prepared for and originally presented at the annual meeting of the American Society of Church History, Chicago, Illinois, 8 January 1995.

the restoration of New Testament Christianity.[2] In their influential *The Disciples of Christ: A History*, W. E. Garrison and A. T. DeGroot stated this thesis clearly: "The initial impulse of the movement, as expressed most clearly by Thomas Campbell, was a desire for the union of all Christians in one undivided church by the restoration of the primitive faith and practice as exhibited in the New Testament."[3]

What the historiographic focus on *restoration* and *unity* (and their interrelation) did was to highlight that which seemed most central, characteristic, and identifying of the internal life of the Disciples. The focus on these two ideas and on the tension between them became such a familiar part of Disciples historiography that by the 1960s it was widely taken for granted.[4]

In the 1970s, Ronald Osborn suggested that this two-idea framework needed to be expanded to include an emphasis on the idea of *freedom*. A significant part of the argument for this expanding of the interpretive formula relates to the importance of the United States and its political culture and values in the development of the Disciples of Christ.[5] The addition of freedom to the basic framework for interpreting the history of the Stone-Campbell movement helps to draw attention beyond its internal life to the contextual factors of American social and political culture and its religious interpretation. One of the things that scholars of the Stone-Campbell tradition who have turned their gaze in those directions have been rediscovering is early Disciples *eschatology*.

---

[2]The overview of Disciples historical/interpretative traditions in the next several paragraphs draws on my article "Evangelization and Eschatology: Lost Link in the Disciples Tradition?" *Lexington Theological Quarterly* 28,1 (Spring 1993):44-49.

[3]Winfred Ernest Garrison and Alfred T. DeGroot, *The Disciples of Christ: A History* (St. Louis: Bethany Press, 1958) 550.

[4]See W. E. Garrison, "An Overview: The Main Stream of Disciple Thought," in *Disciple Thought: A History*, Alfred T. DeGroot (Fort Worth TX: By the Author, 1965) 3.

[5]Ronald E. Osborn, *Experiment in Liberty: The Ideal of Freedom in the Experience of the Disciples of Christ, The Forrest F. Reed Lectures for 1976* (St. Louis: Bethany Press, 1978) 13, 118-19, n. 3, 19-45. Osborn's suggestion has been taken with some seriousness by Mark G. Toulouse who organized much of the first half of his *Joined in Discipleship: the Maturing of an American Religious Movement*, with a foreword by Martin E. Marty (St. Louis: Chalice, 1992) around the *three* themes of "the interpretation principle," "the restoration principle," and "the ecumenical principle." "The interpretation principle" is defined, in part, as "the freedom to embrace diversity." The opening chapter, "Born in America," of *Joined in Discipleship* also places the beginnings of the Disciples story in the context of the early American commitment to freedom (17-38).

The trajectory for this rediscovery was set, to a degree, by Churches of Christ scholar David Edwin Harrell, Jr. In his *Social History of the Disciples of Christ*, Harrell details the millennialist eschatology of early Disciples leaders and its rootage in a "God-centered philosophy of history" as well as its close relationship to belief in the special destiny of the American nation.[6] Richard T. Hughes and C. Leonard Allen have described the "Millennial Odyssey of Alexander Campbell" from an early focus (prior to the mid-1830s) on the primitive (restored) Church to a later belief that America (as the Protestant nation) would play a crucial role in ushering in the millennium.[7] (Both authors have continued their reflections on millennialism and closely related themes in the early Stone-Campbell movement.)[8] In spite of differences in Stoneite and Campbellite eschatology,[9] it is clear that both Barton W. Stone's associates and the later Campbell movement shared the widely held conviction that God was very much present and active in history. Barton Stone was so convinced of the near approach of Christ's millennial reign that in 1843 he told the

---

[6]David Edwin Harrell, *A Social History of the Disciples of Christ*, vol. 1, *Quest for A Christian America: The Disciples of Christ and American Society to 1866* (Nashville: Disciples of Christ Historical Society, 1966) 39-53. Harrell also notes that early Disciples eschatology was frequently racist—a belief that millennialistic triumph of freedom and pure religion was to be accomplished in God's Providence by Protestantism, America, and the white [race] (53).

[7]Richard T. Hughes and C. Leonard Allen, *Illusions of Innocence: Protestant Primitivism in America, 1630-1875* with a foreword by Robert N. Bellah (Chicago and London: University of Chicago Press, 1988) 170-87. The authors also mention eschatology in the Stone movement (111). Stephen V. Sprinkle has made the case that "the eschatological impulse drove Campbell to free himself and his church of any excess ecclesiastical baggage that would impede the journey towards the future of Jesus Christ" ("Alexander Campbell and the Doctrine of the Church," *Discipliana* 48,2 [Summer 1988]: 24-25).

[8]Richard T. Hughes, "The Apocalyptic Origins of Churches of Christ," *Religion and American Life: A Journal of Interpretation* 2,2 (Summer 1992):184; C. Leonard Allen, "'The Stone That the Builders Rejected': Barton W. Stone in the Memory of Churches of Christ," in *Cane Ridge in Context: Perspectives on Barton W. Stone and the Revival*, ed. Anthony L. Dunnavant (Nashville: Disciples of Christ Historical Society, 1992) 43-62.

[9]Richard T. Hughes and C. Leonard Allen have highlighted differences in nature of Barton Stone's and Alexander Campbell's millennialism. They have depicted Stone as a pessimistic pre-millennialist and Alexander Campbell as an optimistic post-millennialist: see Hughes, "Apocalyptic Origins of Churches of Christ," 181-214, and Allen, "'The Stone that the Builders Rejected': Barton W. Stone in the Memory of Churches of Christ," 43-62.

280   *Christian Faith Seeking Historical Understanding*

readers of his paper, *The Christian Messenger*, that if they did not work for the reformation, it would be "done by others" for "the millennium approaches."[10] Thomas Campbell believed that the United States of America, in this nation's early days, offered a rare opportunity for persons to move in and with God's *mission*.[11] Millennialism and the discernment of mission were closely intertwined.

Hiram Lester has noted that the "triumph of the Christian Gospel, the promised conversion of the *whole* world" was the "central Millennial issue for [Alexander] Campbell."[12] Campbell's own words make this quite clear, especially when he comments on the intercessory prayer of Jesus as found in John 17—an especially formative text for the movement[13]:

A person possessing the spirit of Christ, cannot, in my judgment, read that prayer with an understanding of what is expressed, and not feel the most intense interest in the accomplishment of that union by which the world was to be convinced and to be assured that Jesus of Nazareth is the Son and the Apostle of God ....[14]

Because Campbell believed with so much conviction in a God who was the maker of ordered systems,[15] he believed that (*systematically*) union would only come on the basis of the restoration of New

[10]B[arton] W[arren] S[tone], "Reflections of Old Age," *Christian Messenger* 13 (August 1843): 126.

[11]See, for example, Thomas Campbell's statement about the "favorable opportunity which Divine Providence has put into your hands, in this happy country" in *Declaration and Address, by Thomas Campbell; Last Will and Testament of the Springfield Presbytery, by Barton W. Stone and Others*, introduction by F. D. Kershner (St. Louis: Bethany Press, 1960) 30.

[12]Hiram J. Lester, "Alexander Campbell's Millennial Program," *Discipliana* 48,3 (Fall 1988): 36.

[13]See Anthony L. Dunnavant, "United Christians, Converted World: John 17:20-23 and the Interrelation of Themes in the Campbell-Stone Movement," *Discipliana* 46,3 (Fall 1986): 44-46.

[14]Editor [Alexander Campbell], "To Elder William Jones, of London. Letter VIII.," *Millennial Harbinger* 7 (1836): 27.

[15]The obvious illustration for this point is Alexander Campbell's most renowned book, *The Christian System*. See, especially, his opening paragraphs on "The Universe" (Bethany [West] Virginia: By the Author, 1839; reprint, Nashville: Gospel Advocate Co., 1964).

Testament Christianity and that evangelistic success—the world's being "convinced and assured" of the Messiahship and divine Sonship of Jesus Christ—would follow that kind of Christian union. His vision was for a Bible-based Christian union assumed to be dear to the heart of Jesus Christ himself "because essential to the success of his [Christ's] mission—the salvation of the world."[16]

To the founding generation of the Stone-Campbell movement, using God-given New World *freedom* to *restore* New Testament Christianity as the platform for Christian *unity* was seen in terms of an *eschatological* mandate to participate in God's *mission* of evangelization and world-transformation.

This brief survey of major themes in Disciples historiography thus places the pursuit of unity within a context. Neither Christian unity nor the restoration of New Testament Christianity were the paramount goal of the Stone-Campbell movement. Each, however, was viewed as inextricably related to the movement's ultimate aim: the *tactics* of the restoration of the "ancient faith and ancient order of things" were seen as part of an overall *strategy* of providing a catholic basis for the unification or reunification of the Church. In turn, this strategy was understood as a means to the *objective* or goal of the evangelization (conversion and transformation) of the world. They were seeking not just union, but triumphant union.

The Campbells clearly believed that an evangelistically effective Church and, through it, a gospel-transformed world (this triumph of God and Church) was kept beyond reach by the sin-sickness of division. Disciples were to be those who offered the prescription. How bitterly ironic it has seemed that this religious community, too, became infected with the disease it was born to treat.[17]

The shame of schism has made its impact on the historical self-interpretation of the Stone-Campbell movement. It has contributed a degree of defensiveness and to a good deal of the literature of the movement. But there has also been some healthy self-criticism and valuable reflection on how the Christian unity movement proved to be by no means immune to division—how Disciples, in fact, became infected.

A survey of fifty years of historical interpretation (between 1930

---

[16]Campbell, "To Elder William Jones," 27.

[17]For a fairly mild recent example of the recognition of this irony, see Martin E. Marty's Foreword to *Interpreting Disciples: Practical Theology in the Disciples of Christ*, eds. L. Dale Richesin and Larry D. Bouchard (Fort Worth: Texas Christian University Press, 1987) xi-xiv.

and 1981) of the divisions in the Stone-Campbell movement yields a recognizable and fairly simple pattern in the historians' accounts of the divisions.[18] This pattern might suggest what the harbingers of division among Disciples have been.

In the accounts of the schism between the Churches of Christ and the remainder of the movement three factors emerge frequently: *First, there is the identification of one of the most cherished ideals of the movement as the fracture point.* In the case of the first major division, the ideal was "restorationism," the notion that the New Testament contains a reasonably clear "ancient faith [doctrine] and ancient order of things [structure]," which is the one necessary platform for Christian unity and mission in this and every other age.

Division came between "strict" restorationists (those more inclined to desire an explicit scriptural support for specific church practices) and "progressive" restorationists (those willing to be innovative in practice in order to fulfill a scriptural mandate—such as evangelistic mission). This issue became symbolized in the unwillingness or willingness to use musical instruments in worship. Must organs be avoided because scripture does not mention them (the "strict" view), or may they be used to fulfill the admonition to "make a joyful noise to the Lord" (the "progressive" view)?[19]

---

[18]This literature search was originally conducted for the preparation of "The Recent Polarization in the Christian Church (Disciples of Christ) in Light of the History of Divisions in the Campbell-Stone Movement," a paper presented at the annual meeting of the Association for the Sociology of Religion, Chicago, Illinois, August 14-16, 1987.

[19]Although the evaluation of the restoration idea is quite different from one to another branch of the Stone-Campbell movement and among their scholars, the idea is identified in some way as the fracture-point by writers in each tradition. See, for example, these works by Disciples of Christ writers: Alfred T. DeGroot, *The Grounds of Division Among the Disciples of Christ* (Chicago: By the Author, 1940), 220; W. E. Garrison, *Religion Follows the Frontier: A History of the Disciples of Christ* (New York: Harper and Bros., 1931) 238-39; Allen V. Eikner, "The Nature of the Church Among the Disciples of Christ" (Ph.D. diss., Vanderbilt University, 1962) 182-83, 219-34; Ronald E. Osborn, "Dogmatically Absolute, Historically Relative: Conditioned Emphases in the History of the Disciples of Christ," in W. B. Blakemore, gen. ed., *The Renewal of Church: The Panel of Scholars Reports*, vol. 1, *The Reformation of Tradition*, ed. Ronald E. Osborn (St. Louis: Bethany Press, 1963) 278-79; Lester G. McAllister and William E. Tucker, *Journey in Faith: A History of the Christian Church (Disciples of Christ)* (St. Louis: Bethany Press, 1975) 237. The same basic issue is stressed by Churches of Christ writers: Homer Hailey, *Attitudes and Consequences in the Restoration Movement*, 2d ed. (Rosemead, CA: Old Paths Book Club, 1952) 197; Earl I. West, *The Search for the Ancient Order: A History of the Restoration Movement*, vol. 2, 1866-1906

The second explanatory factor widely given for the first division is the divisive influence of editors and their journals. Laying blame is, of course, either avoided or shaped by the historian's own convictions, but it is widely acknowledged that what were to become Churches of Christ views were given expression by such journals as David Lipscomb's *Gospel Advocate*, whereas the editors of *The Christian Standard* (Isaac Errett) and *The Christian-Evangelist* (James Harvey Garrison) voiced and helped to shape the views of much of the rest of the movement. The journalism of the movement, in short, was neither unified nor simply diverse. Rather, it became increasingly clearly divided.[20]

A third factor that links many of the historical accounts of the first division is the importance of opposition to, or support of, the American Christian Missionary Society. Of course this factor is very much related to the other two, but it is often given a distinctive emphasis in the histories. Some opponents of the American Christian Missionary Society (ACMS) argued against its legitimacy on "strict" restorationist grounds from its very beginning. According to this argument no missionary society was allowed by the New Testament. But the feelings against this particular missionary society began to run higher after a series of loyalty-to-the-Union resolutions were passed during the Civil War. These resolutions were regarded with growing bitterness in the Reconstruction-era South, and this translated into

---

(Indianapolis: Religious Book Service, 1950, 448; LeRoy Garrett, *The Stone-Campbell Movement: An Anecdotal History of Three Churches* (Joplin, MO: College Press, 1981) 610. Undenominational fellowship of Christian Churches and Churches of Christ (informally called "Independents") scholar James DeForest Murch also locates division at the point of divergence on the restoration ideal in *Christians Only: A History of the Restoration Movement* (Cincinnati: Standard Publishing, 1962) 359-74.

[20]Virtually all historians who have commented on the first division have made mention of the impact of journalism--of the facts that editors and journals became divisive in their influence. However, such Disciples writers as Edward Coffman (in "The Division in the Restoration Movement" [M.A. thesis, Vanderbilt University, 1930], 19); W. E. Garrison (in *An American Religious Movement: A Brief History of the Disciples of Christ* [St. Louis: Bethany Press, 1946] 122); J. Brooks Major (in "The Role of Periodicals in the Development of the Disciples of Christ, 1850-1910 [Ph.D. diss., Vanderbilt University, 1966] 143-44); and Arthur V. Murrell (in "The Effects of Exclusivism in the Separation of the Churches of Christ from the Christian Church [Ph.D. diss., Vanderbilt University, 1972] 10-11) give special prominence to this factor in the division. Churches of Christ writers such as West (in *1866 to 1906*, 22) and Garrett (in *Stone-Campbell Movement*, 610) have also pointed to the importance of editors and periodicals. Since the editors articulate divergent interpretations of the movement's ideals, the first and second themes do overlap.

disaffection with the ACMS and its convention.[21]

We may now turn to the second major division in the Stone-Campbell movement with the three factors in mind that came to the fore in two generations of written histories: disagreement on a basic ideal of the movement, a divided journalism, and disaffection with the general Missionary Society. Do these factors reappear in explanations of the second division?

Each factor reappears in a form unique to this second schism. The "restoration" ideal becomes focused on the issue of "open membership" or the question of how Disciples were to view the "pious unimmersed"—those baptized as infants (as Presbyterians, Methodists, etc.) and not as confessing adult believers in keeping with the traditional Disciples practice. The accusation arose that Disciples missionaries were regarding the "pious unimmersed" on the mission field as Christians and including such persons in their congregations. Thus, the missionaries were "opening" the "membership" of their churches to unimmersed persons. Again, "strict" restorationists viewed such a practice with alarm. It seemed to them to be an abandonment of an essential plank in the New Testament platform— what they viewed as scriptural baptism.[22] The "progressive" missionaries were more inclined to see visible unity and cooperation with Christians of any baptismal tradition as more essential when their situation was that of being part of a small Christian presence in largely non-Christian cultures.

The factor of a divided journalism also reappears powerfully in the second division. In the years after the turn of the century, *The Christian Standard* increasingly became the voice of dissent from the practices and policies of the Disciples at the "general" level who, by the 1920s, had created the United Christian Missionary Society, the International Convention of Disciples of Christ, and other agencies.[23]

---

[21]A comprehensive treatment of the "war resolutions" and their reception is in William Lee Miller "The Role of the Disciples of Christ During the Civil War" (B.D. thesis, College of the Bible, 1961). West also comments on the "war resolutions'" contribution to the Society's unpopularity in the South (*1866-1906*) 46.

[22]For an articulation of what was felt to be at stake in these matters by those who became disaffected with the Disciples missionary societies, see Edwin V. Hayden, *Fifty Years of Digression and Disturbance: A Review of Stephen J. Corey's Book, "Fifty Years of Attack and Controversy"* (Joplin, MO: By the Author, 1953).

[23]The role of *The Christian Standard* and of Standard Publishing Company in contributing to the second division in the Stone-Campbell movement is, perhaps, the best known factor in Christian Church (Disciples of Christ) historiography. W. E. Garrison's works, those of his sometime collaborator A. T. DeGroot, and McAllister

Meanwhile, *The Christian-Evangelist* took up the task of advocacy for, and primarily favorable reporting on, the ministries of these agencies. The third factor, disaffection with what is now called the "general manifestation" of the Christian Church (Disciples of Christ) has already been mentioned in connection with the divided journalism. In the second division, however, this disaffection went beyond simply criticizing and withholding support from the Disciples conventions and agencies. Beginning just prior to the 1920s, dissident "Restoration Congresses" began to be held by the "strict" restorationists and before the end of that decade a North American Christian Convention had been formed.

Neither the Congresses nor the North American Christian Convention (NACC) were originally promoted as alternatives to participation in the "general" life of the Disciples. In fact, it was positively denied that such was the intention of the promoters of these bodies. The NACC was to be a time for "strict" restorationists to gather for fellowship and mutual encouragement because the Disciples International Convention and its related agencies had disappointed and alienated this group. Nonetheless, over time fewer and fewer persons participated in both the NACC and the International Convention of the Disciples of Christ. The NACC became essentially the convention of a different body—the undenominational fellowship of Christian Churches and Churches of Christ.[24]

There are a number of "recent polarities" within the Christian Church (Disciples of Christ). Much of the remainder of this paper, however, will focus on the case of *Disciple Renewal* and on the question: "How do the actions and proposals of *Disciple Renewal* look in light of the historical pattern of divisions that has been suggested here?

In January of 1986 the first issue of the newsletter *Disciple*

and Tucker's *Journey in Faith* all give attention to Standard's influence in the second schism. Unquestionably, however, Stephen J. Corey's *Fifty Years of Attack and Controversy: The Consequences Among Disciples of Christ* (St. Louis: Christian Board of Publication, 1953) is the most thorough and single-minded work in this explanatory category. Churches of Christ author LeRoy Garrett basically concurs with this point of view (see *Stone-Campbell Movement*, 626-50).

[24]For a general overview of the development of the North American Christian Convention from the perspective of a sympathetic writer, see Robert O. Fife, "The North American Christian Convention: 1927-1977," *Discipliana* 77/2 (Summer 1977): 19, 20, 29.

Renewal appeared. Its avowed purpose was to "offer a forum for thought, discussion, and sharing among conservative Disciples." The paper's editors denied being "Independent" in affiliation, but stressed that "being evangelicals, we have some clear areas of disagreement with the policies and directions of our General church." They also denied explicitly the desire to "be exclusive."[25] The view was also expressed that, "at this time in our church's history, we felt that conservatives do not have full access to present denominational institutions."[26]

Disciple Renewal opened its first issue (volume one, number one, page one) with an article by Donald McGavran.[27] McGavran's disaffection with the character and recent direction of ecumenically oriented missions is well known.[28] In fact, it was this disaffection that led McGavran from the Disciples' United Christian Missionary Society (eventually) to Fuller Theological Seminary. By the 1980's, McGavran was widely hailed as the "father" of the "Church Growth Movement"—a movement with missiological assumptions clearly at odds with those of the ecumenical mainline.[29] The first issue of *Disciple Renewal* contained a brief but clear reflection of McGavran's missiology in a critique of the missionary policies of the Disciples Division of Overseas Ministries.[30]

Editors or contributors to *Disciple Renewal* included the pastors of congregations which had sponsored (Disciples)) General Assembly resolutions: (1) against "political resolutions" at the Disciples General Assembly, (2) against the General Board recommending adoption or non-adoption of resolutions, and (3) in favor of affirming biblical

---

[25]"What Is Disciple Renewal?" *Disciple Renewal* 1 (January 1986): 8.

[26]Richard M. Bowman, "Our Aim," *Disciple Renewal* 1 (January 1986): 6.

[27]Donald McGavran, "The Essential Element in Renewal," *Disciple Renewal* 1 (January 1986): 1.

[28]Don A. Pittman and Paul A. Williams cite one example in "Mission and Evangelism: Continuing Debates and Contemporary Interpretations," in *Interpreting Disciples*, 244, n. 1.

[29]Tim Stafford, "The Father of Church Growth," *Christianity Today* 30 (February 21, 1986): 20, 22; Donald A. McGavran and Winfield C. Arn, *Ten Steps for Church Growth* (San Francisco: Harper and Row Publishers, 1977) 2-6; Ralph H. Elliott "Dangers of the Church Growth Movement," *The Christian Century* 98 (April 12-19, 1981): 799-801.

[30]Doug Harvey, "The Evangelical Challenge to Disciple Pluralism," *Disciple Renewal* 1 (January 1986): 7.

infallibility.[31] The failure of the General Assembly to adopt these resolutions and, especially its rejection of a 1987 resolution affirming "that Jesus Christ is the only Savior of the world and that apart from him there is no salvation,"[32] have underscored the alienation of *Disciple Renewal* from the effective leadership of the assemblies.

The editors of *Disciple Renewal* have worked to become the leaders of a "network" for conservative Disciples, to facilitate new dimensions of local organization (Disciple Renewal Covenant congregations), and within the present regional and General Assembly structures, a new regional and general presence (booths and sessions at assemblies, for example). There seems to be considerable consciousness of the part of *Disciple Renewal*'s editors that their efforts might be, or be construed as, divisive. In this vein, McGavran's praise of the Methodist movement within Anglicanism (with its rather obvious outcome) may be more than a casual historical illustration.[33]

How does this publication appear in terms of the historical pattern? First, the "restoration" ideal is not as clearly at the forefront of the basic disagreement this time. "Evangelistic mission," another fundamental concern of the Disciples movement, however, is at the heart of this polarity. The featuring of Church Growth founder Donald McGavran, criticism of the Division of Overseas Ministries (especially of its grant to the African National Congress in South Africa), and the approving publication of a letter defining mission as "the preaching of the Gospel and winning souls to Jesus Christ" all indicate *Disciple Renewal*'s disagreement with their denomination's official missiology.[34] Because the Stone-Campbell movement's ultimate aim was to contribute (triumphantly!) to the conversion and transformation of the world, to disagree about missiology is to disagree about a fundamental issue.

---

[31]Bowman was the minister of First Christian Church, Decatur, Illinois, the sponsor of the first two resolutions. Jerry L. Briscoe, pastor of Rocklane Christian Church, which sponsored the third of these resolutions, writes about renewed efforts along the same lines in "A Resolution from Rocklane," *Disciple Renewal* 2 (Winter 1987): 7.

[32]"General Assembly Resolutions," *Disciple Renewal* 2 (May 1987): 4.

[33]Kevin Ray, "General Assembly News," *Disciple Renewal* 2 (June 1987): 1; Doug Harvey, "Are You For or Against?" *Disciple Renewal* 1 (January 1986): 4; McGavran, "Essential Element," 1.

[34]Richard Bowman, "South Africa Update," *Disciple Renewal* 1 (Summer 1986): 6; letter from Robert Tripp *Disciple Renewal* 2 (Winter 1987): 2.

Second, *Disciple Renewal* began as a quarterly publication in January of 1986. The content of this publication is quite varied, but within this variety is enough denunciation of the actions of the General Units, the General Board, and the General Assembly of the Christian Church (Disciples of Christ) to identify *Disciple Renewal* as a journal of dissent.

Finally, it is in keeping with the third feature of the historical pattern that much criticism by *Disciple Renewal* focuses on the general manifestation of the Christian Church (Disciples of Christ). Further, *Disciple Renewal*'s recent call for "alternative" national and regional gatherings and a "seminary alternative"[35] goes beyond criticizing the Disciples structures to the promotion of gatherings that could drift—as unintentionally as did the NACC—toward becoming the structural bones and tissue of a separate body.

Does the fact that this "recent polarity" manifests some of the same features that have been proffered by historians as explanations for the previous splits mean that the Stone-Campbell movement will travel yet farther along the road of bitter irony? It is worth pausing to consider. It seems likely that these points of past fragility, or at least harbingers of division, have some relevance to the present; but it is also important to note other insights in the Disciples historiography of division beyond the three most prominent clusters of explanation. Further, the limitations of this historical tradition must be admitted.

Many factors exist behind and within Disciples divisions beyond the three so far identified. Some of these are no longer present. (1) The Stone-Campbell movement may have been especially fragile in its early years because its roots were far more complex than simply the two groups led by Barton W. Stone and by Thomas and Alexander Campbell.[36] (2) The movement's organization has been, for most of its history, very loose and highly voluntary. (3) Temperamental differences and theological disagreements among the first-generation leaders and changes in their individual views created some "cracks" in the fellowship at the outset.[37] (4) The divisions have been more

---

[35]For both an account of the proposed "alternatives" and a vigorous denial of their divisiveness, see Douglas A. Harvey, "This Is Not a Split," *The Disciple* 131:11 (November 1993): 22-24. My very brief and virtually undocumented version of the case being made in the present paper also appeared in the same issue of *The Disciple* under the title "Diagnosing Disciples Divisions," 19-21.

[36]See, for example, the account of these roots in DeGroot, *Grounds of Division*, 30-31, n. 2.

[37]See, for example, the case made by Hughes that the movement's split is

"processes" than "events." The Churches of Christ emerged as a separate body in a process that spanned most of the second half of the nineteenth century—and a bit beyond. Similarly, the division that yielded a separate "undenominational fellowship of Christian Churches and Churches of Christ" (the Independents) was a process that spanned much of the first half of the twentieth century—and a bit beyond. (5) The divisions have been affected by the wider church and society. Civil War and Reconstruction-era sectional bitterness was surely an element in the first division.[38] Likewise, some of the most acrimonious events in the second division came at the height of the Fundamentalist-Modernist Controversy in American Protestantism in the 1920's. Stone-Campbell movement schisms have, in part, been features of a larger religious and social history. The degree to which division threatens again will be affected by contemporary versions of factors such as these as well as by the threefold pattern most evident in Stone-Campbell movement histories of their divisions.

The foregoing suggests some lessons in history about unity and division for the heirs of Stone and Campbell, but the lessons are not simple. Historical explanations have clustered around three issues, but this is, in part, because these issues are themselves large and complex and multi-faceted. Therefore, even if the focus is kept upon these broad issues—the roles of basic ideals, of journalism, and of extra-local structures—interpretation becomes more "panoramic" than "focused." That is the first conclusion of this exercise: understanding division historically requires a broad vision and the capacity to entertain "multi-genetic" theories of its origins.[39]

Second, the reminder that there were uniquely divisive elements

---

attributable to the differences in the eschatological world views of Stone and Campbell in Hughes, "Apocalyptic Origins."

[38]The studies by William Miller and J. Brooks Major cited above certainly make the point of the sectionalism factor. David Edwin Harrell's *Social History of the Disciples of Christ* also argues strongly for this perspective. Richard Hughes and C. Leonard Allen (in "Apocalyptic Origins" and "'The Stone the Builders Rejected'") and R. L. Roberts have done much to establish the "Stoneite" roots of the Churches of Christ. My suspicion is that their work must be synthesized with that of Harrell. That is, the "fault line" was present because of the Stoneite/Campbellite disparate origins; but the Civil War and Reconstruction certainly appear to have been at least a bit of a tremor.

[39]W. E. Garrison (in *Religion Follows the Frontier*), David E. Harrell (in *Social History of the Disciples of Christ*), and Oliver Read Whitley (in *Trumpet Call of Reformation* [St. Louis: Bethany Press, 1959]) contain strong elements of a sociological explanation of the divisions in the Stone-Campbell movement. This is an interpretive tradition has contributed insights not addressed fully in this paper.

present in the early period of Stone-Campbell history calls attention to the importance of maintaining an historical perspective. That is, there were elements in the first divisions that absolutely cannot be replicated or even very closely approximated in other times.

Third, the Stone-Campbell movement has sometimes suffered from a more-than-usual degree of "exceptionalism" in its historical self-interpretation. The best example of this is how easily many in several generations of Disciples were apparently convinced that the Civil War and Reconstruction did not adversely affect the unity of the movement. A close look at the historiography of division in this tradition at least calls into question "exceptionalist" assumptions.

Fourth, surveying the historical interpretations of divisions in light of the changing foci of Stone-Campbell historiography casts additional dimension of these divisions in sharper relief. For example, the growing attention given to Disciples eschatology in general helps to illuminate its possible impact on divisions.

Finally, the title "Seeking Triumphant Union and Being Found in Schism" is meant to point to another result of this kind of historical reflection. The history of Disciples historical interpretive formulae and the accompanying reconstruction of the Stone-Campbell movement's "Plea" explains the phrase "Seeking Triumphant Union."

The phrase "Being Found in Schism" is intended to capture the haplessness, the shock, the shame, befuddlement, blaming, and denial that have been the result of the "unity movement's" repeated divisions in the past, and the near panic that can accompany impending ones. Historical study that can identify disintegrative factors that are both many and complex can, perhaps, contribute to forms of engagement with these factors that are more constructive than shame or panic.

Christian Faith and the Oneness of the Church: Disciples of Christ and Roman Catholics in Dialogue

Nadia M. Lahutsky

In September 1977 a group of eighteen mostly North American theologians and pastors gathered around a table to hear some papers and to talk with each other about the issues contained in the papers. While this gathering of Roman Catholic and Disciples of Christ may not have attracted national media attention that week, the work begun there has continued for the nearly twenty years since then and shows no immediate signs of halting. The work may have seemed, at first, rather modest, being a joint project sponsored by the Council on Christian Unity of the Christian Church (Disciples of Christ) and the Committee on Ecumenical and Interreligious Affairs of the National Conference of Catholic Bishops. Thus, it was rather like a national ecumenical dialogue, with a number of participants from outside the United States and with official oversight by both the Vatican Secretariat for Promoting Christian Unity and the Disciples Ecumenical Consultative Council. This group met for five years, with some change in personnel, until in 1981 it produced its Final Report, *Apostolicity and Catholicity in the Visible Unity of the Church*.[1]

This Final Report, called "a statement of shared insights and findings" (1-2), reveals some genuine, although limited, results. That Disciples of Christ and Roman Catholics may seem to be rather far removed from each other and only recently come together for dialogue is evident in the Final Report. Topics covered included spiritual ecumenism, baptism, and issues relating to faith and Tradition. The claims made are genuine and significant, but they bear a tone that suggests that even some of the dialogue participants were a bit surprised to find themselves in agreement.

---

[1]*Midstream* 21 (October 1982): 555-69 and Secretariat for Promoting Christian Unity *Information Service* ; also published separately as a pamphlet by the Council on Christian Unity.

The work of this round of talks was deemed promising enough to warrant an increased internationalization of the entire group and the shift from a joint Roman Catholic sponsorship to making it solely the responsibility of the Secretariat. Thus, what might have remained a largely North American event with somewhat limited impact became a group with the status, if not yet the stature, of the other bilateral dialogues in which the Roman Catholic Church was engaged.[2]

This essay will focus on only a small part of the work of this bilateral: namely, the role of the concept of communion in ecclesiology and the sacramental nature of the Church in the Final Report, *The Church as Communion in Christ* (1993)[3] and, where appropriate, in the agreed accounts of the second round of the dialogue (1983-89). Some comparison will be made between the use of the concept of communion and the sacramental character of the Church in the 1943 encyclical of Pope Pius XII, *Mystici Corporis Christi* and *Lumen Gentium* (1964). An attempt will be made also to illustrate how Disciples have used these concepts, if not the terminology. This brief look at how these issues have been treated or not in both of the churches can show how the concepts may be important for both parties to the dialogue.

At the Second Vatican Council, (1962-65) one of the truly astonishing accomplishments was the renewed view of the church that resulted in *Lumen Gentium*. Having received at the outset a text that spoke of the church emphasizing the hierarchy, that identified the visible church with the Roman Catholic Church, and that used a legal/juridical/institutional approach, the council participants rejected this view and eventually presented to the world a text that gave priority of place to the Church as mystery, and as the sacrament of God, that is, "a sign and instrument, that is, of communion with God and of unity among all men"[4] and developed the image of the Church as the People of God.[5] Of course, the matter is much more

---

[2]The Vatican office responsible for ecumenical work has since become the Pontifical Council for Promoting Christian Unity.

[3]This report was completed at the December 1992 meeting, published in *Midstream* 33 (April 1994): 219-39. It was published in pamphlet form by the Council on Christian Unity in 1994. Hereafter, the text will be referred to as CACC and paragraphs numbers used.

[4]*Lumen Gentium* I.1, in Austin P. Flannery, O. P., ed., *The Documents of Vatican II: The Conciliar and Post-Conciliar Documents*, rev. ed. (Grand Rapids, MI: Eerdmans Publishing Co., 1984) hereafter LG.

[5]The dramatic story of the rejection of the preparatory document *De ecclesia* in favor of more discussion and, ultimately, the text of *Lumen Gentium* has been told

complicated than can be simply characterized in a few phrases, but while maintaining continuity with the past, the *Dogmatic Constitution on the Church (Lumen Gentium)* charted a new course for ecumenical activity. The common impression may be to credit the *Decree on Ecumenism* as marking the major change in Roman Catholic ecumenical activity. Indeed, this important document offers a set of guidelines for Roman Catholic understanding of, and involvement in, ecumenical dialogue. But no such activity would be imaginable without the important foundational work of *Lumen Gentium*.

The second round of the Disciples/Roman Catholic dialogue (1983-92) pursued the theme "The Church as Koinonia in Christ." The topics engaged during the annual meetings through 1989 (always in early December) explored the nature of this *koinonia* (communion) in Christ, the centrality of the Church's *koinonia* to the Church's confession, and the means by which the Church is maintained in continuity with its apostolic foundation (specifically, ministry, and Eucharist).[6] The work of all of the seven annual meetings was

---

many times. For a contemporary account, see the reports to the *New Yorker* published later under Xavier Rynne, *Vatican Council II*, (New York: Farrar, Straus and Giroux, 1968). The leavening effect of time on historical judgments will be found in the most recent work on the topic. Guiseppe Alberigo and Joseph Komonchak, eds., *History of Vatican II: 1959-65*, vol. 1, (Maryknoll NY: Orbis Books, 1995) and in the remaining 4 projected volumes.

[6]Each of these discussions resulted in a document, officially called an agreed account. The texts have been published jointly in *Mid-Stream* and the *Information Service* of the Pontifical Council for Promoting Christian Unity. *Mid-Stream* has also published the discussion papers and responses. A reading in chronological order of the agreed accounts would provide a sense of the flow of the meetings. The agreed accounts of the second round are as follows: "Agreed Account of First Meeting [of the Second Round] (1983): Venice," Topic: "The Church as Agent and Realization of Koinonia," *Mid-Stream* 23 (October 1984): 400-407; "Agreed Account of the Seventh Meeting [First and Second Rounds] (1984) Nashville," Topic: "The Nature of Koinonia," *Mid-Stream* 25 (October 1986): 409-419; "Agreed Account of the Eighth Meeting (1985): Mandeville," Topic: "The Church's koinonia as sacrament, demonstration, and communication of the essential content of the faith (i.e., redemption through Christ)," *Mid-Stream* 25 (October 1986): 419-25; "Agreed Account of the Ninth Meeting (1986): Cambridge," Topic: "The Eucharist and the Visibility of the Church's Koinonia," *Mid-Stream* 27 (October 1988):414-19; "Agreed Account of the Tenth Meeting (1987): Duxbury," Topic: "Continuity of the Church in the Apostolic Tradition," *Mid-Stream* 27 (October 1988): 419-27; "Agreed Account of the Eleventh Meeting of the Disciples of Christ and Roman Catholic International Commission for Dialogue (1988): Gethsemani, Kentucky," Topic: "Ministry and Continuity in the Apostolic Tradition," *Mid-Stream* 29 (July 1990): 279-89; "Agreed Account of the Twelfth

gathered together into *The Church as Communion in Christ*. Not merely a summary of all the previous accounts, it takes each of them into a more comprehensive synthesis on the central nature of the Church. Here, in this text, can be seen most clearly the importance of the work of *Lumen Gentium* for ecumenical discussion, especially the work of this particular dialogue.

The Disciples of Christ have been identified in various ways; indeed the Final Report describes them as "distrustful of many of the creeds, confessions and doctrinal teachings within Christian tradition," and acknowleges that this characteristic arose partly out of a concern to overcome denominationalism and find the unity of the Church. They are "suspicious of the structure of episcopal authority" as held by Roman Catholics. The Final Report sets these characteristics in contrast to the Roman Catholic understanding of creeds and doctrinal definitions as guided by the Holy Spirit and, thus, as an essential part of the continuous history of the Church; so also for the episcopal college which maintains continuity with the apostolic community and the See of Rome which serves as a sign of unity in the Church.[7] This characterization of the differences between the two groups has a prominent place early in the text of the Final Report, acknowledging that the two groups are, on the surface, rather unlikely dialogue partners.[8] Clearly, a consensus statement on the primacy of the Bishop of Rome is not likely in the near future. In fact, this is the last topic mentioned under work for the future, following the differing significances and practices surrounding the Eucharist/Lord's Supper, episcopacy as fundamental for the nature of the Church, and the "nature of the rule of faith in a changing history."[9] Apparently, the absence of any formal break between the Disciples of Christ and the Roman Catholic Church means that the search for consensus statements intending to overcome such ruptures will not be the most pressing need.

This need is to be found, rather, in the quest for a shared vision of

Meeting of the Disciples of Christ and Roman Catholic International Commission for Dialogue (1989): Venice, Italy," Topic: "The Involvement of the Whole Church in Handing on the Apostolic Tradition," *Mid-Stream* 29 (July 1990): 290-303.

[7]CACC, para. 11.

[8]This head-on facing of some hard realities is noted by William Henn in his assessment of the Report. "[They] cannot be accused of ignoring important differences in belief and practices between their respective communities." "An Evaluation of *The Church as Communion in Christ*," *Mid-Stream* 33 (April 1994): 159.

[9]CACC, para. 53.

the Church. Thus, the decade of dialogue did not explicitly seek to identify the extent of communion already existing between the two groups or try to work through specific issues on which obvious differences exist.[10] In this search for a shared vision, the importance of *Lumen Gentium* for this kind of ecumenical work can be most clearly seen.

The Church as Communion in Christ echoes the very opening chapter of *Lumen Gentium*. Having begun by noting the fundamental character of the Church as mystery, *Lumen Gentium* then proceeds with a narration, as it were, of salvation history. Those whom the creator raised up for the purpose of sharing in the divine life did soon thereafter fall into sin, but always with the promise of redemption.[11] This salvation history sweep appears in CACC, but much more succinctly. "Christians confess that the same God who created human beings has also redeemed them. God has not abandoned humanity to its sinfulness but, through the plan of salvation, has given the possibility of forgiveness of sin and new life. This plan of salvation culminates in Christ Jesus."[12]

In this rather brief section of the Final Report, titled "New Creation and Communion," appears the very heart of the argument being made.[13] That God's will for humanity appears definitively in Christ Jesus, that God makes of us a new creation, that God's activity has temporal priority over the appropriate human response of thanks and praise—all this seems quite reasonable and even unexceptional. The substantive claim (to call it a surprising claim would be far too strong) is in paragraph 21. "By drawing people out of isolation and into communion (*koinonia*) God makes a new creation—a humanity now established as children of God." The Final Report thus presents its central point: that God's salvific plan for humanity implies the creation of a community. In this point can be heard a virtual echo of *Lumen Gentium*, whose second chapter on the "People of God" begins by saying that God has willed to save human beings "not as individuals without any bond or link between them, but to make them into a people who might acknowledge him and serve him in holiness."

This particular point emerged in the bilateral as something of a breakthrough during the 1985 meeting, whose session bore the rather

---

[10]CACC, para. 20.
[11]*Lumen Gentium*, I. 2.
[12]CACC, 21.
[13]CACC, paragraphs 21-24.

unwieldy title "The Church's Koinonia as Sacrament, demonstration and communication of the essential content of the faith (i.e., redemption through Christ)." The agreed account of that year's meeting put it this way: "The Christian confession, then, includes three aspects: that God intends to save all humankind, that this salvation is offered in the work of Jesus Christ, and that salvation changes human life by remaking it, by drawing it out of isolation into the bonds of reconciliation and love ... Christian communion is at the center of Christian confession."[14] The Christian confession implies the Christian communion and a recognition of the importance of the communion is itself an essential aspect of making the confession.

There can be no authentic confession of Christ that does not involve the community. Indeed, one way of describing what it is to be a Christian is to speak of being part of the Body of Christ, thereby implying a community. That very fact that making this statement together could be seen as a breakthrough should be attributed to the situation in which both churches found themselves in the twentieth century.

Imagining a a time when the Roman Catholic Church would have denied such a claim is impossible. Indeed, it has not. Nevertheless, a teaching may be held by a group and yet obscured by other teachings, or its significance diminished by the context in which it is placed. Such, I would say, is the case with this idea in Roman Catholic teaching and life prior to Vatican II. In 1943 Pope Pius XII issued the encyclical *Mystici Corporis Christi*, which determined Catholic teaching on the nature of the Church for a generation. A look at this letter can illustrate the point. The very title of the encyclical—the Mystical Body of Christ—implies community, and suggests the idea of unity arising out of many parts coming together; indeed, allusions to the Pauline uses of this analogy appear sprinkled about the text. It is impossible to imagine the image of a body being articulated without attending to the issue of communion. This encyclical does that. After asserting the visibility of the one Church and rejecting those who would see unity as only spiritual, it continues. "But a body calls also for a multiplicity of members, which are linked together in such a way as to help one another. ... [So] in the Church, the individual members do not live for themselves alone, but also help their fellows, and all work in mutual collaboration for the common comfort and for the

---

[14]*Mid-Stream* 25 (October 1986): 421.

more perfect building up on the whole Body."[15] This brief passage aside, most of the rest of the encyclical has to do with the proper constitution of the structure of the church, matters of membership, and how the various parts fit together. In fact, the paragraph immediately following this quotation signals the main concern of the text. "Moreover, as in the natural order a body is not made up of a haphazard grouping of members, . . . so the Church with much greater reason is called a Body because she is formed of well-organized and coordinated parts, and made up of different members which are in harmony with one another." This body previously associated with mutual assistance and consolation is, rather quickly, it seems, relegated to concern for "well-ordered structure." And so goes the rest of the first part of the encyclical. This body was founded by Christ in his earthly mission and through his suffering and resurrection he became its head, and his continuing concern for it is seen in the visible governance of this body entrusted through Peter to the Roman Pontiff to whom the individual bishops of particular churches are submissive. And so on. The spiritual beauty and power of the image of the Church as Body of Christ is unmistakable. So too is the emphasis on hierarchy and structure, duties and responsibilities. The material in the second and third parts of the encyclical likewise leaves unexploited the communion aspects of the image of the church as the body of Christ. No surprise, then, that the impression given, especially to outsiders, is of an overwhelming interest in what many people in the late 1960s derisively and dismissively used to call "the institutional church," referring then indiscriminately to Protestant or Catholic expressions.[16]

The idea of the church as communion was, likewise, obscured in Roman Catholic practice, especially in the experience of worship. The people were gathered with their presbyter—representative of their bishop—and the eucharistic sacrifice was offered, but, overwhelmingly, the emphasis was elsewhere. The use of Latin in the Mass and, especially, the encouraging of the laity to engage in private devotions during the Mass may be seen as contributing to this process. One Roman Catholic commentator has described the lived experience of the understanding of church this way: "Except on All Souls Day

---

[15]Pius XII, *On the Mystical Body of Christ and Our Union in it with Christ* (*Mystici Corporis*), Boston: St. Paul Books and Media, n.d.) para. 15.

[16]Pius XII dealt with this, rejecting the pernicious error that pitted the church of charity against the juridical church. His point is clear; you can't have one without the other. See *Mystici Corporis Christi*, 557.

there seemed to be small awareness of a corporate union of the faithful. The Mass was the atoning sacrifice, but not the means or the expression of the community. ... Devotions abounded, subjective and individualistic in tone, with little reference to the liturgical year."[17] The faithful might know quite well the official doctrine of the Roman Catholic Church, and yet still find it almost impossible not to embrace the message communicated by their experience of the faith.

The situation in the Disciples of Christ, in their American expression at least, bears some resemblance to that of the Roman Catholic experience. At its most basic level, an understanding of the church as communion means that any talk about salvation is not to be understood in only individualistic terms: that God has not chosen to save us one by one by one but, rather, by making us into a community. That would be good news—that God saves and does this by means of the community called Church. Or, in the language more commonly identified with Vatican II, by making us part of the People of God. Yet, Disciples of Christ have their own problems with the lived experience of the faith. In no place in the world in which they have established congregations, and especially not in the region of origin, have Disciples of Christ ever experienced being part of an established church. Matters of church and state aside, the established church model provides a kind of givenness to the experience of church (even if it is that body against which one determines to struggle), an experience that corresponds, in some way, to the givenness of one's own people, the community one experiences daily. One might live comfortably with or struggle mightily against this community, but one is hardly likely to imagine having created it. Nor does one live easily apart from it.

A Disciples of Christ founder, Alexander Campbell, was strongly influenced by a Lockean understanding of society with its emphasis on the individual. The church, in this view, has not the quality of givenness. Locke's own definition of a church may be recalled here. "A church, then, I take to be a voluntary society of men, joining themselves together of their own accord to the public worshipping of God in such a manner as they judge acceptable to him, and effectual to the salvation of their souls."[18] While acknowledging the necessary historical circumstances that gave rise to such a definition of a

---

[17]William Leonard, "Popular Devotions Remembered," *America* 145 (September 12, 1981): 120.

[18]John Locke, *A Letter Concerning Toleration*, in *The Works of John Locke*, new ed., vol. VI, (London: G. H. Wooten, 1823) 15.

church, one can also see that it might tend to contribute toward those in that voluntary society stressing the rights of the individual over the community and its givenness.

Alexander Campbell himself used the Body of Christ imagery to discuss the church, even occasionally acknowledging the term "mystical body of Christ." "This institution, called the *congregation of God*, is a community of communities—not a community representative of communities, but a community composed of many particular communities, each of which is built upon the same foundations,"[19] that is, the apostles and prophets. This way of talking about the Church could hardly be mistaken for any particular voluntary society founded simply to achieve a certain social aim. Nevertheless, individual members of these communities would be conscious of having made the decision personally to associate with this kind of community (one congregation) rather than another. Thus, for Disciples, as also for Roman Catholics, the message about Church was twofold, with elements concerning both individual needs and responses and the community's significance and priority.

Early Disciples teaching argued that the community of the Church, the fullness of the life of the People of God, finds itself most completely expressed at the Table of the Lord. In a beautiful passage emphasizing the importance of the Christian community in the process of salvation, Campbell described his understanding of this. "Upon the loaf and upon the cup of the Lord, in letters which speak ... to the heart of every disciple, is inscribed, 'When this you see, remember me,' ... Each disciple, in handing the symbols to his fellow disciple says, in effect, 'You, my brother, once an alien, . . . are now brought home to the family of God. You have owned my Lord as your Lord, my people as your people. Under Jesus the Messiah we are one.'"[20] Often lost in the flurry of talk supporting individual rights and concerns, this decidedly non-individualistic understanding of the Church is being recovered in Disciples of Christ theological writings and in practice.[21] None could deny, however, that its recovery will be

---

[19] Alexander Campbell, *The Christian System*, 6th ed. (Cincinnati: Standard Publishing Co., 1910), 55-56.

[20] Campbell, *System*, 273. This beautiful passage has been adapted into the text for a communion hymn, "When You Do This Remember Me," text by David L. Edwards (1988) and tune Loretto, by David L. Edwards (1988), arr. Jane Marshall (1993), #400 in *Chalice Hymnal* (St. Louis: Chalice Press, 1995).

[21] See Colbert S. Cartwright, *People of the Chalice: Disciples of Christ in Faith and Practice* (St. Louis: CBP Press, 1987) for a description of some of this recovery.

difficult, contrary as it is to the prevailing cultural trends in which people are encouraged to identify themselves according to the type of consumer products they can afford or to the degree of individual success they have attained in a career rather than to the religious community whose fellowship they enjoy.

Thus, when the Final Report of the Disciples of Christ-Roman Catholic dialogue emphasizes the communion aspects of life in God's new creation, it is stressing a theme that is both an ancient Catholic understanding of the Church, but in need of some clearer expression in the twentieth century,[22] and a Disciples view, struggling for greater prominence over against the siren call of contemporary individualism. Neither of the dialogue partners had ever explicitly rejected the notion. Yet work has been needed to bring the idea to greater prominence, both in theological teaching and in the lives of ordinary believers.

In this way, at least, both churches can acknowledge their need for continuous reform, although each is likely to express that need in different ways. In his first encyclical letter, *Ecclesiam Suam*, issued in 1964, Pope Paul VI addressed the issue of the church, with an eye to the ways in which it might better serve the whole world as the bearer of God's good news. Not the essential nature of the church or its basic structure, but, nevertheless, something in the church must admit of correction. He wrote, "Hence, if the term reform can be applied to this subject, it is not to be understood in the sense of change, but of a stronger determination to preserve the characteristic features which Christ has impressed on the Church."[23] Paul VI does not concern himself in this letter with the idea of the Church as communion; nonetheless, a major portion of the text considers the conditions of genuine dialogue with the world—what he calls the "dialogue of salvation." These are the conditions that are essential for the message of the Church to be heard. They are also, perhaps not coincidentally, conditions that would be necessary in any careful nurturing of communion.[24] Almost any Disciples call for a reform of a particular

---

[22]There is an enormous amount of literature in Roman Catholic theology on this topic. A particularly clear and recent example is George H. Tavard, *The Church, Community of Salvation*, New Theology Studies, vol. 1, (Collegeville, MN: The Liturgical Press, 1992).

[23]Pope Paul VI, *Ecclesiam Suam*, (Boston: St. Paul Books and Media, n.d.) para. 47.

[24]*Ecclesiam Suam*, para. 70-83. Notable among Paul VI's list of necessary conditions is charity, that the dialogue be without coercion and carried out in

church practice is unlikely to display such fear at using the word *change*, without in the least intending to imply that the previous practice being raised for elimination means the lack of God's presence with the Church.[25]

The argument of *The Church as Communion in Christ* moves toward its climax in the section titled "The Church." The intervening sections on Eucharist and teaching as means of continuity with the apostolic community and the gifts of the Spirit for the Church are interesting both for what is said and what is not said, but will not be considered here. They take the text toward the other of its major claims. This comes in a three-part form:

—a person is saved by being introduced into this communion of believers, described in the New Testament by images of the body of Christ, the temple of God, the vine, the household of God;

—this communion is never given to the believer without the involvement of other believers, some of them being the ministers of the Church, having a specific responsibility for preaching the Word of God and presiding at the celebration of the sacraments. Through the Word and the sacraments the Church is the servant or instrument of God's plan of salvation;

—this communion is ultimately with the apostolic community....[26]

These three shared truths undergird the claim that "the Church is at one and the same time an epiphany of the destiny which God wills for all humanity and a means to achieve that destiny." The Church is "the sacrament of God's design."[27]

The idea of the Church as the sacrament of God's plan for humanity figures prominently in *Lumen Gentium*, occupying the very first paragraph of the opening chapter on the mystery of the Church. This point sets up the urgency of the Church to give a clear expression of its nature and mission and, indeed, drives the logic of the chapter. Is the idea of the Church as the sacrament of God's design absent from the earlier *Mystici Corporis Christi*? Surely not; indeed, it is implied everywhere in the text as it presents the Church

---

meekness and with trust and prudence.

[25]By way of an example, see James O. Duke and Richard L. Harrison, Jr., *The Lord's Supper*, Council on Christian Unity Nature of the Church Study Series, no. 5 (St. Louis: Christian Board of Publication, 1989), in which a host of current Disciples practices and understandings of the Lord's Supper are discussed, some of them criticized and *change* encouraged.

[26]CACC, para. 46.

[27]CACC, Para. 52.

as the bearer of the life-giving means of sanctification.[28] Yet, as with the Church as communion, here too this point is obscured. The weight of the text is to declare and defend the divine origin of particular aspects of the Roman Catholic Church. This concern so dominates the text that some readers might have to supply for themselves this implied reason. Most Protestant readers probably had trouble getting beyond the blunt claim that "this true Church of Christ . . . is the One, Holy, Catholic, Apostolic, Roman Church."[29] As things turned out, ecumenical ground was paved at Vatican II in at least two ways: the explicit articulation of the sacramental nature of the Church and the substitution, in *Lumen Gentium*, of *subsists* for *is* to explain the relation between the Church and the Roman Catholic Church.[30]

What of Disciples? Is not the language of Church as sacrament strong, perhaps even foreign, terminology for them to hear? After all, Alexander Campbell didn't like even the sacraments to be called sacraments, preferring to use the term *ordinances* to describe them. Of Campbell's many pronouncements on the Church, none that I know of actually speak of the Church as the sacrament of God. Yet his life work was an attempt to get the Church right. Surely this was because getting it right mattered. Furthermore, Campbell seems to have possessed the conviction that getting it right was—in all essential parts—an attainable goal.

Disciples today do not share Campbell's aversion to speaking of Baptism and the Lord's Supper as sacraments, having in that regard been influenced by any number of twentieth-century concerns—a deeper view of the language of symbol, the liturgical revival that affected many of the churches, and an ever deepening involvement in the Ecumenical Movement. Neither does one commonly hear on Disciples' lips the language that calls the "Church the sacrament of God's design." Yet, the concept itself may be implied from the fact that Disciples of Christ have expressed an overwhelming concern to understand the Church. In nineteenth-century terminology, the effort was to restore the ancient church, that denominationalism might be overcome. The language of restoration has fallen away and with it, perhaps, much of the certainty accompanying particular forms.

---

[28] *Mystici Corporis Christi*, para. 18-21.

[29] *Mystici Corporis Christi*, para. 13.

[30] Quite a lot of ecumenical effort has been built on the difference between *subsists* and *is*, a distinction that has, thankfully, not been spelled out. See Tavard, *Church*, 182-3, for an interesting discussion of how this phrase can be the basis for ecumenical promise.

In the last half of this century, Disciples of Christ, especially those in the United States, have been preoccupied with such questions. From the bitter internal disputes over the growing commitment to cooperative work to the process completed in 1968 and formally called "Restructure," American Disciples have given considerable attention to the question of the Church. This "new reformation movement," begun to bring about an end to denominationalism and factionalism, has resulted in the institutionalization of particular forms that make up a new denomination. The irony has probably not been lost on most of the participants in this process. While the effort was never understood to be producing the final word on churchly structures, some Disciples must have worried that the very existence of such hard-won forms might lead to a hardening of structures, making future change more difficult. Such fears may not have been unfounded, as struggles in the last decade of the century are showing. Once in place, institutions and structures are extraordinarily hard to change significantly or remove. The test for all church structures should be, Disciples would argue, the effectiveness of the work of such a body or group toward the corporate proclamation of the gospel. Any structure that seems no longer to contribute toward greater faithfulness and effectiveness should become a candidate for change. Thus, whatever forms church life might take at any given time are important, even necessary, for the work of the Church, but the forms themselves would never be seen by Disciples as irreformable.

Disciples' restorationist language and conviction is gone, but as strong as ever is the concern to present the gospel in such a way that it is both faithful to God's Word and plausible to those who might hear it. This concern to announce the gospel implies a parallel concern for the means by which the message is kept alive and lived out.[31] This means or instrument is, of course, the Church which, in its

---

[31]Disciples history can be seen as a series of episodes of seeking to identify the nature of the Church: Alexander Campbell's passion for restoring the ancient church; mid-nineteenth-century debates about the possibility of cooperation in societies beyond the local congregation, early twentieth-century disputes about agencies and accepting into congregational membership the unimmersed, mid-twentieth-century work on restructure. Any faithful analysis of these events would have to be accompanied by a look at the effects of theological discussion of the time. Disciples experienced internal disputes inspired by the fundamentalist-modernist controversy of the 1920s and in the 1990s have had their share of denominational dissension rooted in the liberal-conservative differences sometimes characterized as resulting from the culture wars.

communion, is "an effective sign given by God also to the world,"[32] witnessing to the possibility of overcoming the divisions that afflict humanity. This point is the practical reason why the work of ecumenism is seen by many to be so urgent today. The claim that the gospel offers communion with God *and with each other* must ring hollow to outsiders when it comes from churches that will not be reconciled with each other.

The Disciples-Roman Catholic dialogue and its work in producing *The Church as Communion in Christ* surely did not introduce the Roman Catholic Church or the Disciples of Christ to the ideas of the Church as communion or that of the Church as the sacrament of God's plan. Yet, a helpful task has been accomplished in the articulating of these two points in the recent Final Report. The rather blunt expression of these ideas can be an occasion for each of the churches to look at their own current situation and that of their dialogue partner more clearly. Perhaps such careful looking will help each to see the other ever more deeply as fellow-sharers in the new life given by Christ Jesus. Even if there is to be found no other immediate result from this dialogue's work, it will, then, not have been in vain.

---

[32]CACC, ¶50.

Select Bibliography of Scholarly Writings by H. Jackson Forstman

1960

"The Nonchalance of Faith." *The Pulpit*, 1960.

"A Protestant Conception of Christian Liberty and Some Observations of its Implications for Human Creativity." Commencement and Alumnae College Addresses, Randolph-Macon Women's College, 1960.

"What Does It Mean to 'Preach from the Bible'?" *Encounter* 21,2 (Spring 1960): 218-31.

Review of *Academic Market Place*, by Theodore Caplow and Reece V. McGhee. In *Encounter* 21,1 (Winter 1960): 107-9.

1961

"Have the Disciples Become Irrelevant to Today's World?" *The Christian* 99 (1961): 8-9.

"The Subject-Object Relation: Its Relevance to the Problem of Authority." *Encounter* 22,3 (Summer 1961): 248-64.

"Theology in the American University: To Teach and to Learn." *Encounter* 22,4 (Autumn 1961): 435-44.

1962

Word and Spirit: Calvin's Doctrine of Biblical Authority. Palo Alto, CA: Stanford University Press; Oxford: Oxford University Press, 1962.

Review of *Faith and Learning: Christian Faith and Higher Education in 20th Century America*, by Alexander Miller. In *Encounter* 23,3 (Summer 1962): 365-66.

Review of *Logic of the Humanities*, by Ernst Cassirer, Translated by C. S. Howe. In *Encounter* 23,4 (Autumn 1962): 473-74.

1963

"Bultmann's Conception and Use of Scripture." *Interpretation* 17,4 (October 1963): 450-64.

1964

"Paul Tillich and His Critics." *Encounter* 25,4 (Autumn 1964):

476-81.

"The Relevance of the Church and its Theology." *The Christian* 102 (1964): 4-6.

"Samuel Taylor Coleridge's *Notes Toward the Understanding of Doctrine (Aids to Reflection).*" *Journal of Religion* 44 (October 1964): 310-27.

"Theology and Other Disciplines: A Basis for Conversation." *Encounter* 25,2 (Spring 1964):145-61.

1965

Christian Faith and the Church. St. Louis: Bethany Press, 1965.

1966

"Barth, Schleiermacher, and the Christian Faith." *Union Theological Seminary Quarterly Review* 21 (March 1966): 305-19.

"Luther's Understanding of Christian Liberty and its Implications for Human Creativity." In *One Faith: Essays in Honor of Stephen J. England.* Edited by Robert L. Simpson. Enid OK: Phillips University Press, 1966.

"The Meaning of the Cross and Resurrection in the History of Christian Thought." *Classmate* (April 1966).

"What Does it Mean 'To Preach from the Bible'?" *Encounter* 27,1 (Winter 1966): 28-38.

Review of *The Future of Religions*, edited by Jerald C. Brauer. In *Religion in Life* 35, 4 (Autumn 1966): 798-99.

Review of *Translating Theology into the Modern Age*, by Rudolf Bultmann et al. *Journal for Theology and the Church*, vol. 2, edited by Robert W. Funk et al. In *Interpretation* 20 (July 1966): 364-65.

1967

"*Leben Schleiermachers, vol. 2*: A Review Article." *The Journal of Religion* 47 (1967): 347-55.

Review of *Salvation in History*, by Oscar Cullmann. In *Religion in Life* 37 (Winter 1967-68): 130-31.

1968

"Language and God: Gerhard Ebeling's Analysis of Theology." *Interpretation* 22,2 (April 1968): 187-200.

"The Understanding of Language by Friedrich Schlegel and Schleiermacher." *Soundings* 51,2 (Summer 1968): 146-65.

Review of *God and Word*, by Gerhard Ebeling, translated by John W. Leith. In *Interpretation* 22 (April 1968): 187-200.
Review of *Theology as History: New Frontiers in Theology, vol. 3*, edited by James M.Robinson and John B. Cobb, Jr. In *Interpretation* 22 (April 1968): 217-19.

1969

Review of *Shaftesbury's Philosophy of Religion and Ethics: A Study in Enthusiasm*, by Stanley Green. In *Encounter* 30,2 (Spring 1969): 178-79.
Review of *The Shaping of Modern Christian Thought*, by Warren F. Groff and Donald E. Miller. In *Religion in Life* 38,3 (Summer 1969): 450-51.
Review of *Contours of Faith*, by John Dillenberger. In *Religion in Life* 39, 1 (Winter 1969-70): 131-32.

1970

"Theology as Transcendental Jest? Schlegel's Concept of Irony and the Theology of Schleiermacher." In *Schleiermacher as Contemporary: The Journal for Theology and the Church*, Vol. 7. Edited by Robert W. Funk. 96-124. New York: Herder and Herder, 1970.

1972

Review of *Atheismus und Orthodoxie: Analysen und Modelle christlicher Apologetik im 17. Jahrhundert*, by Hans-Martin Barth. In *Church History* 41,2 (June 1972): 270.

1973

Review of *Albrecht Ritschl: Three Essays*, translated by Philip Hefner. In *Religion in Life* 42 (Autumn 1973): 426.
Review of *Protestant Theology in the 19th Century: Its Background and History*, by Karl Barth, translated by John Bowden. In *Religion in Life* 42 (Winter 1973): 559-60.

1975

"On the History of Christian Doctrine: A Demurral to Jaroslav Pelikan." *Journal of Religion* 55,1 (January 1975): 95-109.
"Thomas Mann's Seance and the Argument from Triviality." *The Disciple* 2,20 (October 1975): 2-4.

1976

"A Beggar's Faith." *Interpretation* 30,3 (July 1976): 262-70.

"Expressing our Common Faith." *Study Encounter* 11,2 (September 1976): 20-22.

"Find the Center--Make It Known." *The Christian Century* 93 (17 November 1976):1007-1010.

"Giving an Account for the Hope That is In Us." *Study Encounter* 12 (1976); reprinted as "Giving an Account of the Hope Today." *Faith and Order Paper No. 81*. Geneva: World Council of Churches, 1977; Indianapolis: Council on Christian Unity, Christian Church (Disciples of Christ) 1977.

1977

Friedrich Schleiermacher's Hermeneutics: The Handwritten Manuscripts. Edited and translated with James O. Duke. American Academy of Religion Texts and Translations Series. Missoula, MT: Scholars Press, 1977.

A Romantic Triangle: Schleiermacher and Early German Romanticism. Missoula, MT: Scholars Press for the American Academy of Religion, 1977.

"The Nicene Mind in Historical Perspective and its Significance for Christian Unity." *Encounter* 38,3 (Summer 1977): 213-26.

1978

"Bangalore: Hope in Our Time." *The Disciple* 5,23 (3 December 1978): 12.

"Reflections on the Academic Climate." *Vanderbilt Gazette* (4 December 1978).

1979

"Is Christian Faith A 'Systematic Negation of Religion'?" *Religion in Life* 48 (Summer 1979): 217-226.

Review of *Schleiermacher the Theologian*, by Robert R. Williams. In *Religion in Life* 48 (Summer 1979): 248-49.

1980

(collab.) "Issues of Ecclesiology for Disciples: An Interim Report [of the Commission on Theology.]" *Mid-Stream* 19,3 (July 1980): 334-37.

Review of *Tradition and the Modern World: Reformed Theology in the Nineteenth Century*, by Brian A. Gerrish. In *Religious Studies Review* 6 (October 1980): 286-88.

1981

"The Faith of the Individual and the Faith of the Church (The Community)." *Mid-Stream* 20,3 (July 1981): 219-27.

(collab.) "A Word to the Church 1980 [on the Nature of Witness, Mission, and Unity]: Report of the Commission on Theology." *Mid-Stream* 20,2 (April 1981): 191-98.

1982

"Early Christian Divisions and the Unifying Power of the Gospel." *Mid-Stream* 21,1 (January 1982): 31-53.

"On the State and Future of Historical Theology." In *In Memory of Wilhelm Pauck (1901-1981)*, edited by David Lotz. *Union Papers*, 2 (November 1982): 41-45.

(collab.) "A Word to the Church 1980 [on the Nature of Witness, Mission, and Unity]: Report of the Commission on Theology." *Mid-Stream* 20,2 (April 1981): 191-98.

1983

(collab.) "A Word to the Church on Authority: Report of the Commission on Theology and Christian Unity." In *What is Our Authority?*, by William Baird, St. Louis: Council on Christian Unity by Christian Board of Publication, n.d. [1983].

Review of *Ecclesial Reflection: An Anatomy of Theological Method*, by Edward Farley. *Encounter* 44,3 (Summer 1983): 301-3.

1986

"The Church as Sacramental Community and as Community of Faith." *Mid-Stream* 25,4 (October 1986): 393-402.

"Coherence and Incoherence in the Theology of John Calvin: Reflections on Word and Spirit after 25 Years." In *Calvin Studies*, edited by John Leith, 3: 47-62; also "Coherence and Incoherence in the Theology of John Calvin." In *Revisioning the Past: Prospects in Historical Theology*. Edited by Mary Potter Engel and Walter E. Wyman, Jr., 113-30. Minneapolis: Fortress Press, 1992.

"The Nature of Koinonia: A Disciples of Christ Understanding." *Mid-Stream* 25,4 (October 1986): 354-63.

Review of *Christian Trade Unions in the Weimar Republic, 1918-1933: The Failure of "Corporate Pluralism*," by William L.

Patch, Jr. In *Journal of the American Academy of Religion* 54,3 (Fall 1986): 603-4.

1987
(collab.) "A Word to the Church on Baptism: Report of the Commission on Theology, 1987." In *Baptism: Embodiment of the Gospel*, by Clark Williamson, St. Louis: Christian Board of Publication for Council on Christian Unity, 1987; reprint, *Mid-Stream* 26,2 (April 1987): 222-39.

1988
"Continuity of the Church with the Apostolic Tradition." *Mid-Stream* 27,4 (October 1988): 375-86.

1989
"A Chapter in Theological Resistance to Racism: Rudolf Bultmann and the Beginning of the Third Reich." In *Justice and the Holy: Essays in Honor of Walter Harrelson*. Edited by Douglas A. Knight and Peter J. Paris. Atlanta: Scholars Press, 1989.
(collab.) "Report of the Commission on Theology, Concerning Salvation in Jesus Christ." In *Business Docket and Program, General Assembly of the Christian Church (Disciples of Christ)*, Indianapolis, Indiana 28 July-2 August 1989, 337-43; reprint, *Mid-Stream* 28,4 (October 1989): 421-33.

1990
"The Church of Jesus Christ, always itself and never the same *(Ecclesia Jesu Christi semper ipsa et nunquam eadem)*." *Mid-Stream* 29,3 (July 1990): 231-43.

1991
Review of *The Melody of Theology: A Philosophical Dictionary*, by Jaroslav Pelikan. *Church History* 60,1 (March 1991): 149-50.
(collab.) "Progress Report of the Theology Commission: On Relations Between Jews and Christians." In *Business Docket and Program, General Assembly of the Christian Church (Disciples of Christ)*, 25-30 October 1991, 304-7.
(collab.) "Report of the Theology Commission: On the Lord's Supper." In *Business Docket and Program, General Assembly of the Christian Church (Disciples of Christ)*, 25-30 October, 1991, 296-303.

1992

Christian Faith in Dark Times: Theological Conflicts in the Shadow of Hitler. Louisville, KY: Westminster/John Knox Press, 1992.

1993

Review of *Christianity and Western Thought: A History of Philosophers, Ideas, and Movements*, Vol. 1, From the Ancient World to the Age of Enlightenment, by Colin Brown. In *Church History* 62,4 (December 1993): 564-65.

Review of *For the Soul of the People: Protestant Protest against Hitler*, by Victoria Barnett. In *Cross Currents* 43 (Fall 1993): 424.

(collab.) "Report of the Theology Commission: A Statement on Relations Between Jews and Christians." In *Business Docket and Program,General Assembly of the Christian Church (Disciples of Christ*, 15-20 July 1993, 366-69.

1994

"Foreword" to a new printing of Friedrich Schleiermacher, *On Religion: Speeches to its Cultured Despisers.* Louisville, KY: Westminster/John Knox Press, 1994.

1995

"A Historical Theologian in Ed Farley's Court." In *Theology and the Interhuman: Essays in Honor of Edward Farley*, 125-43. Edited by Robert R. Williams. Valley Forge, PA: Trinity Press International, 1995.

(collab.) "The Church for Disciples of Christ, A Progress Report of the Commission on Theology." In *Business Docket and Program, General Assembly of the Christian Church (Disciples of Christ)*, 20-24 October 1995, 289-93.

1996

"The Gospel and the Church: A Probe for Understanding." *Mid-Stream* 35,4 (October 1996): 377-94.

CONTRIBUTORS

DUKE, JAMES O.
Professor of Historical Theology
Brite Divinity School

DUNNAVANT, ANTHONY L.
Professor of Church History
Lexington Theological Seminary

EARL, RIGGINS R., JR.
Professor of Ethics and Theology
Interdenominational Theological Center

FARLEY, EDWARD
Professor of Theology
Vanderbilt University

FOREMAN, TERRY H.
Associate Professor of Religion
Murray State University

GORDY, STEVE R.
Associate Professor of Religion
Moravian College

GREEN, GARRETT
Professor of Religion
Connecticut College

HARRISON, RICHARD L., JR.
President and Professor of Church History
Lexington Theological Seminary

HARRELSON, WALTER
University Professor
Wake Forest University

HENRY, KENNETH E.
Professor of Church History
Interdenominational Theological Seminary

JONES, PAUL H.
Associate Professor of Religion
Transylvania University

LAHUTSKY, NADIA M.
Associate Professor of Religion
Texas Christian University

PLUMMER, JOHN P.
Ph.D. Candidate
Vanderbilt University

STEWART, CYNTHIA
Ph.D. Candidate
Vanderbilt University

WILLIAMS, D. NEWELL
Dean and Professor of Church History
Christian Theological Seminary

Published by Mercer University Press, in
    association with Disciples of Christ
    Historical Society
November 1997

Book design by Marc A. Jolley
Camera-ready pages composed on a MacIntosh
    Performa 636CD, via Microsoft Word 6.0.1.
Text font: Times New Roman 11/12, 9/11.
Printed and bound in the United States.
Cased and covered with cloth, smyth-sewn, and
    printed on acid-free paper.